The Behavioral Economics of Brand Choice

Also by Gordon R. Foxall

CONSUMER BEHAVIOUR: A PRACTICAL GUIDE

MARKETING BEHAVIOUR

STRATEGIC MARKETING MANAGEMENT

CONSUMER CHOICE

INNOVATION: MARKETING AND STRATEGY

ADVERTISING POLICY AND PRACTICE (*with John Driver*)

MARKETING IN THE SERVICE INDUSTRIES

CONSUMER PSYCHOLOGY FOR MARKETING (*with Ronald Goldsmith and Stephen Brown*)

CONSUMERS IN CONTEXT: THE BPM RESEARCH PROGRAM

MARKETING PSYCHOLOGY: THE PARADIGM IN THE WINGS

CONSUMER BEHAVIOUR ANALYSIS: CRITICAL PERSPECTIVES IN BUSINESS AND MANAGEMENT

CONTEXT AND COGNITION: INTERPRETING COMPLEX BEHAVIOR

UNDERSTANDING CONSUMER CHOICE

The Behavioral Economics of Brand Choice

Gordon R. Foxall, Jorge M. Oliveira-Castro, Victoria K. James and Teresa C. Schrezenmaier

palgrave
macmillan

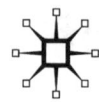

Gordon R. Foxall, Jorge M. Oliveira-Castro, Victoria K. James and
Teresa C. Schrezenmaier 2007

All rights reserved. No reproduction, copy or transmission of this publication
may be made without written permission.

No paragraph of this publication may be reproduced, copied or transmitted
save with written permission or in accordance with the provisions of the
Copyright, Designs and Patents Act 1988, or under the terms of any licence
permitting limited copying issued by the Copyright Licensing Agency,
90 Tottenham Court Road, London W1T 4LP.

Any person who does any unauthorized act in relation to this publication
may be liable to criminal prosecution and civil claims for damages.

The authors have asserted their rights to be identified as the authors of this
work in accordance with the Copyright, Designs and Patents Act 1988.

First published 2007 by
PALGRAVE MACMILLAN
Houndmills, Basingstoke, Hampshire RG21 6XS and
175 Fifth Avenue, New York, N. Y. 10010
Companies and representatives throughout the world

PALGRAVE MACMILLAN is the global academic imprint of the Palgrave
Macmillan division of St. Martin's Press, LLC and of Palgrave Macmillan Ltd.
Macmillan® is a registered trademark in the United States, United Kingdom
and other countries. Palgrave is a registered trademark in the European Union
and other countries.

ISBN-13: 978–0–230–00683–6   hardback
ISBN-10: 0–230–00683–3   hardback

This book is printed on paper suitable for recycling and made from fully
managed and sustained forest sources. Logging, pulping and manufacturing
processes are expected to conform to the environmental regulations of the
country of origin.

A catalogue record for this book is available from the British Library.

A catalogue record for this book is available from the Library of Congress.

10 9 8 7 6 5 4 3 2 1
16 15 14 13 12 11 10 09 08 07

Printed and bound in Great Britain by
Antony Rowe Ltd, Chippenham and Eastbourne

HF5415.32 .B44 2007

0134110545941

The behavioral economics
of brand choice
2007.

2008 02 28

This is for

David (VKJ)
Karina, Cristina and Maria Eduarda (JMO-C)
Melanie and Michael (TCS)
Helen and Robin (GRF)

Contents

List of Tables	ix
List of Figures	xi
Preface	xiii
Acknowledgements	xix

1 Brand Choice in Behavioral Perspective   1
Gordon R. Foxall, Jorge M. Oliveira-Castro, Victoria K. James and Teresa C. Schrezenmaier

2 The Substitutability of Brands   25
Gordon R. Foxall

3 Behavior Analysis of Consumer Brand Choice: A Preliminary Analysis   54
Gordon R. Foxall and Victoria K. James

4 The Behavioral Ecology of Consumer Choice: How and What Do Consumers Maximize?   71
Gordon R. Foxall and Victoria K. James

5 The Behavioral Economics of Consumer Brand Choice: Establishing a Methodology   100
Gordon R. Foxall and Teresa C. Schrezenmaier

6 The Behavioral Economics of Consumer Brand Choice: Patterns of Reinforcement and Utility Maximization   125
Gordon R. Foxall, Jorge M. Oliveira-Castro and Teresa C. Schrezenmaier

7 Patterns of Consumer Response to Retail Price Differentials   165
Jorge M. Oliveira-Castro, Gordon R. Foxall and Teresa C. Schrezenmaier

8 Dynamics of Repeat-Buying for Packaged Food Products   198
Jorge M. Oliveira-Castro, Diogo C. S. Ferreira, Gordon R. Foxall and Teresa C. Schrezenmaier

9	Consumer Brand Choice: Individual and Group Analyses of Demand Elasticity *Jorge M. Oliveira-Castro, Gordon R. Foxall and Teresa C. Schrezenmaier*	223
10	Deviations from Matching in Consumer Choice *Sully Romero, Gordon R. Foxall, Teresa C. Schrezenmaier, Jorge M. Oliveira-Castro and Victoria K. James*	256

Author Index 290

List of Tables

2.1	Annual Performance Measures for Eight Leading Brands	34
2.2	Annual Penetration and Average Purchase Frequencies (Leading Brands in Order of Market Share)	35
2.3	Duplications of Purchases between Brands	36
4.1	Schedules of Reinforcement (Prices) for Butter	80
4.2	Schedules of Reinforcement (Prices) for Cola	82
4.3	Adjusted R^2s, Betas (Sensitivity) and Intercepts (Bias) Results for Matching Analyses for Butter	85
4.4	Adjusted R^2s, Betas (Sensitivity) and Intercepts (Bias) Results for Matching Analyses for Cola	86
6.1	Levels of Informational Reinforcement	138
6.2	Number of consumers, total and average (per consumer) number of purchases, total and average (per consumer) amount spent, average (per quantity) price, average unit price, total and average number of brands purchased, and percentage brand loyalty, calculated for each product category	139
6.3	Matching Analysis	142
6.4	Relative Demand Analyses	142
6.5	Maximization Analyses	143
6.6	Parameters of Equation (log Quantity = $a - b$ [log Price]), calculated for each consumer group, the significance level of the regression (p), and the standard error of the estimate of b	152
6.7	Parameters of *Log Quantity = a – b1 (Log Intra-Brand Price) – b2 (Log Informational Level) – b3 (Log Utilitarian Level)*, calculated for each consumer group, the significance level of the regression (p), and the standard error of the estimates of *b1, b2, and b3*	155
7.1	Number of consumers, total purchases, average number of purchases, average total amount spent, average amount spent per shopping trip, average price per standard amount, average price per package, total number of brands, average number of brands bought, for each product category	180

x List of Tables

7.2	Parameters of Equation 7.1 (log Quantity = $\alpha + \beta$ [log Price]), calculated for each product category	181
7.3	Parameters of Equation 7.2 (log Quantity = $\alpha + \beta_1$ (log Utilitarian) + β_2 (log Informational) + β_3 (log Relative Price)) calculated for each product category	183
7.4	Parameters of Equation 7.2 (log Quantity = $\alpha + \beta_1$ (log Utilitarian) + β_2 (log Informational) + β_3 (log Relative Price)) calculated for each of two samples of the biscuits product category	185
8.1	Equation 8.1 parameters for the brand groups classified at each informational level and for all product categories	208
8.2	Equation 8.2 parameters for the brand groups classified at each informational level and for all product categories	211
9.1	Number of consumers, total purchases, average number of purchases, average total amount spent (British pounds), average amount spent per shopping trip, average price per standard amount (e.g., 100 g), average price per package, total number of brands, average number of brands bought, for each product category	229
9.2	Parameters of Equation 9.2, including all data points from all consumers, calculated for each product category	233
9.3	Parameters of Equation 9.3, including one data point per consumer, calculated for each product category	235
9.4	Parameters of Equation 9.4, including all data points for each consumer across product categories, calculated for each individual consumer	236
9.5	Parameters of Equation 9.4, calculated for each individual consumer for each of the following three product categories: biscuits (cookies), cheese, and breakfast cereals	240
9.6	Parameters of Equation 9.4, calculated for each consumer using data from Split-sample 1 (weeks 1–8) and Split-sample 2 (weeks 9–16)	246
10.1	Frequencies (fr) and Percentages (%) of consumers for product combination within FR and VR	266
10.2	Generalized equation: Aggregated level	272

List of Figures

1.1	The Behavioral Perspective Model of Consumer Choice	5
3.1	Matching Analyses for Catfood100	61
3.2	Relative Demand Curves for Catfood100	62
3.3	Maximization Analyses for Catfood100	62
3.4	Matching Analyses for Bottled Soft Drinks (BSD1)	63
3.5	Relative Demand Analyses for Bottled Soft Drinks (BSD1)	64
3.6	Maximization Analyses for Bottled Soft Drinks (BSD1)	65
3.7	Matching Analyses for Wine/Cola	65
3.8	Relative Demand Analyses for Wine/Cola	66
3.9	Maximization Analyses for Wine/Cola	66
4.1	C1 – Butter: Results of the Matching Analysis	83
4.2	C2 – Cola: Results of the Matching Analysis	84
4.3	C1 – Butter: Results of the Demand Analysis	87
4.4	C2 – Cola: Results of the Demand Analysis	88
4.5	C1 – Butter: Results of the Maximization Analysis	89
4.6	C2 – Cola: Results of the Maximization Analysis	90
5.1	Matching Analyses for Fruit Juice	111
5.2	Relative Demand Analyses for Fruit Juice	113
5.3	Maximization Analyses for Fruit Juice	114
6.1	Matching analysis: "FR" schedules	140
6.2	Matching analysis: "VR" schedules	141
6.3	Relative demand analysis: "FR" schedules	144
6.4	Relative demand analysis: "VR" schedules	145
6.5	Maximization analysis: "FR" schedules	146
6.6	Maximization analysis: "VR" schedules	147
6.7	Percentage of quantity purchased of brands at each informational level (Level 1: black bars; Level 2: empty bars; Level 3: striped bars) by each consumer of each product category as a function of average price paid per consumer	149
6.8	Price elasticity coefficients calculated for each group of consumers classified according to the informational and utilitarian level of the brands they predominantly purchased	153

xii *List of Figures*

6.9	Intra-brand, informational inter-brand and utilitarian inter-brand price elasticity coefficients calculated for each group of consumers, classified on the basis of the informational/utilitarian level of the brands they predominantly purchased	156
8.1	Probability of Sequential and Non-Sequential Buying in each Informational Level	213
8.2	Summary of the Data from Information Level 3 for Baked Beans	215
9.1	Log of quantity bought divided by the average quantity bought in the category as a function of log of price paid divided by the average price paid in the category, calculated with all data points from all consumers (Equation 9.2), for each product category	232
9.2	Log of quantity bought divided by the average quantity bought in the category as a function of log of price paid divided by the average price paid in the category, calculated with one pair of data points from each consumer (Equation 9.3), for each product category	234
9.3	Demand curves for each of six consumers, calculated with all data points across all products for each consumer (Equation 9.4)	238
9.4	Demand curves for six consumers, two for each of the three products, calculated with data points from each of the products for each consumer	244
10.1	FR Schedule: Patterns of Matching Analysis (%)	267
10.2	VR Schedule: Patterns of Matching Analysis (%)	269
10.3	Matching Analysis for subject 93182: Substitutable Products *(*log10)*	271
10.4	Matching Analysis for subject 93182: Independent Products *(*log10)*	271
10.5	Matching Analysis for subject 93182: Complementary Products	271
10.6	Matching Analysis: Substitutable Products	274
10.7	Matching Analysis: Independent Products	274
10.8	Matching Analysis: Complementary Products	274

Preface

The central intellectual problem of academic marketing is the explanation of consumer choice at the level of the brand. A brand is any version of a product or commodity that competes in the market place with other such versions: it may be a variety of a product, supermarket, or person, or of a place, ideology or creed. By and large, marketing inquiry has been confined to the first three. But, however broad or narrow our definitions of it, the brand uniquely defines the marketing level of analysis, one in which members of other academic communities show little if any direct interest. It is marketing's response to the need to explain consumer brand choice that will ultimately determine its success as a legitimate domain of academic inquiry.

Understanding consumer brand choice is, therefore, central to modern marketing thought and practice. Successful marketing management inheres in the accurate anticipation of consumer behavior by means of the marketing mix, while academic marketing as a separate subject matter is defined largely in terms of the intellectual explanation of brand choice and marketing response. A great deal is known about the patterns of brand choice exhibited by consumers of fast-moving products such as foods. The work of Ehrenberg and his colleagues is of paramount importance in this regard. But while marketing texts are not short on prescriptions for marketing action based on surmises about the behavior of consumers, there is a singular lack of understanding of the underlying causes of brand choice won by painstaking empirical investigation of consumer markets of the kind Ehrenberg has produced at the purely descriptive level. Consumer research requires novel insights into the dynamics of consumer market structure and this book reports on a research program that has sought and found such insights in the field of behavioral economics.

The particular source of behavioral economics on which we draw has its origins in behavioral psychology and experimental economics where it has proved highly successful in predicting the behavior of animals and humans according to the principles of basic economic analysis. For the first time we have extended this methodology to cope with the complexities of consumer purchase behavior in national markets. Our work has three purposes:

- To demonstrate that the methodology of behavioral economics can be meaningfully applied to the analysis of consumer choice; this has meant showing that the full complexity of the marketing-oriented economy can be incorporated in the analysis, so that the influences of both price and non-price elements of the marketing mix on consumer behavior can be understood in terms of the basic behavioral economic theory;
- To advance academic consumer research by using the insights of our findings to the causal analysis of brand choice, and thereby to extend understanding of consumer choice in marketing economies in ways that the purely descriptive approach has not achieved;
- To draw conclusions for marketing practice.

In general, our empirical work has been marked by two phases: an ad hoc analysis of a convenience sample of consumers in order to demonstrate that the principles of behavioral economics actually apply to consumer choice analysis, and a study based on consumer panel data for 80 consumers for weekly purchases of eight product categories over a period of 16 weeks. In the course of the research program on which the book is founded, the authors have published extensively in refereed marketing and psychology journals and will draw on these sources as well as adding entirely new material.

The early chapters (particularly Chapters 1 and 2) present a detailed account of the form that consumer choice takes in advanced marketing-led economies and compares our empirical knowledge of these affairs with the prescriptions for marketing action put forward in marketing managerial texts. Drawing particularly on the work of Andrew Ehrenberg and his colleagues, it describes patterns of consumer choice in terms of such concepts as frequency of purchase, penetration level, duplication of purchases, and double jeopardy, and relates the findings of research on consumer choice to the limited scope that marketing managers have to influence brand selection other than by means of short-term price promotions. Attention is drawn to the restrictions placed on consumer research by a purely descriptive approach and the consequent need to seek appropriate conceptual and methodological insights from the social sciences.

Behavioral economics is presented as a methodology that promises considerable theoretical and practical avenues for the advancement of consumer research. Specifically, it brings to the analysis of consumer choice a set of proven techniques and theories for the analysis of repetitive behavior such as brand purchasing which systematically relates market choices to the economic variables that control them. The investigation and explanation of animals' economic behavior which has been the major – but not the sole – focus of this work raises fascinating theoretical and philosophical questions for marketing science such as the role of cognition in choice. As a result, our research program is not confined to a search for managerial advantage but examines continuing issues in the social sciences. This part therefore describes the technical and methodological implications of matching theory, maximization theory, economic analysis and marketing science as a prelude both to our empirical research findings and their implications for consumer research and marketing practice, and to our subsequent conclusions with respect to the nature and explanation of choice.

Chapters 3, 4, 5 and 10 are concerned with the establishment of a new methodology of consumer analysis. Although the behavioral economics paradigm described above provides a sound starting point for the deeper understanding and explanation of patterns of brand purchasing, it is limited by its having investigated situations of choice that lack in some respects clear analogues of the realities of the marketing economy. These include competition, exchange, and the influences on brand selection of the non-price elements of the marketing mix such as advertising. The positive implications of a technique of behavior analysis known as matching theory are discussed, together with the search for a viable explanation of the behavioral equilibrium to which matching leads in situations of choice. Such explanations include maximization (which is discussed in some detail relative to its importance in economic theory and marketing science) and melioration in which the consumer selects the local choice alternative that provides the higher or highest return rather than maximizing globally. Melioration is discussed in relation to diminishing marginal returns to economic behavior, satisficing, and incremental maximization.

Having set the theoretical scene, we turn to our first researches that showed the relevance of matching to consumer brand choice, describing how the methods of behavioral economics need to be adapted if they are to provide realistic means of analyzing consumer choice in competitive markets. Our first studies of matching among individual consumers, followed by work with a larger sample of brand purchasers within the matching framework, and on deviations from the matching law are all described here. In addition, we seek a broader understanding of the patterns of choice unearthed in this way by reference to the literature on foraging and behavioral ecology. These chapters also act as a prelude to the later work on behavioral economics of consumer choice by describing our studies of consumer brand choice in terms of relative demand analysis and maximization analysis, and conclusions are drawn with respect to the competing explanations of consumer choice put forward by economics and marketing science.

The methods of analysis derived from behavioral economics are also extended by introducing a marketing model of consumer choice, the Behavioral Perspective Model (BPM), which explains consumer behavior by reference to the utilitarian and symbolic rewards that products and brands confer on their purchasers. This model permits a powerful account of consumer brand choice as behavior shaped by the promotional/advertising influences available to marketing managers as well as price differentials.

Chapters 6, 7, 8 and 9 describe our further analyses of brand choice based on behavioral economics, extending the scope of the study by considering how groups of consumers, defined by their propensity to choose different patterns of utilitarian and symbolic reward show distinct susceptibilities to price differentials among brands. The question what consumers maximize can now be answered in terms of these discrete combinations of customer benefit identified by the BPM.

Moreover, since buyers of consumer non-durables tend to buy several brands of a product category in the course of a year, though a few are exclusive buyers of particular brands, we investigated the dynamics of successive repeat-buying and penetration levels of groups of brands belonging to similar levels of brand differentiation (defined in BPM-derived terms of utilitarian and symbolic customer benefit). We specifically examined the probability of consumers' buying brands belonging to the same level of differentiation on successive shopping occasions. Since the number of exclusive buyers of a brand decreases as the duration of sales increases, we hypothesized a decrease in the probability of sequential repeat-buying of brands belonging to the same level of brand differentiation with increases in the number of successive shopping occasions. Similar analysis was undertaken to examine the penetration level of groups of similar brands, which were expected to increase with the period chosen for analysis. Two equations, constructed to describe the dynamics of repeat-buying for groups of brands, were applied to the description of the dynamics of repeat-buying and penetration level of particular brands. The results suggest several managerial applications including the estimation of the proportion of sequential repeat buyers and non-repeat buyers during the product shopping cycle.

An additional dimension to the study of consumer brand choice stems from the disaggregation of overall price elasticity of demand. Several marketing strategies depend upon knowledge of consumers' responsiveness to changes in price. Studies that have decomposed price elasticity suggest that the major impact of promotions is on brand switching rather than increased consumption. Some of these results also indicate that consumers tend to buy smaller quantities of more expensive brands when compared to cheaper ones (i.e., inter-brand elasticity). Our research attempted to verify whether such inter-brand elasticities occur and to measure the relative importance of intra- and inter-brand elasticities in determining overall category elasticity. Brands were classified according to the level of programmed informational (i.e., socially mediated) and utilitarian (i.e., mediated by the product) reinforcement, proposed by the BPM. This classification was used to calculate inter-brand elasticities. Regression analyses indicated that, for most product categories, intra-brand elasticity was higher than utilitarian inter-brand elasticity, which, in turn, was higher than informational inter-brand elasticity. These results suggest that overall category elasticity observed for supermarket products reflects different choice patterns: buying larger quantities of a promoted brand and buying smaller quantities of more differentiated, usually more expensive, brands.

Finally in this part of the research, we considered individual consumers and the possibility that inter- and intra-consumer levels of price elasticity could be identified. Following the behavior-analytic tradition of analyzing individual behavior, we investigated demand elasticity of individual consumers purchasing supermarket products, and compared individual and group analyses of elasticity. Elasticity coefficients were calculated for individual consumers with data from all or only one product category (intra-consumer elasticities), and for each product category using all data points from all consumers (overall product elasticity) or one average data point per consumer (inter-consumer elasticity). In addition to this, split-sample elasticity coefficients were obtained for each individual. The results suggest that: (1) Demand elasticity coefficients calculated for individual consumers purchasing supermarket food products are compatible with predictions from economic theory and behavioral economics; (2) Overall product elasticities, typically employed in marketing and econometric research, include effects of inter-consumer and intra-consumer elasticities; (3)

When comparing demand elasticities of different product categories, group and individual analyses yield similar trends; and (4) Individual differences in demand elasticity are relatively consistent across time, but do not seem to be consistent across products. These results demonstrate the theoretical, methodological and managerial relevance of investigating the behavior of individual consumers.

Overall the volume establishes that utilitarian and informational reinforcement, derived from the BPM, can serve as a basis to elucidate consumer brand choice with respect to both sources of benefits. In the course of this, we have suggested a refined concept of substitutability, which seeks the reason for substitutability in price and in non-price marketing factors, i.e., utilitarian and informational reinforcement. Thus, our analyses suggest that demand for substitute goods is not only price-related but can also be related to informational, more symbolic, benefits. First, the matching analysis confirmed that brands within a product class are functionally substitutable. Second, it has been demonstrated that brand choice of frequently-bought supermarket goods reflects, via consumers' responses to price differentials, their preferences for combinations of utilitarian and informational reinforcement. Third, the analysis has shown that consumers tend to choose brands within the same or the adjacent price tier as these are reflected by different combinations of utilitarian and informational benefits.

Acknowledgements

G. R. Foxall thanks The Nuffield Foundation, London, for financial support (SGS/LB/0431/A and SGS/00493/G/S1).

J. M. Oliveira-Castro thanks the Brazilian institutions, CAPES (Ministry of Education), CNPq (Ministry of Science and Technology), and FINATEC (Fundação de Empreendimentos Científicos e Tecnológicos Brasília, DF) for financial support.

1
Brand Choice in Behavioral Perspective[1]

Gordon R. Foxall, Jorge M. Oliveira-Castro, Victoria K. James and Teresa C. Schrezenmaier

The study of consumer behavior has been given increasing attention in the context of the expansion of the study of marketing and marketing research over the past decades (e.g., Kotler et al., 2001; Jobber, 2004; Keith, 1960). Today, consumer researchers account for almost half of all marketing faculty in business schools (Simonson et al., 2001) and it is a growing area of research in other disciplines such as sociology, communication and anthropology (e.g., Miller, 1995). One of the reasons for the interest in the subject has been that markets and companies have been growing in size and hence there is no longer a great deal of proximity between sellers and buyers. Whereas selling for the most basic commodities like food used to be an everyday social experience, it largely has become an anonymous process with minimal personal interaction, possibly even without any face to face contact when shopping over the Internet. Most purchases for food items and other products, at least in urbanized areas, are done in supermarkets where there is little interaction between staff and customers.

However, despite the rapid growth and development in the study of consumer behavior, there are considerable disagreements about what consumer research is, what its objectives are, and how it differs from other disciplines (Simonson et al., 2001). Consequently, the field lacks a universally-accepted theoretical framework or model (Foxall, 2005). The disciplines of economics and psychology (especially cognitive and social) have traditionally provided the theoretical foundations of consumer behavior and have bent their research toward more cognitive approaches (Jacoby et al., 1998). Although several theoretical approaches have influenced consumer research, such as behaviorism, physiological psychology, psychoanalytic psychology, cognitive psychology and interpretative psychology (*cf.* O'Shaughnessy, 1992), social-cognitive theories and models have dominated the field with an increasing emphasis on cognition (e.g., decision making) rather than on social phenomena (e.g., reference groups) (*cf.* Simonson *et al.*, 2001). Hence, many consumer choice models portray consumer behavior as a process where thinking, evaluating and deciding are prevailing (e.g., Engel *et al.*, 1995; Howard & Sheth, 1969). Although the importance of emotions in buying behavior has also received a growing share of attention in recent years (e.g., O'Shaughnessy & O'Shaughnessy, 2002; Bitner, 1992; Dawson *et al.*, 1990; Donovan & Rossiter, 1982), the large majority of studies are designed to investigate consumer decision-making processes, inspired by cognitive, information processing, theories (see Jacoby *et al.*, 1998; Simonson *et al.*, 2001, for comprehensive reviews).

As an example, it has been widely assumed that measuring attitudes and beliefs will enable marketers to predict consumers' behavior. The Theory of Reasoned Action (Ajzen & Fishbein, 1980) and the Theory of Planned Behavior (Ajzen, 1985) have been very influential in this respect and have been used extensively to demonstrate the link between attitudes and action. According to these theories, psychological constructs, such as attitudes and beliefs, which are formed through direct or indirect experience with the attitude object (e.g., a product's attribute), would influence the person's intention to act in relation to the object, which in turn would influence the person's behavior (e.g., buying the product). Such constructs (e.g., attitudes) have been usually measured on the basis of consumers' responses to questionnaires, the results of which are then used to predict consumers' behavior toward the object (e.g., purchasing). However, it has been repeatedly pointed out by scholars that this relationship is in fact much weaker than assumed (e.g., Wicker, 1969; Foxall, 1987). Although such criticisms had some impact on the adoption of these theories, which has declined in use since (Simonson *et al.*, 2001), the most commonly adopted solution to these weak relations between attitude and behavior were to amend slightly the theory or the methodology. One way of doing this was to propose, for example, dual-process theories, according to which consistent relations between attitude and behavior need not always occur for they would depend on other factors, such as level of consumer's involvement (e.g., Chaiken, 1980; Petty & Cacioppo, 1983) or level of correspondence between measures of attitude and measures of behavior (e.g., Kraus, 1995). Since then an enormous number of studies have attempted to identify the variables that influence attitude-behavior consistency, which do not propose any substantial change in the basic theoretical and conceptual framework of the research and, consequently, multiply the number of psychological constructs related to the phenomena of interest (cf. Glasman & Albarracín, 2006). Considering that the field is very akin to marketing where prediction of what consumers will do is of paramount importance, empirical results showing inconsistency between attitudes and behavior may discourage the adoption of cognitive models to explain consumer behavior, or, at least, encourage the search for alternative types of explanation. In fact, a closer examination of the development of this tradition of research indicates that when more emphasis is given to possible effects of situational variables and to measures of behavior, the level of prediction of behavior increases substantially (cf. Foxall, 1997). These findings suggest that approaches of consumer behavior that give more emphasis to situational variables and behavioral measures might be promising alternatives to the prevailing cognitive theories.

There is yet another reason to look for epistemologically different approaches of consumer behavior, namely, the excessive dominance of the social-cognitive way of theorizing. According to some epistemologists, scientific development of a field depends on diversity of ideas, on opposing, incompatible views strongly held by different research groups. According to this position, the overwhelming predominance of one single theoretical perspective may impoverish the intellectual milieu and hinder scientific development of the field (cf. Feyerabend, 1993; for more details of these ideas applied to consumer behavior and marketing, see Foxall, 1997).

Consumer behavior analysis

An alternative approach to consumer behavior that emphasizes the influence of situational variables and direct measures of behavior might be found in behavioral psychology, particularly in Skinner's operant theory (cf. Skinner, 1953, 1969, 1974). Behavior analysis, as this field is usually known, has developed a coherent and systematic set of theoretical concepts, derived from a long tradition of experimental and applied research. It has always emphasized the role of situational variables in the determination of behavior, paying particular attention to events that antecede and follow individuals' responding, and defended the adoption of direct measures of behavior, with little use of hypothetical constructs in their theories. One of the central concepts in operant theory is the three-term contingency ($S^D - R - S^R$), which specifies what responses (R) are reinforced (S^R) or punished in the presence of what situations or discriminative stimuli (S^D). According to the three-term contingency, reinforcing and punishing consequences of responding increase and decrease, respectively, its future occurrence probability in similar situations. Events in the situation would acquire discriminative (or inhibiting) functions by signaling the probability and magnitude of reinforcement that would be contingent upon the emission of a given response. This conceptual framework has been used to analyze and interpret a very broad range of phenomena, including, for example, learning, verbal behavior, clinical interventions, politics, and religion (e.g., Skinner, 1953, 1957). Behavior analysis has also developed a strong tradition of experimental research on choice and consumption that could enrich the investigation of consumer behavior. The field has developed systematic theoretical treatments of choice and consumption, based on results from laboratory experiments and institutional interventions, such as the matching law (Herrnstein, 1970) and laboratory analysis of demand (Hursh, 1984), which are now part of the interdisciplinary area usually known as *behavioral economics*.

Despite the fact that behavior analysis has been heavily criticized since the cognitive revolution entered its ascendancy from the 1960s onwards, the characteristics mentioned above would in themselves justify the exploration of its usefulness in the field of consumer behavior. Moreover, recent research developments in behavior analysis have addressed some of the most common criticisms directed to it. Behavior analysis was much criticized for its excessive use of animal experiments to the exclusion of investigating complex, typically human phenomena. In the last decades behavior analysis has come to treat subject areas that lie at the very heart of cognitive psychology, among them thinking, decision making and language. The distinction between behavior that is simply the result of the individual's direct contact with the environment ("contingency-shaped" behavior) and that which is the result of verbal interventions from others or from the individual him/herself ("rule-governed" behavior) is particularly relevant here. The advent of investigations of stimulus equivalence, and naming, to give two examples, have transformed behavior analysis from a school of psychology that was once easily disparaged to an exciting intellectual and practical exploration of human complexity.

In order to integrate consumer research with behavioral principles, Foxall (1990, 1997) developed a model which has, since its emergence, proved a useful framework: the Behavioral Perspective Model (BPM). Foxall (2002, p. 20) argues that the BPM is a "means of summarizing empirical regularities", in the same way as Skinner has been fundamentally inductive in their approach. Foxall (1998, p. 337) summarizes the model as portraying "the rate at which consumer behaviors take place as a function of the relative openness of the setting in which they occur and the informational and utilitarian reinforcement available or promised by the setting". These components of the model are explained in what follows.

The BPM represents an adaptation of the three-term contingency and locates consumer behavior at the intersection of the consumer's learning history and the current behavior setting, that is, at the consumer situation. Thus, the BPM provides an environmental perspective to consumer behavior and hence includes situational influences in the analysis of purchase and consumption. In behavioral terms, consumer behavior, the dependent variable, is a function of the individual's learning history related to a given type of consumption, the behavior setting and the consequences the behavior produces. Figure 1.1 combines all these variables to provide a general picture of the BPM.

The behavior setting is defined as the social and physical environment in which the consumer is exposed to stimuli signaling a choice situation. A doctor surgery's waiting area, a supermarket or an open-air festival in a public park are all examples of behavior settings, varying in their scope and capacity of evoking consumer responses. This scope translates into a continuum between an open and a closed setting,

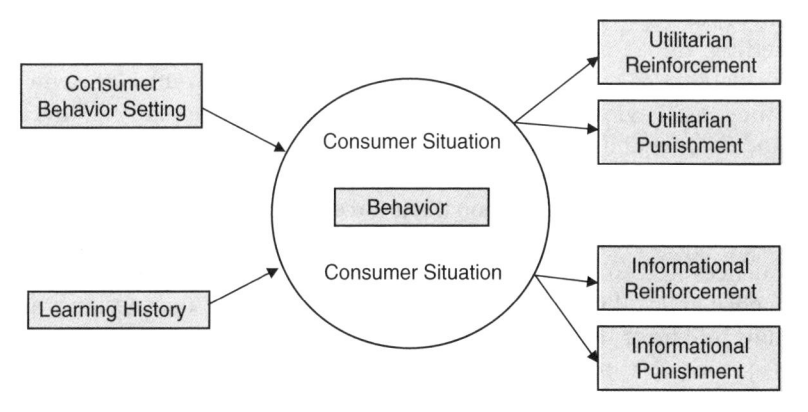

Figure 1.1 The Behavioral Perspective Model of Consumer Choice
Source: (Adapted from Foxall, 1996).

allowing consumers different degrees of control over their behavior. The more open setting, like for instance the park festival, grants consumers to behave in a relatively free way with the option to wander around, talk, listen to music, eat, drink, smoke or even leave the scene. Toward the other end of the spectrum consumers are less free in their choice and are indeed expected to conform to a pattern of behavior set by someone else. Schwartz & Lacey (1988, p. 40) describe a closed setting as where "only a few reinforcers are available, and usually, only one has special salience; the experimenter (behavior modifier) has control over conditions of deprivation and access to reinforcers; there is only one, or at most a few, available means to the reinforcers; the performance of clearly defined, specific tasks is reinforced; [...]; the contingencies of reinforcement are imposed and varied by agents not themselves being subjected to the contingencies; and there are no effective alternatives to being in the situation".

For example, according to society's norms, patients in a surgery's waiting area are expected to sit quietly and wait in a patient manner until they are called for their treatment. Of course, they are free to read magazines, possibly chat with other waiting patients or walk out of the surgery if the waiting time is considered too long (in which case they will not receive treatment).

The other element of the consumer situation, the learning history, refers to the similar or related experiences a consumer has had before encountering the current behavior setting. This previous experience helps the consumer to interpret the behavior setting accurately by predicting the likely consequences her behavior in this situation will incur. In other words, the otherwise neutral stimuli of the behavior setting are transformed into discriminative stimuli, indicating the availability of three types of consequences contingent upon the consumer's behavior. First, utilitarian reinforcement refers to the direct and functional benefits the purchase and/or consumption of a product (or service) involves. These are benefits mediated by the product or service. Secondly, informational reinforcement circumscribes the more indirect and symbolic consequences of behavior, such as social consequences (e.g., social status and self-esteem). These are consequences mediated by other people and function as feedback to the consumer as how well he or she is performing as a consumer. The third type of consequence, costs to the consumer in monetary and non-monetary form, is the aversive outcome of behavior.

As an example, the utilitarian consequence of buying a car is the benefit of owning and using the product afterwards, in a purely functional and hedonic sense, for it gives, for instance, door-to-door transportation, with minimum weather exposure and spare time schedule. Conversely, the informational reinforcement of owning a car might be related to the social status and admiration of others, particularly if it is a prestigious and expensive car make (e.g., a Bentley or Mercedes). The aversive but unavoidable outcome of shopping is the surrendering of money at the cash point but also the time spent searching for an item. Foxall (1990) argues that all products or services contain elements of utilitarian, informational and aversive consequences. Additionally, like the behavioral setting scope, which can vary from highly open to highly closed, the reinforcement patterns of the BPM are arrayed as a continuum from high to low utilitarian reinforcement and from high to low informational reinforcement.

Thus, the probability of purchase and consumption depends on the relative weight of the reinforcing and aversive consequences that are signaled by the elements in the consumer behavior setting (*cf.* Alhadeff, 1982). According to this view, product, brand, and service attributes, including price, may be interpreted as programmed reinforcing (i.e., benefits) and aversive events. Manufacturers, retailers, and brand managers direct all their efforts to modifying and shaping the reinforcing and aversive properties of the attributes of their products and brands, so as to make them more attractive to the consumer. Branding, promotional activities, new product development and product selection are just a few options open to the supply side. These endeavors may or may not work, and this is why they ought to be interpreted as programmed reinforcing (or aversive) events rather then actual reinforcing (or aversive) events. According to this theoretical perspective, one of the main tasks in marketing is to identify what events can function as benefits (or aversive stimuli), to what extent, for what consumers, and under what circumstances (Foxall, 1992).

The theoretical framework has been used to investigate a range of phenomena, such as consumer brand choice (Foxall & James, 2001, 2003; Foxall *et al.*, 2004; Oliveira-Castro *et al.*, 2005; Oliveira-Castro *et al.*, 2005, 2006; Foxall & Schrezenmaier, 2003), consumers' reactions to shopping environments (Foxall & Greenley, 1999; Foxall & Yani-de-Soriano, 2005; Soriano & Foxall, 2002), social responsible consumption (Davies *et al.*, 2002; Foxall *et al.*, 2006a), product search behavior (Oliveira-Castro, 2003), among others. The model has also served as inspiration to philosophical research that attempts to reconcile, in an epistemologically coherent way, behaviorism and cognitive psychology (Foxall, 2004, 2005). As it is not possible to explore all these topics within the present paper, some of the research that has been carried out on brand choice is presented next, as an illustration of the kind of investigation based on this theoretical approach to consumer behavior.

Consumer brand choice

In the last decades, several regularities have been discovered concerning consumer brand choice and the behavior of brands in the market (e.g., Ehrenberg, 1988), which should be considered by any researcher interested in the topic. Using consumer panel data of mainly, but not only, frequently and regularly bought branded consumer products, Ehrenberg and colleagues have analyzed enormous amounts of data and reported interesting and systematic results (for examples of and detail about the research program see Ehrenberg, 1988; Ehrenberg *et al.*, 1990; Ehrenberg & Scriven, 1999; Ehrenberg *et al.*, 2004; Goodhardt *et al.*, 1984; Uncles *et al.*, 1995). One of the important findings stemming from this research program is that most consumers practice multi-brand purchasing, choosing apparently randomly from a small "repertoire" of often three or four brands in a particular product category. Most of the brands are perceived to perform in a functionally similar way and are therefore assumed to be substitutable. Furthermore, during a period of one year, in order to meet their requirements in a product category, consumers of any given Brand A tend to buy other brands more often than they buy Brand A. For example, in the US breakfast cereal market consumers make on average about four purchases of the brand Shredded Wheat in one year, but buy other brands about 37 times in the same period (Ehrenberg & Goodhardt, 1977). By contrast, only a small proportion of consumers (approximately 10%) are exclusive buyers of or 100% loyal to any particular brand during, for example, one year. Sole buyers are described as relatively light users of their favorite brand, disconfirming traditional marketing research which claims that showing exclusive loyalty to one particular brand is equivalent to being a heavy user and therefore a disproportionably valuable to the company. This also contrasts with the widespread belief that higher loyalty rates lead to improved profitability (Reichheld & Sasser, 1990). When comparing across brands, results show that competitive brands differ mainly in the number of buyers they have and not so much in how loyal those buyers are, although there is a "double-jeopardy" (DJ) tendency, that is, brands with smaller market shares do not only attract fewer buyers of the product category but those buyers buy the brand less frequently than buyers of larger brands. All these results have been replicated across more than 50 product categories (for example, grocery products, aviation fuel, store choice, newspapers) and few exceptions have been found in the FMCG market, such as the observed deviations discovered in some US Spanish-language and religious TV stations, which attract heavy viewing from their relatively few viewers (Ehrenberg *et al.*, 1990).

This line of research has enabled the development of a mathematical model to describe the regularities found, the Dirichlet Model (Ehrenberg *et al.*, 2004; Goodhardt *et al.*, 1984), which comprises two main areas: repeat-buying patterns of whole product categories and brand-purchasing patterns. Thus, by making some basic assumptions, the model can specify probabilistically how many purchases in one product category each consumer makes in a time-period and which brand he or she buys on each occasion. Moreover, the performance of single brands can be predicted in different situations such as market introduction or during and after sales promotions (Ehrenberg, 1991; Ehrenberg *et al.*, 1994).

The Dirichlet is described as a "parsimonious" model because it requires limited input for its predictions due to the fact that it is defined for stationary (i.e., showing few or no trends) and unsegmented[2] (i.e., similar brands generally appeal to similar people) markets. The two main inputs into the model are (1) The penetration rate, i.e., the percentage of consumers who buy an item or the product category in a specified time-period; and (2) The average purchase frequency of buyers of the category or a particular brand during the same time. On the basis of these inputs, the three main parameters relating to the product category of the model can be estimated (Ehrenberg *et al.*, 1990): (1) How often consumers buy, (2) Which brands they buy, and (3) The size of the market. Finally, the only brand-specific numerical contribution to be made is the individual brands' market shares.

The model has been criticized mainly for the reason that it does not give attention to the underlying patterns and motivations of consumers and their purchases (Bartholomew, 1984; Jeuland, 1984) or the underlying variables (Popkowski Leszczyc *et al.*, 2000). It is certainly true that Ehrenberg's work has remained largely descriptive and has not questioned why consumers behave in the way that has been repeatedly observed. Goodhardt *et al.* (1984, p. 638) have also supported this: "why one person (or household) generally consumes more toothpaste or soup than others, or somewhat prefers brand j to k or vice versa, is not accounted for by the model and is in fact at this stage still largely unknown".

The following are some of the questions left unanswered by this line of research: (1) It has been assumed that brands within an individual's repertoires are functionally substitutes, but can this be empirically demonstrated or tested? (2) Is the quantity consumers buy on each shopping occasion relatively constant, as assumed by the model? (3) Although it has been assumed that any consumer can have any brand repertoire, how are brand repertoires formed? In what follows, lines of research that have investigated these questions are described.

Substitutability of brands and the matching law

Choice, according to behavioral interpretations, is usually treated as the rate at which a particular behavior is performed, usually in the context of other competing behaviors (Herrnstein, 1997). This view suggests that choice is not a single event but the distribution of behavior over time, for example, the proportion of times that A is chosen over B or B over C. The behavioral explanation for choice is sought not in mental deliberations, as cognitive psychology would suggest, but in the environmental events that accompany the behaviors in question, the pattern of reinforcement and punishment that increases or decreases the probability of those behaviors being repeated and the contingencies encountered. The analysis of any one choice (i.e., any one sequence of behavior) requires the analysis of other behavioral choices that might have been enacted instead and the configurations of reinforcement and punishment that maintain or inhibit them.

In the context of the study of choice in behavioral psychology, the matching law is a quantitative formulation describing a proportional relationship between the allocation of an organism's behavior to two concurrently available response options on the one hand and the distribution of reinforcement between the two concurrent behaviors on the other hand (Herrnstein, 1961). The matching law states that animals or human beings match their behavior in proportion to the reinforcement the behavior produces. In experiments using pigeons as subjects, Herrnstein (1961, 1970) found that organisms distribute their behavior between the two options according to the rate of reinforcement the behavior receives from responding to each option respectively. If animals such as pigeons have the opportunity to choose between pecking one of the keys x or y, where each of which delivers food pellets (reinforcers) on its own concurrent variable-interval schedule,[3] they allocate their responses on x and y in proportion to the relative rate of reinforcement. Hence, distribution of responding is said to "match" the proportion to the reward or punishment this behavior produces. In its general formulation, the matching law can be described by the following equation (Baum, 1974):

$$\frac{B_x}{B_y} = b\left(\frac{R_x}{R_y}\right)^s \qquad (1.1)$$

where B is the behavior the individual allocates to options x and y and R is the reinforcement contingent upon that behavior. The parameters b and s are empirically obtained, and can be interpreted as measures of bias toward one of the alternatives and of sensitivity to changes in reinforcement ratio, respectively.

Rachlin *et al.* (1980) propose that the exponent s in Equation 1.1 represents substitutability between reinforcement sources, that is, when the exponent s is equal to 1.0 there is perfect substitutability between reinforcers. According to this interpretation, after some necessary adaptations related to characteristics of consumer brand choice, the generalized matching law can be used to measure the level of substitutability between different brands. In the case of brand choice, the equation is calculated based upon the ratio of the amount paid (responding) for the preferred brand divided by the amount paid for the other brands as a function of the ratio of the amount bought (reinforcement) of the preferred brand divided by the amount bought of the other brands (*cf.* Chapter 2; Foxall, 1999). The data in this case can be obtained from consumer panels, formed by volunteers who record all their purchases within certain product categories during several weeks and passes the information on to commercial firms or researchers.

Chapters 3 (Foxall & James, 2001) and 4 (Foxall & James, 2003) introduce the use of the matching law and related substitutability measures to the study of brand choice using a small sample of consumers (including qualitative investigations). Chapters 5 (Foxall *et al.*, 2004) and 6 (Foxall & Schrezenmaier, 2003) continue this theme analyzing data from a larger 80-consumer panel purchasing nine different product categories, obtained from a commercial firm. In these studies, exponents of Equation 1.1 tended to be very close to unity, showing matching. These results demonstrate that brands within consumers' repertoires function as substitutes, corroborating the assumption put forward by Ehrenberg and colleagues.

Chapter 10 (Romero et al., 2006) extends the matching analysis of consumer choice to product categories that are not necessarily substitutable, that is, relatively independent and complementary products. Results suggest that for complementary and independent products the occurrence of matching may depend upon the level of analysis adopted, if weekly or across several weeks. However, as the chapter stresses, more research is needed to clarify such findings.

Constant quantity: inter- and intra-consumer demand elasticity

The analysis of demand, which lies at the core of microeconomics, has been one of the most useful and frequently adopted frameworks in behavioral economics. The analysis of demand is usually based on the parameters of demand curves, which plot the quantity purchased or consumed of a commodity as a function of its price. In the case of experiments in behavioral economics, demand curves usually relate amount consumed of a reinforcer as a function of some schedule parameter, such as the number of responses required by a fixed-ratio schedule.[4] The two main parameters of a demand curve are the elasticity and intensity (Hursh, 1984) of demand, which, in its simplest form, can be obtained by using the following equation (*cf.* Hursh, 1980, 1984; Kagel et al., 1995):

$$LogQUANTITY = a + b\ (LogPRICE) \tag{1.2}$$

where *a* and *b* are empirically obtained parameters that represent the intercept and slope of the function, respectively. The advantage of Equation 1.2 is that *a* and *b* can be interpreted as coefficients that measure the intensity and elasticity of demand, respectively. Intensity of demand indicates the level of demand at a given price, whereas elasticity of demand shows how consumption changes with changes in price. Elasticity is said to be inelastic when *b* varies from 0.0 to –1.0, that is, when increases in prices decrease consumption but are accompanied by increases in spending. When *b* is equal to –1.0 decreases in consumption are perfectly proportional to increases in price and spending remains constant. When *b* is smaller than –1.0 (i.e., more negative indicating larger elasticity), demand is said to be elastic, that is, consumption decreases proportionally faster than increases in price and spending decreases. As mentioned previously, the Dirichlet Model assumes that the quantity consumers buy on each shopping occasion is relatively constant.

One way of examining this assumption would be to calculate the elasticity of demand for different product categories. An analysis of demand elasticity, in this case, relates the amount consumers buy on each shopping occasion as a function of changes in price. Values of b significantly different than zero would indicate that the quantity consumers purchase on each shopping trip changes significantly as prices change, suggesting that the quantity individuals buy does change systematically across shopping occasions.

Chapter 7 (Oliveira-Castro *et al.*, 2005) shows the calculation of demand elasticity for each of nine product categories using an 80-consumer sample. As can be seen, the results showed that overall elasticity coefficients were significant ($p \leq .01$) for all nine product categories and ranged from –.23 to –1.01, indicating that quantity bought was not constant and decreased significantly with increases in price.

Although these results refute the constant quantity assumption, they do not clarify the buying patterns associated to changes in quantity. As overall demand elasticity coefficients were calculated by including all data points from all consumers, the observed decreases in quantity bought could be due to different consumers buying different quantities, the same consumers buying different quantities on different occasions, or any combinations of these two patterns. With the purpose of answering this question, Chapter 9 (Oliveira-Castro *et al.*, 2006) contains a study where inter- and intra-consumer elasticities were calculated using the same 80-consumer data set. Inter-consumer elasticity would occur if consumers that buy in average larger quantities pay on average lower prices than consumers that buy on average smaller quantities. Intra-consumer elasticity would occur if consumers were to buy larger quantities when paying lower prices than when paying higher prices, across shopping occasions. The study reported in Chapter 9 also calculated inter-consumer elasticity based on the average quantity and price for each consumer for each product category. Inter-consumer elasticity coefficients were negative for all nine product categories and significant ($p \leq .05$) for seven of them, indicating that consumers that buy in average larger quantities tend to pay lower prices. Intra-consumer elasticity coefficients were calculated for each consumer using all data points from all product categories, normalized according to each consumer's mean quantity and price in each category. Intra-consumer elasticity coefficients were negative for 93.4% of consumers and significant for 75% of them. These results indicate that consumers tend to buy larger quantities when paying lower prices. Taken together, these findings refute the constant quantity assumption and suggest that consumers' choices within their brand repertoires are price sensitive (rather than random).

Brand repertoires: the role of utilitarian and informational benefits

With the purpose of testing if brand repertoires are related somehow to the level of utilitarian and informational reinforcement of the brands, as suggested by the BPM, Foxall and colleagues, included as Chapter 6, developed a classification of brands according to their benefit levels. Based on the already-mentioned 80-consumer panel data set, the authors ranked each brand according to two levels of utilitarian benefit and three levels of informational benefit. Benefit levels were ranked based on the interpretation that brands represent programmed reinforcement contingencies arranged by managers and producers. The choice of two utilitarian and three informational levels was based on the size of the sample (not all brands and brand types were purchased by members of the sample during the period) and with the purpose of making comparisons across product categories. Thus, the different levels of utilitarian and informational benefit cannot be defined absolutely: they ultimately are a result of each researcher's focus and interest. For example, as pointed out in Chapter 6, more levels of utilitarian reinforcement could have been identified for some product categories (e.g., cookies and cheese) in the sample they used, but an equal number of levels across products was considered beneficial for their analysis.

In the marketing context of routinely-bought supermarket food products, higher levels of utilitarian benefit can be identified by the addition of (supposedly) desirable attributes. These attributes are considered to have value-adding qualities for the product or its consumption, they are visibly declared on the package or are part of the product name, and ultimately justify higher prices. Moreover, in most cases, several general brands offer product varieties with and without these attributes. In Chapter 6 (Foxall *et al.*, 2004), utilitarian levels were assigned based on additional attributes (e.g., plain baked beans vs. baked beans with sausage) and/or differentiated types of products (e.g., plain cookies vs. chocolate chip cookies). In the case of differentiated product types, several manufacturers tend to offer the different product types at differentiated prices (e.g., plain cookies were cheaper than more elaborate cookies for all brands examined).

By contrast, informational reinforcement can be linked to brand differentiation, which in turn is usually also related to price differentiation, because the most promoted and best known brands tend to be related to higher levels of prestige, social status, and trustworthiness. In fact, there is a particularly close association between informational reinforcement and brand differentiation in the FMCG context. As an example, when comparing the levels of brand differentiation of Tesco Value and Kelloggs Cornflakes, Kelloggs is clearly the better known, more differentiated and also more expensive brand, with a higher programmed level of informational reinforcement. This type of variation among brands has been translated into different levels of informational reinforcement. It should be noted that the classification of informational reinforcement levels does not rule out the possibility of there also being different degrees of utilitarian reinforcement between two informational levels. Naturally, a company spokesperson for Kelloggs, or for that purpose any other differentiated brand such as Heinz or DelMonte, would claim that their products are distinct from those of other companies in terms of their "utilitarian" attributes, for instance the quality of raw materials and ingredients, production procedures or health aspects. Equally, buyers and users of differentiated brands are likely to confirm such brands' superiority, e.g., the much better taste in comparison the other, cheaper brands.

In the first attempt of categorizing different levels of reinforcement, Foxall *et al.* (2004) took such possibilities into consideration, since most consumer behavior generates both types of consequences. Nevertheless, because brands usually have almost identical formulations (*cf.* Ehrenberg, 1972/1988; Chapter 2, Foxall, 1999), the ranking of informational reinforcement was based on the predominant, more obvious differences between brands. In fact, there is evidence that consumers may not even be able to distinguish between brands of one product category on the basis of their physical characteristics (e.g., in blind tests).

In the study described in Chapter 6 (Foxall *et al.*, 2004), the following criteria were the basis for determining the different levels of informational reinforcement: (1) Increases in prices across brands for the same product type (e.g., plain baked beans, plain cookies or plain cornflakes) were considered to be indicative of differences in informational levels; (2) The cheapest store brands (e.g., Asda Smart Price, Tesco Value, Sainsbury Economy) were considered to represent the lowest informational level (Level 1); (3) Store brands without the add-on good value for money or economy (e.g., Asda, Tesco, Sainsbury) and cheapest specialized brands were thought to embody the medium informational level (Level 2); and (4) Higher-priced, specialized brands (e.g., Heinz, McVities, Kelloggs, Lurpak), were assigned to Level 3, the highest informational level.

After classifying all brands of all nine product categories, consumers' brand choices within and across informational levels were examined. This analysis made clear that most consumers bought mostly brands at one particular informational level, rather than across all levels. The percentage of consumers that bought 70% or more of goods at one particular informational level was: for baked beans 92%, tea 91%, coffee 84%, margarine 84%, butter 81%, cereals 68%, fruit juice 68%, cheese 64%, and biscuits 58%. This showed that the majority of consumers made 70% or more of their purchases within brands at the same informational level. Similar analyses also showed that, for eight of nine product categories, most consumers also made the large majority of their purchases within the same utilitarian level. The percentage of consumers who made 70% or more of their purchases within the same utilitarian level was: for butter 91%, for baked beans 85%, coffee 84%, tea 84%, cheese 82%, fruit juice 77%, margarine 74%, cereals 66%, and biscuits 42%. Taken together, these findings clearly indicate that consumers' repertoires of brands are related to the level of informational and utilitarian benefits offered by the brands. This is a clear step in the direction of understanding the formation of brand repertoires, which can be very useful to marketing segmentation strategies.

The fact that consumers tend to buy mostly brands within the same level of informational/utilitarian reinforcement raised the question of how consumers repeat their purchases of brands belonging to the same or different levels. This investigation is described in Chapter 8 (Oliveira-Castro et al., 2005), where we examined the dynamics of successive repeat-buying and penetration levels of groups of brands belonging to similar levels of brand differentiation. This work presents two equations that describe the dynamic properties of repeat-buying which can be used by managers to estimate, for example, the proportion of sequential repeat buyers and non-repeat buyers at any point of a product shopping cycle.

Intra- and inter-brand elasticities

The previously described tendency of buying larger quantities when paying lower prices still raises questions about the underlying choice patterns. Do consumers buy larger quantities of a given Brand A when Brand A's price is lower or do they buy larger quantities when buying a cheaper Brand B or some combination of both? One of the ways of answering this question would be to analyze intra- and inter-brand elasticities. Intra-brand elasticities would occur if consumers were to buy larger quantities of Brand A when Brand A is cheaper (due to price promotion or regular package size discount). Inter-brand elasticity would occur if consumers were to buy larger quantities when buying a cheaper Brand A than when buying a more expensive Brand B. A theoretically interesting way of looking at inter-brand elasticity would be to consider that inter-brand switching may occur across utilitarian levels, across informational level, or both. This would not only provide information about inter-brand elasticity in general, but would also suggest the type of benefits that may be influencing consumers' choices.

The study described in Chapter 7 (Oliveira-Castro *et al.*, 2005), conducted these analyses using data from the 80-consumer panel described previously. Intra-brand elasticity was calculated considering changes in quantity and price relative to the average quantity and price for each brand. So, intra-brand elasticity measured changes in quantity above and below the average quantity bought for the brand when its price changed above and below the brand average. Two types of inter-brand elasticities were calculated. Informational inter-brand elasticity, measuring changes in quantity bought as a function of changes in the informational level of the brands, and utilitarian inter-brand elasticity, measuring changes in quantity bought as a function of changes in the utilitarian level of the brands.

Multiple regression analyses, with quantity bought as a function of intra-brand price, inter-brand utilitarian level, and inter-brand informational level (all in log scales), revealed that all elasticity coefficients were significant ($p \leq .05$) for at least eight of the nine product categories. These results suggest that the observed overall demand elasticity can be decomposed into these three choice patterns. Moreover, when the types of coefficients were compared, results showed that intra-brand elasticity coefficients were larger than inter-brand utilitarian elasticity coefficients, which, in turn, were larger than inter-brand informational coefficients.

Some conclusions concerning brand choice and future directions

The results presented here answered, at least partially, some of the open questions concerning consumers' patterns of brand choice. One can conclude from this line of research on brand choice that: (1) The vast majority of consumers practice a multi-brand repertoire when purchasing routinely-purchased packaged goods; (2) Brands within the repertoire are functionally substitutable; (3) Brand repertoires are mostly formed by brands belonging to the same level of utilitarian and informational levels; (4) Consumers that buy larger quantities in average tend to pay lower prices in average; (5) Consumers tend to buy larger quantities when paying lower prices; (6) This tendency of buying larger quantities with lower prices is related to three different patterns: buying larger quantities of a given brand when its price is lower (intra-brand elasticity), buying larger quantities when buying a brand with lower utilitarian level (utilitarian elasticity), and buying larger quantities when buying a brand with lower informational level (informational elasticity); (7) Intra-brand elasticity is higher than utilitarian elasticity, which is higher than informational elasticity.

This research fills some of the gaps found in the literature and advances our knowledge of consumers' brand choice, but, as any research program, it also raises several new questions about brand choice. One of them concerns the applicability of matching analyses to identify the level of substitutability of different subcategories of the same product. Research that extends matching measures to product categories is being conducted at the moment.

Another question is related to the relative contribution of each choice pattern to overall changes in the quantity consumers buy. If consumers change the quantity they buy as a function of intra-brand and inter-brand price variations, and if consumers buying different quantities in average tend to pay different prices in average (i.e., inter-consumer elasticity), it would be important to know how much each of these patterns contribute to overall changes in quantity, that is, changes in quantity when all data points of all consumers are included in the analysis, which is what actually happens in the market. One way of doing this would be to decompose total price elasticity into intra-consumer and inter-consumer elasticities, which in turn would be each decomposed into intra-brand and inter-brand elasticities. Unfortunately, the sizes of the samples used in the research we have described so far were too small for such simultaneous analyses of elasticities. Because of that, we are at present conducting these analyses using a much larger sample from a consumer panel.

Other ways of classifying the level of informational reinforcement of brands are also being developed. This is being done with the help of questionnaires that ask large groups of consumers (Dias & Oliveira-Castro, in press; Pohl & Oliveira-Castro, in press) or small groups of experts to rate brands according to their level of quality and familiarity. At present, this new way of measuring brand informational level is being used to evaluate consumer-based brand equity in different product categories, in an attempt to assess the level of *brandability* of products.

The epistemological, theoretical and empirical bases of the BPM are also being refined and expanded. Epistemological work is being developed in the direction of incorporating, in a theoretical consistent manner, the analysis of mental phenomena, such as intentionality, into a behavioral interpretation of consumer choice (Foxall, 2004), and integrating this interpretation with other contemporary behavioral approaches of consumptions, such as teleological behaviorism and picoeconomics (Foxall, 2005). Empirical research is also under way to investigate contextual and temporal consistencies of individual difference in brand choice patterns, such as the disposition of buying brands at different benefit levels.

Conclusion

Consumer behavior analysis is a new and fast growing field of research (*cf.* Foxall, 2002; Oliveira-Castro & Foxall, 2005). The investigation of brand choice presented in this volume includes examples of how the field uses behavior principles, usually gained experimentally, to interpret human economic consumption. In addition, laboratory experiments with human subjects have enabled propositions about matching to be examined empirically in a simulated shopping mall context (Hantula *et al.*, 2001; Rajala & Hantula, 2000), and other experiments have allowed propositions with regard for instance to unit pricing to be examined with human consumers (e.g., Madden *et al.*, 2000).

The area stands academically at the intersection of behavioral economics on one hand, and marketing science – the study of the behavior of consumers and marketers, especially as they interact – on the other. Whilst behavior principles are central to its theoretical and empirical research program, its quest to interpret naturally occurring consumer behavior such as purchasing, saving, gambling, brand choice, the adoption of innovations, and the consumption of services raises philosophical and methodological issues that go beyond the academic discipline known as the "experimental analysis of behavior", "analysis" or "behavioral economics".

However, there remain problems of interpreting the behavior of consumers acting *in situ* and subject to the multiple influences of modern marketing management and the societal influences that shape consumption. Psychology has long attempted to formulate *rules of correspondence* by which the theoretical constructs it employs to denote unobservable operations can be related to observed behavior. The aim of radical behaviorists has generally been to avoid theoretical terms of this kind but different sorts of rules of correspondence are needed: rules that relate the findings of laboratory research to the interpretation of everyday life to which we address ourselves. The full scope of consumer behavior analysis is not yet fixed: diversity of materials and viewpoints is an essential element in the intellectual adventure and what will prove central and what merely useful has yet to be established.

Notes

1. Adapted from Foxall et al. (2006b). "Consumer behavior analysis: The case of brand choice". *Revista Psicologia: Organizac[,]ões e Trabalho*, in press.
2. Goodhardt et al. (1984, p. 634) explain: "Most branded goods markets are largely unsegmented. The structure of buyer behavior is the same for radically different kinds of product-classes (like breakfast cereals or detergents), for different advertised brands (like Kellogg's Corn Flakes and Nabisco's Shredded Wheat), and irrespective of 'exogenous' variables like the interest rate [...]."
3. Interval schedules arrange reinforcement for the first response after a minimum time interval has elapsed since the previous reinforcement. In fixed-interval schedules this time duration remains constant across intervals whereas in variable-interval schedules it varies around an average value. Concurrent schedules arrange two or more reinforcement schedules simultaneously to different responses, for example, a variable-interval schedule of 30 s for pecking key x and a variable-interval schedule of 90 s for pecking key y.
4. Ratio schedules arrange reinforcement for the first response after the emission of a number of responses since the previous reinforcement. In fixed-ratio schedules this number is constant for every reinforcement whereas in variable-ratio schedules it varies around an average value.

References

Alhadeff, D. A. (1982). *Microeconomics and Human Behavior: Toward a New Synthesis of Economics and Psychology*. Berkeley, CA: University of California Press.

Ajzen, I. (1985). "From intentions to actions: a theory of planned behavior", in J. Kuhl & J. Beckman (eds) *Action Control: From cognition to behavior*. Berlin: Springer Verlag, pp. 11–39.

Ajzen, I. & Fishbein, M. (1980). *Understanding attitudes and predicting social behavior*. Englewood Cliffs, NJ: Prentice Hall.

Bartholomew, D. J. (1984). "Discussion: The Dirichlet: A comprehensive model of buying behavior". *The Journal of the Royal Statistical Society Series A (General)*, 147 (5), 643–4.

Baum, W. M. (1974). "On two types of deviation from the matching law: Bias and undermatching". *Journal of the Experimental Analysis of Behavior*, 22, 231–42.

Bitner, M. J. (1992). "Servicescapes: the impact of physical surroundings on customers and employees". *Journal of Marketing*, 56 (2), 57–71.

Chaiken, S. (1980). "Heuristic versus systematic information processing and the use of source versus message cues in persuasion". *Journal of Personality and Social Psychology*, 39, 752–66.

Davies, J., Foxall, G. R. & Pallister, J. (2002). "Beyond the intention-behaviour mythology: An integrated model of recycling". *Marketing Theory*, 2 (1), 29–113.
Dawson, S., Bloch, P. H. & Ridgway, N. M. (1990). "Shopping motives, emotional states, and retail outlets". *Journal of Retailing*, 66 (4), 408–27.
Dias, M. B. & Oliveira-Castro, J. M. (in press). "Comportamento de procura por produtosÇ Efeitos da quantidade de marcas". *Revista Psicologia: Organizações e Trabalho*. [Product searching behavior: Effects of the number of brands]
Donovan, R. J. & Rossiter, J. R. (1982). "Store atmosphere: an environmental psychology approach". *Journal of Retailing*, 58 (1), 34–57.
Ehrenberg, A. S. C. (1972/1988). *Repeat Buying: Facts, Theory and Applications, 2nd edn.* New York: Oxford University Press/London: Griffin.
Ehrenberg, A. S. C. (1991). "New brands and the existing market". *Journal of the Market Research Society*, 33 (4), 285–99.
Ehrenberg, A. S. C. & Goodhardt, G. J. (1977). *Essays on Understanding Buyer Behavior*. New York: J. Walter Thompson and Market Research Corporation of America.
Ehrenberg, A. S. C., Goodhardt, G. J. & Barwise, P. (1990). "Double jeopardy revisited". *Journal of Marketing*, 54, 82–91.
Ehrenberg, A. S. C., Hammond, K. & Goodhardt, G. J. (1994). "The after-effects of price-related consumer promotions". *Journal of Advertising Research*, 34 (4), 11–21.
Ehrenberg, A. S. C. & Scriven, J. (1999). "Brand loyalty", in P. E. Earl & S. Kemp (eds) *The Elgar Companion to Consumer Research and Economic Psychology*. Cheltenham, Gloucestershire: Edward Elgar, pp. 53–63.
Ehrenberg, A. S. C., Uncles, M. D. & Goodhardt, G. J. (2004). "Understanding brand performance measures: Using Dirichlet benchmarks". *Journal of Business Research*, 57, 1307–25.
Engel, J. F., Blackwell, R. D. & Miniard, P. W. (1995). *Consumer Behavior, 8th edn.* Chicago: Dryden Press.
Feyerabend, P. (1993). *Against Method*. London and New York: Verso.
Foxall, G. R. (1987). "Radical Behaviorism and Consumer Research". *International Journal of Research in Marketing*, 4, 111–29.
Foxall, G. R. (1990). *Consumer Psychology in Behavioral Perspective*. London and New York: Routledge.
Foxall, G. R. (1992). "The Behavioral Perspective Model of purchase and consumption: from consumer theory to marketing practice". *Journal of the Academy of Marketing Science*, 20, 189–98.
Foxall, G. R. (1996). *Consumers in Context: The BPM Research Program*. London and New York: International Thomson.
Foxall, G. R. (1997). *Marketing Psychology: The Paradigm in the Wings*. London: Macmillan.
Foxall, G. R. (1998). "Radical Behaviorist Interpretation: generating and Evaluating an Account of Consumer Behavior". *The Behavior Analyst*, 21, 321–54.
Foxall, G. R. (1999). "The substitutability of brands". *Managerial and Decision Economics*, 20 (5), 241–57.
Foxall, G. R. (ed.) (2002). *Consumer Behavior Analysis: Critical Perspectives*. London and New York: Routledge.

Foxall, G. R. (2004). *Context and Cognition: Interpreting Complex Behavior*. Reno, NV: Context Press.
Foxall, G. R. (2005). *Understanding Consumer Choice*. London and New York: Palgrave Macmillan.
Foxall, G. R. & Greenley, G. E. (1999). "Consumers' emotional responses to service environments". *Journal of Business Research*, 46, 149–58.
Foxall, G. R. & James, V. K. (2001). "The behavioral basis of consumer choice: A preliminary analysis". *European Journal of Behavior Analysis*, 2, 209–20.
Foxall, G. R. & James, V. K. (2003). "The behavioural ecology of brand choice: how and what do consumers maximise?". *Psychology and marketing*, 20, 811–36.
Foxall, G. R., Oliveira-Castro, J. M., James, V. K. & Schrezenmaier, T. C. (2006). "Consumer behavior analysis: The case of brand choice". *Revista Psicologia: Organizações e Trabalho*, in press.
Foxall, G. R., Oliveira-Castro, J. M., James, V. K., Yani-de-Soriano, M. M. & Sigurdsson, V. (2006). "Consumer behavior analysis and social marketing: The case of environmental conservation". *Behavior and Social Issues*, 15, 101–24.
Foxall, G. R., Oliveira-Castro, J. M. & Schrezenmaier, T. C. (2004). "The behavioural economics of consumer brand choice: Patterns of reinforcement and utility maximization". *Behavioural Processes*, 66 (3), 235–60.
Foxall, G. R. & Schrezenmaier, T. C. (2003). "The behavioral economics of consumer brand choice: Establishing a methodology". *Journal of Economic Psychology*, 24, 675–95.
Foxall, G. R. & Yani-de-Soriano, M. M. (2005). "Situational influences on consumers' attitudes and behaviour". *Journal of Business Research*, 58, 518–25.
Glasman, L. R. & Albarracín, D. (2006). "Forming attitudes that predict future behavior: A meta-analysis of the attitude-behavior relation". *Psychological Bulletin*, 132, 778–822.
Goodhardt, G. J., Ehrenberg, A. S. C. & Chatfield, C. (1984). "The Dirichlet: A comprehensive model of buying behavior". *Journal of the Royal Statistical Society Series (A General)*, 147, 621–43.
Hantula, D. A., DiClemente, D. F. & Rajala, A. K. (2001). "Outside the box: The analysis of consumer behavior", in L. Hayes, J. Austin & R. Flemming (eds) *Organizational Change*. Reno, NV: Context Press, pp. 203–33.
Herrnstein, R. J. (1961). "Relative and absolute strength of response as a function of frequency of reinforcement". *Journal of the Experimental Analysis of Behavior*, 4, 267–72.
Herrnstein, R. J. (1970). "On the law of effect". *Journal of the Experimental Analysis of Behavior*, 13, 243–66.
Herrnstein, R. J. (1997). *The Matching Law: Papers in Psychology and Economics* (H. Rachlin & D. I. Laibson, eds). Cambridge, MA: Harvard University Press.
Howard, J. A. & Sheth, J. N. (1969). *The theory of buyer behavior*. New York, NY: John Wiley & Sons.
Hursh, S. R. (1980). "Economic concepts for the analysis of behavior". *Journal of the Experimental Analysis of Behavior*, 34, 219–38.
Hursh, S. R. (1984). "Behavioral economics". *Journal of the Experimental Analysis of Behavior*, 42, 435–52.
Jacoby, J., Johar, G. V. & Morrin, M. (1998). "Consumer behavior: A quadrennium". *Annual Review of Psychology*, 49, 319–44.

Jeuland, A. (1984). "Discussion: The Dirichlet: A comprehensive model of buying Behavior". *The Journal of the Royal Statistical Society Series A (General)*, 147 (5), 649–50.

Jobber, D. (2004). *Principles and Practice of Marketing, 4th edn*. London: McGraw-Hill.

Kagel, J. H., Battalio, R. C. & Green, L. (1995). *Economic Choice Theory: An Experimental Analysis of Animal Behavior*. Cambridge: Cambridge University Press.

Keith, R. J. (1960). "The marketing revolution". *Journal of Marketing*, 24 (January), 35–8.

Kotler, P., Armstrong, G., Saunders, J. & Wong, V. (2001). *Principles of Marketing, 3rd European Edition*. Harlow: Prentice Hall Europe.

Kraus, S. J. (1995). "Attitudes and the prediction of behavior: A meta-analysis of the empirical literature". *Journal of Personality and Social Psychology Bulletin*, 21, 58–75.

Madden, G. W., Bickel, W. K. & Jacobs, E. A. (2000). "Three predictions of the economic concept of unit price in a choice context". *Journal of the Experimental Analysis of Behavior*, 73, 45–64.

Miller, D. (1995). "Consumption and commodities". *Annual Review of Anthropology*, 24, 141–61.

Oliveira-Castro, J. M. (2003). "Effects of base price upon search behavior of consumers in a supermarket: An operant analysis". *Journal of Economic Psychology*, 24 (5), 637–52.

Oliveira-Castro, J. M., Ferreira, D. C. S., Foxall, G. R. & Schrezenmaier, T. C. (2005). "Dynamics of repeat buying for packaged food products". *Journal of Marketing Management*, 21, 37–61.

Oliveira-Castro, J. M. & Foxall, G. R. (2005). "Análise do Comportamento do Consumidor", in J. Abreu-Rodrigues & M. Ribeiro (Org.) *Análise do Comportamento: Pesquisa, Teoria e Aplicação*. São Paulo, Brazil: Artmed, pp. 283–304.

Oliveira-Castro, J. M., Foxall, G. R. & Schrezenmaier, T. C. (2005). "Patterns of consumer response to retail price differentials". *Service Industries Journal*, 25, 1–27.

Oliveira-Castro, J. M., Foxall, G. R. & Schrezenmaier, T. C. (2006). "Consumer brand choice: Individual and group analyses of demand elasticity". *Journal of the Experimental Analysis of Behavior*, 85 (2), 147–66.

O'Shaughnessy, J. (1992). *Explaining buyer behavior: Central concepts and philosophy of science issues*. New York: Oxford University Press.

O'Shaughnessy, J. & O'Shaughnessy, N. J. (2002). *The Marketing Power of Emotion*. New York: Oxford University Press.

Petty, R. E. & Cacioppo, J. T. (1983). "Central and peripheral routes to persuasion: Application to advertising", in L. Percy and A. G. Woodside, *Advertising and Consumer Psychology*. Lexington: Lexington Books.

Pohl, R. H. B. F. & Oliveira-Castro, J. M. (in press). Efeitos do nível de benefício informativo das marcas sobre a duração do comportamento de procura. Revista de Administração Contemporânea. [Effects of the level of informational benefit of brands upon the duration of search behavior].

Popkowski Leszczyc, P. T. L., Sinha, A. & Timmermans, H. J. P. (2000). "Consumer store choice dynamics: An analysis of the competitive market structure for grocery stores". *Journal of Retailing*, 76 (3), 323–45.

Rachlin, H. C., Kagel, J. H. & Battalio, R. C. (1980). "Substitutability in time allocation". *Psychological Review*, 87 (4), 355–74.

Rajala, A. K. & Hantula, D. (2000). "The behavioral ecology of consumption: Delay-reduction effects on foraging in a simulated internet market". *Managerial and Decision Economics*, 22, 145–58.

Reichheld, F. F. & Sasser, W. E. (1990). "Zero defections: Quality comes to Service". *Harvard Business Review*, 68 (5), 105–11.

Romero, S., Foxall, G., Schrezenmaier, T., Oliveira-Castro, J. & James, V. (2006). "Deviations from matching in Consumer Choice". *European Journal of Behavior Analysis*, 7 (1), 15–40.

Schwartz, B. & Lacey, H. (1988). "What Applied Studies of Human Operant Conditioning Tell Us about Humans and About Operant Conditioning", in G. Davey & C. Cullen (eds) Human Operant Conditioning and Behavior Modification. Chichester: John Wiley & Sons, pp. 27–42.

Simonson, I., Carmon, Z., Dhar, R., Drolet, A. & Nowlis, S. M. (2001). "Consumer research: In search of identity". *Annual Review of Psychology*, 52, 249–75.

Soriano, M. Y. & Foxall, G. R. (2002). "Validation of a Spanish translation of Mehrabian and Russell's emotionality scales". *Journal of Consumer Behaviour*, 2, 23–36.

Skinner, B. F. (1953). *Science and Human Behavior*. New York: The Macmillan Company.

Skinner, B. F. (1957). *Verbal behavior*. Englewood Cliffs, NJ: Prentice-Hall.

Skinner, B. F. (1969). *Contingencies of Reinforcement: A Theoretical Interpretation*. Englewood Cliffs, NJ: Prentice-Hall.

Skinner, B. F. (1974). *About Behaviorism*. New York: Knopf.

Uncles, M., Ehrenberg, A. S. C. & Hammond, K. (1995). "Patterns of buyer behavior: Regularities, models, and extensions". *Marketing Science*, 14, G71–G78.

Wicker, A. W. (1969). "Attitude versus actions: the relationship of verbal and overt behavioral responses to attitude objects". *Social Issues*, 25, pp. 41–78.

2
The Substitutability of Brands[1]

Gordon R. Foxall

Ehrenberg (1988, for example) has shown that comparatively few purchasers of a product category are 100% loyal to a particular brand. Most consumers show multi-brand purchasing over a sequence of shopping opportunities, choosing within a small "repertoire" of available brands. Ehrenberg explains this in terms of the functional similarities of brands within a product category. Usually, they have near-identical physical formulations and perform identical tasks. The consumer typically exchanges one brand for another because the benefits gained from one are directly substitutable with those provided by others within the repertoire. Ehrenberg is equally known for his approach to theory formulation, resolutely opposing premature theory-building, and favoring instead the detailed observation of buyer behavior and the empirical determination of patterns within the data, especially recurrences of brand choice regularities. Theory can, and should, come later (Ehrenberg, 1993). However, Ehrenberg's assumptions about, and explanations of, the patterns he identifies can be evaluated only if there is a theoretical account of consumer choice that elucidates the meaning of his findings. His work, and that of his colleagues, collaborators and other researchers, spans several decades: it is surely time to move on now to the theory-building phase of this research program.

In this chapter, I draw attention to the resemblance of sequential patterns of brand choice to "matching", a phenomenon that has been extensively analyzed by behavior analysts (notably and originally by Herrnstein, 1961, 1970, 1997; for an extensive review, see Davison & McCarthy, 1988a). The aim is to unite marketing research and behavior analysis by accounting for consumers' choice of brands as a function of the pattern of rewards they confer. According to behavior analysis, behavior is predicted and controlled by environmental events rather than intentional processes. The rate at which a response is repeated is a function of the rewarding (or, more accurately, reinforcing) and punishing consequences it has previously generated. The fundamental explanatory tool is the "three-term contingency" in which a cue (or discriminative stimulus) sets the occasion for a response, which produces rewarding and, or punishing consequences. These consequences, rather than internal deliberation and decision making, explain the behavior. Behavior analysis has been successfully applied to the study of economic behaviors in both human and non-human animals and is an important component of a school of theoretical and empirical research in behavioral economics and economic psychology.

Behavior analysis and behavioral economics can make important contributions to our understanding of patterns of brand choice. Brand purchasing is a behavior that involves choice among a number of alternative forms of the product category. Matching is a relationship between a pattern of behavioral choices among alternatives and the pattern of reward to which those choices lead. In view of the lack of a theoretical account of why multi-brand purchasing takes the form it does, this chapter proposes that matching and melioration (the theoretical behavioral process believed to underlie matching) provide a framework within which consumer choice may be better understood.[2] The chapter also demonstrates the difficulties of using matching, which is delineable with some precision in experimental settings, in behavioral interpretations. It proposes a definition for matching that is appropriate for consumer research and shows that matching theory gives rise to two interpretations of consumer choice, which require further experimental analysis.

Equally, marketing analysis can contribute to behavior analysis by pointing to the marketing-based factors that maintain repeat purchasing, a set of contingencies more complex than behavior analysts usually deal with. The task for the behavioral interpretation of human consumption is to provide an account of patterns of distributed choice for brands of fast-moving consumer goods (FMCG), which are functionally substitutable but differentiated by marketing activity (branding). Behavioral economics has proceeded at the level of the product category (concerning itself with "goods" or "commodities") and has considered functional performance to be the sole source of reinforcement. It thus overlooks the role of brand differentiation in "real-world" consumer markets. The current discussion on the nature of, and the motivation for, patterns of consumer choice suggests that the concept of reinforcement, a central component of behavior analysis, requires further analysis.

Choice as behavior

Matching

Herrnstein (1997) defines choice not as an internal deliberative process but as a rate of intersubjectively observable events that are temporally distributed. In his analysis, the relative frequency of responding becomes the dependent variable. Herrnstein's (1961) initial discovery was that when animals are presented with two opportunities to respond (pecking key A or key B), each of which delivers either reward or reinforcement (access to a food hopper) on its own variable interval (VI) schedule,[3] they allocate their responses to A and B in proportion to the rates of reward available in A and B. In other words, response rate (B1) is proportional to the relative rate of reinforcement (R) (de Villiers & Herrnstein, 1976):

$$B_x/(B_x + B_y) = R_x/(R_x + R_y) \tag{2.1}$$

This phenomenon, which Herrnstein (1961, 1970) refers to as "matching", provides a framework for the behavioral analysis of consumption. As long as there are no differences among reinforcers in terms of bias, i.e., preference for one reinforcer based on characteristics such as its physical position or color, and sensitivity, i.e., responsiveness to the alternative reinforcers, Equation (2.1) simplifies to

$$B_x/B_y = R_x/R_y \tag{2.2}$$

Taking bias and sensitivity into account, Baum (1974) proposed the generalized matching law:

$$B_x/B_y = b(R_x/R_y)^s \tag{2.3}$$

where B is the behavior allocated to alternatives x and y, R is the reinforcers contingent upon that behavior, and the constants b and s represent bias and sensitivity, respectively.

Bias and sensitivity

Bias is absent when b, which is the intercept when Equation (2.3) is re-expressed in logarithmic form, equals unity. Deviations of b from unity indicate a consistent preference for one alternative over the other(s) regardless of the reinforcement rates in operation. As long as the reinforcements for each of the available responses are apparently equal and predict a behavioral indifference between them, *a* measure of *b* greater or less than one indicates that "preference is biased by some unknown, but invariant, asymmetry between the alternatives" (Baum, 1974, p. 233). Bias is the result of a deficiency in experimental design rather than a shortcoming of the experimental subject; it represents a failure to take account of all of the independent variables that influence preference and declines as relevant independent variables are increasingly taken into account (Baum, 1974). Principal sources of bias are undetected response costs imposed in the case of one alternative but not the other(s), such as an additional effort required to shift one lever in an experiment, and a qualitative difference between reinforcers, such as an unanticipated additional value accorded to one reinforcer but not to the rest (Baum, 1979; Pierce & Epling, 1983; Davison & McCarthy, 1988b).

The behavior of a subject who disproportionately chooses the leaner schedule of reinforcement (i.e., who chooses it more often than strict matching would predict) is said to exhibit undermatching; in such cases the exponent *s*, slope, is less than one. The behavior of a subject who disproportionately chooses the richer schedule of reinforcement exhibits overmatching, and $s>1$. Low sensitivity to reinforcement schedules may arise because the subject is unable to discriminate between the alternatives sufficiently well, especially if there is no delay in reinforcement when responses are allocated to a new choice (and are, therefore, controlled by a different schedule), and because rates of deprivation differ between the schedules (Baum, 1974, 1979). The generalized matching law can thus take a variety of data into consideration (Green & Freed, 1993). In contrast to the stimulus response psychologies, Herrnstein's matching equation represents response frequencies as a function of reinforcement frequencies. The resulting choice rule indicates that the average reinforcement rate of response A comes to equal the average reinforcement rate of response B.

Melioration

The empirical findings on matching have been extrapolated from the laboratory to provide an interpretation of complex human economic behavior in terms of melioration, "the process in which a difference between local rates of reinforcement leads to a continuous change in the distribution of behavior in the direction of an equality of local reinforcer rates" (Davison & McCarthy, 1988a, p. 136). An everyday example of melioration involves the way in which drivers on a major highway frequently switch lanes, selecting the clearest and fastest way forward, returning to the original lane or a third when that becomes the most advantageous. Overall, the driver may or may not reach the final destination more quickly than had he/she remained in the one lane for the entire journey, but immediate advantage (the local rate of reinforcement) leads to an averaging of the rates of reinforcement over all choices. An equilibrium is finally reached when the average reinforcement rates of each lane are equalized. Where $T1$ and $T2$ are the times allocated to the two responses, the local difference in reinforcer rates, Rd, is:

$$R_d = (R_1/T_1) - (R_2/T_2) \qquad (2.4)$$

Time allocation changes as a result of the sensitivity of behavior to local rates of reinforcement; stabilization is achieved when $Rd - 0$. Melioration, in which the behavior offering the immediately higher or highest rate of reinforcement is chosen, may result in particular circumstances in the overall maximization of reinforcement, but usually leads to a sub-optimal outcome. Melioration thus provides a molecular level mechanism to explain the behaviors to which matching refers (Herrnstein & Vaughan, 1980).

Marketing, substitutability and matching

Brands and branding

A goal of behavior analysis is the interpretation of complex human behaviors – those not amenable to direct experimental analysis according to principles derived from studies of responding in simpler contexts (e.g., Skinner, 1969, 1988). As Rachlin (1976, p. 569) argued, "even when matching is not directly observed it may still be convenient to assume that matching underlies all choice". Hence, "matching becomes a deductive, rather than inductive law – not a principle derived from experimentation, but a premise with which experimental findings can be interpreted" (p. 570). This working hypothesis does not ignore the multiple sources of influence on consumer behavior. Hursh (1980) wrote nearly 20 years ago that "Because reinforcers differ in elasticity and because reinforcers can be complementary, no simple unidimensional choice rule such as matching can account for all choice behavior" (pp. 219–20). Matching is not the only behavioral framework for dealing with the complexity of choice, as the growth of behavioral economics demonstrates (e.g., Green & Kagel, 1987). Marketing analysis, moreover, has identified a number of influences on consumer choice, which may complicate matching theory in this context. Consumer behavior is shaped by a host of marketing influences such as branding, advertising, sales promotions, and distribution strategies and by social pressures not under the direct control of marketers, which determine the plasticity of demand (Penrose, 1959) and its responsiveness to changes in these non-price variables.

Matching, the tendency of individual organisms to allocate responses among alternatives in proportion to the reinforcement obtained from each, is a well-documented phenomenon of both non-human and human responses in experimental contexts (Davison & McCarthy, 1988a). Matching is a molar process (i.e., concerned with the relationship of the frequency of responding to frequency of reinforcement) which is identifiable from comparison of the rates at which responses are emitted and reinforcement obtained. Herrnstein (1979) pioneered its explanation in terms of the molecular process (i.e., concerned with explaining an individual response), melioration, in which the behavioral option offering the higher local rate of reinforcement is chosen at any time; equilibrium is reached when responses are allocated so as to equalize the average reinforcement rates. The extension of matching to the interpretation of non-experimental consumer behavior in humans is commonplace (e.g., Rachlin & Laibson, 1997). Its further extension to the interpretation of consumers' distributed brand choices within a product category appears, on the face of it, to be a straightforward matter. (A product category is the set of functionally equivalent brands, each member of which embodies all of the essential functional characteristics of the category; indeed, it must do so in order to hope to compete with established brands. Branding is the differentiation of brands within a product category by means of managerial action). Brand choices within a product category, such as the selection of either the Heinz or the Crosse and Blackwell brand from a range of baked beans products on a supermarket shelf, follow well-documented patterns (Ehrenberg, 1988). The impulse to interpret consumers' sequential brand purchasing in terms of matching underlain by melioration is, therefore, compelling.

Moreover, the clearest evidence for the matching law comes from experiments in which the alternative reinforcers are direct substitutes for one another. Davison & McCarthy (1988a); Heyman (1996) argued that both perfect substitutability and confidence that the nominal reinforcement frequencies exclusively control behavior are required for matching to occur.[4] Green & Freed (1993) argued that substitutability inheres in the similarity of the functional attributes of the reinforcers (goods or commodities). Yet in affluent consumer markets, manufacturers and retailers annually incur large expenditures not only on production systems and quality controls to ensure that the physical formulation of their brand is standard for the product category, but also on branding and promotional efforts to differentiate their brand(s) from those of other manufacturers and retailers. While the former expenditure is fully explicable in terms of Green & Freed's (1993) understanding of the substitutability of reinforcers as consequences of purchase that provide a set of functional benefits, the latter expenditure can be understood in behavior analytic terms only as an extension of the meaning of reinforcement. These considerations illustrate the kinds of assumption and procedure that a behavioral interpretation of consumer choice needs to adopt.

Green & Freed (1993, p. 151) point out that work on the matching law generally has used reinforcers that are "qualitatively similar (indeed identical) reinforcers". They also note that "in choices between qualitatively different reinforcers (such as between orange juice and grapefruit juice), relative obtained reinforcement value would not equal relative amount consumed; yet if one assumes the matching relation to be true, then some other factor must be incorporated to preserve the relation between relative obtained reinforcement value and relative amount consumer for qualitatively different reinforcers" (Green & Freed, 1993, p. 151). Rachlin *et al.* (1980) go so far as to claim that substitutability inheres in the measure of sensitivity, s, of the generalized matching law (Equation (2.3)); $s=1$ would, therefore, imply perfect substitutability. They adduce empirical evidence for this view, showing that in the case of pigeons', rats' and monkeys' choices of food versus water, $s \sim -10$ indicating complementary products, whereas for these animals' choices of food versus food and water versus water, $s \sim 1$. Although this is not a universally accepted view, there is general agreement even among its critics that s represents qualitatively different reinforcers (Baum & Nevin, 1981). While economists have generally studied non-substitutes, psychologists have concentrated on substitutes. The assumption of both has been that highly branded versions of a product category (Coca Cola and Pepsi Cola, for instance) are substitutes. The integration of matching research and behavioral economics is desirable in order to combine their ideas of substitutability. A marketing analysis raises additional questions such as "what is the relationship between brands of this sort and those less-differentiated by marketing activity?" (such as own-label colas).

The meaning of matching in marketing

The idea of matching needs to be carefully defined in the context of buyer behavior. It is important to recognize that the matching law says nothing about consumption. All reinforcers obtained are assumed to be consumed. If matching implied simply that the proportion of buying responses for Brand A equals the proportion of reinforcers obtained from that brand, it would be a truism. Assuming that the reinforcement value from consuming a commodity is constant, and that all commodities purchased are consumed (and these seem to be reasonable assumptions), then the proportion of "purchases" would always match the proportion of "reinforcers".

The application of matching to marketing must avoid this tautology. The problem derives in part from the fact that matching was developed on interval schedules (where reinforcement rate can be used as an independent variable) and purchasing behavior is based on a ratio-like schedule.[5] The true independent variable on a ratio-like schedule (price) does not translate nicely into the independent variable of the matching law (reinforcement rate) because reinforcement rate is dependent on response rate on ratio schedules. As a result, translations between the matching law and consumer behavior are not straightforward. More suitable variables for consumer behavior have the advantage that they are readily measurable, however. In the analysis of consumer behavior, an appropriate unit of choice (i.e., the dependent variable) is spending, not purchasing. Spending would be measured in monetary units such as dollars or pounds. An appropriate unit of reinforcement is the number of actual purchases made, given a particular ratio of spending (i.e., price per unit by volume, weight or size). This is not a true independent variable because it is determined by spending patterns. Unfortunately, this is a by-product of using the matching law with ratio-like schedules.

With these adjustments, the matching law comes to state that "The proportion of dollars: pounds spent for a commodity will match the proportion of reinforcers earned (i.e. purchases made as a result of that spending"). Frequency of purchase is thus the independent variable. This avoids the problem of tautology (there are possible conditions under which this would not be true). It also avoids the problem of having varying amounts of reinforcement from each act of consumption. The predicted equilibrium point for behavioral allocation on concurrent variable-ratio schedules is exclusive choice of the richest schedule i.e., that with the lower or lowest ratio requirement (Herrnstein & Loveland, 1974; Herrnstein & Vaughan, 1980), and this has been borne out empirically (Green *et al.*, 1983). The definition captures the essence of a market transaction. We do not know, from the data on multi-brand buying, what the precise pricing schedules are. However, by assuming that functional utility is (a) the sole operative reinforcer (the homogeneity assumption), and (b) constant from brand to brand (the constancy assumption), we can ascertain which is the leaner or richer schedules from relative brand: unit prices. The aggregate data of marketing analyses are then invaluable for indicating how often consumers switch brands and how far they allocate responses between the leaner and richer schedules.

Assumptions and predictions

The brands in a product category are substitutes inasmuch as they are functionally interchangeable; usually, they are of near-identical physical formulation. A new brand, in order to become accepted as a member of the product category into which it is introduced, must incorporate the functional attributes offered by existing members (Ehrenberg, 1991). Assuming homogeneity of reinforcement and constancy of reinforcement across brands, because the schedules involved are conc VR VR, the first prediction is that consumers will show exclusive purchase of the lowest priced alternative.

There is an important exception to the prediction and finding that, for consumers faced with conc VR VR schedules, maximizing reinforcement is the only option consistent with matching. Matching, as has been argued, applies to identical or near-identical reinforcers-substitutes. If, however, choices are non-substitutable, the prediction is of non-exclusive responding on conc VR VR schedules (Green & Freed, 1993, p. 152). Hence, the second prediction is that, if the brands are not perfect substitutes, consumers will purchase several brands within a product category.

In view of the ubiquity of branding in consumer product markets, the third prediction is that the source of any non-exclusive purchasing will be found in the branding activities of firms. This prediction, based on an assumption commonly found in the marketing literature, involves a relationship whose nature needs to be made specific because it is the essence of the behavior analytic account of the substitutability of brands.

Table 2.1 Annual Performance Measures for Eight Leading Brands

Brands	Brand Size Market Share %	Loyalty Percentage buying	Loyalty Purchases per buyer	Percentage buying once	100% Loyal %	100% Loyal rate	Category purchases/buyer	Partitioning % who bought 1st	3rd	5th
1st	27	46	4.6	36	20	4	13	–	32	19
2nd	19	36	4.1	40	15	4	14	52	33	20
3rd	12	26	3.7	47	10	4	15	57	–	22
4th	9	24	3.3	50	10	4	14	56	36	24
5th	7	16	3.7	46	11	3	15	54	35	–
6th	5	15	3.0	55	9	3	15	56	36	21
7th	4	13	3.2	55	8	3	15	57	36	20
8th	3	8	3.9	55	7	3	16	52	32	20
Average	8	23	3.7	48	11	3	15	55	34	21

Source: Ehrenberg & Uncles (1999, p. 13). Product categories: catsup, cereals, cheese, chilled orange juice, gasoline, household cleaners, laundry detergents, paper towels, take-home beer and toothpaste. Based on panel data from Nielsen, IRI, AGB, GfK, TCI.

Patterns of brand choice

Exclusive choice: the sole purchasers

A small proportion of buyers are loyal to one brand over a sequence of 10:15 purchases of the product category (Table 2.1). Each brand attracts exclusive purchasers who are a relatively small proportion of buyers of the product category. Larger, more differentiated brands attract a rather higher proportion of exclusive purchasers than small brands.

Non-exclusive choice: the multi-brand purchasers

Most customers of any brand buy other brands far more often than they buy it. Table 2.2 shows that a coffee customer typically makes three purchases of the brand per year but nine purchases of the product category; each brand displays more or less the same pattern. Similar patterns are found for brands in other product categories: for example, American consumers of breakfast cereals, which tend to be

Table 2.2 Annual Penetration and Average Purchase Frequencies (Leading Brands in Order of Market Share)

Instant coffee, USA, Annual	Market Share %	Penetration %	Average purchases[a] Brand	Any
Any instant	100	67	–	7
Maxwell House	19	24	3.6	9
Sanka	15	21	3.1	9
Tasters Choice	14	22	2.8	9
High Point	13	22	2.6	8
Folgers	11	18	2.7	9
Nescafe	8	13	2.9	11
Brim	4	9	2.0	9
Maxim	3	6	2.6	11
Other	13	20	3.0	9
Average Brand	11	17	208	9

[a] per buyer of the brand.
Source: Ehrenberg & Uncles (1999, p. 6). Although this table refers to instant coffee, the database is comprehensive: The product categories investigated by Ehrenberg et al. include: 30 food and beverage items ranging from cookies to take-home beer; 20 personal care products and cleaners from cosmetics to washing-up liquids; industrial and durable goods including gasoline, aviation fuel and motor cars; stores, store chains, shopping trips; and audience viewership patterns for TV programs and channels. The research summarized here was undertaken, between 1950 and 1995, in the UK, Continental Europe, the USA and Japan.

highly-differentiated, make about five purchases of a brand per year, but 35 purchases of the product category; British consumers of gasoline, a product category which is much more difficult to differentiate, make ten purchases of a given brand annually, but 50 of the product category (Ehrenberg & Goodhardt, 1979). From these figures can be calculated the annual "share of category requirements" (SCR), which is the average number of brand purchases divided by the average number of product category purchases over a year. Breakfast cereals show an SCR of 13%; for gasoline, the SCR is 20%.

Whatever the brand, its customers buy a similar range of other brands and do so in a replicated pattern. Thus, Table 2.3 indicates that Maxwell House was, on average, bought by 41% of the customers of each of the other brands, and Maxim by about 12% of each other brand's customers. These phenomena appear predictable from the penetration (and market share) levels of each brand: hence, Maxwell House's penetration was the highest; Maxim's was the lowest. Finally, it is notable that, apart from those relatively few customers who are 100%-loyal to any brand, buyers tend to restrict their purchases to a small subset of brands rather than spreading them across the entire brand set. Even 100% brand loyal buyers are not particularly heavy buyers of their preferred brand.

The variability in consumers' choices is also borne out by the data on penetration rates and market shares, which diverge markedly from brand to brand (Table 2.2). (Market share records the percentage of product category sales accounted for by each brand. Penetration measures the percentage of potential buyers of a brand who in fact pur-

Table 2.3 Duplications of Purchases between Brands

Instant coffee, USA, annual buyers of	Percentage who also bought							
	1	2	3	4	5	6	7	8
1. Maxwell House	–	32	29	32	38	26	13	13
2. Sanka	36	–	32	40	25	23	20	11
3. Tasters Choice	31	32	–	36	28	20	17	14
4. High Point	34	38	34	–	31	22	18	10
5. Folgers	51	30	35	40	–	25	15	11
6. Nescafe	48	39	34	40	34	–	15	8
7. Brim	33	45	39	44	27	20	–	16
8. Maxim	52	38	51	39	34	17	25	–
Average Duplication	**41**	**36**	**36**	**39**	**31**	**22**	**17**	**12**

Source: Ehrenberg & Uncles (1999).

chased it in a given time period). For instant coffee, which is typical of consumer product categories, annual brand penetrations range from 6% to 24%, and market shares from 3% to 19%. Table 2.1 shows similar results for a wider range of products.

Repeat purchase loyalty tends to be similar for brands that have similar market shares: compare the repeat rates for highly-differentiated versus less-differentiated brands in Tables 2.1 and 2.2. Smaller brands not only attract fewer buyers but those buyers buy less of the brand (or buy it less frequently), a phenomenon known as "double jeopardy" (Ehrenberg *et al.*, 1990). Both the SCRs and the number of sole buyers are lower for smaller brands (Ehrenberg & Uncles, 1999). There is no evidence of rigid market partitioning into clusters of brands that exclusively attract some customers rather than others. However, a buyer of one of the more-differentiated brands is more likely to buy another highly-differentiated brand on a subsequent purchase occasion than a less-differentiated brand (Tables 2.1 and 2.3).

Branding and differentiation

Surveys and field experiments have shown three relationships between purchasing and its consequences that (a) establish the consequences as genuine reinforcers for the consumer behaviors of interest, and (b) will prove of interest in the interpretation of multi-brand purchasing as matching. The first of these relationships is among price, sales and brand differentiation. In this relationship, Ehrenberg (1986) describes an experiment to identify the relationship of price-brand differentiation. Eighteen sales calls were made on consumers who were offered three or four brands or versions of each of three products: cookies, leaf tea and ready-to-eat breakfast cereals. The product categories represented several levels of brand differentiation: physically different product formulations (for cookies: tea biscuit versus shortbread; for breakfast cereals: Corn Flakes versus Rice Krispies); a heavily-advertised brand and a generic: Kellogg's Corn Flakes versus the identical product in a pack simply labelled Corn Flakes; marginally-differing versions of the same advertised brand: United Biscuits' Rich Tea cookie appeared in both standard form and in an otherwise identical pack containing the word NEW; the firm's Pennywise brand was similarly presented in two versions; and identical generics differentiated only by price, sold simply as "Tea" but at three different prices. Bimonthly sales calls were made over an eight-month period at the participants' homes; the participants, all medium-to-heavy users of each product category, formed a quota sample by age and social class in three UK locations. One hundred and eighty-one consumers participated over the entire period, divided into two matched subsamples; participants were allowed to buy none or one pack of each product on each call.

The results indicate that, for near-identical brands, even a small price differential will result in the higher-priced brand receiving only a small share of purchases; however, if the higher-priced brand is markedly differentiated from the other brand in some way (e.g., in flavor, packaging, advertising, or some other marketing variable), it can hold a large share of the market. Brand shares tend to be remarkably stable into the medium term and, following major sales upset caused by promotional activities, the shares tend to resettle at or near to their old levels. This experiment identified a number of components of branding that influence sales: package familiarity, levels of past advertising support, different market shares external to the sales test, and individual respondents' previous brand preferences or buying habits. The author concludes that other elements of the marketing mix, including product quality, availability, branding, promotional and merchandizing activities, relaunches and perhaps media advertising, also seem likely to have demonstrable sales effects that could be identified and measured by experimental means.

The second study establishes that a promotional price reduction has an effect on brand sales (albeit smaller than might be expected) but brand shares and repeat purchase rates return to their prepromotional levels once the promotion has ended. Ehrenberg *et al.* (1994) investigated the after-effects of FMCG promotions based on price in the UK, USA, Germany and Japan. Such promotions are known to increase sales markedly for the duration of the offer; the research question was whether there would be an after-effect of a sales promotion in terms of higher repeat purchase rates. (The authors assumed that sales would rise during the promotion and fall subsequently: indeed, they used a sales blip as evidence for a promotional effect. Their actual research question is more subtle than the mere expectation that sales levels owing to the promotion would not be sustained once the deal had come to an end). Price promotions for packaged grocery products were examined in the four countries, and data were gathered from various kinds of household panel, ranging from scanner output, diaries and garbage diaries; each national sample consisting of between 1,000 and 5,000 respondents. Sales peaks deviations of 25% or more from the usual steady rate of purchases typical of these markets were taken as evidence of major promotions (many peaks exceeded a 50% increase in sales but basing the criterion level of sales increase on this figure did not affect the analysis). Such large sales peaks are generally caused only by promotional campaigns and subsequent checking revealed that price-promotions indeed coincide with the large increases in sales identified. Before and after sales levels could be compared for 175 promotion induced peaks. Small sales differences, both positive and negative, were detected; across the 25 products examined, the average change in sales level was one percentage point. "We interpret this as effectively a nil effect: there was little if any general after-effect on sales" (Ehrenberg et al., 1994, p. 15). Moreover, repeat-buying rates during the eight-week period immediately following each sales peak were unchanged from those recorded for the eight-week period immediately preceding it. Because the sales peaks were clearly the outcome of large numbers of additional consumers purchasing during the promotional periods, why was the increased brand-specific buying observed during the promotions not maintained afterwards? The reason is that some 70% of buyers during the promotional periods were already consumers of the brand, having bought the brand at least once during the preceding six months; 80% had done so in the last year and 93% in the last 2.5 years.

The underlying pattern of buyer behavior is that some consumers who already include the promoted brand within their portfolio temporarily switch to it while it is offered at a price reduction; however, promoted brands that are not part of their portfolio are not tried just because they are offered at a discount. The additional buyers during the promotion period did not remain disproportionately high-level users of the promoted brand once the deal had come to an end; rather, they settled back to their customary rate of purchasing the brand. Even so, only some 10%–20% of the brand's long-term customer base reacts during a promotion by switching purchases; most do not change their buying habits. They buy less frequently than would be required for them to get involved in the short-term promotion. Price promotions reward (some) existing purchasers of the brand, rather than drawing in new buyers. Unfamiliar brands, even when they are highly promoted, tend to draw increased sales only from customers who already feature the brands in their portfolios. Because the usual sales of these brands are lower than for others, the increased purchases induced by the promotion are also relatively low.

The third study indicates that token rewards for repeat-loyalty to brand or store do not affect repeat-buying rates. A particular kind of promotion occurs when retailers attempt to influence repeat-buying rates (or "loyalty") by rewarding consumers for making current purchases of a particular brand or at a particular store in the expectation that this will encourage continued patronage. The rewards usually consist of tokens (coupons) redeemable on subsequent purchase occasions when they lead to a reduction in the consumer's overall bill. Consumers' usual pattern of store choices closely resembles that of their brand choices (Kau & Ehrenberg, 1984). For example, American consumers who in the course of a year bought ground coffee at Safeway purchased it (anywhere) on average 11.1 times. Those who purchased at Safeway did so 3.3 times; they also purchased ground coffee at other retail outlets 7.8 times. Similar patterns of many infrequent buyers and low-repeat loyalty are apparent for chains other than Safeway (Uncles & Ehrenberg, 1990).

Sharp & Sharp (1997) describe and evaluate a store loyalty program in which panel-generated repeat-buying data were compared with predictions obtained from the Dirichlet model.[6] The purpose of a loyalty program is to "lock consumers in" to a specific brand and might, therefore, be expected to generate a longer-term effect than a one-off price promotion. The propensity of consumers to revert to their baseline patterns of brand choices once a sales promotion has ended has been noted (Ehrenberg *et al.*, 1994). The expectation was that the aggregate sample of consumer would: (i) switch less often to non-program stores (those not included in the promotion); (ii) increase the program stores' shares of total product category purchases; (iii) increase repeat-buying rates for the program stores; (iv) increase usage frequency for these stores; (v) show a greater tendency toward exclusive loyalty to these stores; and (vi) increase their switching among program stores while decreasing their tendency to switch to non-program stores (Sharp & Sharp, 1997).

The program Fly Buys is the largest of its type in Australia, and covers all purchases made at participating stores or with the program credit card; in order to accumulate points, consumers are required to present a magnetic strip card when they make payment. Observed variables were close to the Dirichlet predictions; for instance, penetration statistics generally fall within two percentage points of the predictions. The data show no general effect of the Fly Buys program on repeat-buying patterns. Penetrations of brands sold at Fly Buys, measured as average purchase frequencies, were not consistently higher or lower than prior to the program; customers did not allocate a higher share of their purchases to Fly Buys brands than they had prior to the program; nor did program brands attract a higher than expected number of sole-purchasers (100%-loyal consumers). Deviations were found for two of the six program brands investigated in that they produced a higher repeat rate than predicted ("excess loyalty") but they did so for non-program as well as program members. Ehrenberg *et al.* (1994) concluded that "It is difficult to interpret these results as evidence of Fly Buys changing the repeat purchase patterns of these markets" (p. 483).

Interpretation

The focus of interpretation

We have noted that the only behavior consistent with matching on conc VR VR (variable ratio; see note 5) schedules is exclusive choice of the richer:richest schedule. Such maximization is the only strategy consistent with matching in these circumstances (Herrnstein & Vaughan, 1980). In fact, three patterns emerge from the tables, only one of which is consistent with this prediction and even then only partially. This first pattern is exclusive choice or sole buying in which a small proportion of product category users is 100%-loyal to one brand. Sole purchasers presumably maximize something, but all brands attract some sole buyers. The strategy of repeatedly purchasing a single brand minimizes costs of search. Sole purchasers of cheaper, less-promoted brands also minimize their absolute monetary outlay on the product category and may be insensitive to those reinforcers that derive from branding. Other consumers exclusively purchase heavily-promoted brands. The second pattern is multi-brand buying in which a consumer chooses among a small group ("repertoire") of tried-and-tested brands rather than over the entire brand set. Consumers who practice "repertoire buying" might be said to show matching because they apparently select among brands according to some principle of melioration – perhaps responding locally to small price differentials or non-price deals. But there is no direct evidence of this on the present assumptions.

Because the prediction of exclusive purchasing, based on the VR schedules in operation, is not borne out for all consumers, we may at this exploratory stage ask whether matching phenomena other than maximization elucidate the data. If brands provide reinforcers by virtue of their functional substitutability, and do so equally, the consumer who does not, as predicted, settle on one tried and tested brand could be expected to substitute any and all brands in the product category for one another, apparently at random. The brand-indifferent consumer would distribute purchases approximately equally among the brands (and we might refer to them as equitable brand purchasers). Such equitable choice suggests that all brands in a product category would tend toward similar shares of the market. However, the third tendency is a preference for branded goods those heavily-differentiated through marketing and promotional activities; and there are actually large discrepancies in brand shares.[7]

By far the most common pattern is multi-brand purchasing across a number of brands, with a tendency to favor the highly-differentiated brands. These repertoire buyers are of particular interest. They cannot be said to maximize but we have noted that their switching among all brands, including both the highly- and the less-differentiated, is superficially suggestive of melioration and matching. If the homogeneity and constancy assumptions hold, why would these consumers not maximize by becoming sole purchasers of the least expensive brands, or become equitable brand purchasers? Matching research suggests two avenues of interpretation: bias and sensitivity, the b and s of Equation (2.3), i.e., the generalized matching law. Bias and under- or overmatching can be difficult to infer even from rigorous experiments designed to explore matching (Davison & McCarthy, 1988b), however, and it is worthwhile examining the problem in more detail before attempting an interpretation in these terms.

Brand preferences appear to be remarkably resilient to disruptions in the market environment (such as price and sales promotions). Even adverse price differentials do not shift consumers from those preferences as long as the brand is well-differentiated by advertising or other marketing activity. Nor do price deals induce consumers to buy the promoted brand unless they have been buyers of that brand at some time in the past; even then, only relatively few such consumers buy the brand during the promotion. There is no evidence of continuing "excess" allegiance to a promoted brand once the deal comes to an end. Differential rewards in the form of token loyalty points are similarly unable to dislodge consumer brand preferences. Consumers who have never bought the promoted brands seem particularly resistant to trying it as a result of a price promotion.

Why are the consumers who take advantage of price promotions generally those who are already occasional users of the brand who happen to be replenishing their stock of the product category at the moment of purchase? The answer presumably lies in learning history and melioration. Purchase and consumption of the brand in question have presumably been reinforced on several occasions; the brand delivers the functional attributes of the product category; if replenishment is needed, the consumer will make the least expensive choice; the consumer will make this choice for only as long as the price advantage remains. Three further questions are more difficult to answer as long as the assumption is that functional performance is the sole source of reinforcement. First, why does increased value for money attract so few consumers who have previously used the brand? Second, why do non-buyers of a promoted brand not buy it when it provides the required functional rewards more economically? There is no reason to conclude that the learning histories of either group differ significantly from those of consumers who do buy the promoted brand, as long as reinforcement is assumed to be confined to the functional performance of brands. Third, how are we to account for the behavior of many consumers which is not controlled by the contingencies defined by price and functional reinforcement relationships but, apparently, by the elements of branding?

Bias

It will be recalled that bias is a consistent preference for one choice alternative independent of the reinforcement rate. Brand loyalty is a consistent preference for one choice alternative which is independent of relative price. Consistent choice of a highly-differentiated brand is exactly this. If consumers choose the "high status" brand over the cheaper generic brand, this is a clear example of bias.

All three sources of bias suggested by Baum (1974) may have analogs in consumer research. Response bias would occur when search costs for a particular brand increase as a result of shelf positioning in stores or of the failure of a supermarket to carry a wide spectrum of available brands. In reality, response bias on these grounds is unlikely to seriously affect the analysis of aggregate data collected over a three-month period. Moreover, patterns of store choice are similar to those of multi-brand purchasing: exclusive patronage is relatively rare (Kau & Ehrenberg, 1984). No one store's marketing practices are, therefore, likely to bias choice consistently during the measurement period. Discrepancy between scheduled and obtained reinforcement is a more serious candidate for bias. By adopting the homogeneity assumption, we have apparently "scheduled" functional utility as the sole source of reinforcement. If reinforcement is available from some other source, perhaps related to branding, bias will ensue. As Baum (1974, p. 238) argued, choice between qualitatively different reinforcers resembles choice between different amounts of the same reinforcer. Branding may so enhance a particular alternative, perhaps operating as an establishing operation (Michael, 1982) or by presenting rules in the form of augmentals (Zettle & Hayes, 1982), as to render the "intended" schedules of little value in interpreting consumer behavior.

The question of qualitatively different reinforcers deserves comment in its own right. Branding points to reinforcing consequences of ownership and consumption (rather than spending or purchasing), over and above those that inhere in the functional properties of the product category. It appears then that brand differentiation supplies discriminative stimuli for reinforcers that are qualitatively different from functional performance. In fact, a brand always signals two sources of reinforcement: functional utility, the intrinsic properties by which the product reduces physical deprivation, and performance feedback, by which it reduces social deprivation. Utility and feedback are qualitatively different sources of reinforcement, albeit ones which act only in combination. A completely unpromoted brand is unlikely to succeed, no matter how well it provides the functional utility that defines the product category. Established brands, therefore, differ in the amount of differentiation they embody. The capacity of highly-differentiated brands to elicit higher spending would be explicable in terms of their providing different reinforcers, because in addition to functional utility they would confer feedback on the level of social and personal performance that would accrue during consumption. They would increase the opportunities for conspicuous consumption, social status, style, reliability, reputation, and so on; in addition, in as much as the product's reputation is inextricably bound up with that of the consumer, they would continue to denote his or her skill, expertise and (socially-defined) judgment as a consumer. Purchase and consumption of the less-differentiated brands might actually diminish these.

Sensitivity

Given the assumptions of homogeneity and constancy, the pattern of multi-brand purchasing identified by marketing analysis suggests undermatching, because the highly-differentiated brands are generally more expensive. This observation does not, of course, reveal why these consumers do not become either sole or equitable purchasers. It also fails to take branding into consideration. Consumers' habit of switching between highly- and less-differentiated brands is difficult to attribute to melioration while homogeneity and constancy of reinforcers is presumed. I should like to propose the counterhypothesis that if it is the case that branding provides or signals qualitatively different reinforcers from those inherent in the functional performance of the product, then repertoire buyers are showing overmatching (favoring the richer schedules of reinforcement).

The view that many consumers practice overmatching by favoring the more differentiated brands initially seems absurd. Overmatching occurs when the ratio of responses to the choice providing the highest reinforcement rate is greater than the ratio predicted by matching. It is difficult to apply overmatching directly to ratio schedules but one possibility is that overmatching would only be present if the dominant brands also happened to be the lowest in price. An overmatching consumer is spending less on the lower cost alternative. However, because purchasing highly differentiated brands is actually likely to incur a price premium, this is not the case. Differentiated brands are in fact offered on a leaner schedule than the less-differentiated brands, and those who purchase them disproportionately are presumably undermatching. By contrast, consumers who favored the less-differentiated brands, whose prices would presumably be lower, would be overmatching, disproportionately allocating their spending to those versions of the product that were presented on the richer schedule. The attractiveness of this interpretation lies in its consistency with the experimental analysis of matching and the behavior analytic concepts that underpin it. Reinforcement is homogeneous and the behavior of those consumers who show a tendency to favor the differentiated brands can simply be put down to bias. In that case, the question raised by the data for behavior analysis is as follows: Why should consumers spend more on these relatively expensive brands if they offer no greater functional benefits than cheaper alternatives? It may simply be the case that the elements of branding are discriminative stimuli for the benefits to be obtained in consumption rather than purchase: they are claims that augment the anticipated pleasures of consumption.

However, it may be that the elements of branding are rewards in their own right that provide an additional source of reinforcement to that found in the functional characteristics of the product (Foxall, 1998). If this is so, an interpretation in terms of overmatching seems more plausible. In order to establish that overmatching was the case, it would be necessary to show that the favored brands are characterized by richer schedules than other brands. In addition, because there is no evidence that price advantage plays a part in the long-term level of sales for differentiated brands – on the contrary, it suggests that price may be a disincentive to loyalty for such brands – the additional source of reinforcement must be located elsewhere.

In other words, if overmatching is the case, the favored brands must be offered on a richer schedule and, because price is not the source of the richness of these brands' schedules, purchase of these brands must be reinforced by means additional to functional performance. The price: promotion experiments support the view that this additional source of reinforcement inheres in the values provided by branding. The qualitative differences between these reinforcers may lie in their differential satiation rates (Baum, 1979).[8] As Baum stated,

> When the alternatives produce different reinforcers, differential satiation leads to deviation from matching ... Differing rates of satiation ... are probably more common than equal ones ... Increases in the rate of occurrence of one, therefore, will produce increases in responding for the other – the opposite of what occurs in choice between alternatives providing the same reinforcer (Baum, 1979, p. 279).

This is closely related to the definition of the complementarily of goods given above. Perfect substitutability and perfect complementarily are more accurately viewed as poles of a continuum rather than as discrete relationships (Kagel *et al.*, 1995). In light of the large shared component of functional substitutability among the brands in a product category, the most that can be claimed is that brands, considered as combinations of functional attributes and symbolic entities, show less than perfect substitutability. If so, the matching law would reflect that spending on brand i as a proportion of all spending on the product category equals reinforcement (functional, symbolic) for brand i as a proportion of all reinforcement (functional, symbolic) from the product category.

Utilitarian and informational reinforcement

The qualitative differences between economic goods can be explained as follows. Brands within a product category comprise discriminative stimuli that refer to two sources of reinforcement: utility and symbol. Brands differ in combining differing amounts of each type of stimulus. They are generally treated by consumers as substitutable because their functional performances are (near-) identical, but brands differentiated by marketing activity are valued more highly over a stream of purchases than those that are less differentiated. Discriminative stimuli that signal utility and symbolism refer to "utilitarian" and "informational" reinforcements, respectively (Foxall, 1990). Utilitarian reinforcement derives from the functionality of the purchased item, its economic and technical benefits, and is contingency-based. Informational reinforcement is symbolic rather than substantive; it inheres in feedback on the social and personal effectiveness of consumer behavior, resulting in the conferral of social status and/or self-esteem. It functions by showing the consumer how well he or she is doing according to some symbolic scale of value. It involves verbal behavior and is rule-based (Foxall, 1997). Such a qualitative difference between the utilitarian aspects of the product and the symbolic references it makes is widespread in economic studies of conspicuous consumption, in organizational psychology, in the applied behavior analysis of ecologically impacting consumption, and in other fields (Foxall, 1996, 1998). However, it is not generally embraced in behavior analysis, possibly because it seems to require a fundamental conceptual shift. The analysis of consumer brand choice in terms of behavior analysis and behavioral economics suggests that it does not require this.

Conclusions

Summary and implications

Behavior analysis provides empirically-based concepts and conceptual insights to elucidate observed patterns of choice in human consumers. Marketing analyses of consumer choice identify two types of buyer behavior: exclusive purchase of a brand and multi-brand purchasing. Over time, sole buyers may become multi-brand purchasers; those observed may simply buy the product category so infrequently as to rule out multi-brand buying during the time period recorded.

The sole buyers' behavior is consistent with the matching theory prediction for close substitutes presented on conc VR VR schedules in one respect, inconsistent in another. The prediction is that one choice should be exclusively preferred that presented on the most economical schedule. Sole buyers are, by definition, exclusive purchasers of one brand or another, but each brand in the product category has its own set of exclusive buyers. While the theory predicts that one choice will emerge overall as the only brand selected by the entire sample, every brand conforms to this pattern in some degree. Moreover, the larger, more differentiated brands attract a higher proportion of sole buyers. If, as matching theory predicts, these consumers are maximizing, they are presumably maximizing different preferred combinations of functional and non-functional reinforcers. The multi-brand purchasers also show more than one pattern of preference, which require careful interpretation. Although they purchase several brands (a selected "repertoire" in the case of individuals, the entire brand set aggregately), they also show disproportionate preference for the highly-differentiated brands. The first suggests indifference among the brands; the second qualifies this by identifying a systematic pattern of preference.

This may reflect bias-preference based on factors other than the reinforcement contingencies. A local store may stock a limited range of brands; even large supermarkets do not carry all versions of the product. Consumers may simply prefer their baked beans in blue packaging rather than in red or green. Any element of branding and merchandizing might effect some degree of bias. This explanation maintains that only functional utility reinforces and that consumers are indifferent to the schedules on which the competing brands are offered. Price differences, relatively small for affluent customers, may actually have little influence on choice. Hence, preference for promoted brands is accounted for as bias. However, the observed patterns of multi-brand purchasing may yet be owing to sensitivity to one or other of the schedules. If functional performance is the only source of reinforcement and all brands are equal in this respect, then consumers are opting for the leaner schedule. They are certainly buying the strongly promoted brands disproportionately and may be undermatching (only an experimental analysis can unequivocally determine the latter by calculating s). If, however, both functional and non-functional reinforcers control these preferences, the latter deriving from firms' branding activities, then consumers' disproportionate buying of highly-differentiated brands may be evidence of overmatching. The second interpretation supports the conclusion that qualitative differences render brands less than perfect substitutes. The extent of the non-substitutability of brands is extensive: the lack of partitioning indicates that consumers differentiate not only between the broad categories of highly- and less-differentiated brands, but among the brands within each of these categories. While branding differences may be relatively small within each of the broadly defined categories, they are sufficient to allow consumers to discriminate their preferences among the brands within each.

Further research

The analysis suggests that brands within a product category cannot be treated simply as substitutes. The empirical evidence on multi-brand purchasing indicates that many such brands lie closer to the substitutability pole of the substitutability-independence continuum. To this extent, Ehrenberg's explanation of multi-brand purchasing in terms of the essential similarity of brands is upheld; in the degree to which competing brands are functionally similar, they will provide ready replacements for one another and brand loyalty (understood as repeat purchasing rates) will be less than 100%. The relationship among the choices inherent in multi-brand purchasing requires elucidation, however. Are the choices made by individual consumers attributable simply to indifference among the brands in a product category, or can they be linked, by matching research, to specific differences in the reinforcement provided by the various brands? In particular, is it possible to relate choice to price differences or to variations in measurable non-price rewards? A second line of inquiry is intimated by the cumulative proportions of consumers who are totally loyal to one brand or another (sole purchasers who show exclusive choice). Table 2.1 shows that many consumers discriminate among competing brands to the extent that they treat one brand as independent of the others within the product category. What is the relationship of such purchasing to price and non-price sources of reward (or, in terms of the conceptual development proposed above, to utilitarian and informational sources of reinforcement)?

The aggregate level of analysis on which this chapter rests has provided the assignment for behavior analysis and behavioral economics to unravel the underlying patterns of choice that consumers exhibit in their individual behavior. The required level of analysis for further investigation is that of the intensive study of single subjects, which is characteristic of behavioral research. Research in progress which employs this strategy hints that product categories may indeed be allocated along a continuum of substitutability-independence (G. R. Foxall (in preparation) multi-brand purchasing as matching; consumer choice as melioration).

Notes

1. Previously published in: *Managerial and Decision Economics*, 1999, 20, pp. 241–57.
2. Skinner (1947), the architect of behavior analysis, proposes a similar theory-building process: identification of the basic data, expression of the relationships among them, and the emergence of new concepts. Behavior analysis has generally failed to move on to the third stage (Dinsmoor, 1995), a state of affairs to which this chapter may also bring conceptual development, albeit in a specific area.

3. An interval schedule maintains a constant minimum time interval between rewards (or reinforcements). Fixed interval schedules maintain a constant period of time between intervals, while on a variable interval schedule the time varies between one reinforcer and the next (Catania, 1992). The contingencies just described enable behavioral allocation to be controlled and predicted by concurrent variable interval schedules, usually abbreviated to "conc VI VI."
4. Two commodities, X and Y, are substitutes if a reduction in the price of X leads to an increase in the quantity demanded of X and a decrease in the quantity demanded of Y. The usual examples are of highly competitive brands in the same product category such as Coca Cola and Pepsi Cola, Cadbury's Dairy Milk and Galaxy Milk Chocolate (Kagel et al., 1995). (Complementarity is the converse: a reduction in the price of X leads to an increase in quantity demanded of Y; commodities are independent if a change in the price of one has no effect on the quantity demanded of the other). A marketing analysis would emphasize that price is only one aspect of the marketing mix which might influence such changes in quantity demanded. Thus, few if any brands will be perfect substitutes; differentiation is likely to lead consumers to discriminate between them on non-functional grounds.
5. A ratio schedule is one in which a specified number of responses have to be performed before reinforcement becomes available. Fixed ratio schedules keep the number of required responses equal from one reinforcer to the next; variable ratio schedules allow the required number of responses to change from one reinforcer to the next (Catania, 1992).
6. The Dirichlet model (Goodhardt et al., 1984) assumes that the market is stationary, i.e., sales growth of each brand is small and steady in the medium term, and unsegmented, i.e., the brands are independent rather than grouped. The model represents consumer behavior stochastically at the level of the individual household and estimates three parameters of buying for a product: the total number of purchases, consumers' rates of product purchase, and their brand choice probabilities. The model may also be used to estimate patterns of store choice. Its inputs are (i) the penetration and average purchase frequency of the product category and the average brand, and (ii) the market shares of relevant brands. Its output descriptions and predictions refer to any brand's performance or loyalty measures, such as penetration, purchase frequency, repeat buying and switching, all of which are assumed to reflect its market share. These factors form the baseline levels from which purchase behavior is expected (at least by marketing managers) to vary from baseline during and following promotional interventions.
7. One possibility is that the "overpurchased" brands are functionally superior. Because it is unlikely, however, that a brand would be given a functional advantage not reflected in its price, the schedule on which it was offered would remain approximately constant.
8. Of the several sources of deviation from $s-1$ proposed by Baum (1979), differential satiation is the most relevant to marketing-influenced purchasing. Poor discrimination between alternatives is unlikely for experienced consumers dealing with qualitatively different reinforcers; changeover delay, an experimental procedure in which no reinforcer is available for a short period

after a change from one schedule to another, has no obvious analog in consumer behavior; deprivation of itself is unlikely to influence affluent consumers; and asymmetrical pausing, which refers to a subject's pausing for different times after reinforcement on each schedule, again has no obvious analog.

References

Baum, W. M. (1974). "On two types of deviation from the matching law". *Journal of the Experimental Analysis of Behavior*, 22, 231–42.

Baum, W. M. (1979). "Matching, undermatching and overmatching in studies of choice". *Journal of the Experimental Analysis of Behavior*, 32, 269–81.

Baum, W. M. & Nevin, J. A. (1981). "Maximization theory: some empirical problems". *Behavioral and Brain Sciences*, 4, 389–90.

Catania, A. C. (1992). *Learning*, 3rd edn. Englewood Cliffs, NJ: Prentice-Hall.

Davison, M. & McCarthy, D. (eds) (1988a). *The Matching Law: A Research Review*. Hillsdale, NJ: Erlbaum.

Davison, M. & McCarthy, D. (1988b). *The Matching Law: A Research Review*. Hillsdale, NJ: Erlbaum.

de Villiers, P. A. & Herrnstein, R. J. (1976). "Toward a law of response strength". *Psychological Bulletin*, 83, 1131–53.

Dinsmoor, J. A. (1995). "In the beginning …", in J. T. Todd & E. K. Morris (eds) *Modern Perspectives on B.F. Skinner and Contemporary Behaviorism*. Westport, CT: Greenwood Press, pp. 7–24.

Ehrenberg, A. S. C. (1986). "Pricing and brand differentiation". *Singapore Marketing Review*, 1, 5–15.

Ehrenberg, A. S. C. (1988). *Repeat Buying: Facts, Theory and Applications*, 2nd edn. New York: Oxford University Press, London: Griffin.

Ehrenberg, A. S. C. (1991). "New brands and the existing market". *Journal of the Market Research Society*, 33, 285–99.

Ehrenberg, A. S. C. (1993). "Theory or well-based results: which comes first?" in G. Laurent, G. Lilien & B. Pras (eds) *Research Traditions in Marketing*. Dordrecht: Kluwer Academic Publishing, pp. 79–108.

Ehrenberg, A. S. C. & Goodhardt, G. J. (1979). *Essays on Understanding Buyer Behavior*. New York: Market Research Corporation of America: J. Walter Thompson.

Ehrenberg, A. S. C., Goodhardt, G. J. & Barwise, P. (1990). "Double jeopardy revisited". *Journal of Marketing*, 54, 82–91.

Ehrenberg, A. S. C., Hammond, K. & Goodhardt, G. J. (1994). "The after-effects of price-related consumer promotions". *Journal of Advertising Research*, July–August, 11–21.

Ehrenberg, A. S. C. & Uncles, M. D. (1999). *Understanding Dirichlet-type Markets*. London: South Bank Business School.

Foxall, G. R. (1990). *Consumer Psychology in Behavioural Perspective*. London and New York: Routledge.

Foxall, G. R. (1996). *Consumers in Context: The BPM Research Program*. London and New York: Thomson.

Foxall, G. R. (1997). *Marketing Psychology: The Paradigm in the Wings*. London: Macmillan.

Foxall, G. R. (1998). "Radical behaviorist interpretation: generating and evaluating an account of consumer behavior". *The Behavior Analyst*, 21, 321–54.

Goodhardt, G. J., Ehrenberg, A. S. C. & Chatfield, C. (1984). "The Dirichlet: a comprehensive model of buying behaviour". *Journal of the Royal Statistical Society*, A147, 621–55.

Green, L. & Freed, D. E. (1993). "The substitutability of reinforcers". *Journal of the Experimental Analysis of Behavior*, 60, 141–58.

Green, L. & Kagel, J. H. (1987). *Advances in Behavioral Economics*, Vol. 1. Norwood, NJ: Ablex.

Green, L., Rachlin, H. & Hanson, J. (1983). "Matching and maximizing with concurrent ratio-interval schedules". *Journal of the Experimental Analysis of Behavior*, 40, 217–24.

Herrnstein, R. J. (1961). "Relative and absolute strength of response as a function of frequency of reinforcement". *Journal of the Experimental Analysis of Behavior*, 4, 267–72.

Herrnstein, R. J. (1970). "On the law of effect". *Journal of the Experimental Analysis of Behavior*, 13, 243–66.

Herrnstein, R. J. (1979). "Derivatives of matching". *Psychological Review*, 86, 486–95.

Herrnstein, R. J. (1997). *The Matching Law: Papers in Psychology and Economics*, H. Rachlin & D. I. Laibson (eds) New York: Russell Sage Foundation, Cambridge, MA: Harvard University Press.

Herrnstein, R. J. & Loveland, D. H. (1974). "Hunger and constraint in a multiple schedule". *Journal of the Experimental Analysis of Behavior*, 24, 107–16.

Herrnstein, R. J. & Vaughan, W. (1980). "Melioration and behavioral allocation", in J. E. R. Staddon (ed.) *Limits to Action: The Allocation of Individual Behavior*. New York: Academic Press, pp. 143–76.

Heyman, G. M. (1996). "Elasticity of demand for alcohol in humans and rats", in L. Green & J. H. Kagel (eds) *Advances in Behavioral Economics. Vol 3. Substance Use and Abuse*. Norwood, NJ: Ablex, pp. 107–32.

Hursh, S. R. (1980). "Economic concepts for the analysis of behavior". *Journal of the Experimental Analysis of Behavior*, 34, 219–38.

Kagel, J. H., Battalio, R. C. & Green, L. (1995). *Economic Choice Theory: An Experimental Analysis of Animal Behavior*. Cambridge: Cambridge University Press.

Kau, A. K. & Ehrenberg, A. S. C. (1984). "Patterns of store choice". *Journal of Marketing Research*, 21, 399–409.

Michael, J. (1982). "Distinguishing between discriminative and motivational functions of stimuli". *Journal of the Experimental Analysis of Behavior*, 37, 149–55.

Penrose, E. T. (1959). *The Theory of the Growth of the Firm*. Oxford: Oxford University Press.

Pierce, W. D. & Epling, W. F. (1983). "Choice, matching, and human behavior: a review of the literature". *The Behavior Analyst*, 6, 57–76.

Rachlin, H. (1976). *Behavior and Learning*. San Francisco, CA: W.H. Freeman and Co.

Rachlin, H., Green, L., Kagel, J. H. & Battalio, R. C. (1980). "Substitutability in time allocation". *Psychological Review*, 87, 355–74.

Rachlin, H. & Laibson, D. I. (1997). *Introduction to Herrnstein, R.J., The Matching Law: Papers in Psychology and Economics*. New York: Russell Sage Foundation, Cambridge, MA: Harvard University Press, pp. 1–14.

Sharp, B. & Sharp, A. (1997). "Loyalty programs and their impact on repeat-purchase loyalty patterns". *International Journal of Research in Marketing*, 14, 473–86.

Skinner, B. F. (1947). "Experimental psychology", in W. Dennis (ed.) *Current Trends in Psychology*. Pittsburgh: University of Pittsburgh, pp. 16–49.

Skinner, B. F. (1969). *Contingencies of Reinforcement: A Theoretical Analysis*. Englewood Cliffs, NJ: Prentice Hall.

Skinner, B. F. (1988). "Reply to Mackenzie", in A. C. Catania & S. Harnad (eds) *The Selection of Behavior. The Operant Behaviorism of B.F. Skinner: Comments and Consequences*. New York: Cambridge University Press, pp. 113–14.

Uncles, M. & Ehrenberg, A. S. C. (1990). "The buying of packaged goods at US retail chains". *Journal of Retailing*, 66, 278–94.

Zettle, R. D. & Hayes, S. C. (1982). "Rule-governed behavior: a potential framework for cognitive behavioral therapy", in P. C. Kendall (ed.) *Advances in Cognitive Behavioral Research and Therapy*. New York: Academic Press, pp. 73–117.

3
Behavior Analysis of Consumer Brand Choice: A Preliminary Analysis[1]
Gordon R. Foxall and Victoria K. James

Aggregate studies of choice show that most consumers practice multi-brand purchasing, selecting among a small "repertoire" of the brands that compose the product category (Ehrenberg, 1988). Marketing researchers have not suggested an underlying behavioral mechanism to account for the choices of this group or the minority who are entirely loyal to one brand. Price, an obvious source of explanation in behavioral economics (though one which is often overlooked in marketing studies that concentrate on brand differentiation through advertising), has not been systematically related to brand choice other than in the context of promotional campaigns which are short-lived tactical exceptions to marketing strategies (Ehrenberg et al., 1994).

The possibility that the patterns of brand choice identified in these aggregate studies can be investigated at the level of the individual consumer is here explored for the first time in the context of brand and product choices which are analyzed using the techniques employed by matching theorists (e.g., Herrnstein, 1997) and behavioral economists (e.g., Kagel et al., 1995) to demonstrate matching and maximization in laboratory animals' choice behaviors.

Brand choice

The sequential brand choices made by a typical consumer of a product category such as chocolate bars or canned baked beans follow a pattern in which a subset of the brands that constitute the category are selected apparently haphazardly over a series of purchase occasions. Two brands, A and B, might be chosen in the sequence AABABAAAB-BABAB, for instance on successive shopping trips. Such consumers are typical in that they evince multi-brand purchasing, which is the prevailing characteristic of steady-state product-markets, i.e., those with no more than a small trend in sales over the short to medium term. By contrast, a minority of purchasers of the product category are entirely loyal to a single brand over a period such as a quarter and each of the brands in the category attracts its own sole buyers.

The composition of a consumer's repertoire and the precise sequence of brand choices reflects concurrent marketing and promotional campaigns that differ from shopping trip to shopping trip. Sales are augmented for the duration of promotions based on price or provision of extra units (e.g., "Two for the price of one" type deals) because existing brand users who may not have bought the promoted brand for some time are encouraged to purchase or to purchase more units (Ehrenberg *et al.*, 1994), and price premiums may be exacted even in competitive product-markets when the overpriced brand is highly differentiated from its rivals (Ehrenberg, 1986). However, price has not been systematically related to brand purchasing, partly because the small price differentials by which competing brands are usually distinguished are often thought to be too small to affect established patterns of brand choice.

Experiments on choice in behavior analysis and behavioral economics suggest a more general source of explanation for brand purchasing patterns (e.g., Rachlin, 1980, 1989). Behavior analyses of choice have given rise to matching theory based on Herrnstein's (1961, 1970) discovery that when animals are presented with two opportunities to respond (pecking key A or key B), each of which delivers reinforcers (food pellets) on its own variable interval (VI) schedule, they allocate their responses on A and B in proportion to the rates of reward earned respectively from A and B.[2] If, for instance, given a choice of one of two keys, a pigeon in an experimental chamber obtained 70% of the available rewards by pressing key A, it is found that 70% of pecks will have been allocated to that choice. While the maximization theory derived from behavioral economics proposes that consumers will optimize over the sequence of their choices, matching theorists argue that the underlying behavioral mechanism that accounts for observed patterns of choice is *melioration*. The principle of melioration proposes that the individual selects among the available choices such that at equilibrium the average returns from each are equalized; there is no reason to expect that overall returns will thereby be optimized (Herrnstein, 1982, 1990). Although experimental research has generally employed *conc* VI VI schedules, brand choices are like most naturally occurring phenomena involving choice governed by concurrent ratio schedules.[3] In such circumstances, both theories predict that the individual will maximize by exclusively selecting the schedule that provides the higher return (Herrnstein & Loveland, 1975).

Matching phenomena are described by the General Matching Law (Baum, 1974; see also Baum, 1979) – $B_A B_B = b(R_A R_B)^s$ – which relates the ratio of behavioral responses on choice A to responses on choice B (B_A and B_B, respectively) to the reinforcements obtained from each choice R_A and R_B, respectively). The intercept, b, is a measure of biased responding between A and B, usually the result of an experimental artefact that makes one response less costly than the other; the exponent, s, indicates deviation from strict matching as a result of the individual's favoring either the richer schedule of reinforcement, overmatching ($s > 1$) or the less favorable schedule, undermatching ($s < 1$). In behavioral economics research s is sometimes assumed to be a measure of the substitutability of the programmed reinforcers (Baum & Nevin, 1981); strict matching has been found for identical commodities and would not be expected when reinforcers differ qualitatively or require qualitatively different responses for their respective deliveries (Kagel, *et al.*, 1995, p. 53). Kagel *et al.* (1995, pp. 57–9) report results for rats consuming gross complements (food and water) which revealed *anti-matching*, in which the slope coefficients for matching curves were negative, as opposed to the positive coefficients required by Baum's generalized formulation of the matching law.

Behavior analysts and behavioral economists agree that matching results in sub-optimal responding that may reflect melioration. This conclusion is based on experimental studies in which contingencies are constructed in the laboratory; naturally occurring situations are more likely to give rise to maximizing behavior even where the pattern of choice adheres to the matching equation (Vaughan & Herrnstein, 1987; Kagel *et al.*, 1995).

Method

Procedure

Subjects were recruited on a convenience basis among colleagues and acquaintances who were willing to be interviewed and to supply data. Only consumers who shopped weekly at supermarkets were included; no further sampling criteria were applied since this would have restricted unnecessarily the applicability of what was a small scale study. Consumers provided data in the form of supermarket till receipts for weekly grocery shopping at supermarkets. Price data on competing brands were collected independently by the investigators week by week by personal inspection of data provided on the relevant supermarket shelves. Prices of all brands, both within and outside respondents' repertoires, were collected alongside this to allow a more complete analysis. Since one or other of the researchers worked alone on this part of the project, it was not possible to derive interrater agreement data. However, supermarkets that offer Internet-based home-delivery schemes give notice of their current prices on their websites. We used these to corroborate price information gained by the researchers. The participating consumers provided between 17 and 40 weeks of data depending on the product and how their purchase patterns developed.

The investigation was undertaken in two phases, quantitative and qualitative. The quantitative study was designed to examine the occurrence or non-occurrence of matching phenomena and the feasibility of an interpretation of brand choice in terms of maximizing behavior. Each participant in the quantitative study was asked to take part in an initial briefing in which the aims of the study were described and agreement was sought for their providing supermarket till receipts. At the end of the period of investigation, participants took part in a final interview and debriefing which took the form of a straightforward semi-structured interview lasting 20–60 minutes, depending on the number of product classes on which each consumer was asked to provide background information.

This chapter is based on the analysis of data for three product categories and three consumers in order to illustrate that the concepts and methods of behavior analysis and behavioral economics can be applied to the investigation of consumer brand choice. Moreover, the product categories have been chosen to illustrate the incidence and shape of matching and maximization for close substitute brands (cat food), complementary brands (bottled soft drinks) and independent products (cola and wine). In the case of cat food (substitutes) we expected to find precise matching, downward-sloping demand curves and local maximization based on price-quantity relationships. For bottled soft drinks (complements), we expected to find matching and maximization but upward-sloping demand curves. Finally, in the case of cola and wine purchasing (independents), we expected to find anti-matching relationships.

Preliminary briefings and a final debriefing provided information on general shopping and purchasing habits. The specific purpose of the investigation was not fully revealed at the initial interview to avoid a greater degree of price sensitivity than usual. The investigators' interest in specific product categories was determined only at the end of the period of data gathering. The overall priority in the selection of product categories was that they be fast-moving consumer goods since this would facilitate comparison of with the aggregate-level research undertaken by Ehrenberg and his colleagues. In addition, data were selected for analysis which promised to elucidate the buying patterns and price – quantity demanded relationships for types of product class and brand repertoire that would be of interest in terms of the economic analysis of substitutes and non-substitutes as detailed above. As a check on this evaluation of the relationships among brands in a product class, the final interviews provided qualitative information on informants' perceptions of the substitutability of the competing brands which they had bought.

Participants

The first consumer (C1) is middle-aged female, a working wife, who buys on behalf of herself and her husband. Her purchases of premium-priced 100g pouches of cat food (hence "Catfood 100") involved choosing between two brands. In the final debriefing, she described these brands as substitutes and stated that as a rule she purchased the less expensive of the two from week to week. The expectation was that her purchase behavior would exhibit matching and maximization and that relative demand curves would be downward-sloping.

This consumer's husband (C2) bought wine and cola on a weekly basis. Although he described the regular and decaffeinated colas he bought as though they were non-substitutes, changes in their relative prices during the period of investigation meant that they were chosen more as economic substitutes would be: the relative costs per litre of the two colas did not differ sufficiently to produce the expected upward-sloping demand curves (Foxall & James, 2001). However, the wine purchased by C2 during the same period represented a much costlier purchase per litre which allowed his consumption of wine and cola to be modelled as though these products were gross complements or independents which ought to exhibit anti-matching.

The third consumer (C3) is a female, married homemaker who buys on behalf of her household. The item chosen for analysis is bottled soft drinks (this was the first of three investigations we have made of this product; hence the abbreviation BSD(1)). She described these at interview as non-substitutes. The expectation was that we would find matching and maximization but upward-sloping demand curves in this case.

Measures and analyses

The measures and analyses have been drawn from standard behavioral economics and matching research practices (see, especially, Herrnstein, 1982; Herrnstein & Loveland, 1975; Herrnstein & Vaughan, 1980).

Matching analysis. The matching analysis followed the procedures of design and analysis that have become established in matching research with animal and human subjects (Herrnstein, 1997). In consumer research the matching law becomes the proposition that the proportion of pounds and pence (dollars and cents, etc.) spent for a commodity will match the proportion of reinforcers earned (i.e., purchases made as a result of that spending) (Foxall, 1999). In seeking to demonstrate matching, the requirement was to express the amount purchased of each brand as a proportion of the total amount of the product category purchased (the "amount paid ratio") as a function of the amount spent on that brand as a proportion of the total amount spent on the product category (the "amount bought ratio"). This was made operational as follows. The proportion of money spent on Brand A defined as the most frequently purchased brand (*the amount paid ratio*) was calculated as *Amount paid for Brand A / Total amount paid for the product category*. The proportion of that brand bought (the *amount bought ratio*) was calculated as: *Amount bought of Brand A / Total amount bought of the product category*.

Relative demand analysis. The relative demand analysis followed procedures of design and analysis employed in behavioral economics studies (e.g., In order to devise relative demand curves for the product categories, a demand analysis expressed the ratio of amount bought of the dominant brand (A) to the mean value of the remaining brands (the "amount bought ratio" described above) as a function of the ratio of the relative average prices of the dominant and the other brands (the relative price ratio)). In operational terms, the relative price ratio = *Mean price of Brand A / Mean price of other brands in the repertoire*.

Maximization analysis. Finally, an analysis intended to reveal whether the observed consumer behavior was maximizing returns on price expended was undertaken, following procedures discussed by Herrnstein & Loveland (1975) and Herrnstein & Vaughan (1980). On *conc* ratio schedules, there is a fixed probability of reinforcement for each response, which can be expressed as the reciprocal of the schedule parameter. "Thus conc VR40 VR80 describes two response alternatives with reinforcement probabilities of 1/40 and 1/80, respectively". On ratio schedules, the probability of reinforcement is independent of response rate (something not true of VI schedules where the probability of reinforcement is inversely proportional to rate of responding). Faced with *conc* VR40 VR80 schedules, the individual's maximal probability of reinforcement is obtained by responding exclusively on the VR40 schedule. Matching theory makes the same prediction for conc VR VR schedules, claiming that maximization under these circumstances are special case of matching (*cf.* Rachlin, 1980). In order to ascertain whether maximization is occurring, we plotted the amount spent ratio against probability of reinforcement where the latter is operationalized as the reciprocal of the price of brand A over the reciprocal of the price of brand A plus the reciprocal of the mean of the prices of the other brands in the consumer's evoked set (B), i.e. $1/P_A / 1/P_A + 1/P_B$.

The difficulty of ascertaining with precision whether brand choice occurs on a series of fixed ratio schedules (represented by the prices of each brand obtaining on each purchase occasion) or, aggregated over several such occasions, on variable ratio schedules led us to undertake three analysis for each product category studied. The first treated the schedules as a sequence of fixed ratio relationships by expressing measures of amount bought as a function of measures of prices for (a) weekly periods, representing a sequence of FR schedules, and (b) periods of three and five weeks, for which the data were averaged, representing VR schedules.

Results

Substitute brands

As predicted, individual consumers' brand choices in a product category, cat food, whose members are close substitutes exhibit both matching (Figure 3.1) and maximization (Figure 3.3). Although the demonstration of matching may appear at first sight trivial when behavior is controlled by ratio schedules (since amount spent will automatically be directly proportional to amount bought), calculation of *s* from the logarithmic expression of the matching curve indicates the extent to which the alternatives investigated can be considered substitutes or non-substitutes, and that of *b* indicates biases in responding which may reflect qualitative differences between reinforcers (Baum, 1979). The demand curves for these highly-substitutable brands are as predicted downward-sloping (Figure 3.2).

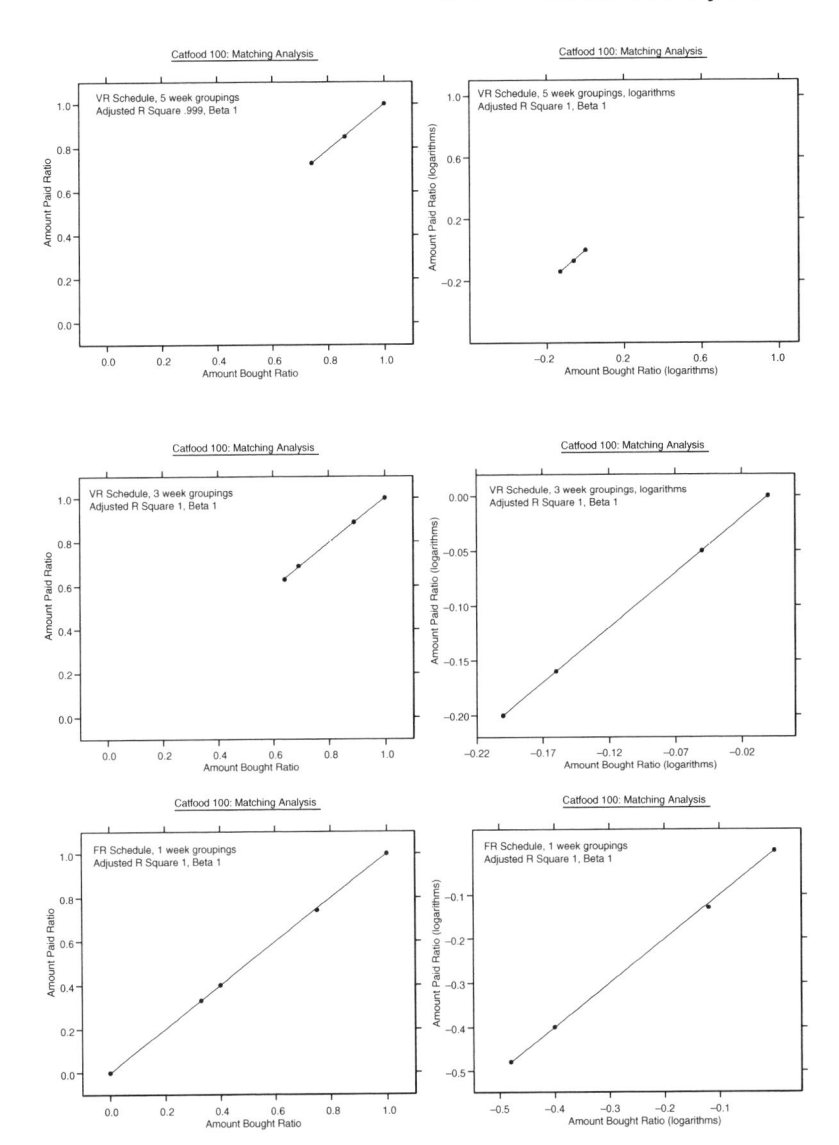

Figure 3.1 Matching Analyses for Catfood100

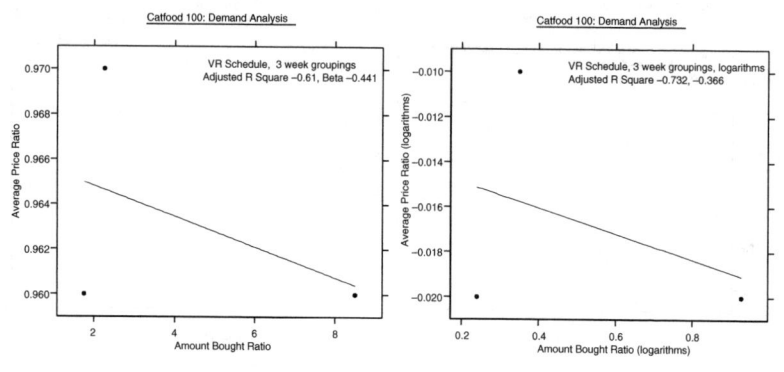

Figure 3.2 Relative Demand Curves for Catfood100

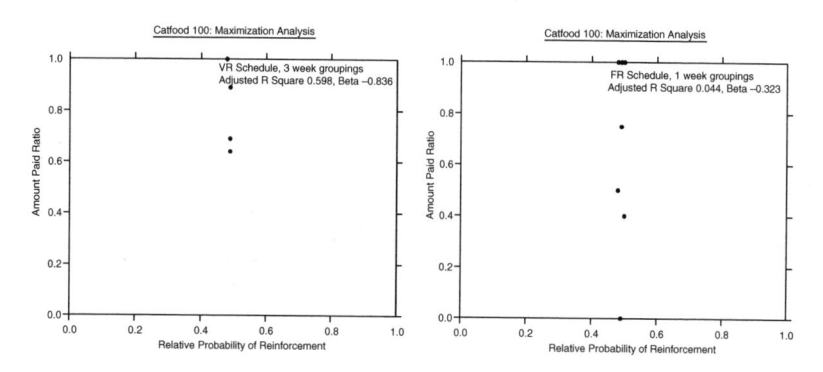

Figure 3.3 Maximization Analyses for Catfood100

Non-substitute brands

In the case of brands that are complementary, bottled soft drinks, similar results are found for matching and maximization (Figures 3.4 and 3.6) but the demand curves are upward-sloping (Figure 3.5).

Gross complements

Finally, in the case of gross complements, cola and wine, anti-matching is observed in the case of the three-week VR schedule (Figure 3.7). In terms of the other two analyses, relative demand and maximization, the gross complements exhibit the predicted patterns which do not differ in their general topography from those of the other product categories investigated (Figures 3.8 and 3.9).

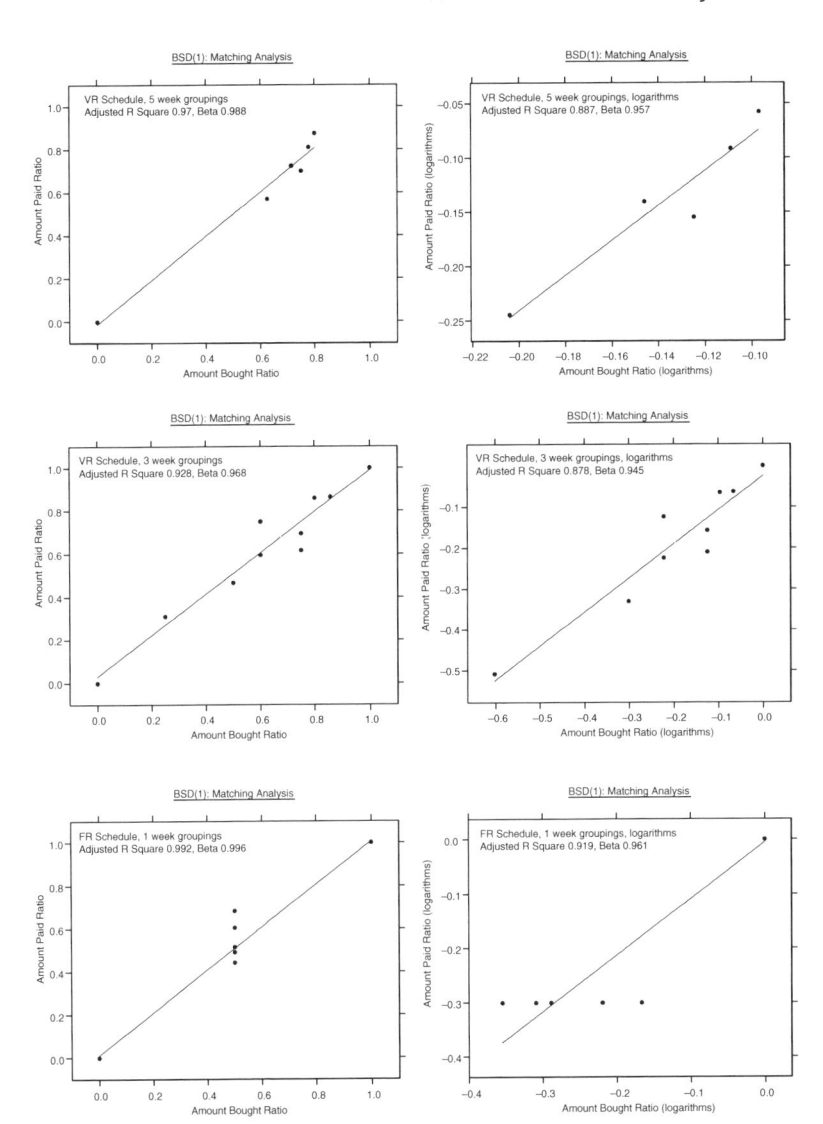

Figure 3.4 Matching Analyses for Bottled Soft Drinks (BSD1)

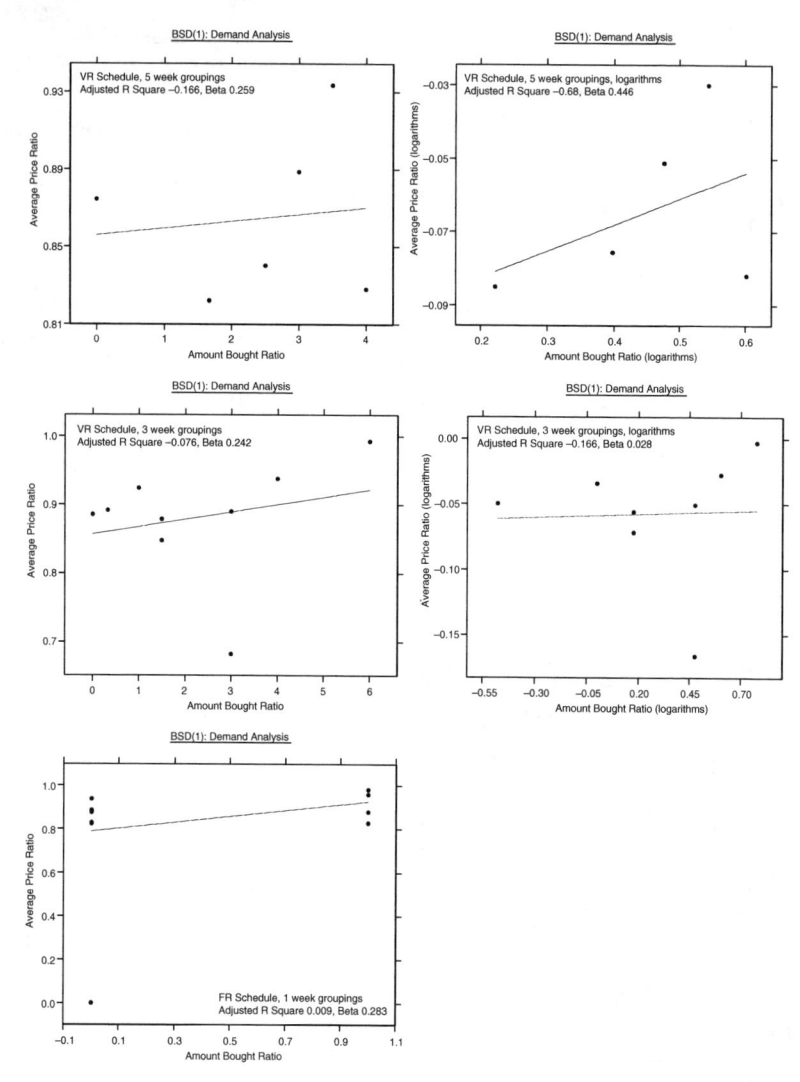

Figure 3.5 Relative Demand Analyses for Bottled Soft Drinks (BSD1)

Discussion

This chapter describes the first application of behavior analysis and behavioral economics to consumer behavior in humans, establishing brand and product choice as a legitimate field for further behavioral

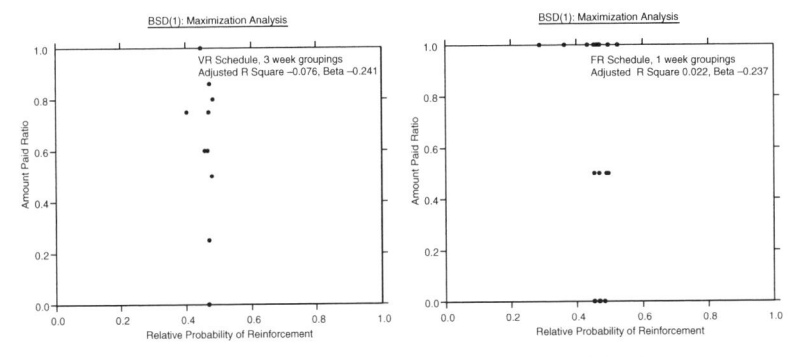

Figure 3.6 Maximization Analyses for Bottled Soft Drinks (BSD1)

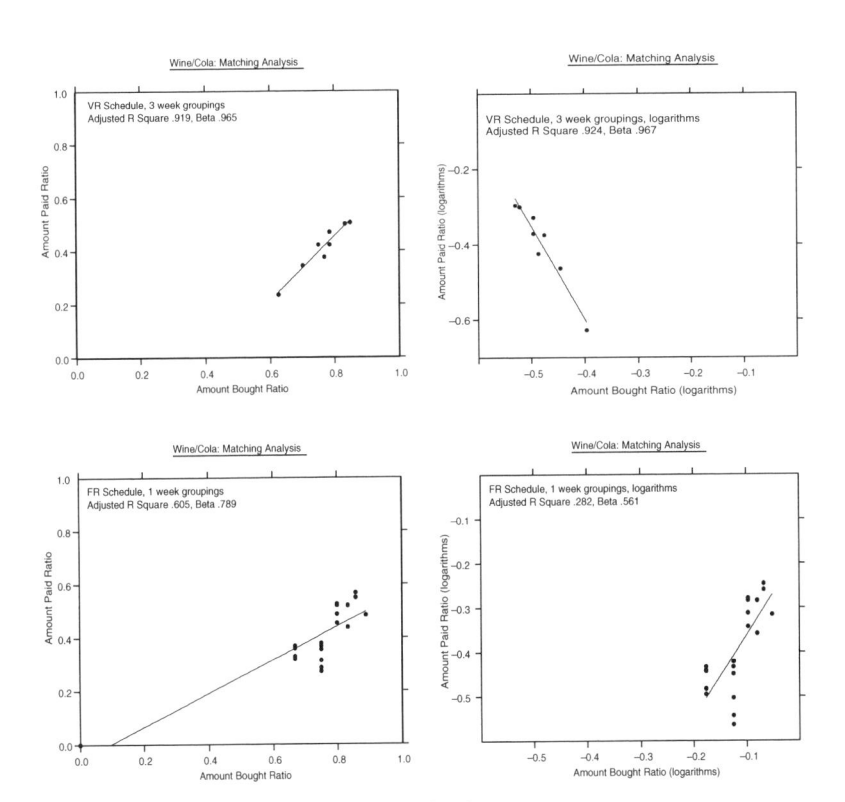

Figure 3.7 Matching Analyses for Wine/Cola

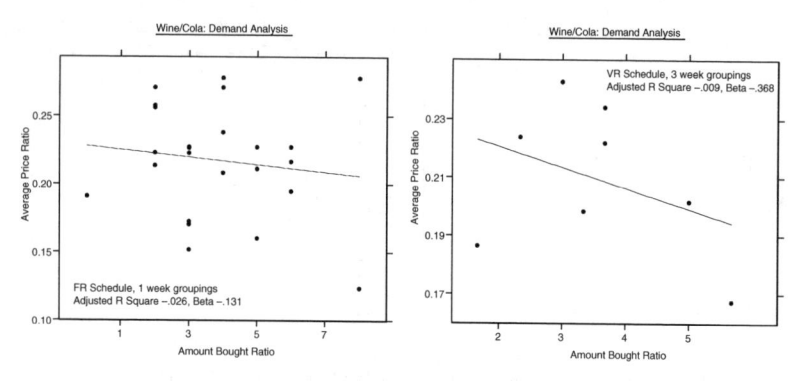

Figure 3.8 Relative Demand Analyses for Wine/Cola

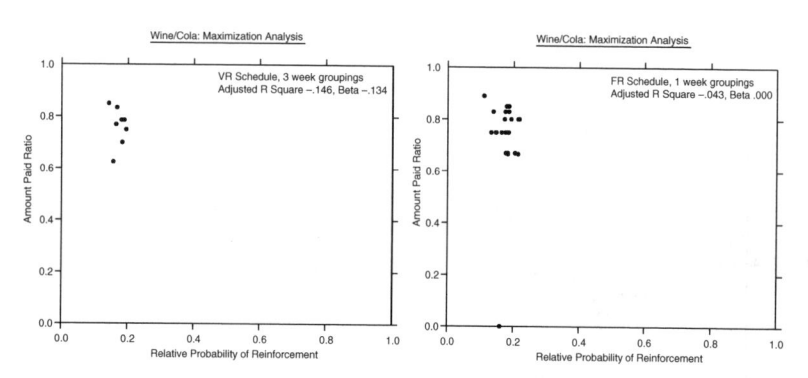

Figure 3.9 Maximization Analyses for Wine/Cola

economics research. The fundamental analytical approaches employed in studies of matching and maximization which have previously used non-human subjects apply equally well to the study of consumers' distributed choices of brands and products.

This preliminary investigation has provided evidence that matching and maximization theories apply to individual consumer choices at both the brand and product levels of analysis. Identification of the differing patterns of matching, relative demand and maximization for substitutes, non-substitutes and gross complements indicates that even relatively small differences in price are a significant variable in the determination of brand and product choice for affluent consumers in marketing-orientated economies. Given the amount of emphasis placed on non-price factors in brand competition, this is a notable finding. The demonstration that competition and pricing play so important a role in the determination of shopping choice suggests that price and value-for-money remain central to the decision-making processes of consumers despite the incidence of advertising and other promotional influences on consumer behavior.

Underlying choice mechanism

We have shown that consumers maximize returns, even when the price differentials among competing brands are small. While we have not reviewed in any detail the models that have been advanced in the literature of behavioral choice to account for observed patterns of choice, we would suggest that in the specific context of consumer brand choice, it occurs in the form of a momentary maximization of both the utilitarian and symbolic benefits promised or provided by immediate brand purchases. Consumers appear to make decisions within the confines of a single shopping trip (purchase opportunity) rather than over a sequence of such occasions. On each separate purchase occasion they behave in ways that maximize the combined reinforcement (the pattern of reinforcement) currently available (given the schedule (prices) in force). This is shown most clearly when we ascribe FR schedules: the maximization apparent from the figures assuming VR schedules appear to show maximization over three- or five-week periods, but care must be taken in interpreting these results.

Further research

Our methodology is consistent with the single-subject research strategy that is characteristic of operant research. As such, it employed a limited number of product categories and consumers, something which renders generalization of the results problematical. Given that the purpose of the study we have described was to show that the principles of operant economic research apply in the context of marketing activity in natural settings, this limitation does not pose insuperable difficulties. However, a larger study is both necessary and, indeed, underway (see Acknowledgement). Our more extensive study of the choices of 80 consumers of eight product categories will enable broader questions to be answered, some of which should be of considerable practical concern in marketing management as well as of scientific significance. This will enable us to gauge more definitively the extent to which consumers' price sensitivity generalizes (a) across all consumers and product categories, (b) for individual consumers across product categories, (c) within and between product categories.

This study and that which we are undertaking at present is concerned almost entirely with contingency-shaped consumer behavior. We recognize the need to investigate the role of consumers' verbal behavior in brand and product choice: the qualitative research that accompanied our main study has provided some access to consumers' rule-following in brand selection and further investigations should seek to comprehend the effects of brand and product preferences, rule-governed behavior, reinforcement histories and the effects of marketing influences such as advertising.

Another issue of practical as well as intellectual interest should be addressed in further research. A major criticism of approaches to the delineation of brand choice based on the analysis of aggregated data is that they record brand choices at the level of the household and hence exaggerate the multi-brand buying which might not be present in individual behavior. Our approach does not eliminate this potential bias since the individuals whose behavior we have analyzed might well be purchasing agents for other household members. However, within the limitations of our small sample, we have found no differences in patterns of multi-brand purchasing for single- and multi-person households. The need now is for a larger sample of consumers by which this can be more extensively tested.

A final theme for further research concerns the effects of ascribed schedules on the analysis of choice. We have argued that in general the techniques of behavior analysis of matching and behavioral economics transferred successfully to the consumer domain. However, the fact that some of the effects we have demonstrated were apparent for some schedules and not others is of considerable interest. Anti-matching was apparent as expected in the case of the gross complements, cola and wine, but is observed only in the case of the three-week VR schedule. Clearly there is a need to use two or three schedules to show all effects. Our inability to do this (for statistical reasons) only emphasizes how future analyses will need to produce multiple schedule data if the effects are to be demonstrated beyond doubt.

Conclusion

The results of this preliminary investigation suggest that the brand choices of individual consumers uphold predictions of both matching (Herrnstein, 1997) and maximization (Kagel, et al., 1995) theories and display expected patterns of price sensitivity for substitute and non-substitute brands. The underlying mechanism of choice is apparently neither the overall maximization predicted by behavioral economics nor the melioration proposed by matching theory but immediate maximization of the utilitarian and symbolic rewards provided by products. Our study, which form part of the broader *consumer behavior analysis research program* (Foxall, 2002), reveals that the methods of behavioral economics previously applied to animals in laboratory settings and humans in therapeutic communities can be applied to human consumer choice in naturalistic settings.

Notes

1. Previously Published in: *European Journal of Behavior Analysis*, 2001, 2 (Winter), pp. 209–20.
2. On an interval schedule, a given period of time must elapse before a response is reinforced. Fixed interval (FI) schedules impose a constant period of time between intervals, while on a variable interval (VI) schedule, the time varies between one reinforcer and the next. Most research on matching utilizes concurrent variable interval (*conc* VI VI) schedules.
3. Under a ratio schedule of reinforcement, a specified number of responses must be enacted before reinforcement becomes available. Fixed ratio (FR) schedules maintain an equal number of required responses from one reinforcer to the next; variable ratio (VR) schedules permit the necessary number of responses to change from one reinforcer to another. Concurrent ("conc") schedules consist of a plurality of schedules that operate simultaneously and independently for separate responses (Catania, 1998, p. 382).

References

Baum, W. M. (1974). "On two types of deviation from the matching law". *Journal of the Experimental Analysis of Behavior*, 22, 231–42.
Baum, W. M. (1979). "Matching, undermatching and overmatching in studies of choice". *Journal of the Experimental Analysis of Behavior*, 32, 269–81.
Baum, W. M. & Nevin, J. A. (1981). "Maximization theory: Some empirical problems". *Behavioral and Brain Sciences*, 4, 389–90.
Catania, A. C. (1998). *Learning*. 4th edn. Upper Saddle River, NJ: Prentice Hall.
Ehrenberg, A. S. C. (1986). " Pricing and brand differentiation". *Singapore Marketing Review*, 1, 5–13.
Ehrenberg, A. S. C. (1988). *Repeat Buying: Facts, Theory and Applications*. London: Griffin, New York: Oxford University Press.
Ehrenberg, A. S. C., Hammond, K. & Goodhardt, G. J. (1994). "The after-effects of price-related consumer promotions". *Journal of Advertising Research*, July/August, 11–21.
Foxall, G. R. (1999). *The Substitutability of Brands, Managerial and Decision Economics*, 20, 241–57.
Foxall, G. R. (2002). *Consumer Behaviour Analysis: Critical Perspectives*. London and New York: Routledge.
Foxall, G. R. & James, V. K. (2001). The behavioural ecology of brand choice: what and how do consumers maximise? Submitted paper.

Herrnstein, R. J. (1961). "Relative and absolute strength of response as a function of frequency of reinforcement". *Journal of the Experimental Analysis of Behavior*, 4, 267–72.

Herrnstein, R. J. (1970). "On the law of effect". *Journal of the Experimental Analysis of Behavior*, 13, 243–66.

Herrnstein, R. J. (1982). "Melioration as behavioral dynamics", in R. L. Commons, R. J. Herrnstein & H. Rachlin (eds) *Quantitative Analysis of Behavior. Vol. II: Matching and Maximizing Accounts*. Cambridge, MA: Ballinger Publishing Company, pp. 433–58.

Herrnstein, R. J. (1990). "Rational choice theory: Necessary but not sufficient". *American Psychologist*, 45, 356–67.

Herrnstein, R. J. (1997). "The Matching Law: Papers in Psychology and Economics" (eds) H. Rachlin & D. I. Laibson. New York: Russell Sage Foundation, Cambridge, Massachusetts and London: Harvard University Press.

Herrnstein, R. J. & Loveland, D. H. (1975). "Maximizing and matching on concurrent ratio schedules". *Journal of the Experimental Analysis of Behavior*, 24, 107–16.

Herrnstein, R. J. & Vaughan, W. (1980). "Melioration and behavioral allocation", in J. E. R. Staddon (ed.) *Limits to Action: The Allocation of Individual Behavior*. New York: Academic Press, pp. 143–76.

Kagel, J. H., Battalio, R. C. & Green, L. (1995). *Economic Choice Theory: An Experimental Analysis of Animal Behavior*. Cambridge: Cambridge University Press.

Rachlin, H. (1980). "Economics and behavioral psychology", in: J. E. R. Staddon (ed.) *Limits to Action: The Allocation of Individual Behavior*. New York: Academic Press, pp. 205–36.

Rachlin, H. (1989). *Judgment, Decision and Choice: A Cognitive–Behavioral Synthesis*. New York: W. H. Freeman and Company.

Vaughan, W. & Herrnstein, R. J. (1987). "Stability, melioration and natural selection", in L. Green & J. H. Kagel (eds) *Advances in Behavioral Economics*, Vol. 1. Norwood, NJ: Ablex, pp. 185–215.

4
The Behavioral Ecology of Consumer Choice: How and What Do Consumers Maximize?[1]

Gordon R. Foxall and Victoria K. James

Although marketing researchers appreciate the significance of branding, they have only a partial understanding of how consumers react to and work with brands in the choices they make from day to day. Aggregate analyses of consumer brand choice show that comparatively few consumers of a product category are 100% loyal to any particular brand. Although each brand in the category attracts some "sole purchasers", most buyers practice multi-brand purchasing, selecting from within a small repertoire or subset of tried and trusted brands (Ehrenberg, 1988). However, marketing research lacks an explanation of the underlying choice mechanisms in the individual consumer that may account for patterns of brand purchasing. Here the authors seek answers from evolutionary psychology, notably behavioral ecology, and from behavior analysis, notably matching studies of choice.

The evolutionary psychology approach comprehends consumer behavior in relation to its environmental contexts, both phylogenic, stemming from the consumer's evolutionary history, and ontogenic, derived from the consumer's learning history acquired in the course of a lifetime of consumption (Skinner, 1966). Evolutionary explanation requires a mechanism that accounts for change as a result of environmental selection and preservation (van Parijs, 1981). Skinner (1981) proposed "selection by consequences" as the causal mechanism for evolution in biology (natural selection), psychology (operant conditioning), and anthropology (cultural selection). What these systems share is the idea that the environment selects genes, responses, or cultural practices, preserving those that are successful (Dawkins, 1986; Flew, 1984).

Van Parijs (1981) identifies the basis of evolutionary explanation in social science as operant conditioning, that is, the process in which the rate at which a response is performed is influenced by the rewarding and punishing consequences such behavior has previously attracted. "Selection by consequences" is the unifying principle that links the contingencies of survival that decide the course of natural selection and the contingencies of reinforcement that shape and maintain operant behavior. As Dawkins (1988, p. 33) puts it, in natural selection, "the replicators are genes, and the consequences by which they are selected are their phenotypic effects …". In operant conditioning, "the replicators are habits in the animal's repertoire, originally spontaneously produced (the equivalent of mutation). The consequences are reinforcement, positive or negative."

The interface of evolutionary theory and operant research synthesizes otherwise disparate lines of investigation: Evolutionary thought presents a broader explanatory framework for the psychology of learning, while behavior analysis provides a means of testing hypotheses derived from evolutionary thought. Together, they elucidate animal and human behavior, not least that of consumers in affluent marketing systems. In particular, evolutionary psychology suggests intellectual underpinnings for the understanding of individual brand choice. Recent experimental research into the behavior of consumers in computer-simulated shopping malls, for instance, reveals an affinity between consumer choice and patterns of animals' foraging in the wild (Hantula et al., 2001; Rajala & Hantula, 2000). Foraging models of consumption generally assume optimality of choice (Charnov, 1976), but there is no obligation in the current context to define this narrowly in terms of the maximization of utilitarian returns for price paid. Indeed, this optimality is not dependent on price (and could be dependent on something as simple as pleasure (Staddon, 1980). Shettleworth (1988) argues, nonetheless, that a theory of foraging behavior must specify the currency or currencies to be maximized. This could take into account not only price but also non-price brand features that include both functional and symbolic features of brands. Given that brands carry both functional and symbolic connotations, there is no conflict between foraging theory and the view that consumers maximize not only utilitarian benefits (which are directly related to function in use) and a broader spectrum of social and personal benefits that have symbolic significance. Various components of foraging research – such as patch assessment and usage (Kacelnik et al., 1987; McNamara, 1982), travel time (Kamil et al., 1982; Roberts, 1993), preference for variety

(Shettleworth, 1988), prey selection (Rashotte *et al.*, 1987; Shettleworth, 1988), and optimum-diet models (Lea, 1982) – have readily found analogies in the analysis of consumer choice (Rajala & Hantula, 2000).

In empirical investigations of the shopping-as-foraging analogy using a simulated Internet mall microworld, Hantula and his colleagues (DiFonzo *et al.*, 1998; Rajala & Hantula, 2000) found support for the matching law (Baum, 1974, 1979) and the delay-reduction hypothesis (Fantino & Abarca, 1985). Their results in general "indicate that human consumption conforms both qualitatively and quantitatively to the predictions of Optimal Foraging Theory and the Delay Reduction Hypothesis in studies of delay in online shopping" (Hantula *et al.*, 2001, p. 215; *cf.* Hantula *et al.*, 1997; Hutcheson & Hantula, 1998). A fascinating proposition arising from these studies is that consumers maximize utility or inclusive fitness (Saad & Gill, 2000) in their purchasing behavior, though this has not been tested empirically in the context of consumers' purchasing behavior that involves brand choice.

Foxall (1999) proposes that consumer choice based on multi-brand purchasing may be explicable in terms of matching theory, derived from operant psychology (behavior analysis) and experimental economics (Herrnstein, 1997; Kagel *et al.*, 1995). This interpretation assumes significance in view of work that casts foraging itself as operant behavior (Shettleworth, 1988). There is a tradition of research to support this view (e.g., Abarca & Fantino, 1982; Dall *et al.*, 1997; Dow & Lea, 1987; Fantino & Preston, 1988; Ito & Fantino, 1986; McCarthy *et al.*, 1994; Mellgren & Brown, 1988; Roberts, 1993; Roche *et al.*, 1996; Williams & Fantino, 1994, 1996). These studies principally involve choices made by non-human animals. However, "the behavioral ecology of consumption," linking as it does the insights of operant psychology, foraging research, and consumer choice, provides an intellectual context for the non-experimental analysis of the brand choices of individual consumers in terms of matching that is the focus of the present chapter.

Matching

Matching is the tendency of animals and humans to distribute their responses between two choices in proportion to the patterns of reward received from the exercise of each choice. Herrnstein's (1961) discovery was that animals presented with two response options (pecking Key A or Key B), each of which delivers reinforcers (food pellets) on its own variable interval (VI) schedule, allocate their responses in proportion to the rates of reward earned from A and B. In general, response rate (B1) is proportional to the relative rate of reinforcement (R) (de Villiers & Herrnstein, 1976):

$$Bx/(Bx - By) - Rx/(Rx - Ry) \qquad (4.1)$$

Matching is well researched in contexts that require an individual to allocate a limited period of time between two choices (Mazur, 1991). Most choices for human consumers differ by requiring the allocation of a fixed income between alternative choices (Herrnstein & Vaughan, 1980). Responses take the form of surrendering money and the reward is the receipt of a fixed amount of the good. Price is the ratio of units of money e exchanged for units of the good. Behavioral economists argue that consumers maximize utility over a sequence of choices while behavior analysts contend that consumer behavior matches. Matching theory proposes that at equilibrium consumers equalize the average returns to each of two (or more) choices; such behavior, in which the individual meliorates, that is, switches to whichever choice provides the greater or greatest reinforcement, may be economically suboptimal (Commons *et al.*, 1982; *cf.* Herrnstein, 1997; Herrnstein & Vaughan, 1980; Rachlin, 1980, 1989; Rachlin *et al.*, 1981). However, both matching and maximizing theories make a similar prediction of behavior on the schedules that apply to consumer brand choice, which is governed by concurrent variable ratio schedules (conc VR VR). Both theories predict that the individual will maximize by exclusively selecting the schedule that provides the higher return (Herrnstein & Loveland, 1975). The relevance of evolutionary psychology here derives from the prediction of matching theory that, under the contingencies of reinforcement presented in common situations such as those of consumer brand choice, consumers will maximize the rewards of purchasing relative to the expenditures they entail (Herrnstein & Vaughan, 1980; *cf.* Herrnstein, 1982; the expectation of maximization may not be an evolutionarily consistent prediction in less common circumstances, however (Vaughan & Herrnstein, 1987).

That most consumers frequently switch brands suggests that they are not maximizing in the manner predicted by matching and maximization theories, both of which lead to the expectation of exclusive choice of the cheapest brand. The theoretical consequences of this have been described elsewhere (Foxall, 1999): what is now required is a means of investigating the behavioral basis of these aggregate patterns of consumer choice. The pilot study described in this article indicates that data from diaries of purchases kept by individual consumers can be used to relate purchase choices over time to the prevailing prices and thus to relate number of responses and reinforcements obtained.

Method

Participants and procedure

The investigation was undertaken in two phases, quantitative and qualitative. The quantitative study was designed to examine the occurrence or non-occurrence of matching and the feasibility of an interpretation of brand choice in terms of maximizing behavior. The overall investigation employed nine participants who provided supermarket till receipts for their weekly grocery purchases. Prices of all brands, both within and outside their repertoire, were collected alongside this to allow a fuller analysis. In total 17 products were analyzed, ranging from bottled soft drinks to butter and cat food. The consumers provided between 17 and 40 weeks of data, depending on the product and how their purchase patterns developed. This article reports in detail on two consumers' product choices, for butter and cola, though the results for these items will be contextualized where appropriate by reference to those for the other consumers and products.

The first consumer (C1) is a woman who buys groceries weekly on behalf of herself and her husband. The selected product category is butter because it emerged in the qualitative research that this consumer buys one or more of up to four brands each week and describes them as substitutes. Although they are interchangeable, she perceives slight differences among them in terms of flavor (one is salted) and color and sometimes selects more than one brand on a given shopping occasion for the sake of variety. Usually, however, one or the other of the four brands is on special offer and she buys that, thereby always selecting the cheapest of the four. The prices she paid during the investigation ranged from 53p to 93p for a 250g pack. (One British penny ("p") equaled c. 1.6 US cents at the time of the study; 250g–9 oz). However, although her repertoire was confined to these four highly differentiated brands, she was aware that what she described as "perfectly acceptable butter" was always available in the supermarket in which she shopped at 49p per 250g.

This consumer's husband (C2) bought cola on a weekly basis and selected two brands: Diet Pepsi was his regular cola of choice for consumption during the day, usually at work. For evening consumption, he chose a supermarket decaffeinated brand, however, typically at a price some 25% lower than that of the regular brand. Diet Pepsi cost 33p per 330ml can at the beginning of the project, compared with 25p per 330ml can for the supermarket's own decaffeinated brand. However, due to price offers, the Diet Pepsi brand was frequently available for 21p, whereas the price of the supermarket's decaffeinated version did not change. Although C2 could have obtained the supermarket's brand of regular cola at the same price as its decaffeinated brand throughout the period of the research, he did not do so on grounds of taste. It was not possible to purchase decaffeinated cola in 330ml cans in the supermarket patronized at a lower price than that paid. He described these brands as non-substitutes and it is clear from his behavior in consuming them that they performed different functions and were qualitatively different also in terms of taste, both from one another and from other competing brands. These two consumer-product examples allow us to investigate the incidence of matching and maximization in consumer brand choice and to relate them to the question of the substitutability of reinforcers (Green & Freed, 1993; Foxall, 1999).

Each consumer who provided data for the quantitative study was asked to take part, initially, in a briefing in which the aims of the study were described and agreement was sought for their providing supermarket till receipts and, subsequently, in a final interview and debriefing. This took the form of a straightforward semi-structured interview which was completed in 20–60 minutes.

Analysis

Matching Analysis. The matching analysis was based on the comparison of the relative amount bought of the most frequently purchased brand and the relative amount paid for that brand. In the context of marketing the matching law states that "The proportion of pounds and pence (dollars and cents, etc.) spent for a commodity will match the proportion of reinforcers earned (i.e., purchases made as a result of that spending)" (Foxall, 1999). The ratio of amount bought of the most frequently bought brand to the average amount bought of the remaining brands was plotted against the ratio of the amount paid for the leading brand to the amount paid on average for the remaining brands. These measures are termed, respectively, the amount bought ratio and the amount paid ratio. Further analysis is possible in light of the generalized matching law (Baum, 1974):

$$Bx/By - b(Rx/Ry)s \tag{4.2}$$

where B is the behavior allocated to alternatives x and y, R is the reinforcer contingent upon that behavior, and the constants b and s represent bias and sensitivity, respectively. Deviations of b from unity indicate a consistent preference for one alternative over the other(s) regardless of the reinforcement rates in operation. As long as the reinforcements for each of the available responses are apparently equal and would predict a behavioral indifference between them, a measure of b greater or less than 1 indicates that "preference is biased by some unknown, but invariant, asymmetry between the alternatives" (Baum, 1974, p. 233). Bias stems mainly from response costs imposed on the choice of one alternative but not the other(s) or from a qualitative difference between reinforcers like an unanticipated additional value accorded to one reinforcer but not the rest (Baum, 1979; Davison & McCarthy, 1988; Pierce & Epling, 1983).

The behavior of a subject who disproportionately chooses the leaner schedule of reinforcement (i.e., who chooses it more often than strict matching would predict) is said to exhibit undermatching; in such cases, the exponent s, slope, is less than 1. The behavior of a subject who disproportionately chooses the richer schedule of reinforcement exhibits overmatching, and $s-1$. Sensitivity to reinforcement schedules arises because the subject is unable to discriminate the alternatives sufficiently well, especially if there is no delay in reinforcement when responses are allocated to a new choice (and are, therefore, controlled by a different schedule), and because rates of deprivation differ between the schedules (Baum, 1974, 1979). Rachlin *et al.* (1980) propose that the exponent s in the generalized matching law represents substitutability.

The matching analysis is subject to the accurate ascription to the behavior in question of an appropriate schedule of reinforcement. There is agreement in the literature that price is a ratio schedule (Hursh, 1984; Hursh & Bauman, 1987; Lea, 1982; Myerson & Hale, 1984): To obtain a product, individuals must provide a certain number of responses; for example, the presentation of, say, 33 pence to obtain a can of baked beans. Given that most consumers are presented with several brands of baked beans on a supermarket shelf, the choices they are offered can be construed in terms of concurrent ratio schedules (usually abbreviated to conc FR FR or conc VR VR depending on the particular contingencies of reinforcement in operation).

Given that prices are prima facie examples of ratio schedules, there remains the dilemma of whether the researcher should treat them as fixed or variable ratio schedules. Hursh and Bauman (1987) suggest that a conc VR VR schedule could be seen as a comparison of prices for two items side by side in one store. Each purchase occasion could be seen as posing a separate price ratio, and this could support the idea that the consumer is presented with separate fixed concurrent ratios (conc FR FR) each time he or she visits the store. It seems intuitively correct to say that a customer compares at best only those prices that are available on a single shopping trip. However, it could also be argued that each product could be a separate schedule, and therefore over a number of weeks including price fluctuations would represent a variable ratio. Predictions of maximization by matching and maximization theorists for conc VR VR schedules apply also to conc FR FR schedules (Davison & McCarthy, 1988). The quantitative data were analyzed both week by week, to represent a FR approach, and in three- and five-week groupings to represent VR.

Demand Analysis. The second analysis was a demand analysis. Again this was a ratio analysis in which the ratio of amount bought of the dominant brand versus the mean value of the remaining brands was plotted against the ratio of the relative average prices of the dominant and the other brands. These data provide individual demand curves. Through the qualitative data collected, it was possible to relate these individual demand curves to the substitutability or independence of the products. This analysis was built on the expectation of a downward-sloping demand curve in the case of substitute brands; that is, the consumer bought less at higher prices because they could substitute other brands. However, in the case of non-substitutable brands, it was expected that the demand curve would be at or upward sloping, because consumers would be less sensitive to moderate price differences under such circumstances. Regression analysis would also provide an idea of the extent to which price plays a part in determining brand purchase behavior.

Maximization Analysis. The final analysis tested for probability matching as opposed to maximization. On conc VR VR schedules, there is a fixed probability of reinforcement for each response, which can be expressed as the reciprocal of the VR schedule. Faced with conc VR40 VR80 schedules, the individual's maximal probability of reinforcement is obtained by responding exclusively on the VR40 schedule.

Matching theory makes the same prediction for conc VR VR schedules, claiming that maximization under these circumstances is a special case of matching (*cf.* Rachlin, 1980).

In order to ascertain whether maximization is occurring, the behavior ratio is plotted against probability of reinforcement where the latter is operationalized as the reciprocal of the price of Brand A over the reciprocal of the price of Brand A plus the reciprocal of the mean of the prices of the other brands in the consumer's evoked set; that is,

$$1/P \ / \ 1/P - 1/P \qquad (4.3)$$

The reasoning is that the price of a brand represents the VR schedule on which the brand is made available: If a can of beans costs 33 pence, the probability of gaining the reinforcer (the can of beans) is 1/33 for each response. (There is a difference from the experimental situation and consumer-choice situations: the consumer does not get the beans until all 33 responses have been made, that is, the asking price has been paid in full). This again relied on a ratio analysis, this time using the relative amount bought and relative average price ratios. By representing these graphically we could ascertain the extent of maximization that would be represented by a step function. As noted earlier it would be possible that we would find evidence simultaneously consistent with both matching and maximization.

Results

Schedule parameters

Tables 4.1 and 4.2 show the parameters of the FR and VR schedules used in the analysis for butter and cola, respectively. The parameters include (a) the rate (arithmetic mean) of the schedule requirement (the product price), and (b) the components (or at least range of possible requirements) of the schedule (the price variation from shopping trip to shopping trip).

Matching analysis

Near-perfect matching is apparent for both consumer products. Figures 4.1 and 4.2 indicate that both R^2 values and betas (which correspond to the exponent s in the general matching equation) are close to unity. The amount spent (the response variable) is entirely explained in terms of the amount bought (the reinforcement variable). This demonstration of

Table 4.1 Schedules of Reinforcement (Prices) for Butter

Week	Kerrygold FR	Kerrygold VR3wk	Kerrygold VR5wk	Anchor FR	Anchor VR3wk	Anchor VR5wk	Country Life FR	Country Life VR3wk	Country Life VR5wk	Lurpak FR	Lurpak VR3wk	Lurpak VR5wk
1	60			83			83			78		
2	60	69.67		75	77		89	87		89	85.33	
3	89		77.4	73		75.4	89		89	89		86.8
4	89			73			95			89		
5	89	89		73	73.3		89	91		89	89	
6	89			74			89			89		
7	89			75			89			89		
8	89	84.3	86.2	75	79.667	77.6	89	89	89	89	89	89
9	75			89			89			89		
10	89			75			89			89		
11	87	87		75	75		83	77		89	89	
12	85			75			59			89		
13	89		87.8	75		75.8	59		69.8	93		91.4
14	89	89		75	76.33		59	69		93	93	
15	89			79			89			93		
16	89			79			89			93		
17	89	89		79	72.33		89	89		93	93	
18	89		89	59		71	89		89	93		91
19	89			59			89			93		
20	89	89		79	72.33		89	89		83	89.667	
21	89			79			89			93		
22	89			89			89			93		
23	89	84	89	79	82.33	83	89	89	87.8	79	83.667	85.4
24	89			79			89			79		
25	89			89			83			83		

Table 4.1 Schedules of Reinforcement (Prices) for Butter – *continued*

Week	Kerrygold FR	Kerrygold VR3wk	Kerrygold VR5wk	Anchor FR	Anchor VR3wk	Anchor VR5wk	Country Life FR	Country Life VR3wk	Country Life VR5wk	Lurpak FR	Lurpak VR3wk	Lurpak VR5wk
26	89	78.667		89	85.667		83			83	86.33	
27	58			79			83			93		
28	58		75.8	79		81	83			93		91
29	87	77.33		79	79		55	64.33		93	93	
30	87			79			55			93		
31	79			79			83			93		
32	87	85		79	80.33		83	73.667		93	93	
33	89		82.6	83		79.8	55		77.4	93		93
34	79			79			83			93		
35	79	79		79	79		83	83		93	93	
36	79			79			83			93		
37	79			79			83			93		
38	79	79	79	79	79	79	83	83	83	93	93	93
39	79			79			83			93		
40	79			79			83			93		
41	79			79			83			93		

Table 4.2 Schedules of Reinforcement (Prices) for Cola

Week	Diet Pepsi			Sainsbury's Own		
	FR	VR3wk	VR5wk	FR	VR3wk	VR5wk
1	28			25		
2	22	26.8		25	25	
3	30.4		28.42	25		25
4	30.4			25		
5	31.3	30.7		25	25	
6	30.4			25		
7	20.3			25		
8	20.3	23.6667	24.34	25	25	25
9	30.4			25		
10	20.3			25		
11	29	26.1		25	25	
12	29			25		
13	19.4		26.56	25		25
14	25	24.9333		25	25	
15	30.4			25		
16	30.4			25		
17	19.4			25		
18	19.4			25		
19	20.3			25		
20	30.4			25		
21	30.4			25		
22	30.4			25		
23	20.3		24.34	25		25
24	20.3			25		
25	20.3			25		

simple matching may seem trivial, given the definition of matching in marketing, which proposes that amount spent is proportional to amount bought, but the logarithmic expression of the observed matching relationship allows the association to be scrutinized in terms of sensitivity and bias.

Three points are apparent from the matching analyses. First, in contrast to the expectation for ratio schedules, the results repeatedly show multi-brand purchasing over a period of weeks to be extensive and significantly more common than exclusive choice. Of the nine consumers and 17 products investigated in the full study there was only one instance of sole brand purchasing. This was for coffee. The debriefing interview revealed, moreover, that even this consumer had purchased other brands of coffee outside the period studied.

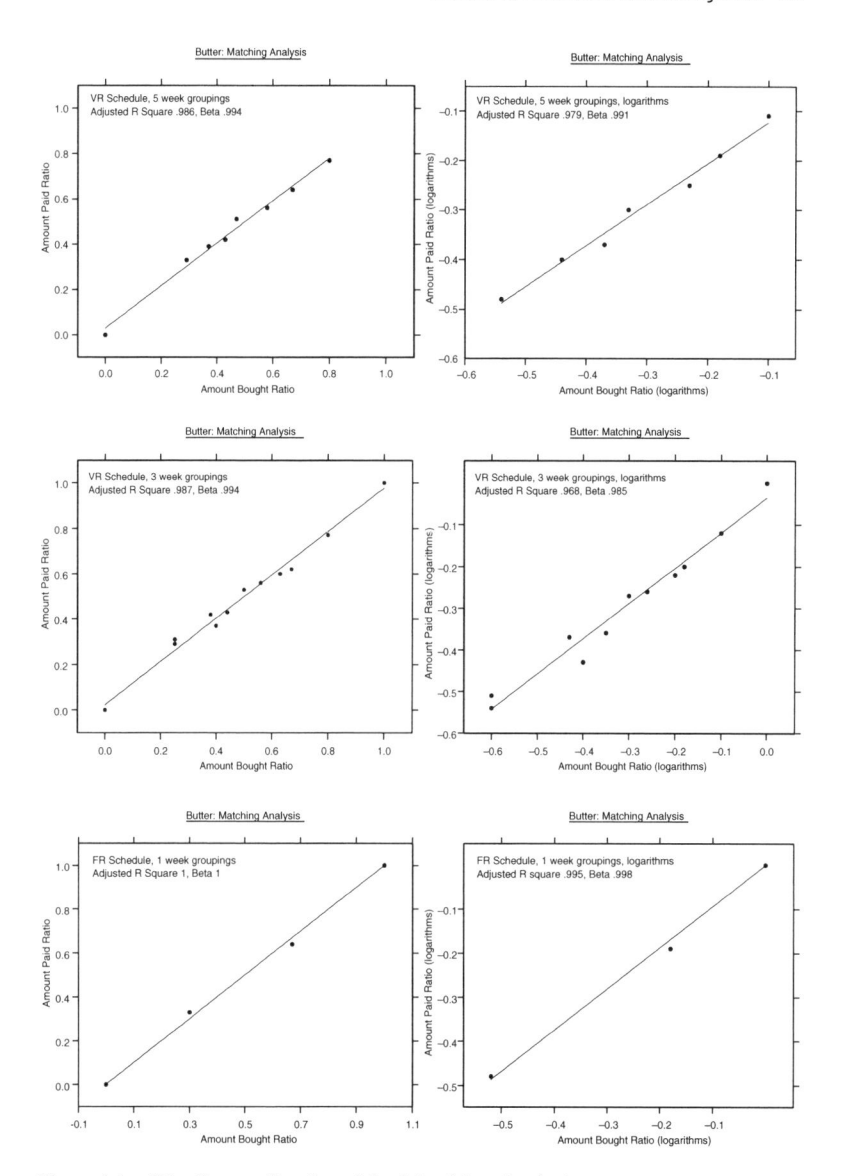

Figure 4.1 C1 – Butter: Results of the Matching Analysis

The proportion of money spent on "Brand A", the most frequently purchased brand (termed the "amount paid ratio") is calculated as
  Amount paid for Brand A / Total amount paid for the product category,
while the proportion of that brand bought (the "amount bought ratio") is:
  Amount bought of Brand A / Total amount bought of the product category.

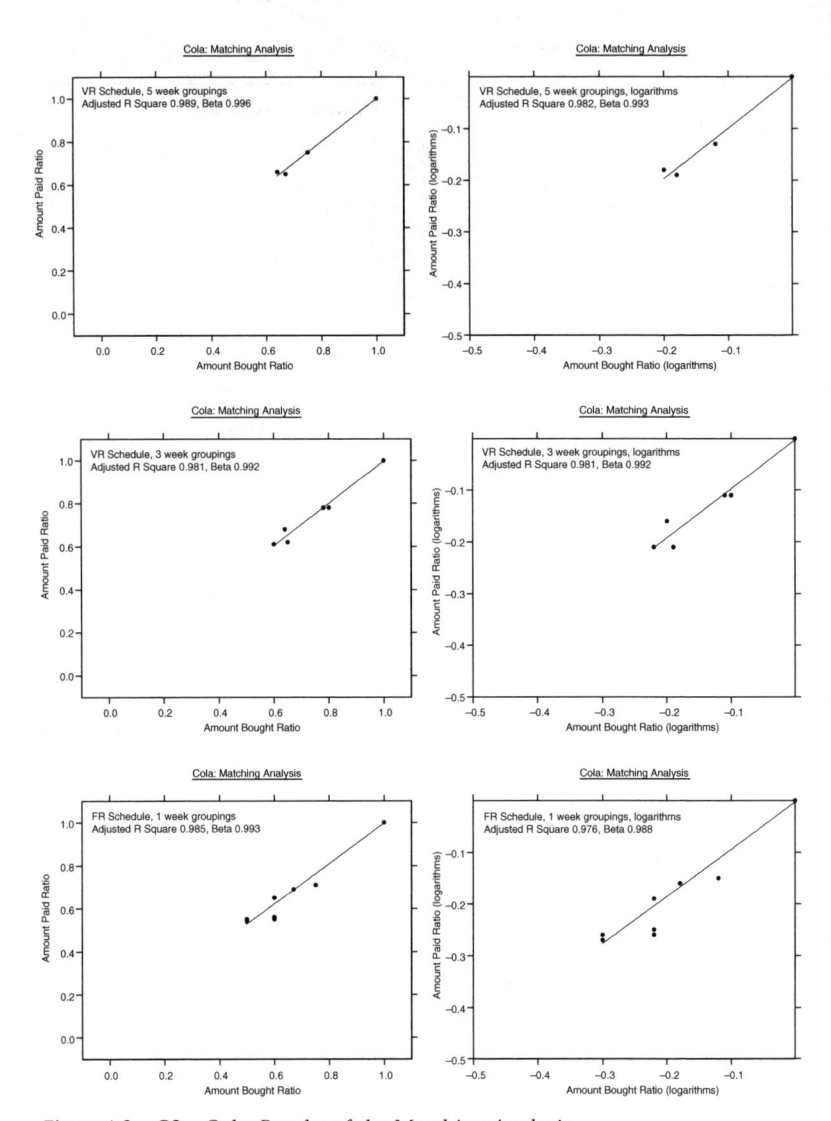

Figure 4.2 C2 – Cola: Results of the Matching Analysis

The basis of calculation is that used for Figure 4.1.

Second, the logarithmic analyses indicate that sensitivity is effectively at unity: There is neither under- nor overmatching; see Figures 4.1(b) and 4.2(b). For sensitivity values, see Tables 4.3 and 4.4. Marked bias (indicated by the *b* of the generalized matching law, the intercept

Table 4.3 Adjusted R^2s, Betas (Sensitivity) and Intercepts (Bias) Results for Matching Analyses for Butter

Analysis	Schedule	Logarithm?	Adjusted R^2	Beta (s)	Intercept (b)
Matching	VR5wk	Non-logarithm	0.986	0.994	-0.0306
Matching	VR5wk	Logarithm	0.979	0.991	0.05365
Matching	VR3wk	Non-logarithm	0.987	0.994	-0.01888
Matching	VR3wk	Logarithm	0.968	0.985	0.03322
Matching	FR1wk	Non-logarithm	1	1	0.0004673
Matching	FR1wk	Logarithm	0.995	0.998	0.0005755
Demand	VR5wk	Non-logarithm	0.789	-0.908	17.438
Demand	VR5wk	Logarithm	0.495	-0.772	-0.363
Demand	VR3wk	Non-logarithm	0.57	-0.778	12.76
Demand	VR3wk	Logarithm	0.456	-0.714	-0.418
Demand	FR1wk	Non-logarithm	0.107	-0.375	4.149
Maximization	FR1wk	Non-logarithm	0.241	-0.51	4.563
Maximization	FR1wk	Logarithm	0.091	-0.364	-1.227
Maximization	VR3wk	Non-logarithm	0.767	-0.887	6.646
Maximization	VR3wk	Logarithm	0.551	-0.772	-3.309

85

Table 4.4 Adjusted R²s, Betas (Sensitivity) and Intercepts (Bias) Results for Matching Analyses for Cola

Analysis	Schedule	Logarithm?	Adjusted R^2	Beta (s)	Intercept (b)
Matching	VR5wk	Non-logarithm	0.989	0.996	-0.00292
Matching	VR5wk	Logarithm	0.982	0.993	-0.00002758
Matching	VR3wk	Non-logarithm	0.981	0.992	-0.01258
Matching	VR3wk	Logarithm	0.972	0.988	-0.00006902
Matching	FR1wk	Non-logarithm	0.985	0.993	-0.04936
Matching	FR1wk	Logarithm	0.976	0.988	0.0006767
Demand	VR3wk	Non-logarithm	-0.215	0.298	-1.031
Demand	VR3wk	Logarithm	-0.229	0.28	0.38
Demand	FR1wk	Non-logarithm	0.362	-0.658	4.003
Demand	FR1wk	Logarithm	0.396	-0.681	0.176
Maximization	FR1wk	Non-logarithm	0.083	-0.351	1.627
Maximization	FR1wk	Logarithm	0.093	0.371	-0.441
Maximization	VR3wk	Non-logarithm	0.089	0.468	2.565
Maximization	VR3wk	Logarithm	0.103	-0.481	-0.777

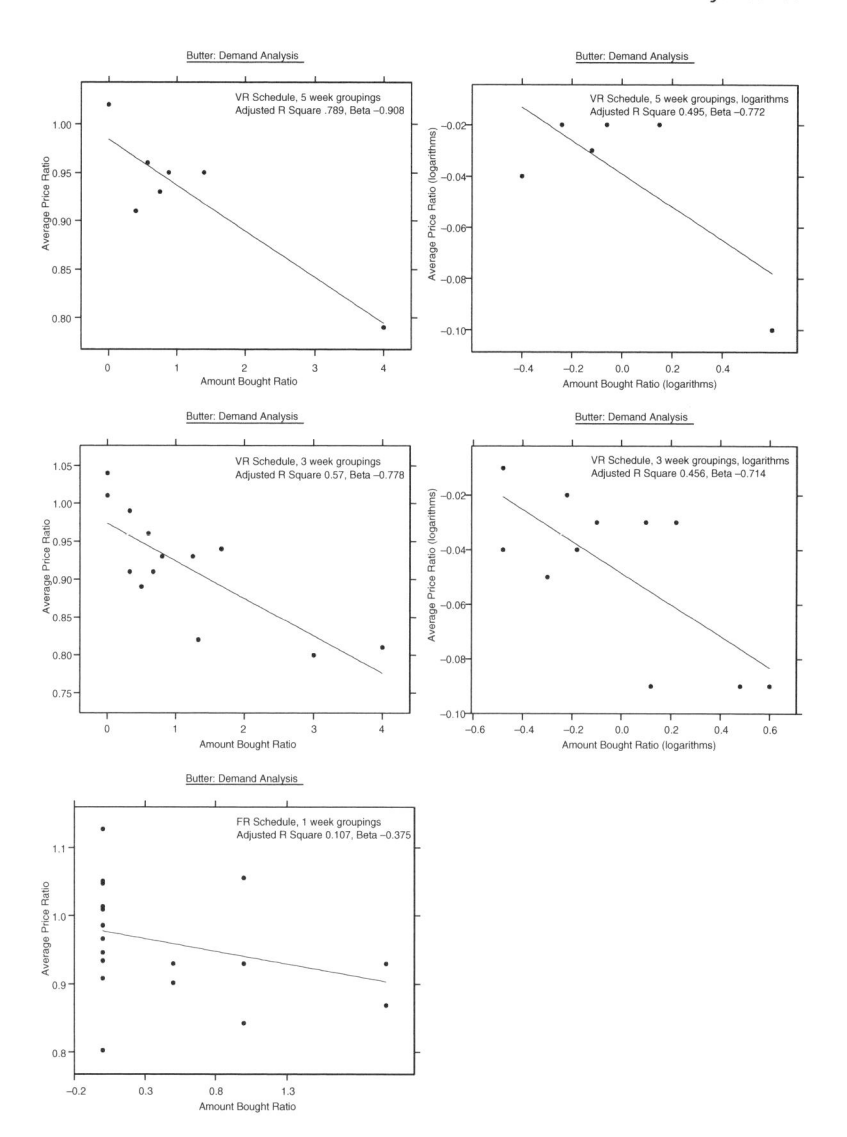

Figure 4.3 C1 – Butter: Results of the Demand Analysis

The amount bought ratio is as defined as in Figure 4.1; the relative price ratio is *Mean price of Brand A / Mean price of other brands in the repertoire* for each of the periods (five-week, three-week, one-week) studied.

of regression analysis) is generally found, however, as shown in Tables 4.3 and 4.4.

Third, in the matching analyses for both butter and cola, Figures 4.1 and 4.2 reveal that there is no difference in the results for each ascribed schedule (conc VR VR five-week, conc VR VR three-week, and conc FR FR one-week).

Demand analysis

Among the nine consumers and 17 products studied in total, there was some support for the expectation that downward-sloping demand curves would be found for brands regarded as substitutes, whereas at or upward-sloping demand curves would be apparent for non-substitute brands. However, results for butter (C1) and cola (C2) both produced downward-sloping curves, but with important differences. Figure 4.3 indicates that butter (C1) exhibits a strong downward-sloping pattern, which was supported in the qualitative analysis when the consumer

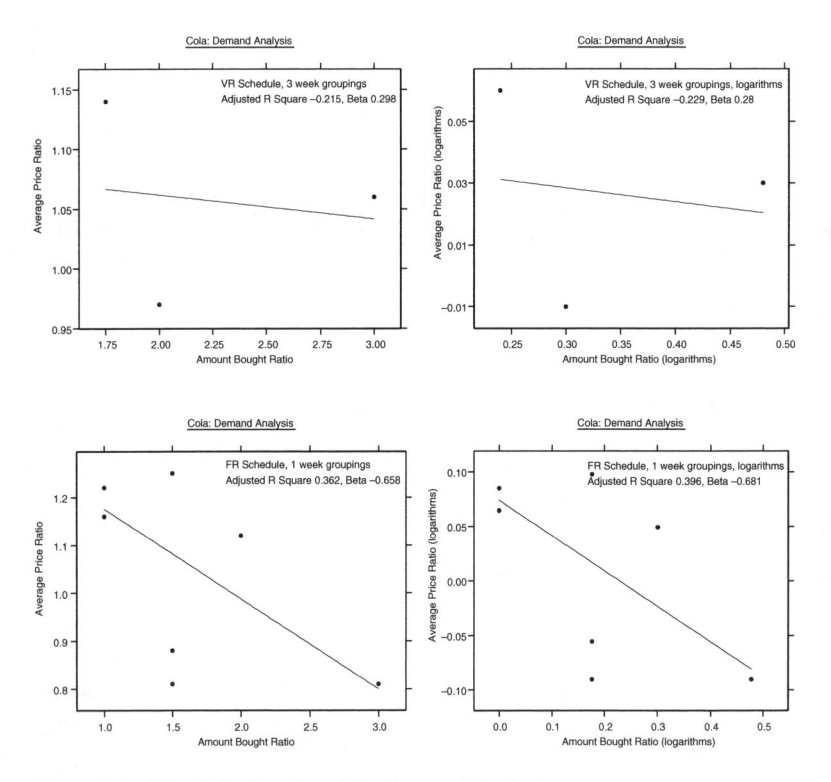

Figure 4.4 C2 – Cola: Results of the Demand Analysis

The basis of calculation is that used for Figure 4.3.

described how she alternated among the four brands in her repertoire (which were those included in the analysis) from week to week, buying one or other because of a price deal or in order to achieve variety of taste. The downward effect is apparent for butter over all ascribed schedules, though R^2 and beta values are rather higher for the conc VR VR five-week grouping than for the conc VR VR three-week groupings, and for the latter than for the conc FR FR one-week groupings of the data.

As Figure 4.4 indicates, cola (C2) also shows a downward-sloping demand curve for the conc VR VR schedule, but this is a much flatter curve than in the case of butter; the weaker relationship here between price and quantity demanded is reflected in the lower R^2 and beta values.

Maximization analysis

The diagonal line in Figures 4.5 and 4.6 shows where the data plots would fall in the case of probability matching. In probability matching, the respondent allocates responses in strict proportion to the programmed reinforcement probabilities of the two schedules in operation. Evidence of probability matching was not found at all. The step function shown at 0.5 indicates maximizing. Consumers' behavior avoided the diagonal; most of the data points were on the vertical step line, indicating maximizing behavior (Herrnstein & Vaughan, 1980).

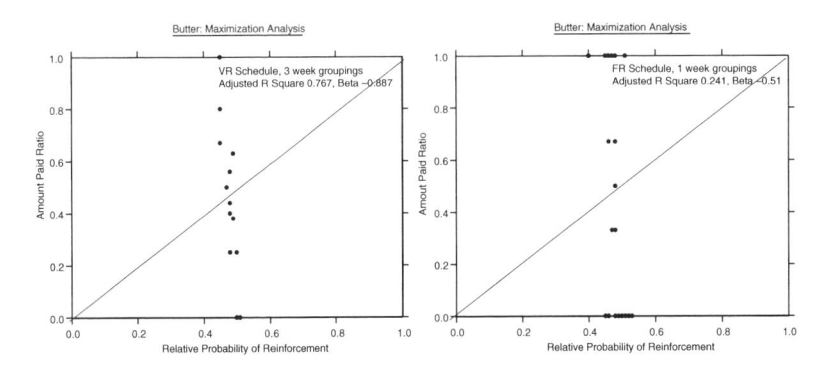

Figure 4.5 C1 – Butter: Results of the Maximization Analysis

The amount paid ratio is defined as in Figure 4.1. Probability of reinforcement is operationalized as the reciprocal of the price of Brand A divided by the reciprocal of the price of Brand A plus the reciprocal of the mean of the prices of the other brands in the consumer's evoked set: i.e., $1/P_A / 1/P_A + 1/P_B$.

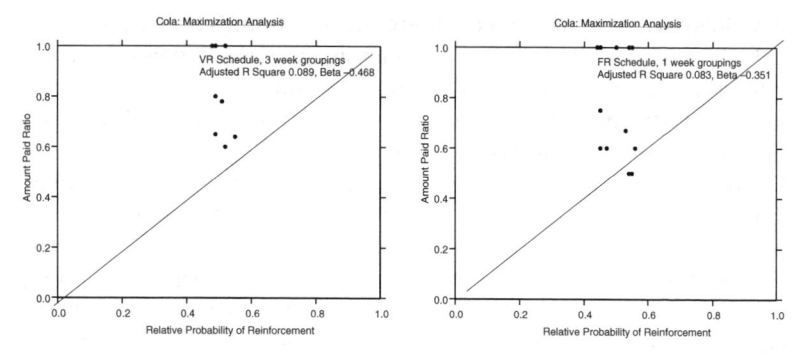

Figure 4.6 C2 – Cola: Results of the Maximization Analysis
The basis of calculation is that used for Figure 4.5.

The patterns for both butter and cola (Figures 4.5 and 4.6) suggest maximization rather than probability matching. There is some evidence that the points cluster closer to the step line for substitute brands of butter (where price differentials are smaller) but deviate from it in the case of non-substitute brands of cola.

Discussion

Matching

The apparently analogous relationship between foraging and response matching in laboratory studies of choice has raised the question of whether behavioral ecology and operant psychology have generated convergent predictions about consumer behavior (Rajala & Hantula, 2000). Foraging researchers' investigations of patch sampling and prey selection suggest ready-made analogues to store and brand choice, and both evolutionary psychology and operant research on matching predict that consumers will maximize. Prior to the research program partially reported here, however, it had not been empirically shown that consumers in fact exhibit matching and/or maximizing in naturalistic environments (Foxall & James, 2002). Given the small differences in price that typically separate competing versions of the same product category, the marketing literature gives little expectation that they will be found to maximize, emphasizing as it does – albeit generally prescriptively rather than on the basis of empirical evidence for the individual consumer – the importance of non-price elements of the marketing mix in determining brand choice.

The results for sensitivity and bias elucidate the relationship between price and quantity demanded. The finding that sensitivity, the s of Eq. (4.2), does not deviate from unity (see Tables 4.3 and 4.4) is especially revealing. Because an assumption of matching theory is that all reinforcement acts as programmed through the schedules in operation, the analysis shows that the relative prices of the brands in question reflect sensitively the total of utilitarian and symbolic reinforcements received by the consumer (Baum, 1974, 1979). Had the s values (the betas of regression analysis) deviated markedly from unity, the implication would have been that the brands were providing qualitatively different reinforcers that were not reflected in the schedules (relative prices) governing the supply of the brands. The finding of bias (Tables 4.3 and 4.4) also requires comment. Bias inheres in a preference for one choice alternative independent of the reinforcement rate (Baum, 1979; Davison & McCarthy, 1988; Pierce & Epling, 1983). This may be due, for instance, to additional response costs imposed in the case of one brand but not another. Response bias of this sort would arise, for instance, if search costs for a particular brand were relatively higher because of its shelf positioning in the supermarket or the failure of a supermarket to stock the full range of repertoire brands. The latter occurred in the case of butter (C1) when the cheapest brand was unavailable. Again in the case of cola, C2 reported that on occasion he had bought decaffeinated Coca-Cola in error because the packaging so resembled that of the supermarket brand. Bias may also arise from a qualitative difference between reinforcers. This, after all, is the prime motivation for branding, which points to reinforcing consequences of ownership and consumption (rather than spending or purchasing), over and above those that inhere in the functional properties of the product class. C1 reported buying an additional brand "just for the taste" or "just for variety," even when this was not consistent with buying the cheapest option; on two occasions, she bought additional butter mid-week at another supermarket, chosen for its convenience on those occasions, where she chose that supermarket's own brand. A third source of bias, discrepancy between scheduled and obtained reinforcement, is also a serious candidate. It has been assumed here, and by matching theorists generally, that scheduled functional utility is the sole source of reinforcement. If reinforcement is available from some other source, related either to branding or to one brand having an additional functional quality (such as saltiness in the case of butter or lack of caffeine in the case of cola), bias may ensue (Foxall, 1999). After all, choice between qualitatively different reinforcers resembles choice between different amounts of the same reinforcer (Baum, 1974).

Further evidence for the role of price differences among brands is provided by the demand analysis. The downward-sloping demand curve for cola is in line with the expectation that brand non-substitutability would be reflected in a lower sensitivity to price. This was supported as the consumer described how he used the different colas for different reasons at different times – regular during the day at work and decaffeinated at home during the evening. However, this pattern is not supported by the analysis for the conc FR FR schedule based on one-week groupings of the data. Moreover, R2 values and betas are higher for the one-week analysis. (As noted, because of price deals, the regular cola was in fact at times less expensive than the supermarket-branded decaffeinated version and this may have affected the relative prices in a way counter to that initially expected).

Maximization

Consumer brand choice evinces not only matching but also maximization; hence, the questions of what and how consumers maximize deserve at least tentative answers. The brand choices exhibited by the consumers in this study reflect not only the value-for-money relationships based on qualitative differences among the reinforcers (brands) within their respective evoked sets – that is, utilitarian reinforcement – but also symbolic differences established by brand marketing techniques-informational reinforcement. C1, for instance, generally selected the least expensive of the four brands that comprised her choice set but always chose brands that were significantly higher in price than the cheapest brand of butter available. The brands in her choice set differed qualitatively from the cheapest brand as well as from one another (in terms, for example, of flavor and color) but were also purchased in preference to the cheapest available brand by virtue of brand differentiation. The theoretical distinction between these two sources of reinforcement proposed by Foxall (1990), one based on contingency shaping, the other on verbal rule governance (Skinner, 1969), is borne out by both the quantitative and qualitative investigations of consumer choice in natural environments. Whatever consumers maximize, it is not simply the utilitarian reinforcement with which the experimental analysis of behavior has been preoccupied because of its specific capacity to deal with this source of consequence in the laboratory settings that are its natural domain but the combination of utilitarian and symbolic reward that require a rather richer interpretative framework (Foxall, 1998).

As to how this process of maximization takes place, it is suggested that in the specific context of consumer brand choice, it occurs in the form of a momentary maximization of the utilitarian and symbolic benefits promised or provided by immediate brand purchases. Hantula *et al.* (2001) raise two possible ways in which consumers might maximize (thereby, conveniently simplifying a complicated set of possibilities: *cf.* Commons *et al.*, 1982; Herrnstein, 1997). They may practice momentary maximization of food intake (product purchasing), always foraging in the patch (perhaps, by analogy, stores) or selecting the prey (brands) with the highest expected rate of reward; or, closer to the expectations of neoclassical microeconomics, they may maximize food intake over the entire foraging period (several weeks or more), sacrificing short term for overall gain. In line with the findings of operant studies (Staddon, 1980), the results presented suggest the former. Consumers appear to make decisions within the confines of a single shopping trip (purchase opportunity) rather than over a sequence of such occasions. On each separate purchase occasion they behave in ways that maximize the combined reinforcement (the pattern of reinforcement) currently available, given the schedule (prices) in force. This is shown most clearly when we ascribe FR schedules: the maximization apparent from the figures assuming VR schedules appear to show maximization over three- or five-week periods, but care must be taken in interpreting these results.

In operant research with non-human consumers, the data points shown to deviate more or less from the step line are, typically, the means of the last ten responses on a programmed schedule to which the subject had become habituated. In this research, these data points are simply and arbitrarily means for various sequences of three or five purchase occasions: The schedule has not been systematically programmed; it is simply that inferred from the prices ruling in the market place at the time of the research. This kind of naturalistic enquiry was the aim and no apology was made for it, but the interpretation of the results in terms of a research paradigm appropriate to the study of non-human consumers must be undertaken with care. Momentary maximization appears to be the best interpretation of the results of the first and third analyses. The demand analysis, however, necessarily relies on the observation of a series of choices made under a variety of price-reinforcer contingencies – that is, what a demand curve is – and the most reliable results, judging by the R^2 values achieved, are indeed for the extended (five- or three-week) analyses.

The foraging analogy

As noted earlier, there are a number of areas of foraging research that could be used to explain consumer brand choice behavior. These are largely supported by the qualitative data collected in the course of this investigation.

Most consumers can give a good idea of why they would choose to leave a patch and those features would encourage them to do so. Consumers rarely entirely abandon a brand they have bought in the past, and would have to become very disappointed with such a brand (probably as a result of its radical physical reformulation or it being offered at an exorbitant price) before permanently switching away from it (Ehrenberg, 1988). Because consumers mostly practice multi-brand purchasing, patch departure is a complicated business in the present context and may be reflected more in frequency of brand selection rather than in an irrevocable turning away from a brand. If a brand which the consumer has chosen to purchase less frequently than previously is offered at a sufficient discount relative to its competitors, the consumer is likely to repurchase it at least for the duration of the deal (Ehrenberg et al., 1994).

The idea of patch departure is linked closely with patch assessment. Consumers must use some form of assessment before making a decision on when or if to depart from the patch/brand or select a different brand. It seems unlikely (and is supported by the qualitative data so far) that any consumer has perfect knowledge of each of any brand or set of brands and will make decisions based on those features most important to them or features they have noted. Because of this imperfect knowledge, it is not certain that the consumer will make an economically rational decision. As foraging animals and also consumers have partial preferences, they may also spread their choices across brands (again practicing multi-brand purchasing) and choose to use a number of patches at once.

Related again to patch choice, assessment, and usage is travel time. Whereas, as one of our respondents said, "a few pence here and there may not make a difference to brand choice," there is certainly evidence (from this quantitative study, for instance) that even small differences in price are noticeable and affect the choice of brands more strongly. In the context of supermarket selection, there is again certainly evidence that travel time is an important choice feature and is only secondary when a consumer desperately wants a particular brand of product that is only available at a store further away.

There is still the question of the accuracy and usefulness of the idea that consumer brand choice is essentially a process of foraging. As noted, Hantula proposes that evolutionary psychology may provide a comprehensive framework for the analysis of consumer behavior. Accommodating the possibilities of his shopping-as-foraging analogy to the complexities of a marketing-oriented economy has been the task of the current article and the investigations of real-time consumer choices that it has described. The present study has shown that with respect to product and price there are certainly relationships between consumer choice and marketing that are analogous with foraging research. The demonstration of matching and maximizing in consumer brand choice is directly analogous to the treatment of schedule-reinforcer relationships. In addition, this work has drawn attention to the relevance of the remainder of the marketing mix, promotions and place, to a behavioral ecological interpretation of consumer behavior.

To an important degree, the examples presented here show that consumer brand choice is highly price sensitive. This is not an emphasis found in the literature of brand marketing, which accords almost mystical prominence to the non-price elements of marketing's effects on consumer choice. Although the small number of cases considered here naturally raises the problem of generalizability, there is now a more comprehensive analysis of some 80 consumers purchasing eight product classes to be drawn upon to show that the results reported here are reliable indications of the general nature of consumer choice (Foxall & James (unpublished)).

However, it must be remembered that the repertoire of brands from which the present consumers purchased were usually those highly differentiated by advertising and other forms of sales promotion and purchased from high-level supermarket outlets rather than corner stores. The consumers in question had clearly made decisions with respect to promotion and place (and the issues of reputation and quality for which they are proxy variables) prior to making price and product decisions in the store. In other words, consumers appear to seek the extrinsic symbolic rewards of consumption as well as – and perhaps prior to – the intrinsic utilitarian rewards thereof (Foxall, 1990).

Hantula's view that the foraging analogy presents a comprehensive approach to consumer behavior must be interpreted within the framework of our findings about the marketing context of consumer choice. Foraging analogies are often essentially qualitative, due perhaps to the largely naturalistic and observational research approaches. Even where quantitative measures or experimentation take place there is often only agreement with the qualitative and not the quantitative predictions (Roberts, 1993). The assumption must be, therefore, that the essentially qualitative marketing mix elements, promotions and place, can be adequately taken care of by the b and s components of the generalized matching law (Foxall, 1999). The present results indicate that both bias and sensitivity may result from qualitative differences between reinforcers and behavior settings, as it is only in cases of qualitative difference that these issues occur. In contradistinction to the marketing-mix elements of price and product that have been the principal subject of this study, the conceptualization of symbolic reinforcers in which promotional and locational stimuli inhere remains at present largely qualitative (Foxall, 2002). Further experimental research, both conceptual and empirical, must be directed toward a closer examination of what the b and s components of generalized matching are actually capturing.

The fact remains that neither foraging theory nor behavior analysis is at present part of the mainstream perspectives in psychology or marketing. Although there is ample evidence to suggest that much of foraging behavior can be interpreted in operant terms, this assertion is still controversial. Further consideration must be given in a wider forum than a single article affords to the ways in which these two areas of analysis complement each other (Dalley & Baum, 1991; Houston, 1991).

Note

1. Previously published in *Psychology and Marketing*, 2003, 20, pp. 811–36.

References

Abarca, N. & Fantino, E. (1982). "Choice and foraging". *Journal of the Experimental Analysis of Behavior*, 38, 117–23.

Baum, W. M. (1974). "On two types of deviation from the matching law". *Journal of the Experimental Analysis of Behavior*, 22, 231–42.

Baum, W. M. (1979). "Matching, undermatching and overmatching in studies of choice". *Journal of the Experimental Analysis of Behavior*, 32, 269–81.

Charnov, E. L. (1976). "Optimal foraging: Attack strategy of a Mantid". *The American Naturalist*, 110, 141–51.

Commons, M. L., Herrnstein, R. J. & Rachlin, H. (eds) (1982). *Quantitative analyses of behavior. Vol. II: Matching and maximizing accounts*. Cambridge, MA: Ballinger.

Dall, S. R., Cuthill, I. C., Cook, N. & Morphet, M. (1997). "Learning about food: Starlings, Skinner boxes, and earthworms". *Journal of the Experimental Analysis of Behavior*, 67, 181–92.

Dalley, J. & Baum, W. M. (1991). "The functional equivalence of operant behavior and foraging". *Animal Learning and Behavior*, 19, 146–52.

Davison, M. & McCarthy, D. (1988). *The matching law: A research review.* Hillsdale, NJ: Lawrence Erlbaum.

Dawkins, R. (1986). *The selfish gene.* Oxford: Oxford University Press.

Dawkins, R. (1988). "Replicators, consequences, and displacement activities", in A. C. Catania & S. Harnad (eds) *Selection of behavior.* New York: Cambridge University Press, pp. 33–5.

de Villiers, P. A. & Herrnstein, R. J. (1976). "Toward a law of response strength". *Psychological Bulletin*, 83, 1131–53.

DiFonzo, N., Hantula, D. A. & Bordia, P. (1998). "Microworlds for experimental research: Having your (control and collection) cake, and realism too". *Behavior Research, Methods, Instruments & Computers*, 30, 278–86.

Dow, S. M. & Lea, S. E. G. (1987). "Foraging in a changing environment: Simulations in the operant laboratory", in M. L. Commons, A. Kacelnik & S. J. Shettleworth (eds) *Quantitative analyses of behavior Vol. 6.* Hillsdale, NJ: Lawrence Erlbaum Associates, pp. 89–113.

Ehrenberg, A. S. C. (1988). *Repeat-buying: Facts, theory and applications.* New York: Oxford University Press.

Ehrenberg, A. S. C., Hammond, K. & Goodhardt, G. J. (1994, July/August). "The after-effects of price-related consumer promotions". *Journal of Advertising Research*, 11–21.

Fantino, E. & Abarca, N. (1985). "Choice, optimal foraging, and the delay reduction hypothesis". *The Behavioral and Brain Sciences*, 8, 315–30.

Fantino, E. & Preston, R. A. (1988). "Choice and foraging: The effects of accessibility on acceptability". *Journal of the Experimental Analysis of Behavior*, 50, 395–403.

Flew, A. (1984). *Darwinian evolution.* London: Granada Publishing.

Foxall, G. R. (1990). *Consumer psychology in behavioral perspective.* New York: Routledge.

Foxall, G. R. (1998). "Radical behaviorist interpretation: Generating and evaluating an account of consumer behavior". *The Behavior Analyst*, 21, 321–54.

Foxall, G. R. (1999). "The substitutability of brands". *Managerial and Decision Economics*, 20, 241–57.

Foxall, G. R. (ed.) (2002). *Consumer behavior analysis: Critical perspectives.* New York: Routledge.

Foxall, G. R. & James, V. K. (2002). "The behavioural basis of consumer choice: A preliminary analysis". *European Journal of Behavior Analysis*, 2, 209–20.

Foxall, G. R. & James, V. K. (unpublished). The behavioural economics of consumer choice.

Green, L. & Freed, D. E. (1993). "The substitutability of reinforcers". *Journal of the Experimental Analysis of Behavior*, 60, 141–58.

Hantula, D. A., DiClemente, D. F. & Rajala, A. K. (2001). "Outside the box: The analysis of consumer behavior", in L. Hayes, J. Austin & R. Flemming (eds) *Organizational Change.* Reno, NV: Context Press, pp. 203–33.

Hantula, D. A., Rajala, A. K. & Bryant, K. (1997). Of mice and men (and women): Studying consumer choice in an on-line mall. Paper presented at the FABA/OBM Winter Meeting, Daytona Beach, FL.

Herrnstein, R. J. (1961). "Relative and absolute strength of response as a function of frequency of reinforcement". *Journal of the Experimental Analysis of Behavior*, 4, 267–72.

Herrnstein, R. J. (1982). "Melioration as behavioral dynamism", in M. L. Commons, R. J. Herrnstein & H. Rachlin (eds) *Quantitative analyses of behavior Vol. II*. Cambridge, MA: Ballinger, pp. 433–58.

Herrnstein, R. J. (1997). In H. Rachlin & D. I. Laibson (eds) *The matching law: Papers in psychology and economics*. New York: Russell Sage Foundation.

Herrnstein, R. J. & Loveland, D. H. (1975). "Maximizing and matching on concurrent ratio schedules". *Journal of the Experimental Analysis of Behavior*, 24, 107–16.

Herrnstein, R. J. & Vaughan, W. (1980). "Melioration and behavioral allocation", in J. E. R. Staddon (ed.) *Limits to action: The allocation of individual behavior*. New York: Academic Press, pp. 143–76.

Houston, A. I. (1991). "Risk-sensitive foraging theory and operant psychology". *Journal of the Experimental Analysis of Behavior*, 56, 585–9.

Hursh, S. R. (1984). "Behavioral economics". *Journal of the Experimental Analysis of Behavior*, 42, 435–52.

Hursh, S. R. & Bauman, R. A. (1987). "The behavioral analysis of demand", in L. Green & J. H. Kagel (eds) *Advances in behavioral economics Vol. 1*. Norwood, NJ: Ablex, pp. 117–65.

Hutcheson, A. M. & Hantula, D. A. (1998). Delay sensitivity to demand moderated by desire in on-line shopping behaviors. Paper presented at the 24th annual meeting of the Association for Behavior Analysis-International, Orlando, FL.

Ito, M. & Fantino, E. (1986). "Choice, foraging, and reinforcer duration". *Journal of the Experimental Analysis of Behavior*, 46, 93–103.

Kacelnik, A., Krebs, J. R. & Ens, B. (1987). "Foraging in a changing environment: An experiment with starlings" (Sturnus vulgaris), in M. L. Commons, A. Kacelnik & S. J. Shettleworth (eds) *Quantitative analyses of behavior Vol. 6*. Hillsdale, NJ: Lawrence Erlbaum, pp. 63–87.

Kagel, J. H., Battalio, R. C. & Green, L. (1995). *Economic choice theory: An experimental analysis of animal behavior*. Cambridge: Cambridge University Press.

Kamil, A. C., Peters, J. & Linsrom, F. J. (1982). "An ecological perspective on the study of the allocation of behavior", in M. L. Commons, R. J. Herrnstein & H. Rachlin (eds) *Quantitative analyses of behavior Vol. 2*. Cambridge, MA: Ballinger, pp. 189–203.

Lea, S. E. G. (1982). *The mechanism of optimality in foraging*, in M. L. Commons, R. J. Herrnstein & H. Rachlin (eds) *Quantitative analysis of behavior Vol. 2*. Cambridge, MA: Ballinger, pp. 169–88.

Mazur, J. E. (1991). "Choice", in E. Iversen & J. Lattal (eds) *Experimental analysis of behavior. Part 1*. Amsterdam: Elsevier, pp. 219–50.

McCarthy, D., Voss, P. & Davison, M. (1994). "Learning patches: Effects of travel requirements". *Journal of the Experimental Analysis of Behavior*, 62, 185–200.

McNamara, J. (1982). "Optimal patch use in a stochastic environment". *Theoretical Population Biology*, 21, 269–88.

Mellgren, R. L. & Brown, S. W. (1988). "Discrimination learning in a foraging situation". *Journal of the Experimental Analysis of Behavior*, 50, 493–503.

Myerson, J. & Hale, S. (1984). "Practical implications of the matching law". *Journal of Applied Behavior Analysis*, 17, 367–80.

Pierce, W. D. & Epling, W. F. (1983). "Choice, matching and human behavior: A review of the literature". *The Behavior Analyst*, 6, 57–76.

Rachlin, H. (1980). "Economics and behavioral psychology", in J. E. R. Staddon (ed.) *Limits to action: The allocation of individual behavior*. New York: Academic Press, pp. 205–36.

Rachlin, H. (1989). *Judgment, decision and choice*. New York: Freeman.

Rachlin, H., Battalio, R., Kagel, J. & Green, L. (1981). "Maximization theory in behavioral psychology". *The Behavioral and Brain Sciences*, 4, 371–417.

Rachlin, H., Green, L., Kagel, J. H. & Battalio, R. C. (1980). "Substitutability in time allocation". *Psychological Review*, 87, 355–74.

Rajala, A. K. & Hantula, D. A. (2000). "Towards a behavioral ecology of consumption: Delay-reduction effects on foraging in a simulated internet mall". *Managerial and Decision Economics*, 21, 145–58.

Rashotte, M. E., O'Connell, J. M. & Djuric, V. J. (1987). "Mechanisms of signal controlled foraging behavior", in M. L. Commons, A. Kacelnik & S. J. Shettleworth (eds) *Quantitative analyses of behavior Vol. 6*. pp. 153–79.

Roberts, W. A. (1993). "Testing a stochastic foraging model in an operant simulation: Agreement with qualitative but not quantitative predictions". *Journal of the Experimental Analysis of Behavior*, 59, 323–31.

Roche, J. P., Stubbs, A. & Glanz, W. E. (1996). "Assessment and choice: An operant simulation of foraging in patches". *Journal of the Experimental Analysis of Behavior*, 66, 327–47.

Saad, G. & Gill, T. (2000). "Applications of evolutionary psychology in marketing". *Psychology and Marketing*, 17, 1005–34.

Shettleworth, S. J. (1988). "Foraging as operant behavior and operant behavior as foraging: What have we learned?". *The Psychology of Learning and Motivation*, 22, 1–49.

Skinner, B. F. (1966). "The phylogeny and ontogeny of behavior". *Science*, 153, 1205–13.

Skinner, B. F. (1969). *Contingencies of reinforcement: A theoretical analysis*. Englewood Cliffs, NJ: Prentice-Hall.

Skinner, B. F. (1981). "Selection by consequences". *Science*, 213, 501–4.

Staddon, J. E. R. (1980). "Optimality analysis of operant behavior and their relation to optimal foraging", in J. E. R. Staddon (ed.) *Limits to action: The allocation of individual behavior*. New York: Academic Press, pp. 101–41.

van Parijs, P. (1981). *Evolutionary explanation in the social sciences*. Totowa, NJ: Rowman and Littlefield.

Vaughan, W. & Herrnstein, R. J. (1987). "Stability, melioration and natural selection", in L. Green & J. H. Kagel (eds) *Advances in behavioral economics Vol. 1*. Norwood, NJ: Ablex, pp. 185–215.

Williams, W. & Fantino, E. (1994). "Delay reduction and optimal foraging: Variable ratio search in a foraging analogue". *Journal of the Experimental Analysis of Behavior*, 61, 465–77.

Williams, W. & Fantino, E. (1996). "Response-dependent prechoice effects on foraging-related choice". *Journal of the Experimental Analysis of Behavior*, 65, 619–41.

5
The Behavioral Economics of Consumer Brand Choice: Establishing a Methodology[1]

Gordon R. Foxall and Teresa C. Schrezenmaier

> I would like to issue a challenge to current and future researchers to find new, creative ways to investigate, outside the laboratory, the quantitative models arising from the Harvard Pigeon Lab... The researchers – as opposed to the clinicians – who have followed in [Skinner's] theoretical footsteps...have very often focused on tight, and then tighter, and then even tighter controls of variables in the laboratory. There is no question that such research is extremely important to our understanding of the principles of behavior. It should not be, however, the only type of research being conducted. There are a great many benefits to an outside-the-laboratory, empirical approach. (Logue, 2002)

It is well established by marketing research that only comparatively few buyers of a product category (such as baked beans or breakfast cereals) are entirely loyal to a single brand (Heinz or Kellogg's Frosties, for instance). Most buyers practice multi-brand purchasing over a period of, say, three months, selecting apparently randomly among a small subset ("repertoire") of tried and tested brands (Ehrenberg, 1988). Data on buyer behavior for ready-to-eat breakfast cereals in the US, reported by consumer panel members are typical: "The average Shredded Wheat buyer in the year buys it about 4 times in that year, and buys other brands about 37 times. About 12 million US households [buy] Nabisco's Shredded Wheat in the year. But it is not obvious whether these households are to be thought of as Shredded Wheat customers, or as other brands' customers who/occasionally bought Shredded Wheat" (Ehrenberg & Goodhardt, 1977). Similar patterns are apparent for the vast majority of fast-moving consumer goods in steady-state markets (i.e., those with only a slight upward year-on-year trend in sales) in most affluent, consumer-oriented economies. Each brand attracts a relatively small proportion of the buyers of the product category who purchase that brand exclusively during the period under review: as that period lengthens, this proportion declines. Multi-brand purchasing is the norm to the extent that even the heaviest purchasers of a given brand buy other brands within the category much more than they buy their favorite brand over the course of say a year.

The broad similarity of this pattern of choice to that found in studies of matching (Herrnstein, 1997) invites a deeper analysis (Foxall, 1999). In order to explain such patterns in terms of the decision mechanisms employed by buyers of such products, this investigation has turned to the work of behavior analysts and experimental economists who have related choices systematically to the schedule of rewards to which they lead. Most of the work of these behavioral economists has been conducted with animals such as rats and pigeons as their subjects, though similar results, which also support the basic axioms of economic analysis, have been found for human participants in token economies and field experiments concerned, for example, with energy conservation. However, with the exception of the pilot studies which led to the present investigation (Foxall & James, 2001, 2003), no work to date has attempted to discover the extent to which these principles of economic behavior apply to brand choice among human consumers.

Those pilot investigations proposed and implemented a means of investigation in which consumers' actual brand expenditures are related to the relative rates of reinforcement they produce. Their results exhibit both matching and maximization and indicate that brand selection is far more sensitive to small price differentials than has generally been acknowledged in the literatures of consumer choice and marketing management. Work of this kind thus promises to answer (Logue, 2002) challenge. The present chapter extends the pilot investigations of Foxall and James by considering the individual buyer behavior of 80 consumers purchasing brands of nine fast-moving consumer goods over a 16-week period. This study is meant to (dis)confirm the results of the pilot work and to provide an assessment of the generality of the pilot findings across consumers and across product categories.

The pilot research identified a contradiction between the findings of marketing science and those of behavioral economics. Although each of the intellectual traditions that have come to form the discipline of behavioral economics have found much to debate (Commons *et al.*, 1982), the principal prediction of both is that when faced with concurrent ratio schedules organisms will exhibit both matching and maximization by exclusive selection of the cheapest (richest) schedule (Green *et al.*, 1983; Herrnstein & Loveland, 1975). We should expect therefore that brand choice will exhibit maximization of returns for expenditure achieved by the exclusive purchase of the cheapest brand. This seems to rule out the multi-brand purchasing that we have seen is the norm in marketing research studies.

A superficial explanation of this paradox is not hard to find. The brand choice data are aggregated: though they are collected at the level of the individual buyer, he or she may make purchases on behalf of several members of a household, each of whom might be loyal to a given brand, albeit a different brand in each case. But this still does not explain why the cheapest brand (richest schedule) is not universally favored: some consumers select exclusively among the highly differentiated, heavily advertised and therefore premium-priced brands, even though such brands differ only slightly if at all in terms of physical formulation and function from retailer-label or economy brands that cost considerably less. Even buyers of the lowest-priced brands seldom purchase wholly within that subcategory: on occasion, in some cases often, they select the highest-priced brands too, sometimes on the same shopping trip. Of course, if a particular brand is offered as part of a money-off or two-for-one deal, its sales rise appreciably but only while the deal is operative and even then it attracts consumers who have previously bought that brand rather than new buyers. Once the deal comes to an end, sales levels and thus market shares return to their previous trend levels. If the findings of behavioral economics are to be shown to apply to human consumers in naturally occurring settings, there is much to investigate and explain.

Hence, the first objective of the research was to explore how far behavioral economic principles formulated in the investigation of simpler systems explain brand choice in consumer markets. It was clear from the outset, however, that the research had the potential to elucidate the role of branding in marketing and consumer behavior, especially with regard to the sensitivity of consumers' decision processes to differences in price. The conventional wisdom in marketing is that brand choices result predominantly from non-price influences on purchase decisions. The view that the typically small price differentials between brands have little or no influence on brand choice, which is also an emphasis in the economics of imperfect or monopolistic competition, is a staple of the marketing literature on branding. It suggests that, far from maximizing, in the simple sense of obtaining the greatest returns for money expended, consumers seek a wide range of satisfactions from the products they purchase which do not result in their habitually buying the cheapest brand available. The underlying assumption is that the brands that compose a product category are similar if not identical in physical formulation and function: the differences which enable marketers to charge – and consumers willing to pay – price differentials stem largely from perceived differences among brands based on the marketing techniques that comprise "branding". In order to examine further these concerns, it was necessary to employ analyses which permitted: (a) the degree of substitutability and (b) the price sensitivity of brands to be ascertained. They also required further consideration of the relationships among basic, applied and interpretive behavior analysis.

Analyses

Our methodology employs three types of analysis derived from the behavioral economics literature: matching analysis, relative demand analysis, and maximization analysis.

Matching analysis has the capacity to show whether the brands within a product category are genuinely substitutes. It also allows us to identify sources of influence on relative response rate that are not programmed into the schedules (i.e., relative prices) of the brands. Herrnstein (1997) defines choice not as an internal deliberative process but as a *rate* of intersubjectively observable events that are temporally distributed. In his analysis, the relative frequency of responding becomes the dependent variable. Herrnstein's (1961) initial discovery was that when animals are presented with two opportunities to respond (pecking key X or key Y), each of which delivers reinforcers (food pellets) on its own variable interval (VI) schedule,[2] they allocate their responses on X and Y in proportion to the rates of reward available in X and Y. In other words, response rate (B) is proportional to the relative rate of reinforcement (R) (de Villiers & Herrnstein, 1976). Hence:

$$B_x/(B_x + B_y) = R_x/(R_x + R_y) \quad (5.1)$$

where B is the behavior allocated to alternatives x and y, and R is the reinforcers contingent upon that behavior. In contrast to the molecular analysis of the stimulus-response psychologies, Herrnstein's matching equation represents response *frequencies* as a function of reinforcement *frequencies*. The resulting choice rule, based on a molar analysis, indicates that the average reinforcement rate of response X comes to equal the average reinforcement rate of response Y (locally, not overall). This phenomenon, which (Herrnstein, 1961, 1970) calls "matching", provides a framework for the behavioral analysis of consumption. Its importance in the context of economic behavior – especially real world economic behavior that is subject to an operant interpretation – is that, on the conc VI VI schedules on which it has generally been found, matching is argued not to indicate maximization. Matching theorists and behavioral economists have long argued whether matching is a special case of maximization or vice versa (Commons *et al.*, 1982).

As long as there are no differences among reinforcers in terms of *bias*, i.e., preference for one reinforcer based on characteristics such as its physical placement or color, and *sensitivity*, i.e., responsiveness to the alternative reinforcers, Eq. (5.1) simplifies to

$$B_x/B_y = R_x/R_y \qquad (5.2)$$

Taking these possibilities into account (Baum, 1974; *cf.* Baum, 1979) proposed the generalized matching law

$$B_x/B_y = b(R_x/R_y)^s \qquad (5.3)$$

in which the constants b and s represent bias and sensitivity, respectively. Expressed logarithmically, the generalized matching law permits further assessments to be made of the data on which the matching analysis is based:

$$\log(B_x/B_y) = s \log(R_x/R_y) + \log b \qquad (5.4)$$

Deviations of b from unity indicate a consistent preference for one alternative over the other(s) regardless of the reinforcement rates in operation: such bias is absent when b, the intercept, equals unity. As long as the reinforcements for each of the available responses are apparently equal and would predict a behavioral indifference between them, a measure of b greater or less than one indicates that "preference is biased by some unknown, but invariant, asymmetry between the alternatives" (Baum, 1974). Bias is the result of a deficiency in experimental design rather than a shortcoming of the experimental subject; it represents a failure to take account of all of the independent variables that influence preference and declines as relevant independent variables are increasingly taken into account (Baum, 1974). Principal sources of bias are undetected response costs imposed in the case of one alternative but not the other(s), such as an additional effort required to press one lever in an experiment, or a qualitative difference between reinforcers, such as an unanticipated additional value accorded to one reinforcer but not the rest (Baum, 1979; Davison & McCarthy, 1988; Pierce & Epling, 1983). In the marketing context with which we are concerned, bias may result from the positioning of alternative brands within the supermarket or other store, the positioning and space allocated to different brands on the shelves given over to the product category, the positioning of substitute and complementary products, stock-outs, and so on.

The behavior of a subject who disproportionately chooses the leaner schedule of reinforcement (i.e., who chooses it more often than strict matching would predict) is said to exhibit undermatching; in such cases, the exponent s, slope, is less than one. The behavior of a subject who disproportionately chooses the richer schedule of reinforcement exhibits overmatching, and $s > 1$. Sensitivity to reinforcement schedules may arise because the subject is unable to discriminate the alternatives sufficiently well, especially if there is no delay in reinforcement when responses are allocated to a new choice (and are, therefore, controlled by a different schedule), and because rates of deprivation differ between the schedules (Baum, 1974, 1979).

The generalized matching law can thus take a greater variety of data into consideration by explaining deviations from the strict matching which is captured by Herrnstein's basic formulation of the matching law (Green & Freed, 1993). Most importantly from our perspective is the possibility that the use of the generalized matching equation in its logarithmic form will indicate the degree of substitutability of the brands under investigation. The demonstration of matching on conc VR VR schedules is otherwise somewhat trite: in a marketing system based on the mutual acceptance by sellers and buyers of stable unit prices rather than haggling, the proportion of funds expended on a product category that go to a specific brand will trivially equal the proportion of that brand purchased. However, the value of s in the generalized matching equation is widely employed as an index of substitutability. Indeed, strict matching (in which s approximates unity) is found only for non-differentiated reinforcers (Green & Freed, 1993).

Relative demand analysis. The sensitivity of demand (more accurately, *quantity demanded*) to price can be demonstrated by the demand curve. Madden *et al.* (2000) reiterate three predictions made by economic theory. First, "Increasing the unit price of a reinforcer decreases consumption of that reinforcer", i.e., demand curves plotted on logarithmic coordinates show consumption to be a positively decelerating function of unit price increases. Second, "Unit price determines consumption and response output regardless of the specific values of the cost and benefits components of the ratio". And, third, "When choosing between two qualitatively identical reinforcers available at different unit prices, ... behavior will be exclusively allocated to the alternative with the lower unit price". Our analysis has extended Madden *et al.*'s use of the economics of demand in experimental situations by employing relative demand analysis which presents the relative amounts of brands A and B as a function of their relative prices.

Maximization analysis. Behavioral economists and psychologists continue to debate whether consumption is characterized by maximization of satisfactions or by some other principle such as satisfying or melioration (e.g., Herrnstein, 1997; Rachlin, 2000). Although most research with non-human animals has proved inconclusive (Schwartz & Reisberg, 1991), researchers have felt confident in proposing how their results apply to human consumption including the choice of products and brands in supermarkets (Green & Freed, 1993). Their assurance seems unwarranted in the absence of data specifically relevant to this facet of consumer behavior. Our basic studies have, we hope, produced evidence which allows the choices of individual consumers to be better understood and thereby to contribute meaningfully to the debate over maximization.

Preliminary research

Foxall & James (2001, 2003) present analyses for several product categories in order to illustrate that the concepts and methods of behavior analysis and behavioral economics can be applied to the investigation of consumer brand choice. Their preliminary research investigated matching and maximization in the brand buying behavior of nine consumers, conducting analyses to establish whether: (1) matching, (2) downward-sloping demand curves, and (3) maximization were present as predicted by behavioral economics. All three expectations were generally upheld, though the results needed to be understood in the context of marketing research studies of brand choice as well as matching and maximization theories. Contrary to the predictions of both matching and maximization theories consumers showed multibrand purchasing, sometimes on a single shopping trip. They also established the importance of qualitative research for understanding the degree of substitutability-in-use of brands within a product category.

In particular, these authors' investigations focused on specific product categories identified in the qualitative research with the respondents with the aim of elucidating the incidence and shape of matching and maximization for close substitute brands (butter), complementary brands (cola in one study and bottled soft drinks in another) and independent products (cola and wine). Single subject analyses were undertaken.

In the case of butter, the consumer (C1) bought one or more of up to four brands each week and described them as substitutes. As expected, the results showed near perfect matching and maximization. The finding of a strong downward-sloping curve was supported in the qualitative analysis when the consumer described how she alternated among the four brands in her repertoire from week to week, buying one or other because of a price deal or in order to achieve variety of taste. The research drew attention to the fact that despite being very close substitutes, the different brands in the consumer's set of consideration were not functionally identical. C1 appreciated that the brands had slight differences in color and taste and although she bought the cheapest brand within her consideration set on each shopping occasion, she occasionally bought one unit of an additional brand for variety of taste (even though this was usually the most expensive in her consideration set by an appreciable amount) or for convenience (i.e., the own brand of a supermarket she happened to be in or passing).

In the attempt to demonstrate differences among brands that were not substantially substitutes, Foxall & James (in press) investigated the behavior of a second consumer, C2, who bought two brands of cola on a weekly basis and described these brands as non-substitutes. Accordingly, the matching analysis exhibited near perfect matching and maximization. However, whereas the research expected upward-sloping demand curves for non-substitutes, cola exhibited a downward-sloping demand curve. This was explained by changes in the relative prices during the period of the investigation: the relative costs per liter of the two colas did not differ sufficiently (Foxall & James, 2002). In the case of bottled soft drinks, where the consumer (C3) emphatically described the brands as complements rather than substitutes, similar results were found for matching and maximization but the demand curves were upward-sloping, suggesting a comparative indifference to relative price.

A final analysis was undertaken in order to attempt further the demonstration of differences in consumer behavior in the case of commodities that were clearly non-substitutes. C2 purchased wine weekly during the same period for which he reported cola purchases; wine represented a much costlier purchase per liter which allowed his consumption of wine and cola to be modeled as though these products were gross complements or independents which ought to exhibit anti-matching (Kagel *et al.*, 1995). In fact, anti-matching was observed in the case of the three-week VR schedule but undermatching was found for the FR (one-week) schedule. In terms of the other two analyses, relative demand and maximization, the gross complements exhibited the predicted patterns which did not differ in their general topography from those of the other product categories investigated.

Three points are apparent from the matching analyses. First, in contrast to the expectation for ratio schedules, the results repeatedly show multi-brand purchasing over a period of weeks to be extensive and significantly more common than exclusive choice. Among the nine consumers and 17 products investigated in the preliminary study, there was only one instance of sole brand purchasing. This was for coffee. The debriefing interview revealed, moreover, that even this consumer had purchased other brands of coffee outside the period studied. Second, the logarithmic analyses indicate that sensitivity is effectively at unity: there is neither under nor overmatching. Marked bias (indicated by the b of the generalized matching law, the intercept of regression analysis) was generally found, however. Third, in the matching analyses for both butter and cola, there was no difference in the results for each ascribed schedule (conc VR VR five-week, conc VR VR three-week, and conc FR FR one-week).

Method

Subjects

The data, for 80 adult consumers, were drawn from the TNS "Superpanel". The panel consists of 10,000 households, randomly selected, to represent Great Britain. All panel members scan their purchases after each shopping occasion into a sophisticated barcode reader. The data are then downloaded onto the TNS mainframe computer where they are grossed up into reports that provide market trends. The data on which this chapter is based are a subsample that tracked purchasing by households over a 16-week period. The prices recorded were actual prices paid for the items. The product categories under investigation are: fruit juice, packet tea/tea bags, margarine, butter, baked beans, instant coffee, cheese, breakfast cereals, and (sweet and savory) biscuits. The data, which included brand name, price-paid and quantity-bought information, were collected initially for clients in the fast-moving consumer goods industry, principally food.

Procedure

The measures and analyses successfully employed in behavioral economics and matching research (see, especially, Herrnstein, 1982; Herrnstein & Vaughan, 1980) were adapted slightly to fit the particular circumstances of consumer brand buying.

Matching analysis

The matching analysis followed the procedures of design and analysis that have become established in matching research with animal and human subjects (Herrnstein, 1997). In consumer research the matching law becomes the proposition that the proportion of pounds and pence (dollars and cents, etc.) spent for a commodity will match the proportion of reinforcers earned (i.e., purchases made as a result of that spending) (Foxall, 1999). In seeking to demonstrate matching, the requirement was to express the amount purchased of each brand as a proportion of the total amount of the product category purchased (the "amount bought ratio") as a function of the amount spent on that brand as a proportion of the total amount spent on the product category (the "amount paid ratio"). This was made operational as follows. The proportion of money spent on brand A defined as the most frequently purchased brand (*the amount paid ratio*) was calculated as *amount paid for brand A/total amount paid for the product category*. The proportion of that brand bought (the *amount bought ratio*) was calculated as: *amount bought of brand A/total amount bought of the product category*.

Relative demand analysis

The relative demand analysis followed procedures of design and analysis employed in behavioral economics studies. In order to devise relative demand curves for the product categories, a demand analysis expressed the ratio of amount bought of the dominant brand (A) to the amount bought of the remaining brands in that category (the "amount bought ratio" described above) as a function of the ratio of the relative average prices of the dominant and the other brands (the relative price ratio). In operational terms, the relative price RATIO = *mean price of brand A/mean price of other brands in the repertoire*.

Maximization analysis

Finally, an analysis intended to reveal whether the observed consumer behavior was maximizing returns on price expended was undertaken, following procedures discussed by Herrnstein & Loveland, 1975 and Herrnstein & Vaughan, 1980. On conc ratio schedules,[3] there is a fixed probability of reinforcement for each response, which can be expressed as the reciprocal of the schedule parameter. "Thus conc VR40 VR80 describes two response alternatives with reinforcement probabilities of 1/40 and 1/80, respectively". On ratio schedules, the probability of reinforcement is independent of response rate (something not true of VI schedules where the probability of reinforcement is inversely proportional to rate of responding). Faced with conc VR40 VR80 schedules, the individual's maximal probability of reinforcement is obtained by responding exclusively on the VR40 schedule. Matching theory makes the same prediction for conc VR VR schedules, claiming that maximization is under these circumstances a special case of matching (*cf.* Rachlin, 1980). In order to ascertain whether maximization is occurring, we plotted the amount spent ratio against probability of reinforcement where the latter is operationalized as the reciprocal of the price of brand A over the reciprocal of the price of brand A plus the reciprocal of the mean of the prices of the other brands in the consumer's consideration set (B), i.e. $1/P_A/(1/P_A+1/P_B)$.

The difficulty of ascertaining with precision whether brand choice occurs on a series of fixed ratio schedules (represented by the prices of each brand obtaining on each purchase occasion) or, aggregated over several such occasions, on variable ratio schedules led us to undertake two analyses for each product category studied. The first treated the schedules as a sequence of fixed ratio relationships by expressing measures of amount bought as a function of measures of prices for: (a) weekly periods, representing a sequence of FR schedules, and (b) periods of three weeks, for which the data were averaged, representing VR schedules.

Results

The two analyses were conducted within each product category for each of the consumers for one-week and three-week periods; in addition, aggregated analyses were conducted for the entire subset of the consumers who purchased each product during the period. We present below the summary of findings for the entire data set, illustrated by the results for the fruit juice product category. Over 50 brands were bought by the 57 consumers who purchased this product, 22 of whom (just short of 39%) purchased fruit juice at more than one supermarket in the 16-week period to which data relate.

Matching

Within each of the nine product categories, matching analysis revealed that the brands purchased were close substitutes. When the matching law is expressed logarithmically as a power function (Eq. (5.3)), unity of the exponent s indicates substitutability. Measures of s that deviated only in the smallest degree from unity were uniformly found. The results are illustrated with data for fruit juice (see Figure 5.1: note that the upper diagrams in this and subsequent figures are for a single, typical consumer, while the lower diagrams are for the aggregated data set for this product). This high degree of substitutability was found for all products and all consumers who practiced multi-brand purchasing. Hence, it

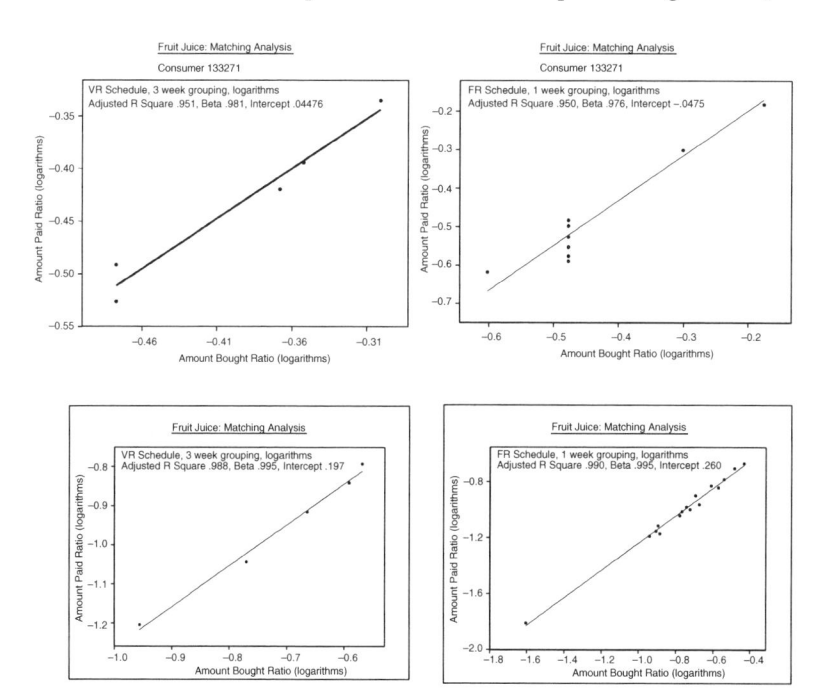

Figure 5.1 Matching Analyses for Fruit Juice

was not possible to compare substitutes and non-substitutes in terms of matching.

Multi-brand purchasing

Multi-brand purchasing was found extensively for all products; a small number of consumers were sole purchasers of each brand. In the case of the product category chosen to exemplify our results, fruit juice, 25 (44%) of the 57 consumers buying this item were sole purchasers; the highest proportion of sole purchasers was found for butter (59%), the lowest for cheese (9%). This result is entirely in keeping with work in marketing research on aggregate patterns of brand choice. Its degree of consistency with the prediction of behavioral economics that under the circumstances exemplified by brand choice ("ratio schedules of reinforcement") consumers would maximize by always selecting the cheapest alternative requires elaboration, and this follows the discussion of maximization.

The multi-brand buying we have seen was the case over a period of weeks. This is what the aggregate studies are picking up. But week by week we have evidence that some consumers buy the cheapest: that is what accounts for their brand switching and switching back. The price incentives to switch are there weekly, not just when a special deal is on.

Relative demand

Relative demand curves for the majority of consumers in most product categories are downward-sloping, indicating price sensitivity. Since the brands investigated within each product category were close substitutes, this is expected.

The results (Figure 5.2) can be addressed in terms of the generalizations advanced by (Madden *et al.*, 2000). (a) "Increasing the unit price of a reinforcer decreases consumption of that reinforcer", i.e., demand curves logarithmically plotted show consumption to be a positively decelerating function of unit price increases. This is precisely what we found for all product classes, the crucial difference being that we found downward-sloping *relative* demand curves. (b) "Unit price determines consumption and response output regardless of the specific values of the cost and benefits components of the ratio". We found this but the R^2s are not high price – alone does not determine consumption and response output in the real world. (c) "When choosing between two qualitatively identical reinforcers available at different unit prices, ... behavior will be exclusively allocated to the alternative with the lower

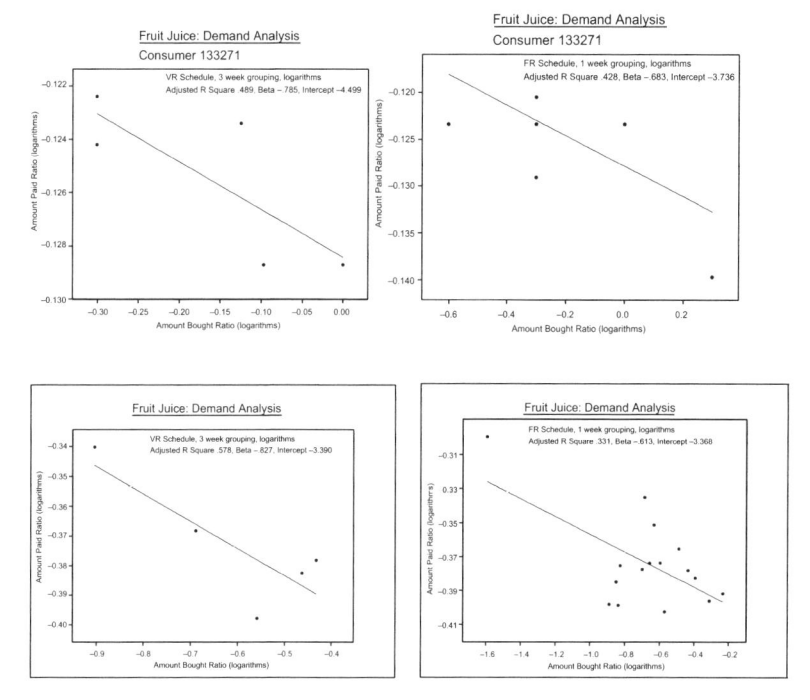

Figure 5.2 Relative Demand Analyses for Fruit Juice

unit price". *This explains brand purchase sequencing when VR is assumed, but we must look to each individual purchasing opportunity (FR) to understand the decision processes used by consumers. Multi-brand purchasing does happen on the same shopping trip but in general it does not.*

Maximization

Maximization analysis would require that consumers purchase the cheapest option on each shopping trip among the brands they purchase. This is indeed what was found in the preliminary studies, at least where consumers were buying close substitutes, but the analysis of the current data suggest a more complicated pattern (Figure 5.3).

Downward-sloping demand curves do not necessarily imply maximization (as continuing controversy in economics attests). The more stringent maximization analysis indicates, however, that consumers consistently chose the cheapest brand on each shopping occasion. This is consistent with the behavioral economics approach. However, the consumers selected the cheapest brand within their consideration set

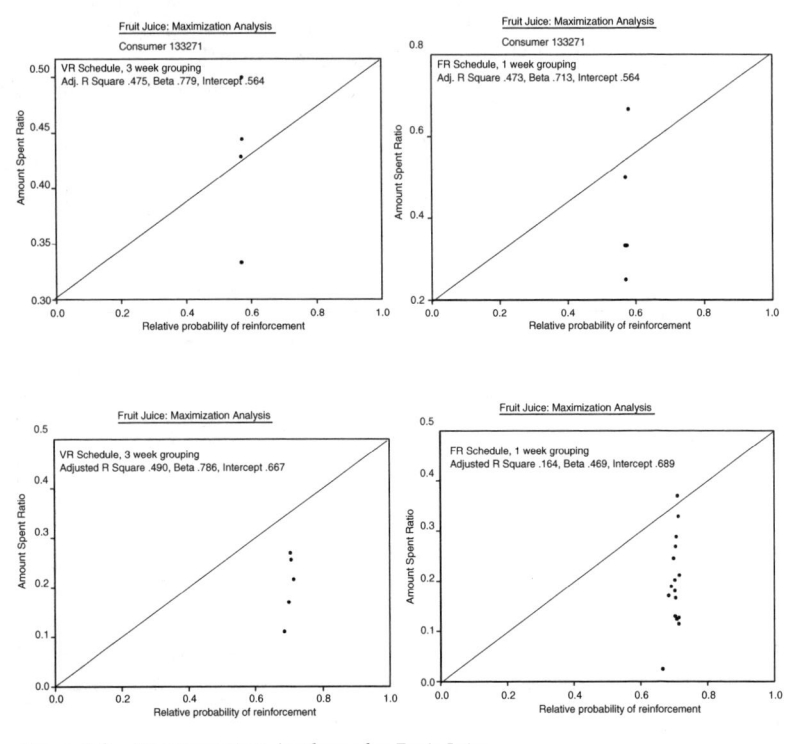

Figure 5.3 Maximization Analyses for Fruit Juice

which in many cases comprised only premium, highly differentiated brands.

Consumers did not maximize in any "absolute" sense, therefore: in each product category, own-label or economy versions existed which were considerably cheaper than those actually purchased. This is consistent with the marketing view of branding: consumers determined their consideration sets according to the level of quality they require and purchase the most price-advantageous brand within that set on each shopping occasion. Minor deviations from this general pattern appear, on the basis of qualitative research at the pilot stage, to result from the convenience of buying at a different store or the desire for variety.

Discussion

The use of FR schedules means that we take account of multi-brand purchasing only when it occurs in a single week. Even here we do find this and we also find maximization at this level of analysis. But when we consider periods of time (the three-week analyses) when multi-brand purchasing is almost certain to appear, we still find maximization despite the fact that the consumer is taking several brands into their consideration and buying sets.

Consumer decision processes: maximization and melioration

As pragmatists we are aware that people do not behave as our models represent their behavior: that we can project that human behavior is maximizing or meliorating and as a result make accurate predictions of their behavior tells us nothing about what that behavior is actually like, what humans are actually like. It merely tells us which models predict aspects of that behavior better or worse. Hence, we are not attempting to say whether consumers actually do this or that as a rule: we are simply saying that if we assume they aim at a particular end we can better predict their behavior. It appears that consumers maximize locally, i.e., on each purchase occasion: this is consistent with melioration, though not with optimization in the economic sense. Yet, the evidence we have also permits the inference that they take long-term consequences into consideration in purchasing premium brands some or all of the time.

How do they maximize?

The integration of behavior and reinforcements is a relevant consideration here. Even if there is evidence that consumers tend to maximize on each shopping trip (typically weekly), it may be useful to study the allocation of behavior over longer periods (i.e., to portray the schedule on which such behavior is enacted as VR as well as FR). The reason for this is that integration may take place at different rates for different bundles of reinforcers and the more we take informational reinforcement (IR) into consideration the more we need to look for longer-term effects as a result of the consumer's increasing the degree of informational reinforcement he or she receives. The judgment that consumers maximize reinforcement on each shopping trip is concerned primarily with their obtaining utilitarian reinforcement (perhaps within a consideration set that is itself determined somewhat by the significance of informational reinforcement like branding effects). Over say a three-week period, the multiple brands purchased may reflect more than the weekly minimization of expenditure: the particular bundle of brands purchased over this period may also reflect issues of variety, for instance see (Rachlin, 1982).

Whilst our results indicate that consumers maximize in some sense, the detailed analysis of cases indicates that they do not do so by the exclusive selection of the cheapest brand, that offered on the richest schedule. When non-human animals select from a number of alternatives, they are physically capable of making only one response at a time, i.e., selecting one and only one of the choices available to them. Consumers on a single shopping trip can buy more than one brand in the same product category. This means that two or more responses can occur simultaneously, that two or more choices can be selected at the same time. Consumers may maximize by choosing the cheapest option more frequently than any other, but they still buy other, more expensive versions of the product sometimes even on a single shopping trip. This is maximizing by means other than exclusive choice and it raises the question of *what* consumers are maximizing.

What are they maximizing?

The results indicate that consumers are maximizing amount bought with respect to unit price. Within their choice sets they make maximizing choices that also show perfect matching ($s = 1$). But since many of them buy premium brands, they can be considered to be actually undermatching when the fact that they could almost certainly buy a much cheaper alternative that is functionally similar and physically identical to the brand(s) they actually buy.

Conclusions

Hursh (1980) drew attention to four elements of economic analysis which he showed to be "useful for the analysis of otherwise conflicting sets of data". Those sets of data were obtained from the experimental analysis of the consumer behaviors of non-human animals. We now need to discuss how far those four tools of analysis apply to the analysis of complex consumer behavior, i.e., the choices of human consumers in the market place.

The scope of consumer behavior settings

Hursh first concludes that, "A behavioral experiment is an economic system and its characteristics can strongly determine the results". In the *open economy*, daily total consumption is independent of response level since food is made available to the organism outside the experimental period; demand is highly elastic with respect to price (response rate declines as price increases). In a *closed* economy, elasticity of demand is low for an essential commodity like food. We need additional concepts to understand consumer behavior in the real world. One of these, derived from the behavioral perspective model (BPM, see Foxall, 1990) is the scope of the consumer behavior setting which has proved relevant to the interpretation (and to some degree the prediction and control) of consumer behavior (Foxall, 1996, 2002; Foxall & Greenley, 1998, 1999, 2000; Foxall & Soriano, 2005; Soriano & Foxall, 2002). The scope of consumer behavior settings, from the most open to the most closed, represents the range of behavioral options available to the individual in a situation, and hence to the would-be interpreter of his or her behavior.

The BPM is an adaptation of the three-term contingency to incorporate the complexity of consumer choice in the environment of the affluent, marketing-oriented economy. Like the three-term contingency it specifies behaviorally antecedent stimulus conditions (the behavior setting) but elaborates the simpler concepts of discriminative stimuli, establishing operations or rules by means of the construct of behavior setting *scope*, the extent to which these setting elements encourage or inhibit the behavior predicted to occur in such settings. Behavior setting scope is conceptualized as a continuum from closed to open in which the former type of setting permits one or at best a very few behaviors to be enacted within its confines, while the latter type permits a whole range of often competing behaviors to be enacted.

The most closed setting likely to be encountered in reality is that of the animal laboratory where the experimental subject has no alternative but to be present and where its behavioral repertoire is severely restricted to serve the purposes of the researcher (see Schwartz & Lacey, 1988). More open than this, but still toward the closed pole of the continuum, is the human operant experiment which the subject is comparatively free to leave at any time even though the social and physical pressures of the experimental space may well act against this.

Toward the other end of the continuum, settings of purchase and consumption are all relatively open compared to this, but still differ from one another along a restricted *continuum of closed-open consumer behavior settings* (Foxall, 1990). Hence, standing in line at the bank to pay in a check takes place in a relatively closed consumer behavior setting: there is probably no alternative to being there and waiting until a teller becomes available, standing in an orderly fashion is encouraged both by the physical style of the building and by the social arrangements, deviation from the established behavior program of the setting is likely to be punished by stares or glares or, if one's fellow customers have succumbed to the latest assertiveness training fad by more direct, and potentially socially embarrassing action. Depending on their learning histories, some customers may actually seek such social disapproval and arrange for calls on their mobile phones to come in at this time but most of us seem to be sufficiently conditioned to conform fairly closely to the behavior patterns laid down by the designers of this closed consumer behavior setting.

An open consumer behavior setting encourages a wider range of alternative behaviors. In a bar, for instance, all manner or beverages and snacks may be available, there may be TV to watch, talking loudly may not be discouraged, even singing and dancing may be possible. The customer is free to leave at any time, even if only to go to another bar in the vicinity – at least far freer than he or she would be to leave the bank and find another at which to present the check.

Unlike open-closed economies which comprise a dichotomous classification, open-closed behavior settings form a continuum, though they are often treated for ease of exposition and research as binary variables. More importantly, open-closed economies reflect only one element of the marketing mix – price-quantity relationships and, hence, elasticity of demand – while consumer behavior settings necessarily involve the other mix elements as well as word-of-mouth and other forms of interpersonal influence – i.e., the *plasticity* of demand, which is further described below.

The plasticity of demand

Hursh's second conclusion is that, "Reinforcers can be distinguished by a functional property called elasticity of demand that is independent of relative value". We have shown in essence the importance of price elasticity of demand. Indeed, we have rescued it in the study of brand choice from the marketers who claim that price differentials as small as we have been concerned with have no impact on brand choice. The burden of our analysis is that they are in fact central to understanding consumer choice. However – and this is a second rule of interpretation drawn from the BPM analysis – patterns of reinforcement can be distinguished according to the degree of utility (functionality) and information (symbolism) they provide. *Utilitarian reinforcement* consists in the direct usable, economic and technical benefits of owning and consuming a product or service, while *informational* reinforcement inheres in benefits of ownership and consumption which are usually social in nature and consist in the prestige or status as well as the self-esteem generated by ownership and consumption.

The driver of a Lada, for instance, is principally concerned with the utilitarian benefits that all cars provide: the most obvious is getting from A to B, door-to-door transportation.[4] *Informational reinforcement*, on the other hand, is more likely to involve a lifestyle statement by which the consumer seeks to convey his or her social status or to bolster esteem and/or reported feelings of self-esteem. The driver of a Mercedes or a Bentley or a Porsche clearly gets from A to B in it but, in addition, gains the social esteem and status provided by friends and acquaintances who admire these prestige products and from members of the general public who see me driving around in a socially desirable vehicle. The social status and esteem that driver is accorded are the symbolic rewards of consumption. Most products have an element of both the instrumental and the symbolic. A mobile phone not only provides communications services when and where the consumer wants them; because it is a Nokia and therefore has interchangeable colored cases, it may also signal to that consumer's social group that he or she is "cool" (or, a year or so later, "not so cool").

These considerations reflect the *plasticity* of demand: the sensitivity of demand not only to price but to all four generic elements of the marketing mix and their interactions and their global influence. Penrose (1959) quotes Alderson and Sessions:

> ... it is essential to distinguish between what the economist has called the elasticity of demand and the *more fundamental* factor of plasticity. The intended difference is suggested by the common meaning of the words. "Elastic" refers to something that can be stretched, and "plastic" to something that can be molded. Economics long pointed out that demand can be stretched to include more units of a product by the simple expedient of reducing the price. Much less attention has been devoted to the fact that demand can often be remolded into quite different forms. The investigation of plasticity of demand has generally been left to the market analyst rather than to the economist. The remolding of demand to make a place for new products has proceeded to spectacular extent in the United States. To make use of the innate plasticity of demand means to find ways of changing the habits and attitudes of consumers. Changing a buying habit means, among other things, making it as convenient as possible for consumers to buy the new product. "Changing buying attitudes means *supplying consumers with reasons for preferring the new product. Cost and Profit Outlook*, Vol. 5, No. 8 (Aug. 1952)". (italics added by Penrose.)

Interesting research can, however, combine economic and marketing variables.

The substitutability of brands

The third conclusion drawn by Hursh is that, "Reinforcers may interact as complements, as well as substitutes". We benefit here from making a distinction between utilitarian and informational or symbolic reinforcement which goes beyond the usual distinction between primary and secondary reinforcers (Foxall, 1997). In the case of brands, it is inevitable that they will tend to be substitutes in so far as they are functionally similar (almost identical in terms of physical formulation), i.e., in terms of utilitarian reinforcement, and complements in so far as they are differentiated by branding, i.e., in terms of informational reinforcement or social symbolism. Branding is an attempt to reduce the perceived substitutability of brands by altering their value to the consumer on the basis of their social significance (e.g., increasing the status of their owners and users) or psychological significance (e.g., enhancing the self-esteem of those who own and use them).

The pattern of reinforcement

"Finally, because reinforcers differ in elasticity and because reinforcers can be complementary, no simple, unidimensional choice rule such as matching can account for all choice behavior". The *pattern of reinforcement* (the pattern of low-to-high utilitarian reinforcement and low-to-high informational reinforcement produced by buying or using a product) is an analytical category that takes the place in interpretive behaviorism occupied by that of the schedule of reinforcement in the experimental analysis of behavior. Because patterns of reinforcement differ and because informational reinforcement increases the complementarity of brands within a product category, non-price elements of the marketing mix come to the fore.

This study of brand choice indicates that the multi-disciplinarity of behavioral economics can usefully be extended by the inclusion of results and perspectives from marketing research. Behavioral economics is supported by the research in that its analyses and conclusions are shown to apply to human consumers in situations of free choice; behavioral economists should appreciate, however, the conclusions of marketing researchers to the effect that most consumers are multi-brand purchasers, and that marketing considerations other than price influence choice. Marketing researchers may need to take note of the import of price differentials in brand choice. The behavioral mechanism of choice that underlies the molar patterns of consumer choice depicted here appears to be momentary maximization of benefit, a result that is consistent with melioration or overall maximization. However, the lesson of the research is that brand choice is reinforced by two sources of reward, *utilitarian* which derives from the functional benefits of the good, and *informational* or *symbolic* which derives from the psychological and cultural meanings which goods acquire through their participation in social interactions and, by derivation, through advertising and other means to branding. The recognition of both sources of reinforcement is the key requirement for both marketing researchers and behavioral economists.

Continuing research

Present effort is concentrated on the completion of the analyses for the remaining product categories in order to make comparison across product categories (for each consumer) and across consumers. Particularly of interest are the questions whether the pattern of there being some maximizers and some non-maximizers for each product is repeated; whether, if so, the proportions of each are similar from category to category; and whether the same consumers maximize from one category to another. However, the combination of economic, psychological, and marketing variables to which the research draws attention suggest some more fundamental research, as a summary of the findings indicates. Purchasers of fast-moving consumer goods generally exhibit multi-brand choice, selecting apparently randomly among a small subset or "repertoire" of tried and trusted brands. Their behavior shows both matching and maximization, though it is not clear just what the majority of buyers are maximizing. Each brand attracts, however, a small percentage of consumers who are 100% loyal to it during the period of observation. Some of these are exclusively buyers of premium-priced brands who are presumably maximizing informational reinforcement because their demand for the brand is relatively price-insensitive or inelastic. Others buy exclusively the cheapest brands available and can be assumed to maximize utilitarian reinforcement since their behavior is particularly price-sensitive or elastic. Between them are the majority of consumers whose multi-brand buying takes the form of selecting a mixture of economy- and premium-priced brands. The implications of this for the conceptualization of brand loyalty are intriguing.

Notes

1. Previously published in the *Journal of Economic Psychology*, 2003, 24, 675–95.
2. An interval schedule maintains a constant minimum time interval between rewards (reinforcements). Fixed interval schedules maintain a constant period of time between intervals, while on a variable interval schedule the time varies between one reinforcer and the next. Concurrent schedules permit simultaneous choice procedures. The contingencies just described enable behavioral allocation to be controlled and predicted by concurrent variable interval schedules, usually abbreviated to conc VI VI.
3. A ratio schedule is one in which a specified number of responses has to be performed before reinforcement becomes available. Fixed ratio schedules keep the number of required responses equal from reinforcer to reinforcer; variable ratio schedules allow the required number of responses to change from one reinforcer to the next. Concurrent variable ratio schedules, usually abbreviated to conc VR VR, allow simultaneous choice to be investigated. It is this arrangement that most clearly resembles the purchases of brand within a product class.
4. The authors are aware of the fact that this may be a sweeping categorization. Some consumers may seek more informational reinforcement in buying the cheaper and traditionally less prestigious Lada for reasons of ethical concern with the environment or the status of making a fashion statement.

References

Baum, W. M. (1974). "On two types of deviation from the matching law". *Journal of the Experimental Analysis of Behavior*, 22, 231–42.

Baum, W. M. (1979). "Matching, undermatching and overmatching in studies of choice". *Journal of the Experimental Analysis of Behavior*, 32, 269–81.

Commons, M. L., Herrnstein, R. J. & Rachlin, H. (eds) (1982). *Quantitative analyses of behavior. II. Matching and maximizing accounts*. Ballinger, Cambridge, MA.

Davison, M. & McCarthy, D. (1988). *The matching law: A research review*. Hillsdale, NJ: Lawrence Erlbaum Associates.

de Villiers, P. A. & Herrnstein, R. J. (1976). "Toward a law of response strength". *Psychological Bulletin*, 83, 1131–53.

Ehrenberg, A. S. C. (1988). *Repeat buying: Facts, theory and applications* 2nd edn. New York, London: Oxford University Press, Griffin.

Ehrenberg, A. S. C. & Goodhardt, G. J. (1977). *Essays on understanding buyer behavior*. New York: J. Walter Thompson and Market Research Corporation of America.

Foxall, G. R. (1990). *Consumer psychology in behavioral perspective*. London and New York: Routledge.

Foxall, G. R. (1996). *Consumers in context: The BPM research program*. London and New York: International Thomson.

Foxall, G. R. (1997). *Marketing psychology: The paradigm in the wings*. London: Macmillan.

Foxall, G. R. (1999). "The substitutability of brands". *Managerial and Decision Economics*, 20, 241–57.

Foxall, G. R. (2002). *Consumer behavior analysis: Critical perspectives*. London and New York: Routledge.

Foxall, G. R. & Greenley, G. E. (1998). "The affective structure of consumer situations". *Environment and Behavior*, 30, 781–98.

Foxall, G. R. & Greenley, G. E. (1999). "Consumers' emotional responses to service environments". *Journal of Business Research*, 46, 149–58.

Foxall, G. R. & Greenley, G. E. (2000). "Predicting and explaining responses to consumer environments: An empirical test and theoretical extension of the behavioural perspective model". *The Service Industries Journal*, 20, 39–63.

Foxall, G. R. & James, V. K. (2001). "The Behavior Basis of Consumer Choice: A Preliminary Analysis". *European Journal of Behavior Analysis*, 2 (2), 209–20.

Foxall, G. R. & James, V. K. (2003). "The Behavioral Ecology of Brand Choice: How and What do Consumers Maximize?". *Psychology and Marketing*, 20 (9), 811–36.

Foxall, G. R. & Soriano, M. Y. (2005). "Situational influences on consumers' attitudes and behavior". *Journal of Business Research*, 58, 518–25.

Green, L. & Freed, D. E. (1993). "The substitutability of reinforcers". *Journal of the Experimental Analysis of Behavior*, 60, 141–58.

Green, L., Rachlin, H. & Hanson, J. (1983). "Matching and maximizing with concurrent ratio-interval schedules". *Journal of the Experimental Analysis of Behavior*, 40, 217–24.

Herrnstein, R. J. (1961). "Relative and absolute strength of response as a function of frequency of reinforcement". *Journal of the Experimental Analysis of Behavior*, 4, 267–72.

Herrnstein, R. J. (1970). "On the law of effect". *Journal of the Experimental Analysis of Behavior*, 13, 243–66.

Herrnstein, R. J. (1982). "Melioration as behavioral dynamism", in M. L. Commons, R. J. Herrnstein & H. Rachlin (eds), *Quantitative analyses of behavior, Vol. II, Matching and maximizing accounts*. Cambridge, MA: Ballinger, pp. 433–58.

Herrnstein, R. J. (1997). In H. Rachlin & D. I. Laibson (eds) *The matching law: Papers in psychology and economics*. Cambridge, MA: Harvard University Press.

Herrnstein, R. J. & Loveland, D. H. (1975). "Maximizing and matching on concurrent ratio schedules". *Journal of the Experimental Analysis of Behavior*, 24, 107–16.

Herrnstein, R. J. & Vaughan, W. (1980). In J. E. R. Staddon (ed.) *Limits to action: The allocation of individual behavior*. New York: Academic Press, pp. 143–76.

Hursh, S. R. (1980). "Economic concepts for the analysis of behavior". *Journal of the Experimental Analysis of Behavior*, 34, 219–38.

Kagel, J. H., Battalio, R. C. & Green, L. (1995). *Economic choice theory: An experimental analysis of animal behavior*. Cambridge: Cambridge University Press.

Logue, A. W. (2002). "The living legacy of the Harvard Pigeon Lab: Quantitative analysis in the wide world". *Journal of the Experimental Analysis of Behavior*, 77, 357–66.

Madden, G. W., Bickel, W. K. & Jacobs, E. A. (2000). "Three predictions of the economic concept of unit price in a choice context". *Journal of the Experimental Analysis of Behavior*, 73, 45–64.

Penrose, E. (1959). *The theory of the growth of the firm*. Oxford: Blackwell.

Pierce, W. D. & Epling, W. F. (1983). "Choice, matching and human behavior: A review of the literature". *The Behavior Analyst*, 6 (1), 57–76.

Rachlin, H. (1980). "Economics and behavioral psychology", in: J. E. R. Staddon (ed.) *Limits to action: The allocation of individual behavior*. New York: Academic Press, pp. 205–36.

Rachlin, H. (1982). "Economics of the matching law", in M. L. Commons, R. J. Herrnstein & H. Rachlin (eds) *Quantitative analysis of behavior, Vol. II, Matching and maximizing accounts*. Cambridge, MA: Ballinger, pp. 347–74.

Rachlin, H. (2000). *The science of self-control*. Cambridge, MA: Harvard University Press.

Schwartz, B. & Lacey, H. (1988). "What applied studies of human operant conditioning tell us about humans and about operant conditioning", in G. Davey & C. Cullen (eds) *Human operant conditioning and behavior modification*. John Wiley & Sons Ltd, Chicester, pp. 27–42.

Schwartz, B. & Reisberg, D. (1991). *Learning and memory*. New York: W.W. Norton & Co.

Soriano, M. Y. & Foxall, G. R. (2002). "Emotional responses to consumers' environments an empirical examination of the behavioural perspective model in a Latin American context". *Journal of Consumer Behaviour*, 2.

6
The Behavioral Economics of Consumer Brand Choice: Patterns of Reinforcement and Utility Maximization[1]

Gordon R. Foxall, Jorge M. Oliveira-Castro and
Teresa C. Schrezenmaier

Introduction

Within marketing science, the analysis of brand choices for fast-moving consumer goods, based on aggregate data, shows that most individuals tend to purchase a variety of brands within a product category. More specifically, such results indicate that, in steady-state markets: (a) only a small portion of consumers buy just one brand on consecutive shopping occasions, that is, few consumers remain 100% loyal to one brand; (b) each brand attracts a small group of 100%-loyal consumers; (c) the majority of consumers buy several different brands, selected apparently randomly from a subset of existing brands; (d) existing brands usually differ widely with respect to penetration level and not so much in terms of average buying frequency (i.e., how often consumers buy it during the analysis period); and (e) brands with smaller penetration levels (or market shares) also tend to show smaller average buying frequency and smaller percentages of 100%-loyal consumers (i.e., "double jeopardy"). These results have been replicated for some 30 food and drink products (from cookies to beer), 20 cleaning and personal care products (from cosmetics to heavy cleaning liquids), gasoline, aviation fuel, automobiles, some medicines and pharmaceutical prescriptions, television channels and shows, shopping trips, store chains, individual stores, and attitudes toward brands (*cf.* Dall'Olmo Riley *et al.*, 1997; Ehrenberg, 1972; Ehrenberg *et al.*, 1990; Ehrenberg & Scriven, 1999; Goodhardt *et al.*, 1984; Uncles *et al.*, 1995).

So sure are the relationships involved that a mathematical model has also been developed to describe such regularities, the Dirichlet Model (e.g., Ehrenberg *et al.*, 1990), which has been used to predict the market insertion of new products (Ehrenberg, 1993), to analyze the effects of promotions (Ehrenberg, 1986; Ehrenberg *et al.*, 1994), and to evaluate patterns of store loyalty (Ehrenberg & England, 1990; Keng & Ehrenberg, 1984; Sharp & Sharp, 1997; Uncles & Ehrenberg, 1990). Nonetheless, despite the wide replication of such patterns, which have been raised by some authors to the status of "empirical generalizations" in marketing (e.g., Uncles *et al.*, 1995), little is known about the variables and the underlying behavioral mechanisms that influence and explain consumers' brand choices. The marketing literature is not forthcoming, for instance, about the factors responsible for shaping the subset of the brands that compose a product category among which consumers choose in practice (their "consideration sets") and what Ehrenberg calls the "repertoire" of such brands actually purchased (their "purchase sets").

It is a basic axiom of modern marketing thought that sales are produced not simply by price acting alone, any more than by product attributes, or advertising and other promotional means, or distribution effectiveness acting singly, but by a combination of all four of these influences on demand that constitute the "marketing mix." As marketing science has developed as a separate discipline, it has de-emphasized the influence of price on demand (the principal focus of the economist's purview) and stressed the non-price elements of the marketing mix, notably the promotional activity involved in brand differentiation (De Chernatony & McDonald, 2003; Jary & Wileman, 1998; Watkins, 1986). Behavioral economics, partly because of the stress it has placed on the economics of animal responding in experimental situations, where the sole reliable analogue of the influences on consumer demand ruling in the market place relates to price, has necessarily followed the reasoning and methodology of the economist rather than the marketing scientist. The non-price marketing mix has, therefore, not featured in the research program of behavioral economics.

The assumption that consumers maximize utility in some way or other – a preoccupation of the economics approach – is, nevertheless, common in the marketing literature. Krishnamurti and Raj (1988), for example, state that "the consumer chooses that alternative which maximizes his (or her) utility," although they recognize that this is a latent or unobservable utility which is assumed rather than tested (*cf.* Rachlin, 1980). Based on this maximization assumption, one could expect consumers to choose the cheapest brands that offer the attributes and characteristics that they are looking for. Although the price of different brands is certainly one variable that is expected to influence brand choice, as exemplified by the literature on the effects of promotions (e.g., Ehrenberg, 1986; Ehrenberg et al., 1994; Bell et al., 1999), empirical evidence showing that consumers tend to maximize when choosing across brands was not available before recent research on the behavioral economics of brand choice (Foxall & James, 2001, 2003; Foxall & Schrezenmaier, 2003). In this chapter, we extend this research from the analysis of single cases to that of panel data for some 80 consumers purchasing nine product categories, examining in detail the relationship between price and quantity demanded in relation to the functional and symbolic attributes of brands which influence the composition of consumers' consideration and purchase sets.

Previous research

Foxall (1999a), Foxall & James (2001, 2003) and Foxall & Schrezenmaier (2003) adopted techniques refined in choice experiments in behavioral economics and behavior analysis to investigate brand choice. Three types of analysis were used: matching, relative demand, and maximization.

Matching analysis

The results of choice experiments with non-human animals in behavior analysis gave support for the development of the matching law, which in its simplest form asserts that organisms in choice situations match the relative distribution of responses to the relative distribution of the reinforcers they obtain (Herrnstein, 1961, 1970). In its more general form, the generalized matching law (Baum, 1974, 1979) states that the ratio of responses between two alternatives is a power function of the ratio of reinforcers, that is,

$$\frac{B1}{B2} = b\left(\frac{R1}{R2}\right)^s$$

where B represents responses, R represents reinforcers, and the subscripts 1 and 2, choice alternatives. The parameter b, obtained from the intercept of the linear log–log formulation of the law, is a measure of biased responding between the alternatives, usually related to asymmetrical experimental factors such as differences in response cost between the alternatives. The parameter s, the slope of the linear log–log formulation, is interpreted as a measure of sensitivity in response distribution with changes in reinforcer distribution, which indicates that the individual favors, more than predicted by precise matching, the richer ($s > 1$) or poorer ($s < 1$) schedule of reinforcement. In behavioral economics, the parameter s can also be used as an estimate of the level of substitutability of the reinforcers in the situation, in which case there is evidence suggesting that it should be equal or close to 1 for substitutable commodities, and negative for complementary commodities (*cf.* Baum & Nevin, 1981; Foxall, 1999a; Kagel *et al.*, 1995).

Foxall & James, 2001, 2003 applied this type of analysis to data obtained from consumers' brand choice. Consumer choice was analyzed for brands that were substitutes, non-substitutes and independent, for one-, three-, and five-week periods. Matching and maximization analyses were based on relative measures of price paid and amount bought, which considered the relation between the amount paid for (or amount bought of) the preferred brand and the amount paid for (or amount bought of) the other brands in the consumer repertoire. As predicted, substitute brands showed matching whereas independent brands showed some evidence of anti-matching. Their results also showed some evidence that consumers tend to maximize the amount they pay in relation to the amount they buy within their brand repertoire by purchasing the cheapest brand (although they sometimes also bought some more expensive brand). Similar results have also been reported by more recent research (*cf.* Foxall & James, 2003; Foxall & Schrezenmaier, 2003).

Relative demand analysis

Whereas matching analysis relates the actual amount of a reinforcer obtained to the actual amount of behavior expended in obtaining it, an understanding of consumer decision making in the face of competing sources or reinforcement offered at a variety of programmed behavioral costs or prices requires a different kind of analysis. Matching analysis plots the quantity obtained of a commodity as a positively accelerating function of the amount paid for it. By contrast, the sensitivity of the quantity demanded of a commodity to its ruling market price is expressed by economists in terms of the demand curve. One of the assumptions underlying the demand curve is that as the unit price of a commodity increases, its consumption will decrease (Madden *et al.*, 2000). This is demonstrated when demand curves plotted on logarithmic coordinates show consumption to be a positively decelerating function of unit price. The sensitivity of quantity demanded to price is expressed in economic terms as "price elasticity of demand" which at its simplest relates the percentage change in amount consumed to the percentage change in price (Houston & McFarland, 1980; see also Hursh, 1980; Hursh & Bauman, 1987).

In an attempt to incorporate some of the features of naturalistic marketing settings involving consumer choices among competing brands whose relative prices might influence selection decisions, Foxall and James (following Kagel *et al.*, 1980) employed relative demand analysis which presents the relative amounts of brands A and B as a function of their relative prices. Their results, albeit for a restricted sample of individual consumers and covering a small number of product categories, found downward-sloping demand curves which indicated a degree of price sensitivity on the part of the buyers investigated (Foxall & James, 2001, 2003).

Maximization analysis

Analyses to reveal whether the observed consumer behavior was maximizing returns on price expended were undertaken following procedures developed by Herrnstein & Loveland (1975) and Herrnstein & Vaughan (1980). On *conc* ratio schedules,[2] there is a fixed probability of reinforcement for each response, which can be expressed as the reciprocal of the schedule parameter. Concurrent VR30 VR60 refers to response alternatives which have respective reinforcement probabilities of 1/30 and 1/60. On ratio schedules, the probability of reinforcement is independent of response rate (something not true of VI schedules where the probability of reinforcement is inversely proportional to the rate of responding). Although most research on matching and maximization has been undertaken in laboratory settings which incorporate VI schedules, VR schedules are more probable in naturalistic settings (Herrnstein, 1982; Herrnstein & Loveland, 1975; Herrnstein & Prelec, 1991; Herrnstein & Vaughan, 1980; Vaughan & Herrnstein, 1987).

Faced with *conc* VR40 VR80 schedules, the individual's maximal probability of reinforcement is obtained by responding exclusively on the VR40 schedule. Matching theory makes the same prediction for conc VR VR schedules, claiming that maximization is under these circumstances a special case of matching (*cf.* Rachlin, 1980). Previous research, subject to the limitations of scope noted above, confirmed that consumers tend to maximize by generally purchasing the least expensive brand available within their consideration set (Foxall & James, 2001, 2003).

Research issues

Taken together, these results indicate that, within their repertoire of brands, consumers show price sensitivity, maximizing (most of the time), and matching (which refers to the relation between the amount they spend and the amount they buy). Based on such findings, one can predict that consumers will buy, more often than not, the cheapest brand among those that they usually buy, although one still does not know why they usually buy a certain set of brands and not others. The fact that consumers tend to buy the cheapest brand within a restricted set of brands rather than the cheapest of all brands available in the product category indicates that not all brands are perfect substitutes for the others. Even though they may be functionally equivalent for the consumer, the brands are not entirely equivalent, that is, consumer preferences reflect more than functional utility. This additional source of utility is usually rationalized in the marketing literature as stemming from rather nebulous "branding" considerations. Branding is not, however, a quantifiable construct and an important objective of the research reported here was to clarify its basis as an extra-functional source of reinforcement.

Although research to date is indicative that the principles and methods of behavioral economics can be usefully applied to consumer brand purchasing, there is clearly need for a more extensive investigation of a larger, systematically-selected sample of consumers purchasing a wider range of products in order to ascertain how far previously reported results are generalizable. It is necessary to take into greater consideration the differences between the typical consumption patterns of laboratory subjects which can be shown to be sensitive to price (or its analogue) and those of consumers in supermarkets who are subject to a much wider spectrum of choice under the influence of the entire array of marketing mix variables available to retailers. For example, an expectation of demand analysis as it is employed in the behavioral economics literature is that when consumers choose between qualitatively identical reinforcers which vary in terms of the unit prices that must be paid for them, the brand with the lower or lowest unit price will be exclusively chosen (Madden *et al.*, 2000). This is the prediction of both matching and maximization theories with regard to choice on conc VR VR schedules. However, research in these theoretical traditions typically takes place within laboratory settings that restrict choice to two alternatives, one or other of which must be selected at any choice point. Consumer brand choice is more complicated than this in that numerous choices are usually available to the consumer within a given product category, more than one of which may be selected on a single shopping occasion (Foxall & Schrezenmaier, 2003).

A source of difference among brands, related to this and other aspects of consumer choice, stems from the distinction between utilitarian and informational benefits offered by different brands, as proposed by the Behavioral Perspective Model (Foxall, 1990, 1994, 1996, 1997, 1998). According to this proposal, the behavior of the consumer can be explained by the events that occur before and after the consumer situation, which influence directly the shaping and maintenance of consumer behavior in specific environments. The consumer situation, in turn, is defined as the intersection between the consumer behavior setting and the consumer learning history. The consumer behavior setting – a supermarket, a bookstore, or a rock concert – includes the stimuli that form the social, physical and temporal consumer environments. As purchase and consumption are followed by different consequences in different settings, the events in the setting become predictive of such consequences, building a learning history that relates elements of the setting to different consequences. According to the proposal, antecedent events present in the consumer behavior setting signal the possibility of three types of consequences: utilitarian reinforcement, informational reinforcement, and aversive events. One major characteristic of economic behavior is that it involves both aversive and reinforcing consequences, for one has to give away money or rights (i.e., loss of generalized reinforcers) in order to get products or services (i.e., reinforcing events).

Utilitarian reinforcement consists in the practical outcomes of purchase and consumption, that is, functional benefits derived directly (rather than mediated by other people) from possession and application of a product or service. It is reinforcement mediated by the product or service and refers to consequences associated with increases in the utility (i.e., use value) for the individual ("pleasant") obtained from the product or service. The utilitarian, most obvious, consequence of owning a car, for example, is to be able to go from one place to the other, door to door, not depending on other people's time schedules and avoiding being exposed to weather conditions, as usually happens when one uses public transportation.

Informational reinforcement, on the other hand, would be symbolic, usually but not exclusively mediated by the actions and reactions of other persons, and would be more closely related to the exchange value of a product or service.[3] It does not consist in information *per se* but in feedback about the individual's performance, indicating the level of adequacy and accuracy of the consumer's behavior. Whereas utilitarian reinforcement is associated with the functional and economic consequences of purchasing and consuming goods or services, informational reinforcement is derived from the level of social status and prestige that a consumer obtains when purchasing or using certain goods. According to Foxall, informational and utilitarian reinforcements would be orthogonal, and most products and services would involve, in different levels or proportions, both types of reinforcement. Then, according to this analysis, the person who drives a Jaguar© or Bentley© gets, in addition to door-to-door transportation (utilitarian), social status and approval from friends and acquaintances who see that car as a prestigious product, and from the general public that sees him or her driving around in a socially desirable car. The social status and prestige received are the informational, symbolic, consequences that the consumer obtains, which are usually related to branding or the level of brand differentiation of the product (*cf.* Foxall, 1999a).

The specific combination of utilitarian and informational reinforcement made available by purchase or consumption of a particular product is known as the "pattern of reinforcement" controlling these responses. Foxall & James, 2001, 2003 argued that pattern of reinforcement influences consumers' brand choices and that it is a key to understanding what consumers maximize. Different consumers might, for example, select brands belonging to different levels of informational reinforcement, some buying mostly highly differentiated whereas others buy relatively undifferentiated brands. The differences in patterns of brand choice, including the set of brands that constitute each consumer's brand repertoire, may be a consequence of individual differences in responsiveness to different types of benefits. This idea gains even more force when we consider that branding is usually related to price, higher-differentiated brands being more expensive than less differentiated ones, and that consumers have different income levels. Then, individual buying patterns may be predominantly related, for example, to minimizing costs, maximizing utilitarian reinforcement, maximizing informational reinforcement, or to particular combinations of these. If this is so, consumers may differ with respect to price responsiveness related to informational and utilitarian benefits.

The research reported here tested predictions arising from these considerations using data from a consumer panel. Panel data are especially valuable for longitudinal studies because changes in purchasing behavior can be monitored very accurately by continuous measurements (Crouch & Housden, 2003). Furthermore, diary panel data are considered to be very precise and less susceptible to errors than those obtained through consumers' reporting their past behavior in surveys (Churchill, 1999). Hence, they are particularly valuable when collecting multifarious information on variables such as price, shopping occasion, brand name, and so on. The special significance of this research technique for the present research lies in the fact that the data were obtained non-experimentally, by electronically tracking real consumers spending their real discretionary income.

The two main purposes of the investigation were as follows. First, in order to ascertain the generalizability of earlier research findings to consumer behavior in marketing-dominated contexts, three analyses were undertaken in order to determine whether the brands in question were in fact close substitutes (matching analysis), whether brand choice was sensitive to price differentials (relative demand analysis), and whether consumers could be said to maximize returns (maximization analysis). Second, in order to gauge consumers' responsiveness to price and non-price marketing mix elements, the brands of nine food product categories were ranked according to their informational and utilitarian levels. The proportion of purchases made by each consumer at each brand level was computed, which served as basis for grouping consumers according to the level of brands they bought most. To test for differences in price responsiveness, price elasticities for consumer groups and individual consumers were compared.

Method

Sample and procedure

The market research company, Taylor Nelson Sofres, provided consumer panel data for 80 British consumers and their total weekly purchases in nine fast-moving consumer goods categories over 16 weeks. Taylor Nelson Sofres is one of the largest and best-known companies in its field and clusters consumer purchasing data on its so-called TNS Superpanel on a range of consumer goods from 15,000 randomly selected British households. Data collection is operationalized as follows: after each shopping trip, members of the panel scan their purchased items into a sophisticated handheld barcode reader by passing the scanner across the barcodes, which nowadays are printed on all packaged supermarket products. The data are then automatically sent to Taylor Nelson Sofres for central processing without any further voluntary contribution from the panel participants. The retail outlets at which purchases were made was also identified for each shopping occasion, and included major UK supermarkets such as Asda (a subsidiary of Wal-Mart), Tesco, and Sainsbury.

The nine product categories that served as basis for this research were: baked beans, cookies, cereals, butter, cheese, fruit juice, instant coffee, margarine, and tea. In more detail, the following information was recorded on each shopping occasion for each consumer: brand specification (i.e., different versions of the same product category were classified as different brands, e.g., Corn Flakes and Rice Krispies© by Kelloggs), package size, name of the supermarket/shop, date, number of units, and total amount spent. As the analysis of brand choice requires information concerning actual purchase across several buying opportunities, data from consumers who bought, within each product category, fewer than four times during the 16-week period were disregarded.

Measures and analyses

Matching: In consumer research, the matching law becomes the proposition that the ratio of amount of money spent for a brand to the amount spent on other brands within the product category will match the ratio of reinforcers earned (i.e., purchases made as a result of that spending) of that brand to the amount bought of other brands within the product category. The first of these, the *amount paid ratio*, was operationalized as the ratio of money spent on "Brand A," defined as the most frequently purchased brand, to money spent on "Brand B," i.e., the amount spent on the remaining brands purchased within the requisite product category: *Amount paid for Brand A/Amount paid for the remaining brands in the product category (B)*. The *amount bought ratio* was calculated, in terms of the physical quantity acquired, as: *Amount bought of Brand A/Amount bought of Brand B (the remaining brands of the product category)*. Logarithmic transformations were used for the analyses.

Relative demand: In order to devise relative demand curves for the product categories, a demand analysis expressed the ratio of amount bought of the dominant brand (A) to the amount bought of the remaining brands in that category (B) as a function of the ratio of the relative average prices of the dominant brand to the average price of other brands purchased from the appropriate product category (the relative price ratio). In operational terms, the relative price RATIO = *mean price of Brand A/Mean price of other brands in the repertoire (B)*. The amount bought ratio was calculated as in the case of the matching analysis. Again, log transformations were used for the analyses.

Maximization: To ascertain whether maximization is occurring, following Herrnstein & Loveland (1975), Herrnstein & Vaughan (1980), we plotted the amount bought ratio against probability of reinforcement. The latter is operationalized as the reciprocal of the price of brand A over the reciprocal of the price of brand A plus the reciprocal of the mean of the prices of the other brands in the consumer's consideration set ("Brand B"): $1/P_A/(1/P_A + 1/P_B)$. If the step function described by the data points falls to the right of the 0.5 line on the abscissa then the purchaser is maximizing by selecting the favorite brand (A) which is also the least expensive (Herrnstein & Loveland, 1975).

Schedule analogies

To ascertain how consumers make decisions, it is necessary to have some idea of how they integrate price data and brand choice responses over time, notably from shopping trip to shopping trip. In the laboratory this can be achieved without undue difficulty by the imposition of a schedule of reinforcement which programs the relationships between dependent and independent variables. Researchers who are concerned with the behavioral analysis and explanation of non-experimental behavior face the difficulty of ascertaining with precision whether brand choice in naturalistic settings occurs, by analogy, on a series of fixed ratio schedules (represented by the prices of each brand obtaining on each purchase occasion) or, aggregated over several such occasions, on variable ratio schedules. The question we are seeking to answer is whether consumers take into consideration only the prices of the brands in their consideration set that are in force on each discrete shopping trip, or whether their behavior (brand choice) reflects the price-quantity relationships for competing brands that are in force over the extended period represented by a series of shopping trips. This led us to undertake two analyses for each product category studied. The first treated the schedules as a sequence of fixed ratio relationships by expressing measures of amount bought as a function of measures of prices for (a) weekly periods, representing (albeit by analogy rather than programming) the situation in which experimental subjects face a sequence of FR schedules, and (b) periods of three weeks, for which the data were averaged, similarly representing an experimental situation governed by VR schedules.

Utilitarian and informational reinforcement

To investigate possible effects of informational and utilitarian reinforcement values on brand choice, an attempt was made to identify different levels or magnitudes of informational and utilitarian reinforcement offered by the brands available (i.e., bought by consumers in the sample) in each product category. The set of alternative brands and product characteristics available in a supermarket within each product category can be interpreted as a set of programmed contingencies of reinforcement, which specify what responses (e.g., how much one has to pay) are followed by what consequences (e.g., product characteristics). A major part of marketing activities, according to this interpretation, is to plan and establish contingencies for the behavior of consumers (Foxall, 1999b). Not all programmed contingencies, however, have the desired or planned influences on behavior, and that is why an important issue for marketing managers and academics is to identify the actual effects of different contingencies (i.e., the effects of the price and non-price elements of the marketing mix on consumer choice). The analyses of informational and utilitarian reinforcement levels presented below follow the same logic, that is, they refer to programmed levels of informational and utilitarian reinforcements, which may or may not influence particular instances of consumer choice. In other words, in the case of marketing activities, an event that was planned to have high reinforcement magnitude, *vis-à-vis* its aversive components (costs), can in fact have low reinforcing value for consumers (e.g., innovations that do not attract people or are too expensive).

Considering that there are no general units to measure utilitarian and informational reinforcement levels, these were identified based on a forced ranking system in which three informational and two utilitarian levels were ascribed to each product category. This classification was chosen due to our interest in making comparisons across product categories and was in part influenced by our sample (not all brands and brand types were bought by our sample during the period). Levels of informational and utilitarian benefit cannot be defined absolutely: they depend ultimately on the interests of researchers. More levels of utilitarian reinforcement, for example, could be identified for some product categories, such as cookies and cheese, but an equal number of levels across products was thought to be desirable for the present analysis.

In the case of supermarket food products like those investigated here, increases in utilitarian level can be identified by the addition of (supposedly) desirable attributes. Such attributes usually add value to the product or its consumption, are mentioned on the package or product name, and justify increases in price. Moreover, in most cases, several general brands offer products with and without these attributes. For the product categories in question, utilitarian levels were identified based on additional attributes (e.g., plain baked beans versus baked beans with sausage) and/or differentiated types of products (e.g., plain cookies versus chocolate chip cookies). In the case of differentiated product types, several general brands usually offer the different product types, charging differentiated prices for them (e.g., plain cookies are cheaper than more elaborate cookies for all brands examined).

Informational reinforcement, by contrast, is strongly associated with brand differentiation in that the most promoted and best known brands are usually associated with higher levels of prestige, social status, and trustworthiness. In the case of the supermarket products investigated here, informational reinforcement level is closely associated with brand differentiation, which in turn is usually also related to price differentiation. If one compares the level of brand differentiation of, say, Asda Smart Price© and Heinz© plain baked beans, Heinz is clearly the better known, more differentiated and consequently more expensive brand, offering a higher level of informational reinforcement. This kind of difference among brands has been interpreted in the present work as differences in informational reinforcement level. It should be noted that informational reinforcement level as specified here does not exclude the possibility of there also being differences in utilitarian reinforcement between two informational magnitudes. Corporate representatives of any differentiated brand would argue strongly that their products differ from those of other companies in terms of their "utilitarian" attributes, such as quality of raw materials and ingredients, production procedures, health control, and such like. Similarly, consumers of differentiated brands may also assert these brands' functional superiority, e.g., that they taste much better than other cheaper brands, which would imply differences in utilitarian reinforcement level. The classification adopted does not exclude such possibilities, since most consumer behavior generates both types of consequences. Nevertheless, the ranking of informational reinforcement is based on the predominant difference that one can find between products, offered by different brands, that usually have almost identical formulations (*cf.* Ehrenberg, 1972; Foxall, 1999a) and may not even be distinguished by consumers on the basis of their physical characteristics (e.g., in blind tests).

Table 6.1 Levels of Informational Reinforcement

The cheapest own (retailer) brands (Asda Smart Price, Tesco Value, Sainsbury Economy).	Level 1
Own (retailer) brands that do not mention good value for money or economy (Asda, Tesco, Sainsbury) and cheapest specialized brands.	Level 2
Specialized brands (Heinz, McVities, Kelloggs, Lurpak) with higher prices.	Level 3

The ranking of informational reinforcement level was based on the following general criteria: (1) Increases in prices across brands for the same product type (e.g., plain baked beans, plain cookies or plain cornflakes) were considered to be indicative of differences in informational levels; (2) The cheapest store brands (e.g., Asda Smart Price©, Tesco Value©, Sainsbury Economy©) were considered to represent the lowest informational level (Level 1); (3) Store brands that do not mention good value for money or economy (e.g., Asda, Tesco, Sainsbury) and cheapest specialized brands were usually considered to represent the medium informational level (Level 2); and (4) Specialized brands (e.g., Heinz©, McVities©, Kelloggs©, Lurpak©), with higher prices, were considered to represent the highest informational level (Level 3). The classification is shown in Table 6.1.

Results and discussion

General statistics for the sample are shown in Table 6.2.

Preliminary analyses

Matching. As has been noted, when the matching law is expressed logarithmically as a power function, unity of the exponent s is frequently interpreted as indicating the perfect substitutability of the alternative reinforcers. Measures of s that deviated only in the smallest degree from unity were generally found (Figures 6.1 and 6.2, Table 6.3). In Tables 6.3, 6.4 and 6.5, we report s values as the output from the regression equations, and the b (bias) values as the intercept from those equations. This general pattern of substitutability (Foxall & Schrezenmaier, 2003) is consistent with the findings of earlier analyses in which anti-matching and substantial undermatching (Kagel et al., 1995) were demonstrable only for gross complements belonging to separate product categories (Foxall & James, 2001, 2003). However, as Table 6.3 indicates, there are two exceptions. Undermatching is appar-

Table 6.2 Number of consumers, total and average (per consumer) number of purchases, total and average (per consumer) amount spent, average (per quantity) price, average unit price, total and average number of brands purchased, and percentage brand loyalty, calculated for each product category

Product	Number of consumers	Total purchases	Average purchases	Total spent	Average spent	Average price	Unit price	Total brands	Average brands	% brand loyalty
Baked Beans	39	265	6.79	4.52	0.62	0.07	0.51	32	2.18	74.59
Biscuits	59	1125	19.07	14.02	0.74	0.30	0.63	230	8.93	28.99
Breakfast Cereals	56	691	12.34	20.09	1.56	0.27	1.46	125	5.64	42.24
Butter	21	174	8.29	9.84	1.17	0.28	0.76	21	2.24	76.91
Cheese	45	447	9.93	13.38	1.38	1.91	2.76	95	5.24	43.66
Fruit Juice	34	336	9.88	13.99	1.52	0.72	1.05	43	2.91	65.77
Coffee	19	144	7.58	18.32	2.51	2.09	2.09	31	2.95	65.29
Margarine	50	401	8.02	8.75	1.12	0.19	1.01	55	2.70	67.77
Tea	32	199	6.22	11.67	2.02	0.61	1.66	30	1.94	77.93

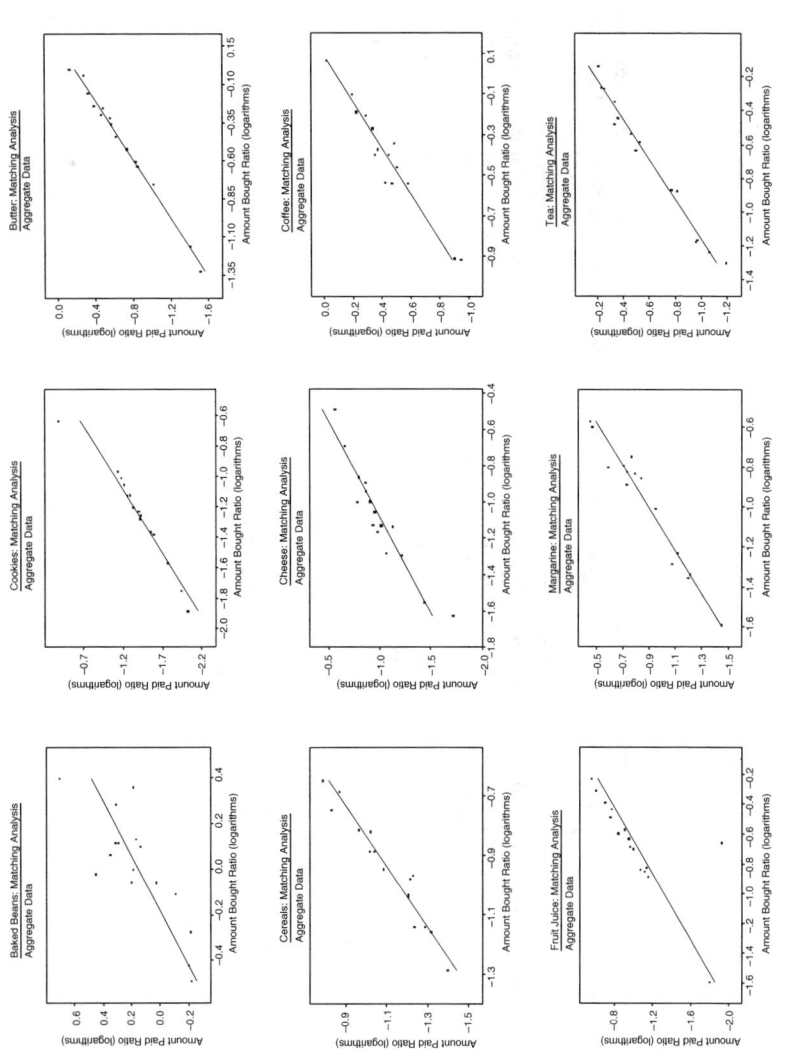

Figure 6.1 Matching analysis: "FR" schedules. Amount paid ratio as a function of amount bought ratio for all nine product types (all data are aggregated across purchasers within a product category)

141

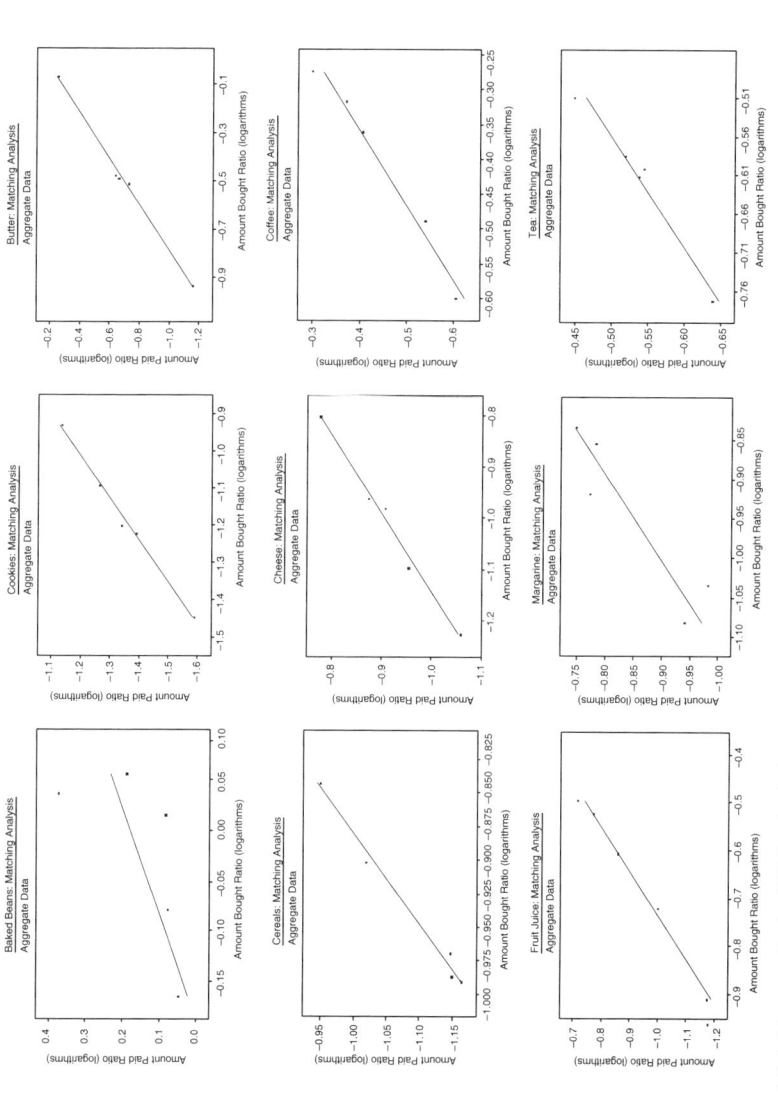

Figure 6.2 Matching analysis: "VR" schedules. Amount paid ratio as a function of amount bought ratio for all nine product types (all data are aggregated across purchasers within a product category)

Table 6.3 Matching Analysis

	"FR" Schedule			"VR" Schedule		
	R^2	β	Intercept	R^2	β	Intercept
Baked Beans	.637 **	.813 **	.152 **	.242	.657	.161
Butter	.991 **	.996 **	−.183 **	.994 **	.998 **	−.172 **
Breakfast Cereals	.928 **	.966 **	−.182 *	.982 **	.993 **	.137
Cheese	.893 **	.949 **	.035	.986 **	.995 **	−.252 **
Cookies	.941 **	.972 **	.112	.992 **	.997 **	−.300 **
Instant Coffee	.934 **	.969 **	−.079 *	.970 **	.989 **	−.069
Fruit Juice	.541 **	.756 **	−.415 *	.990 **	.996 **	−.321 **
Margarine	.952 **	.977 **	.030	.809 *	.925 *	.023
Tea	.978 **	.990 **	−.017	.956 **	.983	−.108 **

*$p < 0.05$ **$p < 0.01$

Table 6.4 Relative Demand Analyses

	"FR" Schedule			"VR" Schedule		
	R^2	β	Intercept	R^2	β	Intercept
Baked Beans	.024	−.211	−.060	.027	−.520	−.099
Butter	.333	−.013	−.834	.077	.009	−.293
Breakfast Cereals	.057	.114	−.871 **	.675	.870	−.559 *
Cheese	.085	.382	−1.072 **	.510	.795	−1.047 **
Cookies	.113	−.415	−2.22 **	.422	−.753	−2.996 *
Instant Coffee	.007	.254	−.243	.142	.379	−.247
Fruit Juice	.319 **	−.604 *	−3.382 **	.612	−.842	−3.219 *
Margarine	.040	−.185	−.928 **	.297	−.165	−.924 **
Tea	.634 **	−.811 **	−1.184 **	.136	−.384	−.975

*$p < 0.05$ **$p < 0.01$

ent in the case of baked beans whether data are integrated over a series of one-week periods (the so-called "FR" schedule) or over three-week periods ("VR"). Consumers in this case selected Heinz© baked beans to an extent disproportionate with that predicted by strict matching: There were in total 265 purchases of baked beans (including baked beans with sausages and other complements), 52% of which were for Heinz plain baked beans alone. Their "favorite" brand was the most expensive. In the case of fruit juice, undermatching is apparent from the "FR" schedule. This anomaly arises from the single outlying value

Table 6.5 Maximization Analyses

	"FR" Schedule			"VR" Schedule		
	R^2	β	Intercept	R^2	β	Intercept
Baked Beans	.015	.284	−2.102	−.020	.485	−1.54
Butter	−.056	−.138	10.75	−.312	−.128	15.67
Breakfast Cereals	−.034	−.188	.378	.633	−.851	.869 *
Cheese	.029	−.307	.315	.595	−.834	.809
Cookies	.462 **	.706 **	−1.26 **	.477	.780	−1.355
Instant Coffee	−.019	−.233	.147	−.080	−.436	2.189
Fruit Juice	.126	.429	−3.092	.426	.754	−4.911
Margarine	−.073	.057	.067	−.310	.132	.062
Tea	.678 **	.836 **	−5.885 **	−.188	.330	−3.345

*p < 0.05 **p < 0.01

shown in Figure 6.1. When this value is excluded from the analysis, the value of R^2 is 0.991, and that for beta is 0.996. The results for fruit juice indicate the merit of integrating the data over three- as well as one-week periods: Even a price-conscious consumer would be expected to "deviate" from matching from time to time in order to secure variety (or because he or she was buying on behalf of another household member). This is consonant with the finding reported by Foxall & James (2003) in the case of single butter purchaser who deviated from her usual highly-price sensitive pattern of choice on occasion simply in order to obtain the flavor advantages of a premium-priced brand.

Relative demand. The expectation that logarithmically plotted demand curves would show consumption to be a positively decelerating function of unit price (Madden et al., 2000) was generally though not universally substantiated. Relative demand curves for six of the nine product categories are, as expected, downward-sloping, though that for butter is approximately horizontal; three were upward-sloping (Figures 6.3 and 6.4, Table 6.4). Moreover, while the curve for baked beans (which were identified as anomalous with respect to matching) is positively decelerating, the R^2 and beta parameters indicate a weak relationship between relative price and relative quantity demanded, which is in keeping with the interpretation of consumers' brand perceptions advanced above. Although the results are generally in line with the expected price-quantity relationship, the wide dispersal of data points reflected in the many low values of R^2 and beta suggest that more precise methods be sought for the demonstration of price-demand associations.

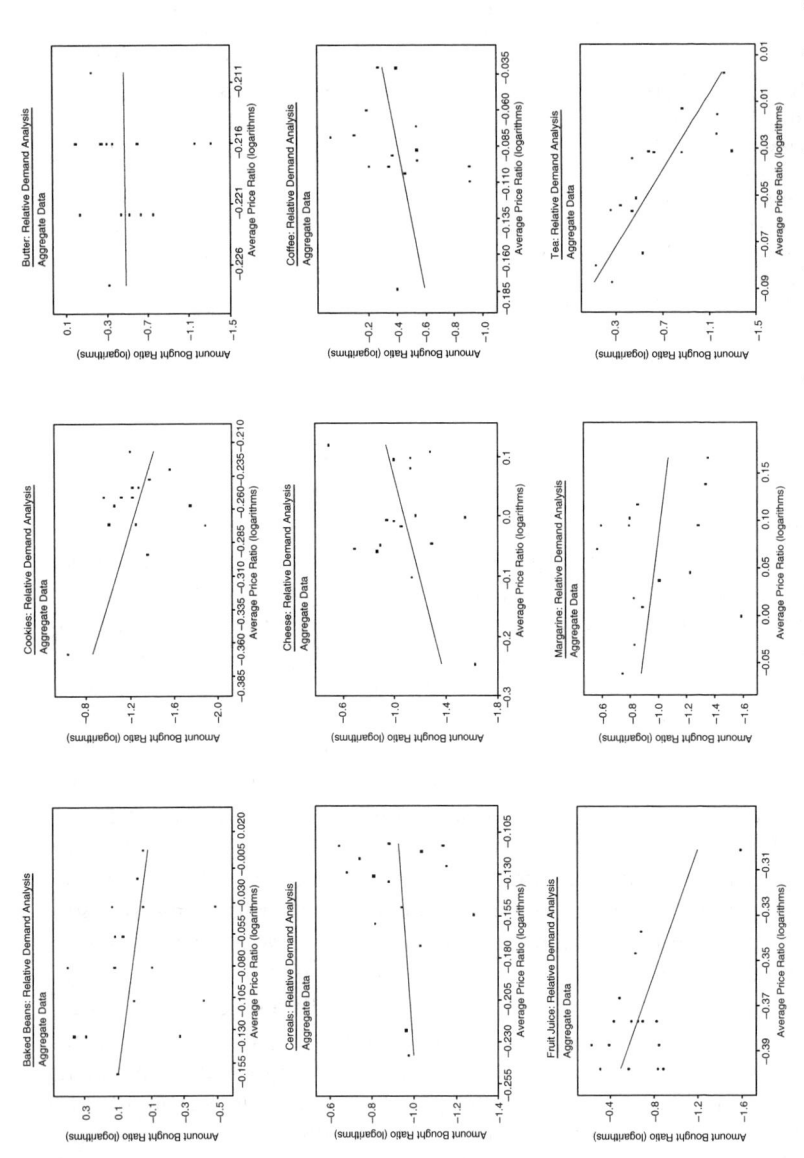

Figure 6.3 Relative demand analysis: "FR" schedules. Amount bought ratio as a function of average price ratio for all nine product types (all data are aggregated across purchasers within a product category)

145

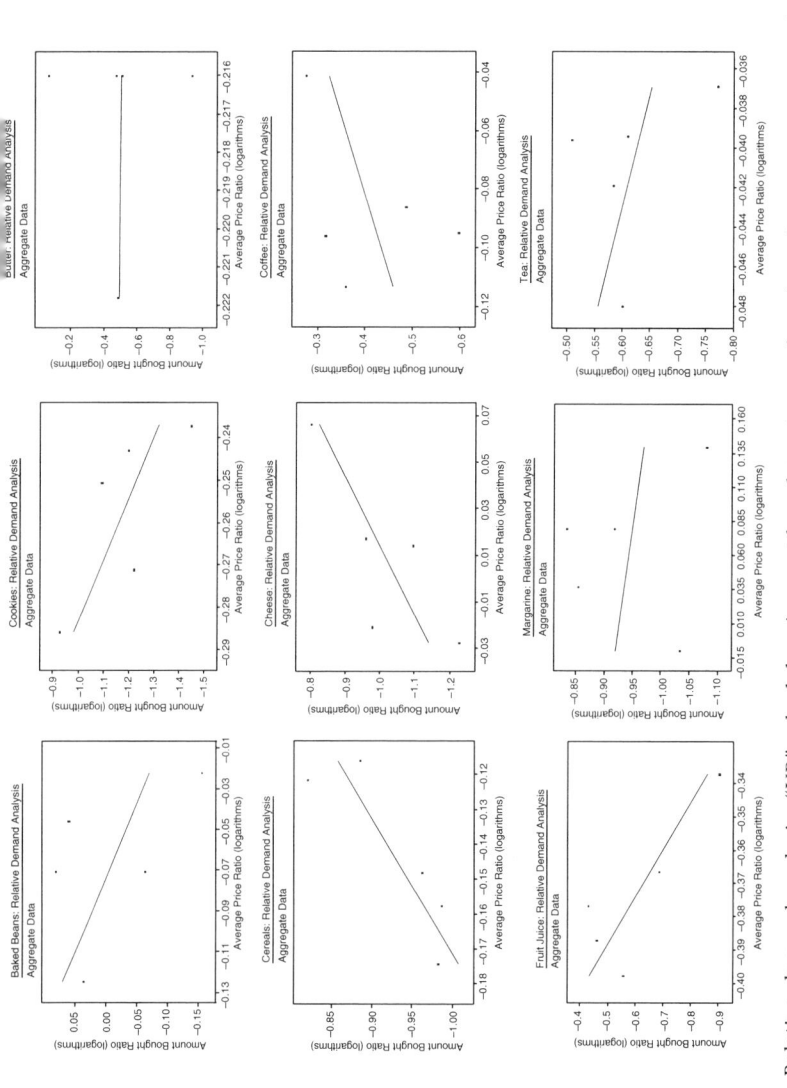

Figure 6.4 Relative demand analysis: "VR" schedules. Amount bought ratio as a function of average price ratio for all nine product types (all data are aggregated across purchasers within a product category)

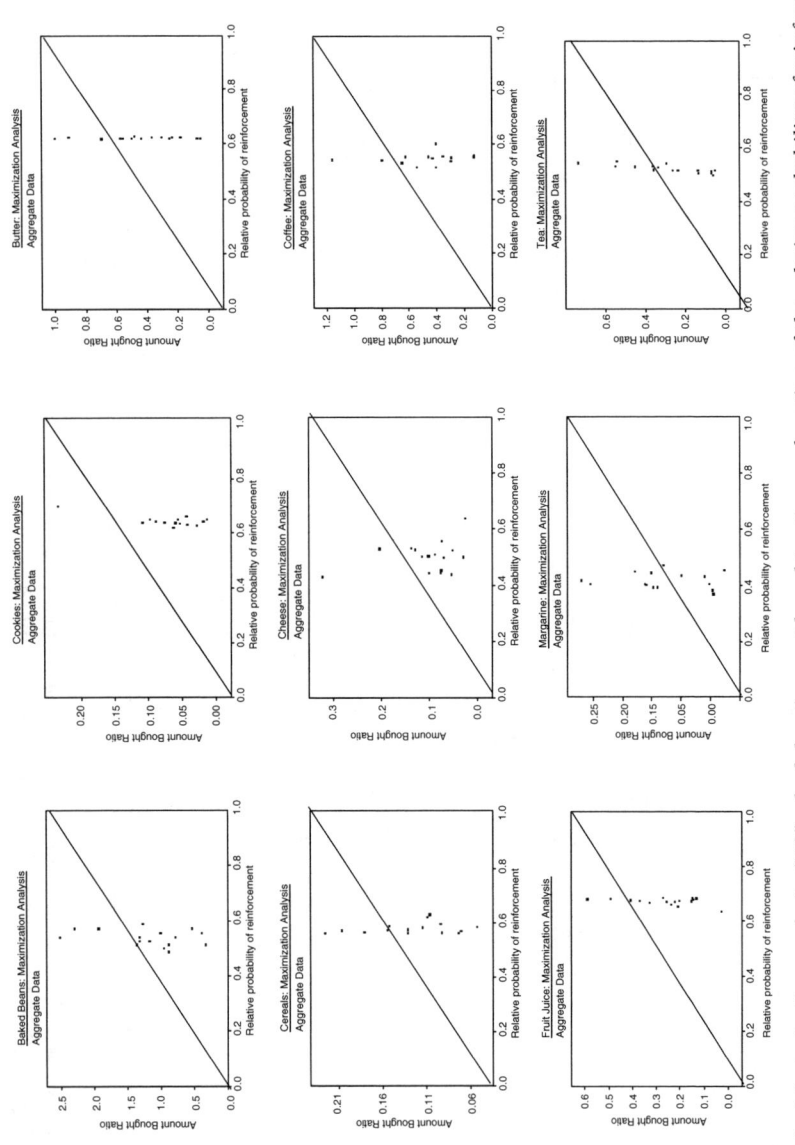

Figure 6.5 Maximization analysis: "FR" schedules. Amount bought ratio as a function of the relative probability of reinforcement for all nine product types (all data are aggregated across purchasers within a product category)

147

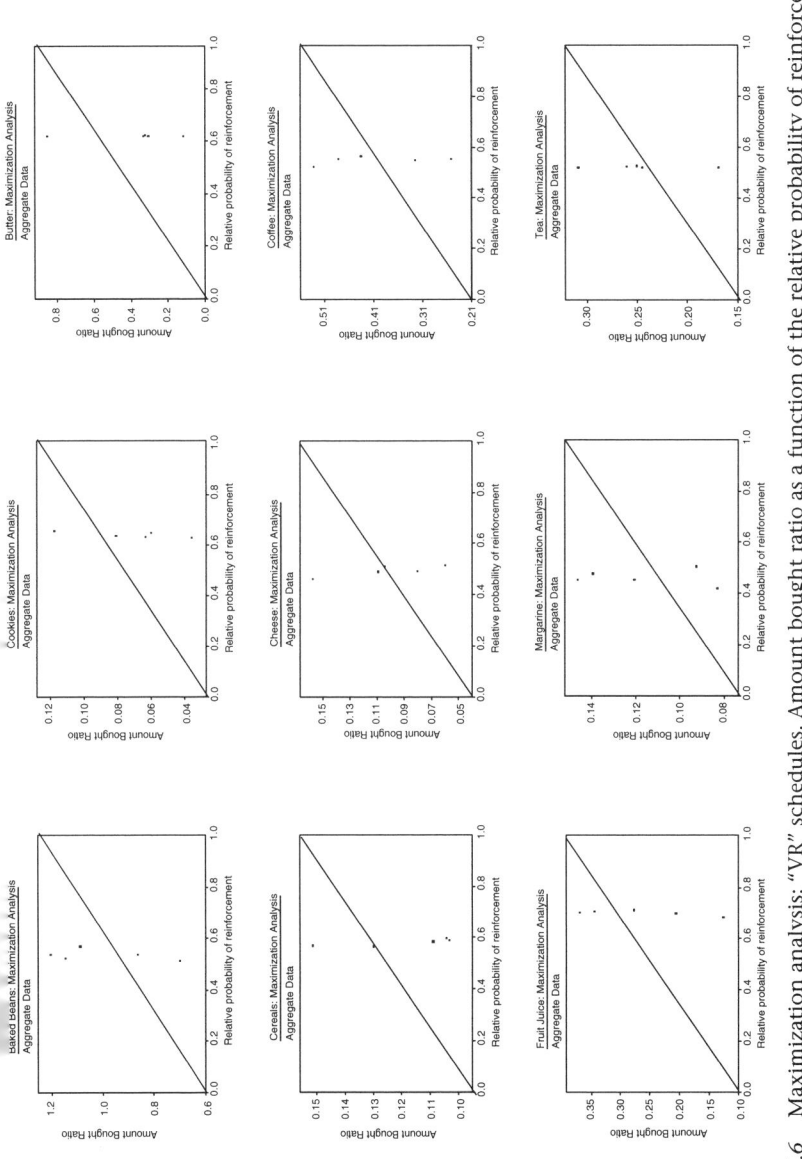

Figure 6.6 Maximization analysis: "VR" schedules. Amount bought ratio as a function of the relative probability of reinforcement for all nine product types (all data are aggregated across purchasers within a product category)

Maximization. The maximization analysis indicates that most consumers consistently chose the cheapest brand on each shopping occasion regardless of product category (Figures 6.5 and 6.6, Table 6.5). This is consistent with the behavioral economics approach pioneered by Herrnstein & Loveland (1975), Herrnstein & Vaughan (1980), but close examination of the results reveals a more complicated pattern of choice than is apparent in the studies of non-humans undertaken by those authors. First, whilst consumers generally selected the cheapest brand within their consideration set, these "repertoires" in many cases comprised only premium, highly differentiated brands. Many consumers did not maximize in any "absolute" sense. In each product category, own-label, or store brand, and economy versions existed which were considerably cheaper than those actually purchased. Second, whilst research with non-human subjects is typically limited to only one choice on each occasion, consumers are able to purchase more than one brand even on a single shopping trip. As is apparent from Figure 6.5 and Figure 6.6, for seven products, consumers in the aggregate maximized by purchasing the favorite (cheapest) brand (Brand A); for two products, however (cheese and margarine), this pattern was not found. This same overall pattern was found for both the "VR" and the "FR" schedules. However, even for the seven product categories where consumers maximized by purchasing Brand A, there is a complication which arises from the nature of consumer choice in the marketplace and which is not encountered in laboratory research with either human or non-human animals in which choice is constrained. Although most consumers maximized in the sense that they purchased the cheapest brand within their consideration set, many also purchased a second brand priced substantially higher on the same occasion. The maximization analyses undertaken based on the behavioral economics literature was thus incapable of indicating comprehensively the pattern of consumer brand choices in relation to a simple value-for-money criterion. (The diagonal lines in Figure 6.5 and Figure 6.6 indicate the distribution of data points that would have occurred if consumers had exhibited probability matching. By contrast, the step function indicated by the vertical distribution of data points indicates a consistent preference for one or other alternative).

These patterns of choice are consistent with findings reported in the consumer research and marketing literatures on branding which portray consumers' consideration sets as a function of the level of quality required for a variety of consumption settings. It was these broader considerations that led to the suggestion that consumers maximize some combination of utilitarian and informational reinforcement and which resulted in the following more detailed analyses.

Individual patterns of choice across informational reinforcement levels

To demonstrate how individuals choose across different informational reinforcement levels, Figure 6.7 shows the percentage of the total quantity of goods bought of brands at each informational level by each consumer for each product category. In the figure, the black, empty, and striped bars represent the percentage bought of brands classified at informational Levels 1, 2 and 3, respectively. Each vertical bar in the figure represents data for one consumer. Data for individual consumers were plotted as a function of the average price (total amount spent divided by total quantity bought) paid by each consumer during the

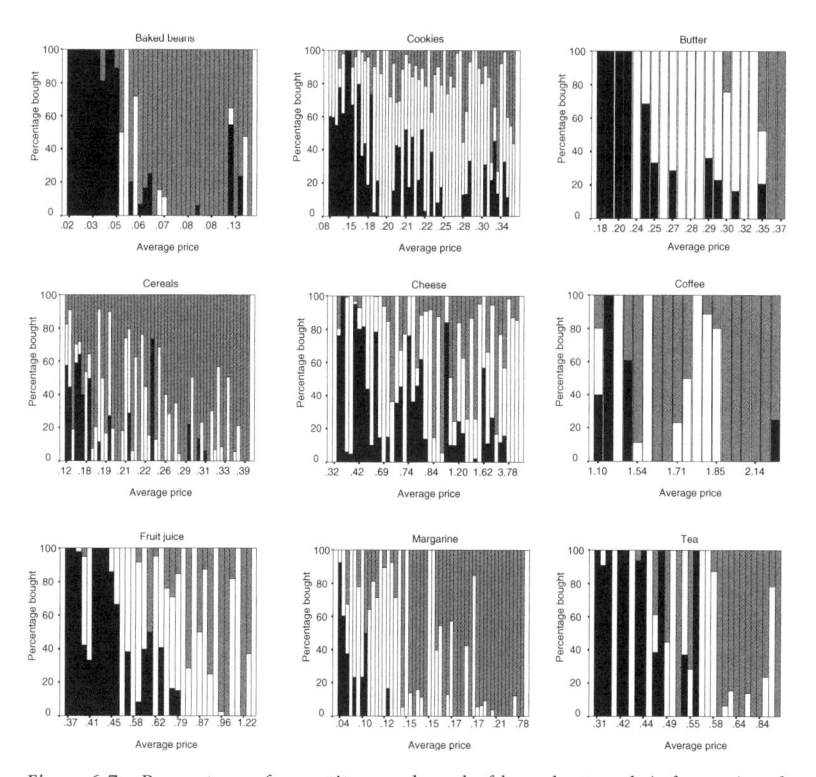

Figure 6.7 Percentage of quantity purchased of brands at each informational level (Level 1: black bars; Level 2: empty bars; Level 3: striped bars) by each consumer of each product category as a function of average price paid per consumer

16-week period. Wider or narrower bars in the figure indicate larger and smaller numbers of consumers included in the analysis of different product categories.

In general, increases in average price paid were associated with decreases in the percentage of brands bought at Level 1 of informational reinforcement and increases in the percentage of brands bought at Level 3. Considering that the average brand price was one of the criteria to classify brands at different informational levels, this may seem a trivial finding: clearly, by definition, the more the consumers buy Level-3 brands the higher should be the average price they paid. However, when one considers that the figure shows data for individual consumers, some non-trivial findings can be noted. First, it becomes clear that most consumers bought mostly brands at one particular informational level, rather than across all levels. The percentage of consumers who bought 70% or more of goods at one particular informational level is: for baked beans 92%, tea 91%, coffee 84%, margarine 84%, butter 81%, cereals 68%, fruit juice 68%, cheese 64%, and cookies 58%. This indicates that the majority of consumers make 70% or more of their purchases within one particular informational level.

A second non-trivial aspect of the data is the fact that, when buying across informational levels, consumers tend to buy more brands at adjacent informational levels than at more distant levels (e.g., buying Levels 1 and 2 more than Levels 1 and 3). A third relevant tendency shown in the figure is the wide difference in the average price paid across consumers, with some consumers buying mostly the cheapest brands while others bought the most expensive ones. This finding could be deduced from the patterns of buying mostly brands at the same informational level, just described above, but it is not a trivial one, for it suggests that consumers' brand-repertoires may be influenced by economic variables such as consumer's budget. This has not been reported in the literature that describes consumers' multi-brand buying patterns. Similar analyses also indicate that, for eight of nine product categories, most consumers also made the large majority of their purchases within the same level of utilitarian reinforcement. The percentage of consumers that bought 70% or more of brands belonging to the same utilitarian level is: for butter 91%, baked beans 85%, coffee 84%, tea 84%, cheese 82%, fruit juice 77%, margarine 74%, cereals 66%, and cookies, 42%.

Consumer groups

These findings invite comparison of the buying patterns of consumers grouped by their predominant purchasing of brands having specific patterns of informational and utilitarian reinforcement. Hence, consumers were classified in one of six groups, derived from the combination of the three levels of informational and the two levels of utilitarian reinforcement, on the basis of the informational-utilitarian level of the brands they bought more frequently. The six groups were named as follows: Group 1 – Informational Level 1 and Utilitarian Level 1; Group 2 – Informational Level 1 and Utilitarian Level 2; Group 3 – Informational Level 2 and Utilitarian Level 1; Group 4 – Informational Level 2 and Utilitarian Level 2; Group 5 – Informational Level 3 and Utilitarian Level 1; and Group 6 – Informational Level 3 and Utilitarian Level 2.

Groups' buying patterns were compared in terms of elasticity of demand, using the equation:

$$\log \text{Quantity} = a - b(\log \text{Price})$$

as suggested by Kagel *et al.* (1995). Some modifications of the measures of quantity and price were necessary for the following reasons. First, price variation throughout the 16-week period was not very wide and can be expected to be even less so within each consumer group, since the classification of individuals in such groups was dependent upon the informational level of the brands they bought most frequently, which in turn were classified in part based on their average price. Therefore, each consumer group can be expected to have a different price average within a relatively restricted range of prices. Second, the analysis of purchases of brands by a particular consumer group for each product category would reduce dramatically the number of data points available to calculate price elasticities. For example, in the case of baked beans, there was no consumer classified in consumer Group 2, which would restrict the analysis for the product category. One possible solution for this problem would be to aggregate all the data obtained from all the products and then calculate price elasticities for each consumer group. This solution would pose another type of measurement problem. Considering that the measurement scales (and even units) of quantity and price varied greatly among product categories, it would be difficult to calculate one single regression line using data from different products.

One way of overcoming all such problems would be to use measures of quantity and price relative to the average of each consumer group (e.g., Bell *et al.*, 1999). These relative measures can be calculated by dividing the quantities bought (and prices paid) on each purchase by the average quantity bought (and average price paid) of each product within each consumer group. The resulting data would provide an estimate of price elasticity relative to the consumer group mean, that is, it would provide an estimate of changes in quantities as a function of changes in prices above and below the mean of each consumer group. Data from each product would be "standardized" to the product mean for each group, yielding unitless ratio values above and below 1.0. Data from all products and groups would become comparable in terms of responsiveness around the mean.

This procedure was adopted in the analyses described next. Each quantity data point for the regression was calculated by dividing the quantity bought on a shopping occasion by the average quantity for that specific consumer group for that specific product. Analogously, each price data point for the regression consisted of the price paid on a given shopping occasion divided by the average price paid by that specific group when buying that specific product. Then, for example, the quantity bought of Tesco Value© instant coffee by a specific consumer on a given shopping trip was divided by the average quantity of instant coffee bought by all consumers in Group 1 (Informational and Utilitarian Level 1). This same procedure was used to calculate the correspondent measures of price. A regression analysis was then conducted with all data points obtained for all consumers classified in Group 1, including data points from all product categories. The same was done with the data for the other five consumer groups (the number of paired data points, N, for the six groups ranged from 179 to 897).

The results are shown in Table 6.6. All regressions, using the above equation (calculated with relative measures of quantity and price), were statistically significant (i.e., $P < 0.000$ for all groups). The values of R^2 were not very large and ranged from 0.22 to 0.46, indicating that other variables that did not enter the equation also influenced the quantities consumers bought. The values of standard error were all ten

Table 6.6 Parameters of Equation (log Quantity = $a - b$ [log Price]), calculated for each consumer group, the significance level of the regression (p), and the standard error of the estimate of b

Consumer Group	r^2	a	b	Std. error	p
Group 1	.22	−.13	−.50	.038	<.000
Group 2	.42	−.15	−.86	.076	<.000
Group 3	.46	−.17	−.73	.027	<.000
Group 4	.35	−.13	−.59	.030	<.000
Group 5	.25	−.12	−.66	.041	<.000
Group 6	.22	−.06	−.41	.033	<.000

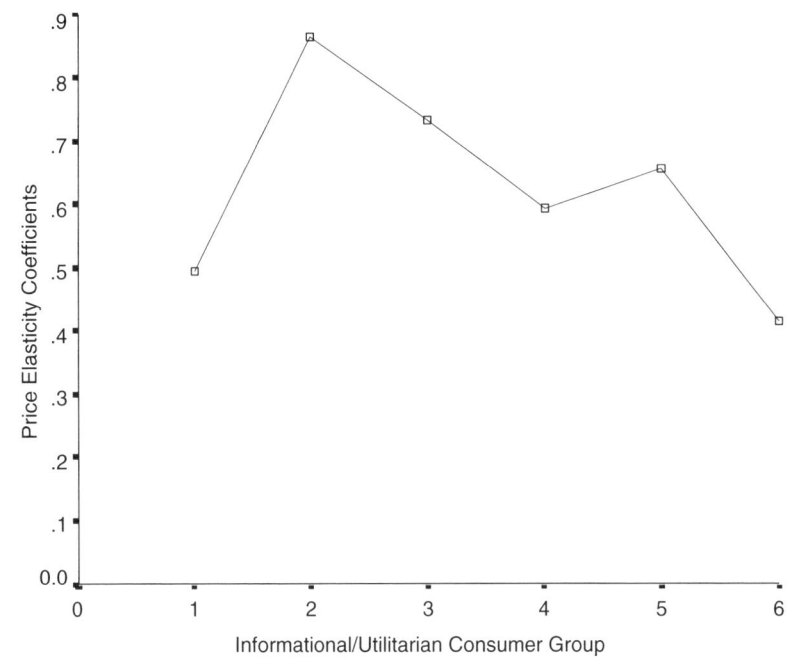

Figure 6.8 Price elasticity coefficients calculated for each group of consumers classified according to the informational and utilitarian level of the brands they predominantely purchased

or more times smaller than the corresponding coefficients of price elasticity, b, suggesting accurate estimations of the latter. All price elasticity coefficients were negative indicating that the quantity consumers bought tended to decrease with increases in price. Moreover, all coefficient values were between 0 and −1.0, indicating that demand was inelastic for all consumer groups. Despite these similarities, the absolute values of elasticity coefficients, shown in Figure 6.8, were lower for the extreme groups, Groups 1 and 6, than for the other groups, suggesting that consumers that buy predominantly intermediate-level brands showed higher price responsiveness than those buying predominantly the least- and highest-differentiated brands (split-sample reliability analyses confirm this trend).

Intra- and inter-brand elasticities

The observed decreases in the quantity bought with increases in prices, indicated by negative elasticity coefficients, may, however, have been associated with different response patterns by different groups. The tendency to buy larger quantities when prices are lower may be related to one or more of the following three patterns: (1) Buying larger quantities of a product when its price was below its usual, average, price rather than when its price was above its average price (i.e., intra-brand or absolute elasticity); (2) Buying larger quantities when buying brands belonging to cheaper, lower informational levels than when buying brands belonging to more expensive, higher informational levels (i.e., informational inter-brand or relative elasticity); and (3) Buying larger quantities when buying brands belonging to cheaper, lower utilitarian levels than when buying brands belonging to more expensive, higher utilitarian levels (i.e., utilitarian inter-brand or relative elasticity). One way of measuring such patterns is to decompose the global price elasticity coefficient into three different coefficients, namely, intra-brand, informational inter-brand, and utilitarian inter-brand coefficients. This analysis would yield an equation in which the quantity bought would be a function of intra-brand changes in price, informational reinforcement levels of the purchased brands, and the utilitarian reinforcement levels of the purchased brands, that is,

log Quantity $- a - b$(log Intra – Brand Price) $- b2$(log Informational level) $- b3$(log Utilitarian Level)

Intra-brand price was obtained by dividing the price paid for the brand by the average price for that same brand in the sample. Relative values of quantity, intra-brand price, informational level and utilitarian level with respect to their respective consumer group averages, analogous to those used to obtain global elasticity coefficients, were used. Regression coefficients were obtained for each consumer group.

The results are summarized in Table 6.7. All regressions were statistically significant (i.e., $P < 0.000$ for $b1$ for all groups). The values of R^2 were not very large and ranged from 0.06 to 0.36, indicating that other variables that did not enter the equation also influenced the quantities consumers bought. Only three, out of 18, values of standard error were ten or more times smaller than the corresponding coefficients of price elasticity, b, suggesting that coefficient estimations were not very accurate (although split-sample reliability analyses corroborated the observed patterns). Collinearity analyses yielded values of tolerance and variance inflation factor close to 1.00, suggesting that there was no significant covariance among variables included in the equation (Hair et al., 1995). All price elasticity coefficients were negative indicating that the quantity consumers bought tended to decrease with increases

Table 6.7 Parameters of *Log Quantity* = *a* − *b1* (*Log Intra-Brand Price*) − *b2* (*Log Informational Level*) − *b3* (*Log Utilitarian Level*), calculated for each consumer group, the significance level of the regression (*p*), and the standard error of the estimates of *b1*, *b2*, and *b3*

Consumer Group	r^2	a	b1	Std. error	p	b2	Std. error	p	b3	Std. error	p
Group 1	.17	−.11	−.53	.084	<.000	−.33	.061	<.000	−.61	.082	<.000
Group 2	.36	−.13	−1.51	.252	<.000	−.84	.113	<.000	−.32	.141	.024
Group 3	.30	−.13	−.92	.067	<.000	−.52	.078	<.000	−.72	.063	<.000
Group 4	.15	−.10	−.74	.078	<.000	−.39	.072	<.000	−.24	.070	.001
Group 5	.21	−.12	−.70	.063	<.000	−.29	.080	<.000	−.69	.074	<.000
Group 6	.06	−.05	−.58	.117	<.000	−.09	.083	.291	−.23	.074	.002

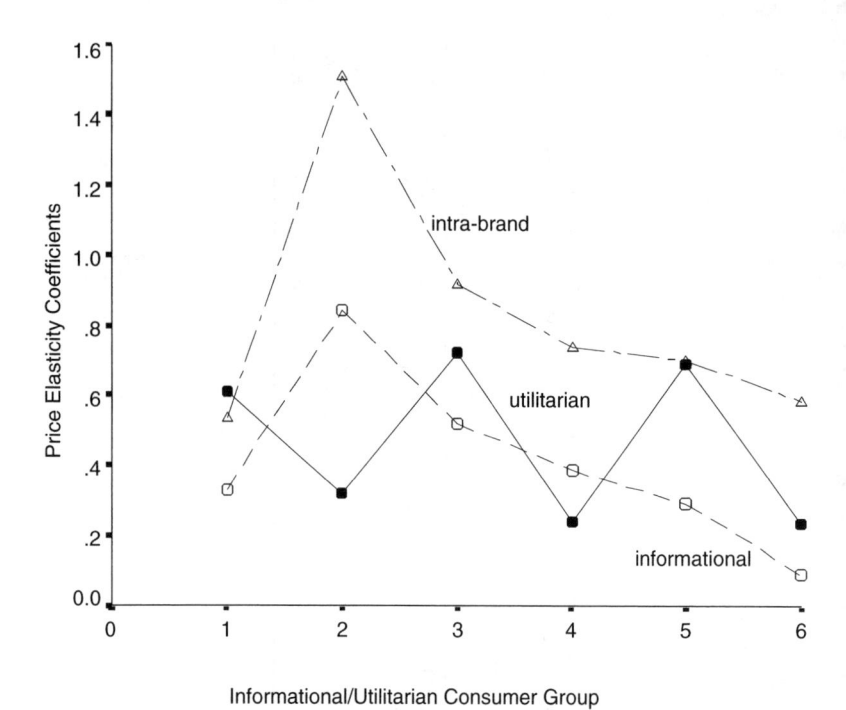

Figure 6.9 Intra-brand, informational inter-brand and utilitarian inter-brand price elasticity coefficients calculated for each group of consumers, classified on the basis of the informational/utilitarian level of the brands they predominantly purchased

in intra-brand price variations, informational level, and utilitarian level. Moreover, with the exception of the intra-brand coefficient for Group 2 (−1.51), all coefficient values were between 0 and −1.0, indicating that all three types of demand tended to be inelastic for all consumer groups. Despite such similarities, the absolute values of intra-brand, informational inter-brand, and utilitarian inter-brand elasticity coefficients differed across consumer groups, as shown in Figure 6.9.

Intra-brand elasticity coefficients were lower for Groups 1 and 6 than for the intermediate groups, showing a decreasing trend from Group 2 to Group 6. This suggests that consumers buying predominantly the cheapest, least-differentiated brands (i.e., Group 1) do not change much the quantity they buy as a function of changes in brand price relative to their usual (average) price. This result suggests a tendency toward buying the cheapest brands, irrespective of other, slightly more expensive, brands. If this interpretation is correct, the observed pattern for intra-brand elasticity, which was largest for Group 2 and decreased systematically as group classification increased up to Group 6, can be interpreted as suggesting that responsiveness to intra-brand changes in price decreases as group classification increases. In other words, if the low intra-brand elasticity observed for Group 1 is a consequence of buying the cheapest brands most of the time, these findings point to the conclusion that as the level of differentiation of the purchased brands increases (i.e., as the price of purchased brands increases), the responsiveness of consumers to changes in prices decreases.

Informational inter-brand elasticities were smaller than intra-brand elasticities for all six groups and followed a similar pattern, with Group 1 showing a low coefficient, Group 2 showing the largest one which decreases systematically with increases in group classification up to Group 6. This suggests that consumers buying mostly the least-differentiated, cheapest brands do not change much the quantities they buy as a function of informational brand level, whereas the responsiveness to informational reinforcement of those buying intermediate-level brands decreases systematically with increases in the informational level of the predominantly purchased brands. This value is close to zero for Group 6, suggesting that consumers that already usually buy the highest informational and utilitarian level brands are not sensitive to changes in informational level (similar to a "satiation" effect, since satiated animals are not expected to be responsive to food, i.e., to do things to get food).

Utilitarian inter-brand elasticity, indicated by the filled circles, was higher for the three groups that bought predominantly low utilitarian-level brands (i.e., Groups 1, 3 and 5) than for the other three that bought high utilitarian-level brands. This finding indicates that consumers who buy predominantly brands with low utilitarian levels tend also to buy smaller quantities of higher utilitarian brands, whereas those that buy predominantly brands with high utilitarian levels do not seem to vary much the quantities they buy as a function of utilitarian brand level. Hence, the utilitarian inter-brand elasticities followed a slightly different pattern from the informational inter-brand elasticities, though like them they were mostly smaller than intra-brand elasticities. Group 1 is the only exception with a coefficient larger than that of the intra-brand elasticities, if only marginally. Whereas the other two curves follow a similar pattern, the shape of the utilitarian curve is different in that it follows a zigzag course with Group 2 showing a lower coefficient than Groups 1 and 3, and similarly Groups 4 and 6 displaying a lower coefficient than their neighbor groups. The implications of this pattern are more complicated because it suggests that consumers buying mostly at utilitarian Level 1, i.e., Groups 1, 3 and 5, are more sensitive to changes in utilitarian level than consumers with a preference for utilitarian Level 2, independent of the informational level of the brand. For example, consumers who mostly buy the least-differentiated, cheapest brands (i.e., Group 1) are more likely to buy larger quantities than consumers who buy at a higher utilitarian but at the same informational level (i.e., Group 2). Consumers of Group 3 however, with a lower utilitarian level than Groups 2 and 4 but a higher informational level than Group 2 and the same informational level as Group 4, is in turn more responsive to utilitarian reinforcement than both Groups 2 and 4.

General discussion

As predicted by both matching theory and maximization theory, we have confirmed that choice on conc VR VR schedules exhibits both matching and maximizing. However, the examination of consumer choice in naturalistic environments raises a number of complications for behavior analysis and behavioral economics that are not evident from the experimental analysis of choice. While the realities of consumer behavior in affluent, marketing-oriented economies have implications for behavioral economics, the techniques of analysis which behavioral economics makes available to the marketing researcher also elucidate the nature of brand choice in the market place.

A common assumption in aggregate studies of consumer choice conducted by marketing scientists is that brands within a product category are functional alternatives and that consumers will include a brand within their repertoire or purchase set only if it embodies the physical and functional benefits that are common to all members of that category (Ehrenberg, 1972, 1993). This proposition is seldom supported by empirical evidence. Although the discovery of matching on conc VR VR schedules is both expected and perhaps in some respects trivial, it is important for the sort of analysis we have undertaken in that it confirms that the alternative brands considered are indeed substitutes in the assumed sense. The very-nearly perfect matching that we have found is a characteristic of choices that are near-perfect substitutes (Kagel *et al.*, 1995).

Another common assumption in the marketing literature is that price plays a relatively small part in the determination of consumer choice: brands that are highly differentiated by advertising command a premium but the consumer is generally portrayed as relatively insensitive to such differentials. Non-price elements of the marketing mix (i.e., promotional tactics, brand attributes, and distribution strategies) are thought to be more influential than price factors for affluent consumers operating within marketing-oriented economies (Foxall, 1999b). The relative demand and maximization analyses, which were intended to shed light on the sensitivity of consumer demand to price differentials among competing brands, present an equivocal impression of the relationship between market prices and quantity demanded. While Figure 6.3 and Figure 6.4 indicate the expected relationship, denoted by downward-sloping relative demand curves, the evidence for the remaining product categories is mixed. The maximization analysis suggests that consumers are in some respects sensitive to price levels when making decisions about how much of a brand to buy relative to other brands in the consideration set. However, the interpretation of the data summarized in these figures and in Figure 6.5 and Figure 6.6 must include the phenomenon of single shopping trip multi-brand purchasing. Although a consumer may exhibit economically rational price sensitivity by purchasing the cheapest brand in her consideration set, her general sensitivity to price may be confounded by her purchasing a premium-priced alternative at the same time. Hence, our results are equivocal on the question whether consumer brand choice is sensitive to price. The consequent need to attend to non-price elements of the marketing mix led us to the analyses of price elasticity of demand which take into consideration both the utilitarian (functional) and informational (symbolic) benefits gained by consumers from the brands they purchase and use.

The evidence is that consumers choose their repertoire of brands on the basis of the informational and utilitarian level of reinforcement programmed by the brands. This is likely to be related, among other things, to their budgets, which we were not able to take into consideration. However, it is also of marketing significance in that it provides opportunities for the partitioning (segmentation) of markets. There do seem to be clearly definable segments based on combinations of the utilitarian and symbolic benefits of purchase and consumption and the cost minimization. These factors encourage consumers to choose brands within a given range defined in terms of these variables. Most purchasing takes place within a fairly narrowly defined range and consumers who switch out of that range generally move only to an adjacent range.

Consumer groups, classified on the basis of the informational/utilitarian level of the brands they buy mostly, show different responsiveness to changes in prices, with extreme groups showing the lowest levels of responsiveness (possibly for different reasons). Price elasticities can be decomposed into intra-brand and at least two types of inter-brand elasticities, informational and utilitarian, according to the type of reinforcing events that influence consumer choice. Intra-brand elasticity can be interpreted as a measure of responsiveness to the aversive consequences of giving up money (Alhadeff, 1982). Therefore, choice patterns can be interpreted as being determined by different combinations of the tendencies to avoid aversive consequences, maximize informational reinforcement and maximize utilitarian reinforcement. A pattern that minimizes financial loss, showing minimum responsiveness to informational attributes and some to utilitarian ones, seems to characterize choices of consumers in Group 1. The responsiveness to informational and utilitarian attributes related to changes in price seems to be an inverse function of how much of these the consumer obtains regularly. So, the results showed increasing responsiveness to informational reinforcement from Group 6 (who obtain higher levels of it) to Group 2 (who obtain lower levels of it). The same was observed for utilitarian attributes, for those groups buying lower levels of utilitarian attributes (Groups 1, 3, and 5) showed higher responsiveness to this aspect of the brands than those that buy higher levels of utilitarian attributes more regularly (Groups 2, 4, and 6).

Elasticity coefficients can be interpreted as measures of consumer "satiation" level, since the less frequently consumers purchase a given reinforcing dimension the higher their responsiveness to that dimension. In the case of intra-brand elasticity this tendency is probably related to available budget. The only exceptions were obtained for consumers that buy the least differentiated brands most of the time, for whom elasticity coefficients seem to reflect a pattern of buying the cheapest products in the category.

From the point of view of the *Behavioral Perspective Model*, the analysis has demonstrated that relatively high and low utilitarian and informational reinforcement can be used to classify consumer behavior even within the narrow range represented by fast-moving consumer goods. In previous analyses, these variables, along with the relative openness of the consumer behavior setting, have been employed to categorize broader patterns of consumer behavior. Within that categorization, the purchase of food products is classified in terms of low utilitarian and low informational reinforcement in a relatively open setting. That categorization is meaningful when buying fast-moving consumer goods is compared with buying and using other kinds of product and service (Foxall & Yani-de-Soriano, 2004), but the demonstration of this chapter is that these structural elements of the consumer situation also provide means of classifying consumer behavior within those broader categories.

The results for the elasticities of demand, especially those for intra-brand, inter-utilitarian and inter-informational elasticities, suggest that the explanatory variables investigated are far from the only influences on brand choice. Nevertheless, along with the results for the inter-group elasticities of demand which provide somewhat stronger evidence of a link, they indicate that utilitarian and informational reinforcement have distinct effects on brand choice and that they may form the basis of the partitioning of markets and strategies of market segmentation.

Notes

1. Previously published in *Behavioral Processes*, 2004, 66, 235–60.
2. A ratio schedule is one in which a specified number of responses has to be performed before reinforcement becomes available. Fixed ratio schedules keep the number of required responses equal from reinforcer to reinforcer; variable ratio schedules allow the required number of responses to change from one reinforcer to the next. Concurrent variable ratio schedules, usually abbreviated to conc VR VR, allow simultaneous choice to be investigated. It is this arrangement that most clearly resembles the purchases of brand within a product class.
3. Following Wearden (1988), we use "informational reinforcement" to refer to performance feedback. The term "informational" carries excess baggage for many behavior analysts since it may appear to make cognitive inferences. Given the examples we provide in the text, it may appear that "social" would be a more acceptable and accurate alternative. However, "social" does not entirely capture what we mean by "informational" which includes rewards for adhering to social mores, *and* physical sources of feedback such as lines on the road that convey an impression of speed, or the fullness of one's shopping trolley. A concomitant consideration arises in the functional definition of rules as "plys," which involve the mediation of other people and which are therefore social, or as "tracks," which depend on the rule-follower's "reading" the physical environment, e.g., in the process of following directions to get to a supermarket (Zettle & Hayes, 1982). Informational reinforcement thus remains our designation of choice for this phenomenon since it includes both personally-mediated and non-personally-mediated performance feedback.

References

Alhadeff, D. A. (1982). *Microeconomics and Human Behavior: Toward a New Synthesis of Economics and Psychology*. Berkeley, CA: University of California Press.

Baum, W. M. (1974). "On two types of deviation from the matching law". *Journal of the Experimental Analysis of Behavior*, 22, 231–42.

Baum, W. M. (1979). "Matching, undermatching, and overmatching in studies of choice". *Journal of the Experimental Analysis of Behavior*, 32, 269–81.
Baum, W. M. & Nevin, J. A. (1981). "Maximization theory: some empirical problems". *Behavioral and Brain Sciences*, 4, 389–90.
Bell, D. R., Chiang, J. & Padmanabhan, V. (1999). "The decomposition of promotional response: an empirical generalization". *Market. Sci*, 18, 504–26.
Churchill Jr., G. A. (1999). *Marketing Research: Methodological Foundations*. Fort Worth, TX: The Dryden Press.
Crouch, S. & Housden, M. (2003). *Marketing Research for Managers*. Oxford: Butterworth-Heinemann.
Dall'Olmo Riley, F., Ehrenberg, A. S. C., Castleberry, C. B., Barwise, T. P. & Barnard, N. (1997). "The variability of attitudinal repeat-rates". *International Journal of Research in Marketing*, 14, 437–50.
De Chernatony, L. & McDonald, M. (2003). *Creating Powerful Brands*. Oxford: Elsevier/Butterworth-Heinemann.
Ehrenberg, A. S. C. (1972). *Repeat-Buying: Theory and Applications*. Amsterdam: North-Holland Publishing Company.
Ehrenberg, A. S. C. (1986). "Pricing and brand differentiation". *Singapore Marketing Review*, 1, 5–13.
Ehrenberg, A. S. C. (1993). "New brands and the existing market". *Journal of Market Research Soc*, 33, 285–99.
Ehrenberg, A. S. C. & England, L. R. (1990). "Generalising a pricing effect". *Journal of Industrial Economics*, 39, 47–68.
Ehrenberg, A. S. C., Goodhardt, G. J. & Barwise, P. (1990). "Double jeopardy revisited". *Journal of Market*, 54, 82–91.
Ehrenberg, A. S. C., Hammond, K. & Goodhardt, G. J. (1994). "The after-effects of price-related consumer promotions". *Journal of Advertising Research*, July/August, 11–21.
Ehrenberg, A. S. C. & Scriven, J. (1999). "Brand loyalty", in P.E. Earl & S. Kemp (eds) *The Elgar Companion to Consumer Research and Economic Psychology*. Gloucestershire: Edward Elgar, Cheltenham, pp. 53–63.
Foxall, G. R. (1990). *Consumer Psychology in Behavioural Perspective*. New York: Routledge.
Foxall, G. R. (1994). "Environment-impacting consumer behaviour: a framework for social marketing and demarketing", in M. J. Baker (ed.) *Perspectives on Marketing Management*. Chichester: Wiley, pp. 27–56.
Foxall, G. R. (1996). *Consumers in Context: The BPM Research Program*. New York: Routledge.
Foxall, G. R. (1997). *Marketing Psychology: The Paradigm in the Wings*. London: Macmillan.
Foxall, G. R. (1998). "Radical behaviorist interpretation: generating and evaluating an account of consumer behavior". *Behavior Anal*, 21, 321–54.
Foxall, G. R. (1999a). "The substitutability of brands". *Managerial and Decision Economics*, 20, 241–58.
Foxall, G. R. (1999b). "The marketing firm". *Journal of Economic Psychology*, 20, 207–34.
Foxall, G. R. & James, V. K. (2001). "The behavioral ecology of brand choice: a preliminary analysis". *European Journal of Behavior Analysis*, 2, 209–20.

Foxall, G. R. & James, V. K. (2003). "The behavioral ecology of brand choice: how and what do consumers maximize?" *Psychology and Marketing*, 20, 811–36.

Foxall, G. R. & Schrezenmaier, T. C. (2003). "The behavioral economics of consumer brand choice: establishing a methodology". *Journal of Economic Psychology*, 24, 675–95.

Foxall, G. R. & Yani-de-Soriano, M. Y. (2004). "Situational influences on consumers' attitudes and behavior". *Journal of Business Research*.

Goodhardt, G. J., Ehrenberg, A. S. C. & Chatfield, C. (1984). "The Dirichlet: a comprehensive model of buying behaviour". *Journal of the Royal Statistical Society*, A147, 621–43.

Hair, J. F., Anderson, R. E., Tatham, R. L. & Black, W. C. (1995). *Multivariate Data Analysis*. Englewood Cliffs, NJ: Prentice-Hall.

Herrnstein, R. J. (1961). "Relative and absolute strength of response as a function of the frequency of reinforcement". *Journal of the Experimental Analysis of Behavior*, 4, 267–72.

Herrnstein, R. J. (1970). "On the law of effect". *Journal of the Experimental Analysis of Behavior*, 13, 243–66.

Herrnstein, R. J. (1982). "Melioration as behavioral dynamism", in M. L. Commons, R. J. Herrnstein & H. Rachlin (eds) *Quantitative Analyses of Behavior. Vol. II: Matching and Maximizing Accounts*. Cambridge, MA: Ballinger, pp. 433–58.

Herrnstein, R. J. & Loveland, D. H. (1975). "Maximizing and matching on concurrent ratio schedules". *Journal of the Experimental Analysis of Behavior*, 24, 107–16.

Herrnstein, R. J. & Prelec, D. (1991). "Melioration: a theory of distributed choice". *J. Econ. Perspectives*.

Herrnstein, R. J. & Vaughan, W. (1980). "Melioration and behavioral allocation", in J. E. R. Staddon (ed.) *Limits to Action: The Allocation of Individual Behavior*. New York: Academic Press, pp. 143–76.

Houston, A. I. & McFarland, D. J. (1980). "Behavioral resilience and its relation to demand functions", in J. E. R. Staddon (ed.) *Limits to Action: The Allocation of Individual Behavior*. New York: Academic Press, pp. 177–204.

Hursh, S. R. (1980). "Economic concepts for the analysis of behavior". *Journal of the Experimental Analysis of Behavior*, 34, 219–38.

Hursh, S. R. & Bauman, R. A. (1987). "The behavioral analysis of demand", in L. Green & J. H. Kagel (eds) *Advances in Behavioral Economics, vol. 1*. Norwood, NJ: Ablex, pp. 117–65.

Jary, M. & Wileman, A. (1998). *Branding: The New Wealth Creators*. Basingstoke: Palgrave Macmillan.

Kagel, J. H., Battalio, R. C. & Green, L. (1995). *Economic Choice Theory: An Experimental Analysis of Animal Behavior*. Cambridge: Cambridge University Press.

Kagel, J. H., Battalio, R. C., Green, L. & Rachlin, H. (1980). "Consumer demand theory applied to choice behavior of rats", in J. E. R. Staddon (ed.) *Limits to Action: The Allocation of Individual Behavior*. New York: Academic Press, pp. 237–67.

Keng, K. A. & Ehrenberg, A. S. C. (1984). "Patterns of store choice". *J. Market Res.*, 21, 399–409.

Krishnamurti, L. & Raj, S. P. (1988). "A model of brand choice and purchase quantity price sensitivities". *Marketing Science*, 7, 1–20.

Madden, G. W., Bickel, W. K & Jacobs, E. A. (2000). "Three predictions of the economic concept of unit price in a choice context". *Journal of the Experimental Analysis of Behaviour*, 73, 45–64.

Rachlin, H. (1980). "Economics and behavioral psychology", in J. E. R. Staddon (ed.) *Limits to Action: The Allocation of Individual Behavior*. New York: Academic Press, pp. 205–36.

Sharp, B. & Sharp, A. (1997). "Loyalty programs and their impact on repeat-purchase loyalty patterns". *Int. J. Res. Market*, 14, 473–86.

Uncles, M. & Ehrenberg, A. S. C. (1990). "The buying of packaged goods at US retail chains". *Journal of Retailing*, 66, 278–93.

Uncles, M., Ehrenberg, A. S. C. & Hammond, K. (1995). "Patterns of buyer behavior: regularities, models, and extensions". *Marketing Science*, 14, G71–G8.

Vaughan, W. & Herrnstein, R. J. (1987). "Stability, melioration and natural selection", in L. Green & J. H. Kagel (eds) *Advances in Behavioral Economics, vol. 1*. Norwood, NJ: Ablex, pp. 185–215.

Watkins, T. (1986). *The Economics of the Brand*. London: McGraw-Hill.

Wearden, J. H. (1988). "Some neglected problems in the analysis of human operant behavior", in G. C. L. Davey & C. Cullen (eds) *Human Operant Conditioning and Behavior Modification*. Chichester: Wiley, pp. 197–224.

Zettle, R. D. & Hayes, S. C. (1982). "Rule-governed behavior: a potential framework for cognitive-behavioral therapy", in P. C. Kendall (ed.) *Advances in Cognitive-Behavioral Research and Therapy*. New York: Academic Press, pp. 73–117.

7
Patterns of Consumer Response to Retail Price Differentials[1]

Jorge M. Oliveira-Castro, Gordon R. Foxall and Teresa C. Schrezenmaier

Introduction

Consumers' responsiveness to changes in price is of primary interest to marketing researchers and retail managers since it influences a variety of strategic and tactical decisions, including pricing, promotion, and segmentation. It is particularly relevant for routinely purchased packaged goods, where price variations that occur during a year are in most part related to tactical marketing activities associated with competing brands, notably short-term price promotions, which may lead consumers to modify their purchase patterns. From the point of view of retail executives, it is vital to know whether and how such changes can impact brand and category sales.

Patterns of consumer brand choice are also of interest to marketing scientists, for the general reason that the brand defines as no other entity does the marketing (as opposed to economic, sociological or psychological) level of analysis, and for the more particular reason of understanding consumer choice in relation to the specific influences of marketing variables. In the research reported here, marketing influence is categorized in terms derived from the Behavioral Perspective Model (BPM) (Foxall, 1990) as the provision of *utilitarian* benefit and *informational* benefit, which refer respectively to the intrinsic functional rewards of owning and using a product, and the symbolic or status-conferring outcomes of purchase and consumption which inhere in the brand. Although it is a fundamental tenet of marketing thought that both utilitarian and symbolic factors shape consumer decision making, previous research on patterns of brand choice has not attempted to incorporate these variables in a manner that shows on the basis of theoretical reasoning how they are systematically related to consumer behavior.

We report an analysis of panel data for purchases of nine routinely-bought food products which classifies brands into groups based on the relative level of utilitarian and informational benefits they are planned to offer, and shows the extent to which quantity demanded per shopping occasion is determined by buyers' responsiveness to price and benefit differentials. Our research incorporates a novel method for calculating price elasticities of demand for products based on relative measures that employ mean product category quantities and prices. This technique permits comparisons across product categories which are designated in widely differing units of quantity and price. Moreover, the results indicate that product quantity elasticities per shopping occasion can be usefully decomposed into *intra-brand* elasticities which relate consumers' propensity to purchase a brand when its price differs from its average over a period of time, *utilitarian inter-brand* elasticities which refer to consumers' sensitivity to brands that offer higher utilitarian benefits, and *informational inter-brand* elasticities which refer to their propensities to select different quantities of brands that offer higher informational benefits. Each of these patterns of brand choice has implications for both retailing strategy and the theoretical depiction of consumer choice.

Literature review

Effects of price promotions

Several marketing studies have investigated the effects of price promotions for routinely purchased packaged goods on brand price elasticity. As consumers have to decide what, how much and when to buy, the increase in sales usually observed during price promotions may be associated with a variety of purchase patterns (Gupta, 1988). Brand sales may increase, for instance, because consumers switch across brands (i.e., secondary demand), or because they buy larger quantities of the promoted brand (primary demand), or as a result of a combination of both. If they buy larger quantities, they may be accelerating their purchases or stockpiling, which may or may not be associated with long-term increases in consumption (i.e., in primary demand). Uncles *et al.* (1995) are strong advocates of the thesis that price promotions engender temporary sales increases by encouraging customers who are already buyers of the brand to purchase more rather than non-buyers to buy at all. Their own research and other empirical investigations have reported effects of price promotions on brand choice, purchase incidence and purchase quantity. Several of these studies have attempted to model such effects, either in isolation or in combination (e.g., Krishnamurti & Raj, 1988; Gupta, 1988; Bell *et al.*, 1999; Guadagni & Little, 1983). In those cases where brand price elasticity, associated with promotions, was decomposed into primary and secondary demand effects, results indicated that the predominant effect of promotions is on brand switching (75% to 84%) rather than on primary demand (16% to 25%) (*cf.* Gupta, 1988; Bell *et al.*, 1999).

Another line of research has investigated relationships among promotional brand price elasticity and market characteristics, brand-specific factors and consumer characteristics (e.g., Bolton, 1989; Fader & Lodish, 1990; Narasimhan *et al.*, 1996). Bolton (1989), for example, has reported significantly more price inelastic brand sales for brands with larger market shares, with more frequent brand or category display in the store, and within categories with less feature activities (i.e., newspapers and flyers). In these studies, the main dependent variable has typically been a summary measure of brand elasticity, which has not been decomposed into primary and secondary demand effects.

In an effort to relate these two lines of research, Bell *et al.* (1999) attempted to determine the extent to which the effects of promotions on primary and secondary demand varies across product categories. These authors also investigated possible relations between market, brand and consumer characteristics and the three components of elasticity, namely, brand choice, purchase incidence, and purchase quantity. They found that the effects of price promotions on primary and secondary price elasticities varied across product categories, and that category-specific variables, such as share of household budget and stockpiling potential, were more powerful in explaining variability in elasticities than brand-specific factors or consumer characteristics like demographics.

The investigation of undecomposed price elasticity at the brand level is particularly relevant to marketing managers who seek improvements in the effectiveness of their promotional activities. The findings of such research are, however, of limited value for retailers practicing "category management," a strategy that "views whole categories as individual business units and seeks to coordinate promotion, merchandising, distribution, and product allocations to enhance overall category performance" (Walters & Bommer, 1996, p. 1). For these retailers, studies that examine the determinants of category-level price elasticities may be more useful, since changes in category sales are more directly related to their economic performance. Based on this reasoning and stressing the lack of research on category elasticity, Walters & Bommer (1996) investigated the association between product category price elasticities and brand and promotion-related characteristics for a large number of product categories (*cf.* Hoch *et al.*, 1995). Using 52 weeks of scanner data from a large supermarket chain, and defining category elasticity as the change in category unit sales relative to a 1% change in the price of a brand that is a member of the product category, they found that product-specific factors, such as brand market share and price, had a significant impact on category elasticity, whereas most promotion-related factors did not.

Inter- and intra-brand choice patterns

When decomposing price elasticity into primary and secondary demand effects, Gupta (1988) reported a curious negative relationship between the regular price of brands and purchase quantity, which may have several implications for the analysis and understanding of product category elasticity. His results suggest that consumers tend to buy smaller quantities of brands that have higher regular prices than brands that have lower regular prices. This finding does not reflect the typical intra-brand or own price elasticity, where purchase quantity of a particular brand decreases with increases in price of that specific brand. As regular prices, in Gupta's research, were defined as shelf prices that remained the same for four or more consecutive weeks and were separated from price cuts, the observed relationship suggests a pattern of brand choice not previously emphasized in the literature. This pattern might consist of an inter-brand elasticity, selecting smaller quantities of higher-priced brands, that occurs independently of price promotions and in addition to the typical intra-brand or own elasticity pattern. These results become even more intriguing when one considers that they were not replicated in subsequent research conducted by Bell *et al.* (1999). These authors hypothesized that relative price position of brands, as indicative of premium brand level, would be positively related to both primary and secondary demand. Their results did not show significant relationships between relative price position and purchase quantity or purchase incidence, and in fact disconfirmed their hypothesis concerning brand switching since higher-priced brands showed lower switching elasticities than lower-priced brands.

Taken together, these contradictory results and divergent hypotheses concerning the effects of brand regular price or "premium" level on the quantity consumers buy suggest the need for more detailed investigations of such phenomena. This kind of knowledge may be particularly relevant for product category management, since this strategy depends, for its successful application, on information concerning brand choice patterns across differently priced brands (*cf.* Hoch *et al.*, 1995; Walters & Bommer, 1996). If, as Gupta's (1988) results suggest, consumers tend to buy smaller quantities of more expensive brands, this pattern may confound calculations of price elasticity per shopping occasion at the category level (which is different than overall changes in the category sales as a function of prices). The expected overall decreases in purchase quantity per shopping occasion as a function of increases in prices, observed at the category level, may be related to two quite different consumer choice patterns.

First, consumers would tend to buy larger quantities of a particular brand when its price decreases, an intra-brand or own elasticity that should be observed, in varying degrees, for all brands. The second of these choice patterns would be a tendency to buy smaller quantities of brands with higher regular prices, an inter-brand elasticity that might be related to a pattern of buying smaller amounts of more differentiated brands on different shopping occasions. This second choice pattern would also call into question the assumption that the quantity consumers buy varies little across shopping occasions (*cf.* Ehrenberg, 1988).

The present study examines quantity price elasticity per shopping occasion at the category level with the purpose of verifying whether or not such intra- and inter-brand choice patterns occur and, if so, separating their relative effects on disaggregate (i.e., per shopping occasion) quantity price elasticity observed at the category level. In order to do so, two points concerning the relations between brand pricing and brand differentiation must be addressed. First is the tendency of several authors to use the regular prices of brands as measures of brand differentiation (or premium brands) or brand strength, without discussing some of the difficulties in establishing such association (e.g., Gupta, 1988; Walters & Bommer, 1996). More expensive brands are not necessarily the stronger brands in the category, if "stronger" refers to brands having larger market shares. Although there is usually a positive correlation between these two measures in most product categories, the magnitude of this kind of correlation may vary significantly from product to product. Another difficulty derived from measuring brand differentiation solely on the basis of regular price is that, when using scanner or panel data, regular prices are usually obtained from shelf prices. This may bias the results, since, in many product categories, the most differentiated and most expensive brands are also the most frequently price-promoted brands. Regular prices, calculated in this manner, may not, therefore, be the most precise indicator of brand differentiation. A second point that may complicate the use of regular price as a measure of brand differentiation is the fact that brand price may differ on the basis of other attributes not related to brand differentiation. For example, cars with air-conditioning are usually more expensive than cars without air-conditioning independently of the make of the car, that is, this occurs both for a Fiat and a BMW. In such cases, regular prices might be related to additional or special attributes of the products, which may or may not be associated to the strength or level of differentiation of the brand.

These points suggest that brand differentiation should not be measured solely on the basis of regular prices and should be separated from other types of benefit offered by different brands. In the present chapter, we use the distinction between utilitarian and informational benefits, proposed in the BPM of consumer choice (Foxall, 1990), to analyze the different types of benefit offered by different brands.

Utilitarian and informational benefits

Foxall (1990) argues that consumer behavior occurs at the intersection of a consumer-behavior setting and an individual's learning history of consumption. The setting contains events in the consumption environment that signal the different consequences for different consumer responses. These events in the setting may be physical (e.g., alternative brands, point-of-sale advertisement), social (e.g., other shoppers, store staff members), temporal (e.g., store opening hours, short-term promotions), and regulatory (e.g., rules concerning shopping). They function as stimuli that signal to the consumer, based on his or her past learning history, the kind of consequences that are likely to follow each type of response, such as buying, postponing the purchase, accelerating the purchase, searching, and saving. Consumer responses may produce three types of consequences, namely, utilitarian reinforcing events, informational reinforcing events, or aversive events. Utilitarian benefit consists of practical outcomes of purchase and consumption, derived from the use of the product itself. This is related to the functional outcomes, to the value-in-use of a product or service, to the economic/pragmatic/material satisfaction derived from acquiring, owning, and/or using it.

Informational benefit, by contrast, is symbolic, social, mediated by the actions and reactions of other people. It is more akin to exchange value. It consists of feedback on the performance of the individual as consumer. Whereas utilitarian benefit is related to economic and functional benefits of products or services, informational benefit is related to social status and prestige, associated to buying, owning, or using products or services. For example, the major utilitarian benefit of owning a car is to be able to get door-to-door transportation, which any car can offer. But driving a Bentley or a Mercedes may offer its owner prestige and social status, in addition to door-to-door transportation. Owning a car itself, independently of its make, might give its owner some social status, the degree of which will depend, primarily, upon the cultural and economic context in which the individual lives. But, in that same context, owning a Bentley will probably give its owner more social status than simply owning a more popularly-available car. Informational benefit may be thus related to brand differentiation, in the sense of brands that are well known as high-quality brands. By the same token, a Bentley and a Mercedes will probably offer more utilitarian benefits (e.g., security items, longer warranty) than less prestigious makes, but even a Mercedes may be acquired with more or fewer utilitarian benefits (e.g., air-conditioning, leather seats).

In addition to these two types of rewarding consequence, consumer responses also produce aversive consequences, such as spending money and time when searching and buying. The probability of purchase and consumption depends on the relative weight of the reinforcing and aversive consequences that are signaled by the elements in the consumer behavior setting (*cf.* Alhadeff, 1982). According to this view, product, brand, and service attributes, including price, may be interpreted as programmed reinforcing and aversive events. Much of what manufacturers, retailers, and managers do is directed toward changing the reinforcing and/or aversive properties of the attributes of their products and brands, so as to make them more attractive to the consumer. They attempt to accomplish that by creating, modifying, and/or promoting brands and products. These manipulations may or may not work, and this is why they should be interpreted as programmed reinforcing (or aversive) events rather then actual reinforcing (or aversive) events. According to this theoretical perspective, one of the main tasks in marketing is to identify what events can function as reinforcers (or aversive stimuli), to what extent, for what consumers, and under what circumstances (Foxall, 1992).

Separating intra- and inter-brand elasticities

Based on this distinction between utilitarian and informational benefit and using consumer panel data, we classified all the brands of nine supermarket food products according to the level of utilitarian and informational benefits that they offer. The purpose was to examine whether and how consumers tend to buy smaller quantities of brands offering higher utilitarian and informational benefits (i.e., inter-brand elasticity), separating such possible tendency from the tendency of buying larger quantities of price-promoted brands (i.e., intra-brand elasticity). The brands in each product category were ranked according to a two-point scale of programmed utilitarian benefits, such as baked beans with sausage *versus* plain baked beans, which was based on the analysis of product attributes. The brands were also ranked according to a three-point scale of programmed informational benefits, which was based on an analysis of brand positioning, such as good-value-for-money own brands, higher-level own and lower-level national brands, and higher-level national brands. Brand average prices were considered in distinguishing lower- and higher-level national brands. Using this classification, we decomposed quantity price elasticity per shopping occasion calculated for each product category, by relating the quantity bought by each consumer on each purchase occasion to the brand informational level, the brand utilitarian level, and the brand promoted price (i.e., price relative to the brand average price). These elasticity measures may help describe intra- and inter-brand consumer choice patterns, suggested by previous results, and determine their relative contribution to overall disaggregate category elasticity. In this sense, the present investigation can be characterized as descriptive and exploratory in nature rather than explanatory. By comparing intra- and inter-brand elasticity measures across nine product categories, the present research tests if the consumer choice patterns examined should be interpreted as an empirical generalization, that is, a "pattern and regularity that repeats over many different circumstances" (Bass, 1993, p. 2). Due to its descriptive and exploratory nature, the research makes no attempt to model price elasticity, that is, it does not include all the possible and/or known variables that might influence it, as some authors have done previously. Elasticity equations are adopted here as measures of consumer behavior patterns.

Considering the need to compare elasticity results across product categories, the measures used to calculate elasticity parameters (quantity, informational level, utilitarian level, and price) were all relative to each product category average. To test for possible distortions derived from the use of relative measures, overall disaggregate elasticity coefficients, based on data from each shopping occasion, obtained for each of the nine product categories were calculated, with the purpose of comparing them with those found in the literature for similar food categories.

Overall elasticity for food categories

Using consumer panel data and regression analyses, Telser (1962) analyzed price elasticities of the leading brands (four to six) of four different food products (frozen orange juice, regular coffee, instant coffee, and margarine). The author found negative coefficients for elasticity, indicating that increases in price, relative to the average price of all brands, were associated with decreases in market share. The values of price elasticity varied considerably across products and brands and depended on the price measures used (short- or long-run, or relative or differential). For instant coffee and margarine, for example, the average short-run relative price elasticities were –1.8 and –1.3, respectively. Long-run elasticities tended to be higher than short-run elasticities.

Using supermarket scanner data, Walters & Bommer (1996) also calculated elasticity coefficients for food categories. Although the authors reported the values of price elasticity for only nine groups of products, rather than for the 89 product categories studied, promotional price elasticities ranged from 0 to –1. Similar elasticity coefficients for food products were also reported by the National Food Survey (Lechene, 2000), using the Almost Ideal Demand System model, in which weekly family expenditure on food was interpreted as a function of the price of food, family income and other variables. The survey was based on data collected from 1988 to 2000 for more than 20 food items, such as milk, cheese, meat, fish, eggs, potatoes, vegetables, fresh fruits, fruit juices, and beverages. With only one exception (prepared fish), the own price elasticity of all these products were negative and inelastic, varying between 0 and –1.

Method

Sampling and procedure

Consumer panel data for 80 consumers, including total weekly purchases of each of nine product categories (i.e., baked beans, biscuits, breakfast cereals, butter, cheese, fruit juice, instant coffee, margarine, and tea) during a period of 16 weeks were obtained. The data were drawn from the TNS (Taylor Nelson Sofres) "Superpanel", which consists of 10,000 randomly selected British households and provides data on a range of consumer goods. The voluntary participant members scan their purchases into a sophisticated handheld barcode reader after each shopping trip by simply passing the scanner across the product codes on the packages. The data are then sent electronically to Taylor Nelson Sofres for central processing. Panel data were chosen as they are especially advantageous for longitudinal studies: changes in the behavior, in this case purchasing behavior, can be well monitored by the continuous measurements (Crouch & Housden, 2003). Moreover, diary panel data are also believed to be very accurate and freer from errors intrinsic to reporting of past behavior (Churchill, 1999) and therefore are particularly valuable when collecting information on many variables such as price, shopping occasion, brand name and so on. The noteworthy reliability of the study is that the data were obtained in a non-experimental, computer-assisted way, by monitoring real-world consumers spending their real disposable income on fast-moving consumer goods. The following information was recorded for each purchase of each consumer: brand specification (i.e., different versions of the same product category were classified as different brands, e.g., Corn Flakes and Rice Krispies by Kelloggs), package size, shop, date, number of units, and total amount spent. As the analysis of brand choice requires information concerning actual purchase across several buying opportunities, data from consumers who bought, within each product category, fewer than four times during the 16-week period were disregarded.

Measures

In order to investigate possible effects of informational and utilitarian benefit values on brand choice, an attempt was made to identify different levels or magnitudes of informational and utilitarian benefit offered by the brands available (i.e., bought by consumers in the sample) in each product category. As mentioned previously, the analysis of informational and utilitarian benefit levels presented below refer to programmed levels of informational and utilitarian benefits, which may or may not influence consumer choice. In other words, in the case of marketing activities, an event that was planned to have high benefit magnitude, *vis-à-vis* its aversive components (e.g., costs), can in fact have low reward value or benefit for consumers (e.g., innovations that do not attract people or are too expensive). So, in the present work, brand classification was based on an analysis of brand positioning from the manufacturer's point of view, rather than based on consumer's perception of benefits. The informational and utilitarian benefit levels are therefore programmed or planned to function as benefits for the majority of consumers. This is confirmed by the fact that manufacturers usually charge higher prices for this planned benefits. Needless to say they may not work as such for particular consumers (e.g., a consumer may not like baked beans with sausage, despite the fact that they are programmed to be something better than plain baked beans).

Since there are no general units to measure utilitarian and informational benefit levels, these were assessed by means of a forced ranking system in which three informational and two utilitarian levels were ascribed to each product category. This classification was chosen on account of our interest in making comparisons across product categories and was in part influenced by our sample (not all brands and brand types were bought by our sample during the period). According to our proposal, there is no correct or definite level of analysis of informational and utilitarian levels, for it all depends on research or managerial interests. More levels of utilitarian benefit, for example, could be identified for some product categories, such as biscuits and cheese, but an equal number of levels across products was thought to be desirable.

Levels of utilitarian benefit. As mentioned previously, utilitarian benefit consists in the practical outcomes of purchase and consumption, that is, functional benefits derived directly (rather than mediated by other people) from possession and application of a product or service; it is benefit mediated by the product or service. In the case of supermarket food products like the ones investigated here, increases in utilitarian level can be identified by the addition of, supposedly desirable, attributes. Such attributes usually improve some aspect of consumption, are mentioned in the package or product name, and justify increases in price. Moreover, in most cases, several general brands (e.g., Kelloggs, Asda and Tesco) offer products with and without these attributes. For the product categories examined here, utilitarian levels were identified based on additional attributes (e.g., plain baked beans vs. baked beans with sausage; plain vs. light product formulations) and/or differentiated types of products (e.g., plain biscuits vs. cookies; corn flakes vs. rice cereals). In the case of differentiated product types, several general brands usually offer the different product types, charging differentiated prices for them (e.g., digestive biscuits are cheaper than cookies for all brands examined). Plain versions of products and simpler types of products were classified as belonging to Level 1 of utilitarian benefit whereas more differentiated versions and types of products were classified as Level 2. Examples of the attributes used to classify Levels 1 and 2 of utilitarian benefit are presented in Appendix A.

Levels of informational benefit. Informational benefit, in contrast to utilitarian benefit, is symbolic, closely akin to exchange value, usually mediated by the actions and reactions of others with respect to one's consumption-related behavior. It consists in feedback on one's performance as a consumer and results from social status, prestige, and acceptance derived from the individual's consumer behavior. In the case of supermarket products investigated here, informational benefit level is closely associated to brand differentiation, which in turn is usually also related to price differentiation. More differentiated brands are usually brands that are better known and perceived by consumers as being of higher quality. If one compares the level of brand differentiation of, let us say, Asda Smart Price and Heinz, as brands producing plain-baked beans, Heinz is clearly a better known, more differentiated baked-beans brand. It also offers a more expensive product. This kind of difference among brands has been interpreted in the present work as differences in informational benefit level. Again, as in the case of utilitarian benefit, these have been interpreted as programmed (or planned) differences in informational benefit magnitude which may or may not have the expected effects on buying behavior (it would be difficult anyway to predict the outcome of different reinforcing and aversive magnitude combinations). It should be noted that informational benefit level as specified here does not exclude the possibility of there also being differences in utilitarian benefit between two informational magnitudes. Representatives of Heinz, or any other differentiated brand, would be the first to defend that their products differ from those of other brands with respect to "utilitarian" attributes, such as quality of raw materials and ingredients, production procedures, health control, and such like. Consumers of differentiated brands could also assert, for example, that they taste much better than other "inferior" brands, which might imply differences in utilitarian benefit level. The classification adopted here does not exclude such possibilities, since most consumer behavior generates both types of consequence. Nevertheless, the ranking of informational benefit is based on the predominant difference that one can find between products, offered by different brands, which have, in many cases, almost identical formulations (*cf.* Ehrenberg, 1972).

The ranking of informational benefit level was based on the following general criteria: (1) The cheapest store brands (e.g., Asda Smart Price, Tesco Value, Sainsbury Economy) were considered to represent the lowest informational level (Level 1); (2) Store brands that do not mention good value for money or economy (e.g., Asda, Tesco,

Sainsbury) and cheapest specialized brands were usually considered to represent the medium informational level (Level 2); and (3) Specialized brands, with higher prices, were considered to represent the highest informational level (Level 3). So, differences in prices across brands for the same product type (e.g., plain baked beans offered by Heinz vs. Tesco Value, digestive biscuits by McVities vs. Asda Smart Price, or plain cornflakes by Kelloggs vs. Sainsbury Economy) were considered to be indicative of differences in informational level. Examples of brands classified in different informational levels for each product category are presented in Appendix B.

Analyses

Classification reliability. With the purpose of checking the level of reliability of the adopted brand classification criteria, two UK residents (male and female) served as judges and were asked to classify the brands of all product categories using the criteria as described in this chapter (Method and Appendix).

Overall product price elasticity. Overall price elasticity coefficients were calculated for each product category in order to compare the results with those found in the literature for similar products. Despite the fact that some authors have modeled quantity as a discrete variable (e.g., Gupta, 1988), we followed other investigators, such as Bell *et al.* (1999) in interpreting quantity and prices as continuous variables (e.g., 100 grams and pounds/100 grams). The following equation was used to calculate the overall elasticity coefficients for each product category:

$$\log Q_{it} = \alpha + \beta (\log P_{it}) + \varepsilon_{it} \qquad (7.1)$$

where:

Q_{it} = the quantity bought by consumer i on shopping occasion t divided by the average quantity bought in the product category, calculated across all consumers on all shopping occasions,

P_{it} = the price paid by consumer i on shopping occasion t divided by the average price paid in the product category, calculated across all consumers on all shopping occasions,

with α and β being estimated regression coefficients, and ε_{it} representing the error term. The equation is similar to that used by Kagel *et al.* (1995), where β can be interpreted as a direct measure of elasticity. The use of relative values, that is, each quantity (and price) value divided by the average quantity (price) in the category, ensures that all categories are measured in their respective purchase units, which allows for comparisons across product categories (*cf.* Bell *et al.*, 1999). This "normalization" with respect to the category mean also favors the interpretation of the relations between quantity and price. In doing this, the equation can be interpreted as measuring whether purchases of quantities above (or below) the mean quantity bought in the product category are associated to prices above (or below) the average price paid in the category. As mentioned previously, we have not attempted to elaborate price elasticity models. We adopted elasticity coefficients as measures of some possible consumer choice patterns. One consequence of this descriptive approach is that we do not expect to obtain high levels of explained variance (R^2) associated with any of the equations.

Intra- and inter-brand elasticities. Overall category elasticity was decomposed into intra-brand, utilitarian inter-brand, and informational inter-brand elasticities with the purpose of identifying consumer choice patterns. The following equation was used:

$$\log Q_{it} = \alpha + \beta_1 (\log U_{it}) + \beta_2 (\log I_{it}) + \beta_3 (\log RP_{it}) + \varepsilon_{it} \qquad (7.2)$$

where:

Q_{it} = the quantity bought by consumer i on shopping occasion t divided by the average quantity bought in the product category, calculated across all consumers on all shopping occasions,

U_{it} = the utilitarian level (1 or 2) of the brand bought by consumer i on shopping occasion t divided by the average utilitarian level of the brands bought in the product category, calculated across all consumers on all shopping occasions,

I_{it} = the informational level (1, 2 or 3) of the brand bought by consumer i on shopping occasion t divided by the average informational level of the brands bought in the product category, calculated across all consumers on all shopping occasions,

RP_{it} = the price paid by consumer i on shopping occasion t divided by the average price of the chosen brand; the result of this calculation being divided by this same measure (i.e., price paid/brand price) calculated for the product category (i.e., average across all consumers on all shopping occasion), that is, [(price paid/brand price)$_{\text{shopping occasion}}$ /(price paid/brand price)$_{\text{category}}$],

with α, β_1, β_2, and β_3 being estimated regression coefficients, and ε_{it} representing the error term. As in the case of Equation 7.1, the dependent and independent variables included in Equation 7.2 are relative measures, obtained by dividing each of them by the product category average. As mentioned previously, this was done with the purpose of "normalizing" the variables and making them comparable across categories. Even in the case of the intra-brand variable (RP_{it}), whose numerator is a relative measure, this procedure may help standardize measurement scales across categories. In the remainder of this chapter, β_1, β_2 and β_3 will be referred to as *utilitarian, informational* and *intra-brand* elasticity coefficients, respectively.

Results

Reliability analysis

The analysis of reliability was conducted by comparing the informational and utilitarian levels attributed to the brands in the chapter with those attributed by each of the two independent judges. This comparison was based on the percentage of brands for which there was perfect agreement between the classification adopted here and the classification proposed by each judge. The percentage of agreement was calculated separately for informational and utilitarian benefits, for all products, and for each product separately. In what follows, the average percentages of agreement, calculated across the percentage of agreement obtained for each of the two judges, are reported.

The analyses showed (i.e., average across the two judges) that 70.9% and 74.6% of all the brands of all the product categories (i.e., 660 brands) were attributed the same levels of informational and utilitarian benefits, respectively. For each product category, the percentages of agreement for the informational classification were equal to 79.7%, 71.2%, 79.5%, 67.2%, 63.2%, 74.5%, 69.4%, 77.3% and 63.4%, for baked beans, biscuits, breakfast cereals, butter, cheese, fruit juice, instant coffee, margarine, and tea, respectively. The percentages of agreement for the utilitarian classification were equal to 96.9%, 73.6%, 87.1%, 78.6%, 69.5%, 63.5%, 64.5%, 65.5% and 78.4%, for baked beans, biscuits, breakfast cereals, butter, cheese, fruit juice, instant coffee, margarine, and tea, respectively.

Descriptive statistics

Table 7.1 presents information concerning the number of consumers, purchases, amount spent, and brands for each product category. As can be seen in the table, most of these measures varied considerably across product categories. The number of consumers with four or more pur-

Table 7.1 Number of consumers, total purchases, average number of purchases, average total amount spent, average amount spent per shopping trip, average price per standard amount, average price per package, total number of brands, average number of brands bought, for each product category

Product	Number of consumers	Total purchases	Average purchases	Total spent	Average spent	Average price	Unit price	Total brands	Average brands
Baked Beans	39	265	6.79	4.52	0.62	0.07	0.51	32	2.18
Biscuits	59	1125	19.07	14.02	0.74	0.30	0.63	230	8.93
Breakfast Cereals	56	691	12.34	20.09	1.56	0.27	1.46	125	5.64
Butter	21	174	8.29	9.84	1.17	0.28	0.76	21	2.24
Cheese	45	447	9.93	13.38	1.38	1.91	2.76	95	5.24
Fruit Juice	34	336	9.88	13.99	1.52	0.72	1.05	43	2.91
Coffee	19	144	7.58	18.32	2.51	2.09	2.09	31	2.95
Margarine	50	401	8.02	8.75	1.12	0.19	1.01	55	2.70
Tea	32	199	6.22	11.67	2.02	0.61	1.66	30	1.94

chases during the 16-week period within each product category, for example, ranged from 19 for coffee to 59 for biscuits, whereas the total number of purchases ranged from 144 to 1,125 also for coffee and biscuits, respectively. These wide differences across categories suggest the need to adopt relative measures to calculate category elasticities, as we do in the present chapter.

Overall product elasticities

Table 7.2 presents Equation 7.1 parameters for each product category. The F statistics indicate that all regression analyses were significant (p ≤ .01), indicating a linear relation between changes in (log of) price and changes in (log of) quantity. The values of R^2 varied from .05 to .76, suggesting that there are wide differences across product categories in the influence of variables other than price, which were not investigated here. The values of the intercept (α) were close to zero and ranged from −.46 to −.07 across product categories. These values indicate that at the average price of the category (i.e., log P_{it} = 0) consumers tended to buy a little less than the average quantity for that category. Elasticity coefficient estimates (β) were all significant (as shown by the t statistics with $p \le .01$), and varied from −.23 to −1.01 across product categories, indicating an inverse relationship between price and quantity demanded. These values also indicate that the demand for all the products was inelastic, that is, increases in prices were accompanied by decreases in quantity demanded, although the decreases in quantity

Table 7.2 Parameters of Equation 7.1 (log Quantity = $\alpha + \beta$ [log Price]), calculated for each product category (See text for details).

Product category	r^2	F	α	β	Std. Error	t	Durbin-Watson
Baked beans	.05	14.39 c	−.12	−.23 c	.06	−3.79	.85 c
Biscuits	.41	764.44 c	−.14	−.54 c	.02	−27.65	1.08 c
Breakfast Cereals	.32	326.66 c	−.07	−.55 c	.03	−18.07	.91 c
Butter	.06	10.46 c	−.09	−.52 c	.16	−3.23	.53 c
Cheese	.76	1399.79 c	−.46	−1.01 c	.03	−37.41	1.19 c
Fruit juice	.18	74.01 c	−.12	−.55 c	.06	−8.60	.74 c
Instant Coffee	.35	76.33 c	−.11	−.58 c	.07	−8.74	1.01 c
Margarine	.15	69.78 c	−.08	−.31 c	.04	−8.35	.92 c
Tea	.30	84.76 c	−.12	−.97 c	.11	−9.21	.82 c

c: p <= .01
b: p <= .05
a: p <= .10

were proportionally smaller than the correspondent increases in price. The standard errors associated with the estimation of β were all at least three times smaller than the estimated value of b, suggesting probabilities of correct estimation much above $p = .90$. Considering that the regression analyses were based on time series data, Durbin-Watson statistics were calculated to check for the existence of significant autocorrelated residuals. As can be seen from Table 7.2, these values were all significant ($p \leq .01$) indicating the existence of positively autocorrelated residuals which may raise suspicion about the estimates of individual coefficients (a point which is discussed further below).

Utilitarian, informational and intra-brand elasticities

Table 7.3 presents Equation 7.2 parameters for each product category. All regression analyses (F statistics) were significant ($p \leq .01$). R^2 values ranged from .05 to .62, suggesting again that there are wide differences across product categories for the influence of variables other than those included in the equation. The values of the intercept (α) were close to zero and ranged from $-.37$ to $-.06$ across product categories, indicating that at the average values of relative price, informational level and utilitarian level of the category (i.e., log $RP_{it} = 0$, log $I_{it} = 0$, and log $U_{it} = 0$), consumers tended to buy a little less than the average quantity for that category. Elasticity coefficient estimates (β_1, β_2, and β_3) were all significant (as shown by the t statistics with $p \leq .05$), with the exception of informational elasticity for baked beans and intra-brand elasticity for butter. Utilitarian elasticity coefficients were negative for eight product categories and ranged from $-.21$ to -1.70. The only significant positive coefficient was observed for butter (.34), which was one of the categories with the smallest number of purchases (i.e., data points). Informational elasticity coefficients were negative for eight product categories and varied from $-.19$ to $-.94$. The only non-significant and positive coefficient was observed for baked beans. Intra-brand elasticity coefficients were significant and negative for eight product categories and ranged from $-.51$ to -1.99. The only non-significant coefficient observed was for butter.

For 24 out of 25 significant coefficients, the standard errors associated with the estimation of β_1, β_2, and β_3 were all at least two times smaller than the estimated value of the coefficient, suggesting probabilities of correct estimation above .90. The only exception was observed for fruit juice where the utilitarian coefficient was equal to $-.21$ with a standard error of .11, a value that is very close to half the coefficient value. Multicollinearity analyses, calculated for all coefficients, indicated that the value of *Tolerance* ranged from .82 to

Table 7.3 Parameters of Equation 7.2 (log Quantity = $\alpha + \beta_1$ (log Utilitarian) + β_2 (log Informational) + β_3 (log Relative Price)) calculated for each product category (See text for details).

Product category	r^2	F	α	β_1	Std. Error	t	β_2	Std. Error	t	β_3	Std. Error	t	Durbin-Watson
Baked beans	.26	30.56 [c]	-.13	-1.00 [c]	.15	-6.50	.02	.07	.33	-1.31 [c]	.16	-8.27	1.13 [c]
Biscuits	.19	87.27 [c]	-.09	-.40 [c]	.04	-9.15	-.38 [c]	.04	-9.11	-.51 [c]	.05	-10.20	1.07 [c]
Breakfast Cereals	.24	70.58 [c]	-.06	-.44 [c]	.05	-8.43	-.39 [c]	.05	-7.79	-.94 [c]	.10	-9.30	1.01 [c]
Butter	.05	3.12 [b]	-.08	.34 [b]	.16	2.13	-.29 [c]	.11	-2.66	-.06	.56	-.10	.54 [c]
Cheese	.62	242.40 [c]	-.37	-1.70 [c]	.09	-18.31	-.94 [c]	.08	-11.59	-.94 [c]	.06	-15.20	1.25 [c]
Fruit juice	.17	22.55 [c]	-.12	-.21 [b]	.11	-2.00	-.33 [c]	.08	-4.26	-1.07 [c]	.18	-6.01	.86 [c]
Instant Coffee	.14	7.27 [c]	-.08	-.39 [c]	.13	-3.02	-.30 [b]	.12	-2.54	-.88 [b]	.34	-2.56	.75 [c]
Margarine	.08	11.65 [c]	-.06	-.23 [c]	.06	-3.57	-.19 [b]	.08	-2.48	-.62 [c]	.15	-4.16	.95 [c]
Tea	.32	31.07 [c]	-.12	-.39 [c]	.13	-3.00	-.50 [c]	.09	-5.50	-1.99 [c]	.25	-7.88	1.02 [c]

a: $p \leq .10$
b: $p \leq .05$
c: $p \leq .01$

1.00 whereas the values of *Variance Inflation Factor* (VIF) ranged from 1.00 to 1.23, from which one can conclude that there was no problem of multicollinearity in the data used. As in the case of overall elasticity measures, Durbin-Watson statistics were calculated with the purpose of detecting possible autocorrelated residuals. As shown in Table 7.3, the test indicated significant (p ≤ .01) autocorrelations in all product categories (which are discussed below).

A comparison among different statistically significant coefficients shows that intra-brand elasticity was larger (more negative) than utilitarian elasticity and informational elasticity for eight out of nine product categories. Utilitarian elasticity was larger than informational elasticity for six of the nine categories. Taken together, these results suggest that intra-brand elasticity was larger than utilitarian elasticity, which, in turn, was larger than informational elasticity.

In order to test the reliability of these elasticity coefficients, a split-sample analysis was conducted using the data from the product category with the largest number of data points (purchases), which was the category of biscuits (see Table 7.1). After ordering consumers' data in an ascending order on the basis of consumers' identification number, two samples were created by separating two groups of consumers with similar number of data points. Samples A and B included 578 and 547 purchases, respectively. Table 7.4 shows Equation 7.2 parameters calculated for each of these samples.

Regression analyses (*F* statistics) for both samples were significant (p ≤ .01). The values of R^2 for Samples A and B were equal to .18 and .21, respectively, very similar to the value obtained for the entire sample (.19). The values of the intercept (α) were equal to –.08 and –.11 and similar to the one obtained with all data points (–.09). Elasticity coefficient estimates (β_1, β_2, and β_3) were all significant (*t* statistics with $p \leq .01$), with standard errors five or more times smaller than the coefficient values. Multicollinearity analyses, calculated for all coefficients, indicated that the value of *Tolerance* ranged from .97 to .99 whereas the values of *Variance Inflation Factor* (VIF) ranged from 1.01 to 1.04, from which one can conclude that there was no problem of multicollinearity in the data used. Again, Durbin-Watson statistics indicated significant (p ≤ .01) autocorrelations in both samples (which are discussed below). The most interesting result is related to the values of elasticity coefficients. As it was observed for the entire category of biscuits, in both samples, intra-brand elasticity was larger than utilitarian elasticity, which, in turn, was larger than informational elasticity.

Table 7.4 Parameters of Equation 7.2 (log Quantity = $\alpha + \beta_1$ (log Utilitarian) + β_2 (log Informational) + β_3 (log Relative Price)) calculated for each of two samples of the biscuits product category (See text for details).

Biscuits – Sample	r^2	F	α	β_1	Std. Error	t	β_2	Std. Error	t	β_3	Std. Error	t	Durbin-Watson
A	.18	41.77 c	-.08	-.36 c	.06	-6.34	-.34 c	.06	-6.13	-.41 c	.06	-7.02	1.03 c
B	.21	48.28 c	-.11	-.47 c	.07	-6.99	-.41 c	.06	-6.62	-.68 c	.09	-7.74	1.13 c

a: p ≤ .10
b: p ≤ .05
c: p ≤ .01

Autocorrelated residuals

All regression analyses showed significant autocorrelated residuals (Durbin-Watson statistic), which may raise suspicions over the tests of hypothesis, including the *t*-tests for individual predictors (*cf.* Kvanli *et al.*, 1996). This is a problem frequently encountered when using linear regression analysis on time series data, particularly when few predictors are included in the equation, as is the case here. If more predictors had been included in the equation, as it is done when one attempts to develop an explanatory model, they might have explained more variance in the data and reduced the autocorrelation of residuals. Since elasticity equations were adopted here as descriptive measures of consumer choice patterns, no attempt was made to model quantity elasticity.

Despite the possible problems that autocorrelated residuals might raise concerning the stability of the estimated parameters, several aspects of our results suggest that they are reliable and replicable. First, overall category price elasticity coefficients were very similar to those obtained by previous authors for similar product categories, despite the adoption of different methods (see Discussion). Second, the relative values of intra- and inter-brand elasticity coefficients were replicated across most product categories. Third, these values were replicated across samples of a split-sample analysis and were similar to the values obtained for the entire sample. And, fourth, one of the main purposes of the present research was to compare the relative values of elasticity coefficients (i.e., intra-brand elasticity larger than informational inter-brand) rather than their absolute values.

Discussion

Overall product category elasticity

The present results yielded lower category price elasticities than those reported by Telser (1962), who used panel data on a monthly basis, from 1954 to 1957, for a period of 36 months. The author estimated price elasticity coefficients relative (i.e., by subtraction and by division) to the average price of other brands and used equations that included a variable that measured the lagged market share of the brand. In that study, only data from the four to six leading brands were included which may perhaps explain in part why the author obtained higher values of elasticity than the ones observed here. Considering that "a distinction needs to be made between *market* ... price elasticity ... and *brand* price elasticity" (Diamantopoulos, 2003, p. 352, emphasis in the original), and that "there are literally hundreds of brands in all of these product classes" (Telser, 1962, p. 315), the small number of brands analyzed in the study may not represent adequately the price elasticity of the respective markets.

The above hypothesis is reinforced by the fact that the values of price elasticity for product categories obtained here corroborate those reported by Walters & Bommer (1996) and the U. K. National Food Survey (NFS) (Lechene, 2000). These two studies reported negative coefficients ranging from 0 to –1, despite several differences in the measures and calculations used. Walters and Bommer used weekly-obtained store-level scanner data for 1,500 universal product codes, which were reduced to 89 product categories, during a period of 52 weeks between 1990 and 1991. The model adopted related the logarithm of the quantity sold in a product category as a linear function of the reciprocals of brand prices. In the NFS report, weekly information was aggregated to the monthly level for the period 1988–2000, each monthly aggregate being based on information from around 600 households. As mentioned previously, the equation used to estimate price elasticity included family income in addition to food price. Despite all these procedural differences, price elasticity coefficients obtained in those studies and in the present research were very similar, all in the range 0 to –1. In the case of fruit juice, the elasticity coefficients obtained in the NFS and by us were identical (–.55).

These similarities between such results and the ones obtained in the present research suggest that price elasticity can be estimated on the basis of relative measures, in which case the elasticity may be calculated at the average category price, as it was done here. The adoption of relative measures allows for comparisons across product categories that may differ widely with respect to quantity and price units. The similarities between category elasticities reported in previous studies, using aggregate data, and the present ones also suggest that category elasticities may be calculated from individual purchases of many individuals during relatively short time periods (16 weeks).

One advantage of this type of analysis is that it incorporates the typical panel data available from commercial firms with very little transformation, which make them particularly practical. One disadvantage of this kind of analysis is that it does not separate intra- and inter-consumer elasticities. Intra-consumer elasticity would measure the relations between quantity and price using data from the same consumer across shopping occasions. Inter-consumer elasticity would measure the relations between quantity and price using data from the same shopping occasions across different consumers. Overall category price elasticity, as calculated here, might be a resulting combination of consumers buying more when prices are lower and some consumers buying smaller quantities of more expensive brands than other consumers. Future research might attempt to separate these two possible choice patterns.

Inter- and intra-brand elasticities

The present results indicate that, when buying routinely purchased packaged goods, consumers show at least three choice patterns. First, they tend to buy larger quantities of a brand when its price is below its average price (i.e., intra-brand elasticity). Secondly, they tend to buy smaller quantities of brands that offer higher utilitarian benefits (i.e., utilitarian inter-brand elasticity). And thirdly, they tend to buy smaller quantities of brands that offer higher informational benefits (i.e., informational inter-brand elasticity). Each of these patterns was observed in eight of nine product categories investigated here. Considering that brands that offer higher levels of utilitarian and informational benefits are usually more expensive than brands offering lower levels of such benefits, the present results corroborate those reported by Gupta (1988), which suggest that consumers tend to buy smaller quantities of brands with higher regular prices.

Although consumers showed responsiveness to price promotions, utilitarian benefits and informational benefits, the results also suggested that intra-brand elasticity was higher than utilitarian elasticity, which, in turn, was higher than informational elasticity. This indicates that, when buying routinely purchased packaged goods, consumers are more responsive to price promotions than to utilitarian benefits, and more responsive to utilitarian benefits than to informational benefits. The highest responsiveness to brand price seems compatible with the extensive use of price promotions of supermarket products, whereas the lowest responsiveness to informational benefits does not seem surprising considering the lack of social status and prestige associated to the product categories investigated here. On the contrary, it seems remarkable to find that even when purchasing supermarket food products consumers show significant responsiveness to informational benefits, changing the quantity they buy in order to acquire, occasionally, brands with higher level of informational benefits. In fact, this responsiveness to informational benefits seems to depend on the price of the product, for correlation analyses among elasticity coefficients and product category characteristics (shown in Table 7.1) indicated that informational elasticity was significantly correlated with average unit price of the product ($r = -.80$, $p = .01$, $n = 9$), suggesting that informational elasticity was higher (i.e., the coefficients, still negative, were larger) for products with higher average unit prices. In other words, consumers showed to be more responsive to informational benefits in categories with higher unit prices. The replication of these findings across several different product categories suggests that they display robust consumer choice patterns, at least for routinely purchased packaged goods. Whether similar patterns occur for other types of products remains a question for future empirical studies.

Theoretical considerations

Taken together, the results demonstrate the usefulness of the BPM as a conceptual framework to analyze consumer behavior. The model provides tools to analyze the relationships between consumer choices and situational variables, including the attributes offered by different brands. One advantage of this approach is that instead of assuming that consumers maximize subjective utility, it encourages the investigation of the influence of actual attributes of brands and products, which are planned to affect consumers' choices. As predicted by the model, consumer behavior was influenced by aversive consequences (price), utilitarian benefits, and informational benefits. These observed choice patterns suggest that consumers may be described as maximizing utilitarian and informational benefits while minimizing aversive consequences, such as spending money.

These results may help explain the multi-brand buying pattern so often described in the literature (*cf.* Uncles *et al.*, 1995). These investigations have reported that, for many different products and some services, the majority of consumers of routinely purchased packaged goods show low levels of brand loyalty (e.g., 10%) during, say, one year, and that they usually choose apparently randomly from a subset of brands. "The picture is that people often have one or two favorite brands, but also buy other brands less frequently, but still more or less habitually" (Ehrenberg, 1991, p. 292). The present findings suggest that their choice is not random, for they might buy, every now and then, small quantities of more differentiated brands. This could be interpreted as an attempt to maximize utilitarian and informational benefits, while minimizing costs. Ehrenberg and colleagues have also reported another well replicated finding that seems to support the present interpretation. They have found that, for many different product categories, the brands with the largest market share are also the ones that are the most frequently bought as second choice by customers of other brands (*cf.* Uncles *et al.*, 1995). Considering that the brands with the largest market shares are often the most differentiated brands, which offer the highest levels of informational and/or utilitarian benefits, it would make sense to think that they are the brands bought in small quantities by customers of other brands.

This tendency of small-brand (low quality) buyers to buy small quantities of brands offering high levels of informational and/or utilitarian benefits is also compatible with two other findings frequently reported in the literature. One of these is the phenomenon of "double jeopardy", the tendency of buyers of small market-share brands to be less loyal (e.g., lower buying frequency) to these brands than are buyers of large market-share brands (*cf.* Ehrenberg, 1988; Ehrenberg *et al.*, 1990; Uncles *et al.*, 1995). If buyers of small brands, which offer less informational and utilitarian benefits, also buy small quantities of large brands, one could expect higher average purchase frequencies for the large brands. The second phenomenon is the asymmetrical effect of price promotions, the finding that price promotions of more-differentiated, higher-priced brands attract consumers of less-differentiated brands more so than the reverse (*cf.* Blattberg & Wisniewski, 1989).

It may be worth noting that, rather than a simple re-description of the findings, this supposition is based on a theoretical premise that consumer behavior tend to maximize informational and utilitarian benefits and minimize aversive consequences (e.g., spending money), as proposed by the BPM. According to the explanation advanced here, almost all consumers would prefer, if there were no budget constraints, to buy the brands offering the highest levels of informational and utilitarian benefits. The exception would probably be those consumers for which the programmed "benefits", in the eyes of the brand manager, are not perceived as benefits at all or, at least, are not perceived as worth the money charged for them. These consumers might, for example, prefer one brand over all others, despite all marketing activities designed to change their preferences. Such consumers who are not influenced by the typical promotions may be part of the group of consumers who show 100% of brand loyalty, which do not represent much more than 10% of all consumers of a brand during one year (*cf.* Ehrenberg, 1988).

Although the present investigation was restricted to routinely purchased packaged goods, the type of analysis proposed by the BPM could in principle be applied to any consumer situation. This idea is reinforced by the fact that the buying patterns described by Ehrenberg, which seem compatible with the present results, have been replicated across many different categories of products and services.

Research limitations

Two aspects of the present research may limit the generalization and applicability of its results. The relatively small sample size is one of them. Although the data concerning the purchases of relatively small samples of products and consumers over a relatively short period of time has proved sufficient to identify some general consumer choice patterns, this sample size may hinder the external validity of the findings, particularly to other samples of consumers and other product categories. The replication across nine food categories gives some reliability to the findings but leaves open the question of whether such intra- and inter-brand elasticities would be observed for non-food categories or, even, for other kinds of products (e.g., durables). The small sample size also precluded some further quantitative analyses. For example, due to the small number of consumers and of data points for each consumer, it was not possible to examine if the observed inter-brand elasticities resulted from intra-consumer elasticities, that is, the tendency of the same consumer to buy smaller quantities of brands with higher informational/utilitarian levels, or from inter-consumer elasticities, that is, the tendency of different consumers to buy larger or smaller quantities of lower- or higher-level brands, or from a combination of these two tendencies. Future research should increase the number of consumers and product categories in order to test the external validity of the findings and to clarify such intra- and inter-consumer elasticities.

The second limiting aspect of the research was the obtained level of reliability for the brand classification criteria. Overall, for all product categories, inter-judge agreement was above 70%, whereas for specific categories they were above 60%. These levels are not as high as one would expect, for they mean that there was no agreement in the classification of 30% of all 660 brands, and of as much as 40% of all brands in some product categories. On one hand, this may of course hinder future attempts to replicate the findings and may be pointed out as a serious limitation of the present study. On the other hand, considering that this was the first attempt to operationalize and measure informational and utilitarian benefits offered by different brands, that the results were replicated across nine different product categories and across two split-samples of one category, and that the results show new patterns of consumer choice not previously reported in the literature, this level of reliability may serve as a reference point to be improved by future research efforts.

Managerial implications

The potential managerial implications of these results are intriguing for both retail and brand management provided both sides recognize the significant value of categorizing products and brands into groups of utilitarian, informational and promotional benefits. First, the results can be instrumentalized to help category management at retail level. With the knowledge that price elasticity can be estimated and calculated on the basis of the average category price, the performance of different product categories, the development of their sales levels and other vital market insights can be better understood or even predicted. This can then in turn lead to more effective stock planning and the more effective use of price promotions. Second, the results suggest that price promotions can indeed have an important role in retail and brand management. This finding deviates to some extent from recent literature which has repeatedly criticized the overuse of price promotions (e.g., Ehrenberg et al., 1994). However, despite the controversial after-effects of price promotions, the present results reiterate that promotions tend to have verifiable, positive effects on the quantities bought by consumers. Therefore, brand managers may after all consider including regular promotions in their repertoire of marketing strategies rather than attempting to add utilitarian or even informational benefits to their brands. In this line of argument, it would be more advisable, for instance for a Tesco Value Baked Beans brand manager, to sell the brand below its normal, average price rather than to seek adding value to the product and "lift" it from utilitarian benefit Level 1 to Level 2 if the desired effect was to be increased levels of sales. Conversely, it appears advisable for management to extend brand lines to include brands with low and high utilitarian reinforcement as well as two or three different degrees of informational benefit. In doing so, a greater number of customers, each striving for different levels of differentiated brands, can be catered for, a strategy that increases capacity utilization and promotes the resulting economies of scale.

Correspondingly, on the retail management side, the results imply that it is imperative to have brands of all different utilitarian and informational benefit levels on offer in order to meet customers' needs in their effort to maximize utilitarian and informational benefits and minimize costs at the same time. It is, therefore, essential to understand that two brands with two different utilitarian levels are not likely to obtain the same level of sales in terms of quantity. For example, our data show that plain Heinz Baked Beans sales outperform the sales levels of Heinz Baked Beans and Sausages by far. Similarly, managers ought to recognize that brands classified as informational Level 3, for instance President Cheese, naturally receive lower levels of sales than brands on informational Level 2 or even 1 (e.g., Tesco Finest Cheese or Tesco Value Cheese, respectively). As pointed out before, this is not surprising considering that the examined product categories in this study are fast-moving consumer goods and are therefore somewhat low in social prestige and status. However, it is important to emphasize that sales levels measured in quantity is only one possible parameter to consider. Brand or retail managers may be, for different reasons, rather interested in sales figures in monetary terms, in which case brands on utilitarian Level 2 or informational Level 3 could contribute a larger share to the aspired sales target.

Also at the retail management side, the present results suggest that brands belonging to the same informational/utilitarian group may show higher levels of substitutability among themselves than brands belonging to different groups. Although this is an empirical question that should be tested for each product category, these brand groupings may help managerial decisions concerning stock replacement and supplier renegotiation.

The results also suggest new ways of looking at category elasticity on the grounds that different categories are likely to include different maximization patterns as well as different intra- and inter-brand elasticities. From that point of view it is not differentiated enough to think in terms of only one elasticity coefficient for a whole product category, which exhibits in fact several distinct subcategories in terms of elasticity when looked at more closely, using the proposed measures of this chapter. Furthermore, the intra- and inter-brand elasticity coefficients presented may in practice be interpreted as measures of consumer responsiveness to such attributes. In this sense, the quantity consumers buy changes as a function of changes in such attributes, for example, larger, more negative coefficients indicate higher responsiveness. Consequently, the relative importance of the utilitarian, informational and promotional elasticity coefficients could be identified and evaluated across different product categories. Following from that, management would be in a position to compare the performance of different subgroups across product categories much better than the performance of a whole product group just on its own. This could be particularly valuable in the very competitive fast-moving consumer goods market where profit margins are shrinking and therefore other parameters like the relative achievement of brands or groups of brands are becoming more pressing and significant. Especially brand portfolio managers, responsible for a range of different brands in different product categories, ought to be interested in this tool enabling them to draw comparisons and set realistic targets. For example, propositions like the responsiveness to informational attributes is larger for coffee than for biscuits, whereas brand price appears to be more important for biscuits than for cheese could be made. Based on the distinction of utilitarian, informational and promotional brand benefits, the issue of consumers' price sensitivity has been tackled from a new angle and this can lead to theoretical and managerial insights that previous research has not identified.

Note

1. Previously published in *Service Industries Journal*, 2005, 25, 309–27.

References

Alhadeff, D. A. (1982). *Microeconomics and human behavior: Toward a new synthesis of economics and psychology*. Berkeley, CA: University of California Press.

Bass, F. M. (1993). "The future of research in marketing: marketing science" (JMR 30th anniversary guest editorial). *Journal of Marketing Research*, 30, 1–6.

Bell, D. R., Chiang, J. & Padmanabhan, V. (1999). "The Decomposition of Promotional Response: An Empirical Generalization". *Marketing Science*, 18, 504–26.

Blattberg, R. C. & Wisniewski, K. J. (1989). "Price induced patterns of competition". *Marketing Science*, 8, 291–309.

Bolton, R. N. (1989). "The relationship between market characteristics and promotional price elasticities". *Marketing Science*, 8, 153–69.

Churchill Jr., G. A. (1999). *Marketing Research: Methodological Foundations* 7th edn. Orlando: The Dryden Press.

Crouch, S. & Housden, M. (2003). *Marketing Research for Managers* 3rd edn. Oxford: Butterworth-Heinemann.

Diamantopoulos, A. (2003). "Pricing", in M. J. Baker (ed.) *The Marketing Book*, 5th edn. Oxford: Butterworth-Heinemann.

Ehrenberg, A. S. C. (1972). *Repeat-buying: Theory and applications*. London: North-Holland Publishing Company. (Second edition 1988).

Ehrenberg, A. S. C. (1988). *Repeat Buying: Facts, Theory and Applications*, 2nd edn. London: Edward Arnold, New York: Oxford University Press.

Ehrenberg, A. S. C. (1991). "New brands and the existing market". *Journal of the Market Research Society*, 33, 285–99.

Ehrenberg, A. S. C., Goodhardt, G. J. & Barwise, T. P. (1990). "Double jeopardy revisited". *Journal of Marketing*, 54, 82–91.

Ehrenberg, A. S. C., Hammond, K. & Goodhardt, G. J. (1994). "The After-effects of price-related consumer promotions". *Journal of Advertising Research*, 34 (July/August), pp. 11–21.

Fader, P. S. & Lodish, L. M. (1990). "A cross-category analysis of category structure and promotional activity for grocery products". *Journal of Marketing*, 54, 52–65.

Foxall, G. R. (1990). *Consumer Psychology in Behavioural Perspective*. London and New York: Routledge.

Foxall, G. R. (1992). "The Behavioral Perspective Model of purchase and consumption: from consumer theory to marketing practice". *Journal of the Academy of Marketing Science*, 20, 189–98.

Guadagni, P. M. & Little, J. D. C. (1983). "A logit model of brand choice calibrated on scanner data". *Marketing Science*, 2, 203–38.

Gupta, S. (1988). "The impact of sales promotions on when, what, and how much to buy". *Journal of Marketing Research*, 25, 342–55.

Hoch, S. J., Kim, B. D., Montgomery, A. J. & Rossie, P. E. (1995). "Determinants of store-level price elasticity". *Journal of Marketing Research*, 32, 17–29.

Kagel, J. H., Battalio, R. C. & Green, L. (1995). *Economic Choice Theory: An Experimental Analysis of Animal Behavior*. Cambridge: Cambridge University Press.

Krishnamurti, L. & Raj, S. P. (1988). "A Model of Brand Choice and Purchase Quantity Price Sensitivities". *Marketing Science*, 7, 1–20.

Kvanli, A. H., Guynes, C. S. & Pavur, R. J. (1996). *Introduction to Business Statistics* 4th edn. New York: West Publishing Company.

Lechene, V. (2000). National Food Survey, Section 6. Institute of Fiscal Studies Working Papers (www.ifs.org.uk). London: Institute of Fiscal Studies, pp. 89–108.

Narasimhan, C., Neslin, S. A. & Sen, S. K. (1996). "Promotional elasticities and category characteristics". *Journal of Marketing*, 60, 17–30.

Telser, L. G. (1962). "The demand for branded goods as estimated from consumer panel data". *The Review of Economics and Statistics*, 44, 300–24.

Uncles, M., Ehrenberg, A. S. C. & Hammond, K. (1995). "Patterns of Buyer Behavior: Regularities, Models, and Extensions". *Marketing Science*, 14, G71–G78.

Walters, R. G. & Bommer, W. (1996). "Measuring the impact of the product and promotion-related factors on product category price elasticities". *Journal of Business Research*, 36, 203–16.

Appendix A: examples of the attributes used to classify levels 1 and 2 of utilitarian benefit

Baked beans: Level 1 – plain; Level 2 – with sausages, low-sugar, diet, all day breakfast, or meal. *Biscuits*: Level 1 – digestive, rich tea, cream cracker, ginger, jam/cream filled, sweet, coconut nice; Level 2 – shortcake, reduced-fat digestive, chocolate-chip digestive, cookie, sesame cracker, fig roll, jaffa cake, chocolate digestive, chocolate-rich tea, wafers/fingers, caramel, teacake, mini cheddar, biscuits with special shapes (e.g., animals), special packages (e.g., snack packs). *Breakfast Cereals*: Level 1 – porridge, muesli, cornflakes; Level 2 – wheat biscuits, fruit and fiber, honey/frosted/chocolate cornflakes, bran cereal, rice cereal, specially shaped or thematic cereals. *Butter*: Level 1 – plain butter; Level 2 – spreadable or creamery. *Cheese*: (many data points from purchases of "random weight" packages were discarded) Level 1 – plain, processed, plain light; Level 2 – cheese spread, organic, special packages (e.g., snacks or lunchables, some containing biscuits). *Fruit Juice*: Level 1 – plain pure juice; Level 2 – juice drink, organic juice, reduced calories. *Instant Coffee*: Level 1 – plain instant coffee; Level 2 – decaffeinated, cappuccino, special blends (e.g., gold). *Margarine*: Level 1 – plain soft margarine, sunflower spread, reduced fat spread; Level 2 – olive margarine, soy margarine, organic, baking margarine. *Tea*: Level 1 – plain bags, green label bags; Level 2 – red label bags, specialty/flavor bags, decaffeinated.

Appendix B: examples of brands classified in different informational levels for each product category

Baked beans: Level 1 – Sainsbury Economy, Morrisons Bettabuy, Tesco Value, Asda Smart Price; Level 2 – Aldi, Tesco Standard, Sainsbury Standard, Asda Healthy Choice, Morrisons; Level 3 – H. P. Standard, Heinz, WeightWatchers. *Biscuits*: Level 1 – Tesco Value, Sainsbury Economy, Somerfield Basics, Morrisons Bettabuy, Asda Smart Price; Level 2 – Sainsbury, Burtons, Somerfield, McVities, Asda, Safeway, Tesco, Morrisons, Co-op, Jacobs, Crawfords; Level 3 – Cadburys, Foxs, Hellema, Ritz, Nabisco, St Michael, Boulevard. *Breakfast Cereals*: Level 1 – Tesco Value, Somerfield Basics, Asda Farm Stores/Smart Price, Sainsbury Economy; Level 2 – Tesco, Asda, Somerfield, Sainsbury, Marshalls, Cheshire, Scotts, Co-op, Morrisons; Level 3 – Weetabix, Kelloggs, Jordans, Quaker, Nestle. *Butter*: Level 1 – Asda Smart Price, Tesco Value, Hollybush, Acorn, St Ivel; Level 2 – Anchor, Asda, Tesco, Kerrygold, Olivio, Country Life; Level 3 – Lurpak, President, Wheelbarrow. *Cheese*: Level 1 – Anchor, Asda Smart Price, Best Ever, Lidl, Longley, Safeway Savers, Tesco Value; Level 2 – Asda, Tesco, Sainsbury, Morrisons, Somerfield, Safeway, Crackerbarrel, Dairylea, Primula, Golden, Iceland, Hochland, Horlicks, Arla, Laughing Cow; Level 3 – Benecol, Philadelphia, President, St Ivel, Kerrygold, Pilgrims, Babybel, Boursin, Buitoni, Kraft, store brand. *Fruit Juice*: Level 1 – Sainsbury Economy, Tesco Value, Morrisons Bettabuy, Somerfield Basics, Asda Smart Price, Safeway Savers, Lidl; Level 2 – Tesco, Sainsbury, Asda, Safeway, Morrisons, Sunny Delight, St Ivel; Level 3 – Del Monte, Ribena, Ocean Spray, Waitrose, Tropicana, St Michael. *Coffee*: Level 1 – Asda Smart Price, Sainsbury Economy, Everyday, Tesco

Classic; Level 2 – Kenco Standard, Maxwell House, Sainsbury, Asda, Nescafe Fine Blend; Level 3 – Nescafe (e.g., Original, Gold), Kenco (e.g., Really Rich), Grandos Cappucino. *Margarine*: Level 1 – Asda Smart Price, Safeway Savers, Somerfield Basics, Tesco Value, Morrisons Bettabuy; Level 2 – Asda, Co-op, Lidl, Morrisons, Sainsbury, Stork, Tesco, ICBINB, Safeway, Vitalite; Level 3 – Anchor, Benecol, Clover, Flora, Golden, Carapelli, Olivio, St Ivel. *Tea*: Level 1 – Morrisons, Asda, Tesco, Sainsbury, Co-op, Somerfield; Level 2 – Typhoo, Lift, Lyons, Tetley; Level 3 – Yorkshire, P.G. Tips, Twinings, store brand, Brooke Bond.

8
Dynamics of Repeat-Buying for Packaged Food Products[1]

Jorge M. Oliveira-Castro, Diogo C. S. Ferreira, Gordon R. Foxall and Teresa C. Schrezenmaier

Knowledge of consumers' patterns of brand choice is crucial to well-grounded managerial decisions. From the point of view of brand manufacturers, the success of positioning strategies involving pricing, promotions and innovations, is more probable when they are based on information about which brands consumers buy, how often they buy them, and how loyal they are to them. Such information is also relevant to retailers, when they make decisions about brand assortment, type and frequency of promotion, and stock replacement. There is no doubt that the marketing strategies of many effective manufacturers and distributors are already based firmly on information of this kind. The aim of this chapter is to show how knowledge of the dynamics of consumers' brand choice behavior, and therefore marketing responses, may be further improved.

Consumers' patterns of brand choice have been extensively investigated in marketing, especially for purchases of fast-moving consumer goods, for which data are available from consumer panels maintained by commercial firms. This literature shows that most consumers buy several brands of a product category during a year and comparatively few of them are exclusive buyers each of the brands that comprise the category. Moreover, as the time period selected for analysis increases, the penetration level of each brand increases and the number of exclusive buyers decreases (e.g., Ehrenberg *et al.*, in press). Recent research has also found that consumers tend to choose the cheapest brand out of a particular consideration set of brands, and that the brands that make up their consideration set have similar levels of differentiation (Foxall *et al.*, 2004). In such research, the measure of brand differentiation was based on distinctions suggested by the Behavioral Perspective Model (Foxall, 1997, 1998, 2004/1990, 2005) and involved methodological initiatives derived from experimental behavioral economics (e.g. Kagel *et al.*, 1995).

Bringing together these two lines of enquiry, the present research investigates the dynamics of successive repeat-buying and penetration level of groups of brands belonging to similar levels of brand differentiation. In order to do this, the probability of buying brands belonging to the same level of differentiation, on successive shopping occasions, was examined. In view of the finding that the number of exclusive buyers of a particular brand decreases with increases in the time period chosen for analysis, and on the understanding that finding may be extensible to groups of brands, one would expect a decrease in the probability of sequential repeat-buying of brands belonging to the same level of brand differentiation with increases in the number of successive shopping occasions. The same kind of analysis was adopted to examine the penetration level of groups of similar brands, which one would expect to increase with increases in the time chosen for analysis. By graphing both these curves, two equations are proposed to describe the dynamics of repeat-buying for groups of brands. These equations are then applied to the description of the dynamics of repeat-buying and penetration level of particular brands. The results suggest several possible managerial applications, such as the estimation of the proportion of sequential repeat buyers and non-repeat buyers during the product shopping cycle.

Patterns of brand choice

Some characteristics of consumers' brand choice have been well documented in the marketing literature. Research based on panel data has shown that most individuals purchasing fast-moving consumer goods buy several brands within a product category over a period of one year, comparatively few of whom are exclusive buyers of one single brand. As the period of time chosen for analysis increases, for example from four to 54 weeks, the penetration levels of brands increase while the number of sole buyers of each brand decreases. The brands bought are usually chosen from a repertoire of three or more brands, which is different for different consumers (otherwise there would be only three or four brands surviving within each product category). In the overall product category, brands may differ widely with respect to penetration level but only slightly in terms of purchase frequency. Such results also show that brands with smaller penetration levels tend to be bought by their customers less frequently than brands with larger penetrations (i.e., "double jeopardy", Ehrenberg *et al.*, 1990). These patterns have been observed for some 30 food and drink products (from cookies to beer), 20 cleaning and personal care products (from cosmetics to heavy cleaning liquids), gasoline, aviation fuel, automobiles, some medicines and pharmaceutical prescriptions, television channels and shows, shopping trips, store chains, individual stores, and attitudes toward brands (*cf.* Dall'Olmo Riley *et al.*, 1997; Ehrenberg, 1972/1988; Ehrenberg *et al.*, 1990; Ehrenberg & Scriven, 1999; Ehrenberg *et al.*, in press; Goodhardt *et al.*, 1984; Uncles *et al.*, 1995). A mathematical model has also been developed to describe such regularities, the Dirichlet Model (e.g., Ehrenberg *et al.*, 1990), which has been used to predict the market insertion of new products (Ehrenberg, 1993), to analyze the effects of promotions (Ehrenberg, 1986; Ehrenberg *et al.*, 1994), and to evaluate patterns of store loyalty (Ehrenberg & England, 1990; Keng & Ehrenberg, 1984; Sharp & Sharp, 1997; Uncles & Ehrenberg, 1990).

The relevance of this literature is to demonstrate that different measures of brand performance (penetration, loyalty, buying frequency, purchase duplication) tend to vary together showing regular buying patterns. In addition to this, the primary determinant of these patterns seems to be the penetration level of the brand: that is, purchase frequency, attitude toward the brand (i.e., its evaluative attributes), and perception of differentiation all seem to be a consequence of how many people buy the brand rather than any brand characteristics (Dall'Olmo Riley *et al.*, 1997; Ehrenberg *et al.*, in press; Romaniuk *et al.*, 2004; Scriven & Ehrenberg, 2003; *cf.*).

However, despite these widely replicated results, this line of research has not identified the variables that influence consumers' selection of brand repertoires (i.e., their consideration set of brands), nor the variables that influence their brand choices within their brand repertoires, from one shopping occasion to the next. In fact, some authors have stated that, on each shopping occasion, consumers' choice of a particular brand within their consideration set is apparently random or can be assumed, for pragmatic purposes, to be so (Ehrenberg, 1972/1988; Ehrenberg *et al.*, in press).

The composition of consumers' consideration sets

Recent research on consumer brand choice has shown that consumers tend to buy the cheapest brand within their consideration set (or "repertoire"), rather than the cheapest of all brands available in the product category (Foxall & James, 2001, 2003; Foxall & Schrezenmaier, 2003; Foxall et al., 2004). This suggests that not all brands are perfect substitutes for the others. Although brands of fast-moving consumer goods may have similar physical formulations, consumers are not indifferent to the particular brands they buy. Their choices reflect more than the functional utility of what they purchase, embracing in addition marketing considerations that seek to differentiate brands.

This additional source of utility, arising from the branding or brand differentiation activities of firms, has not been precisely defined or quantified. A theoretically consistent way of interpreting this distinction between functional attributes and branding can be found in the Behavioral Perspective Model (BPM) of consumer choice (Foxall, 2004/1990). Research based on this model has been able to shed some light on the variables that influence consumers' choice of consideration set. This model proposes that consumer behavior produces both utilitarian benefits and informational benefits, and these consequences influence the rate at which the behavior have produced them is repeated. Utilitarian benefits are functional results of buying and using products and services: they derive from the practical application of the product itself in some consumption situation. They therefore reflect the value-in-use of a product or service, the economic, pragmatic or material satisfaction derived from acquiring, owning, and using it. Informational benefit, however, is socially-derived and symbolic, depending above all on the actions and reactions of other people. It may consist of feedback on the performance of the individual as a consumer. Thus, while utilitarian benefit is related to the technical benefits of products or services, informational benefit is related to considerations of the social status and prestige. For instance, the utilitarian benefit of an extended holiday in an exotic location is the rest, relaxation and recuperation it provides, whereas the informational benefit derives from the personal feelings of satisfaction, self-esteem and prestige conferred by knowing that one can afford this kind of recreation and communicating the fact to one's friends.

On the basis of these distinctions and using consumer panel data, Foxall et al. (2004) classified all brands of supermarket food categories into levels of informational and utilitarian benefits. The brands in each product category were ranked according to a two-point scale of programmed utilitarian benefits, which was based on the analysis of product attributes. Additional attributes or more sophisticated formulations, such as plain baked beans *versus* baked beans with sausages or rich tea *versus* chocolate-cookie biscuits, for which all brands charge higher prices, were indicative of higher levels of utilitarian benefits. The brands were also ranked according to a three-point scale of programmed informational benefits, which was based on an analysis of brand positioning, such as good-value-for-money own brands (e.g., Asda Smart Price or Tesco Value), higher-level own (e.g., Asda or Tesco) and lower-level national brands, and higher-level national brands (e.g., Kelloggs or Heinz). Brand average prices were considered in distinguishing lower- and higher-level national brands.

Their major finding, concerning consumers' consideration set of brands, was that the majority of consumers made 70% or more of their purchases within the group of brands classified at the same level of informational benefit. Similar patterns were observed with respect to utilitarian brand level, i.e., the majority of consumers bought 70% or more of products belonging to the same utilitarian level. These results suggest that consumers' consideration sets of brands are related to the level of benefits offered by the brands, which, in turn, may be related to other variables such as income level.

Dynamics of repeat-buying

Considering that most consumers make most of their purchases within brands at the same level of informational benefit, it would be relevant to know whether and how they keep buying brands at the same level on successive shopping occasions. This would amount to the investigation of consumers' loyalty (conceived as repeat-buying) to groups of similar brands across time. In view of the finding that the number of exclusive buyers of a brand decreases with increases in the time period chosen for analysis, one would also expect a decrease of repeat-buying of groups of brands as the number of successive shopping occasion increases. Hence,

Hypothesis 1: the probability of successive repeat-buying a group of brands, belonging to the same level of differentiation, should decrease as the number of shopping occasions increases.

This analysis of sequential repeat-buying within each informational benefit level can yield relevant information concerning the dynamics of brand choice across time. It could show, for example, the proportion of total sales of a group of brands that are associated to sequential repeat-buying and to non-sequential buying, at any point in time during the product shopping cycle. In 1972, referring to the decrease in the percentage of sole buyers of a brand with increases in time, Ehrenberg asserted that "it is not yet fully known how to describe or model or predict the quantitative rate of its decrease" (p. 211). To the best of our knowledge, this has not yet been done for either particular brands or groups of brands.

Therefore, it was a central aim of the present study to investigate the rate of decrease of repeat-buying of brands within groups of brands belonging to different informational levels. In order to do so, brands from eight supermarket food categories, which appeared as having been bought, at least once, in a data set obtained from a consumer panel, were classified according to three levels of informational benefits, using the same criteria adopted by Foxall *et al.* (2004). The probability of repeat-buying was calculated, for each of the three groups of brands with different informational level, across successive shopping occasions. Considering previous results in the literature that indicate that the penetration level of a brand is the primary determinant of its purchase frequency in the category, of consumers' attitude toward the brand and of their perception of brand differentiation, the following hypotheses was tested in the present study. Hence, since the amount of sales due to successive repeat-buying across shopping occasions is influenced primarily by the penetration level of brands or groups of brands,

Hypothesis 2: higher penetrations should be related to higher sales due to sequential repeat-buying.

The same literature that reports decreases in the number of sole buyers of a brand with increases in the time period chosen for analysis also shows that the penetration level of brands increases with increases in the time period chosen for analysis. Considering, moreover, that in steady markets the penetration level of brands remains relatively constant (e.g., Ehrenberg *et al.*, in press), one would expect to observe, simultaneously to the decrease in sequential repeat-buying hypothesized above, an increase in the penetration level of groups of brands. For example, as exclusive buyers of Level-3 brands purchase brands from other brand groups, repeat-buying probability for Level 3 decreases, while the number of non-sequential buyers of Level 3 should increase. Analogously to the measures of sequential repeat-buying, the probability of non-repeat buyers buying a brand belonging to a particular informational level (i.e., penetration) was calculated, for each of the three groups of brands, across successive shopping occasions. Hence,

> Hypothesis 3: *the probability of non-sequential buying of a group of brands (i.e., penetration level) should increase as the number of shopping occasions increases.*

With the purpose of testing the generalization of the findings to specific and generic brands (rather than groups of brands), the same analyses were conducted for individual brands. This led to our final hypothesis:

> Hypothesis 4: *patterns of decrease in successive repeat-buying and of increase in non-sequential buying, with increases in successive shopping occasions, should be similar for groups of brands and for specific brands.*

Method

Sampling and procedure

The TNS (Taylor-Nelson Sofres) "Superpanel" consists of 15,000 British households and provides data on a range of consumer goods. From this panel, we obtained a subsample of 80 of the voluntary participant members, chosen randomly (i.e., not so as to be geographically or otherwise representative), who had purchased within each of the product categories at least four times over the duration of the investigation. The panel operates as follows. Purchased items are scanned by panel members using a sophisticated handheld barcode reader after each shopping trip, after which data are sent electronically to TNS for central processing. Weekly purchases of eight product categories (i.e., baked beans, biscuits, breakfast cereals, cheese, fruit juice, instant coffee, margarine, and tea) over a 16-week time span were obtained. For each purchase by a member of our subsample, we obtained information on brand specification (i.e., different versions of the same product category were classified as different brands, e.g., Corn Flakes and Rice Krispies by Kelloggs), package size, shop, date, number of units, and total amount spent.

Brand classification

In order to investigate repeat-buying for groups of brands offering different levels of utilitarian and informational benefit, the criteria used by Foxall *et al.* (2004) were adopted to classify all brands in all product categories. These criteria and the measures of utilitarian and informational benefit which were based upon them, and which were summarized in the Introduction, are further elaborated and evaluated in Oliveira-Castro *et al.*, 2005).

Analysis

Considering that the present data set included only data from consumers who bought four or more times within each product category, it was possible to examine the probability of buying brands at the same informational level over four consecutive shopping occasions for each. The probability for the first shopping occasion was calculated by dividing the number of consumers that bought, on their first shopping trip recorded in our sample, brands at each informational level by the total number of consumers that bought four or more times the product category. On the first shopping occasion, this measure is similar to a percentage of penetration of brands at each informational level. It does differ from usual measures of penetration based on the fact that it was calculated across shopping occasions which did not necessarily occurred in the same week. The probabilities of buying brands at the same informational level on the second, third, and fourth shopping occasions were analogously calculated, by dividing the number of consumers that kept buying brands at the same informational level on successive shopping trips by the total number of consumers in the product category. When consumers bought more than one brand on the same shopping occasion, both brands were considered in the analyses. Then, for example, if the consumer on the second shopping occasion bought two different brands belonging to the same informational level of the brand bought on the first shopping occasion, this episode counted as two occurrences of repeat-buying on the second shopping occasion.

Results

Sequential repeat-buying

Figure 8.1 shows the probability of repeat-buying brands (i.e., solid lines with black circles) at each informational reinforcement level as a function of consecutive shopping occasions, for each product category. As can be seen in the figure, probabilities decreased with increases in shopping occasions for all informational levels and all product categories, except for Informational Level 1 for biscuits and margarine.

Within each product category, the probability for each informational level shows, for the large majority of cases, a similarly-shaped, negatively-accelerated decreasing function. These results corroborate Hypothesis 1, which states that *the probability of successive repeat-buying a group of brands, belonging to the same level of differentiation, should decrease as the number of shopping occasions increases.*

Comparisons of the curves obtained for different informational levels within each product category (i.e., comparing adjacent graphs) reveal, in general, two different patterns of curves. The first of these shows the highest probability curve for brands at Level 2 of informational reinforcement, followed by the probability curve for Level 1, in the middle, and Level 3, at the bottom of the graph. This occurred for fruit juice, biscuits and cheese. The other pattern shows in a descending order curves for Level 3, Level 2, and, then Level 1. This was observed for tea, cereals, margarine and coffee. The pattern observed for baked beans was a little different, showing in descending order curves for Level 3, Level 1, and then Level 2. These patterns suggest that the height of the curves were related to the penetration level of each brand group, which would be compatible with interpreting the probability on the first shopping occasion as a measure of penetration level. As the probability curves have similar shapes (i.e., with few exceptions they would not intersect), these patterns could be expected. The results also suggest that the level of penetration of each informational level seems to be the major determinant of the positioning of the probability curve in relation to the others, that is, the larger the penetration level the higher the probability curve depicted in the figure.

However, this basic finding can be elaborated. Additional information, related to the rate of decrease in the probability of repeat-buying brands within the same informational level, can be extracted from the analysis summarized in Figure 8.1. The similar and "parallel" curves observed in the figure suggest that despite the wide differences in penetration levels, that is, the height of the curves in the graph, the decrease in probability across informational levels may be described by the same function. Some desirable characteristics for such a function would be the following: (1) It should describe negatively accelerated decreases; (2) When shopping occasion is equal to one (i.e., the first shopping occasion), it should return a value of probability similar to penetration level; (3) It should allow for the value of probability to be equal to zero, for it does in fact reach such value; and (4) It should make possible to estimate the shopping occasion on which repeat-buying probability is equal to zero, even if it is not within the range of observed shopping occasions. One candidate to describe this type of data is a semi-logarithmic function such as the following:

Repeat Probability = P − R (log Shopping Occasion)   (8.1)

where P and R are empirically derived parameters that give estimates of the probability of purchasing brands at a particular informational level on the first shopping occasion and the rate of decrease in repeat-buying probability across shopping occasions, respectively. Lower values of R (absolute value) would be associated with lower rates of decrease in repeat-buying probability. Equation 8.1 also makes possible the estimation of the shopping occasion on which repeat-buying probability is equal to zero (Z), which is given by $10^{P/R}$.

Using the data shown in Figure 8.1, Equation 8.1 parameters, P and R were calculated for each informational level of each product category, which are presented in Table 8.1. As can be seen in the table, average determination coefficients (r^2) were equal to .81 (SD = .28), .94 (SD = .05), and .93 (SD = .05) for Informational Levels 1, 2 and 3, respectively, indicating that the equation adequately fitted the data. The smaller values of r^2 observed for Informational Level 1 may be related to the smaller number of data points used to calculate such functions, which, in turn, were associated to the lower penetration levels of Level-1 brands. Values of R varied from −.04 to 0.80 across all informational levels and products, and showed an increase, on average, with increases in informational levels (Level 1 = .20, SD = .15; Level 2 = .38, SD = .24; Level 3 = .41, SD = .19). Twenty out of 24 values of R were three times or more the size of their standard errors. The only negative value of R (i.e., positive slope) was observed for margarine (Level 1), and was derived from a non-significant regression analyses. It was interpreted as an exception, probably related to a small number of data points used to calculate the equation.

Values of P varied from 0.03 to 0.75 across all informational levels and products, and also showed an increase, in average, with increases in informational levels (Level 1 = .19, SD = .13; Level 2 = .35, SD = .18; Level 3 = .43, SD = .23). In order to examine the relation between P and penetration level, the level of penetration of each informational level of each product was calculated for each of the four four-week periods of the sample. The average penetration proportion of each informational level for each product was then calculated across four-week periods. The correlation (Pearson) between this average penetration level and P was significant and equal to .68 (N = 23, p < .000). With the

Table 8.1 Equation 8.1 parameters for the brand groups classified at each informational level and for all product categories (See text for details).

Product	Info level	r^2	R	Stand. Error	P	Z
Juice	1	0.98	0.23	0.03	0.31	21.76
Cheese	1	0.96	0.31	0.04	0.23	5.52
Margarine	1	0.21	−0.04	0.05	0.03	0.15
Coffee	1	0.78	0.08	0.03	0.09	11.79
Biscuits	1	–	–	–	–	–
Tea	1	0.97	0.34	0.04	0.30	7.54
Baked beans	1	0.95	0.34	0.05	0.33	9.28
Cereals	1	0.83	0.11	0.04	0.06	3.43
Juice	2	0.95	0.30	0.05	0.42	24.03
Cheese	2	0.95	0.71	0.11	0.53	5.68
Margarine	2	0.84	0.32	0.10	0.39	15.94
Coffee	2	0.89	0.15	0.04	0.20	23.30
Biscuits	2	1.00	0.80	0.01	0.62	5.97
Tea	2	0.96	0.39	0.06	0.37	8.93
Baked beans	2	0.95	0.16	0.03	0.09	3.57
Cereals	2	1.00	0.22	0.01	0.18	13.35
Juice	3	0.98	0.29	0.03	0.24	6.80
Cheese	3	0.87	0.27	0.07	0.19	5.17
Margarine	3	0.83	0.58	0.19	0.57	9.31
Coffee	3	0.95	0.58	0.10	0.68	14.58
Biscuits	3	0.96	0.27	0.04	0.18	4.54
Tea	3	0.89	0.16	0.04	0.31	86.60
Baked beans	3	0.97	0.45	0.06	0.56	17.22
Cereals	3	0.96	0.67	0.09	0.75	7.02
Kelloggs Corn.		0.99	1.05	0.09	0.09	1.22
Kelloggs brand		0.96	1.00	0.15	0.23	1.70
Nescafe Original		1.00	1.09	0.04	0.30	3.93
Nescafe brand		0.89	0.66	0.16	0.65	28.97
Heinz Bkd Beans		0.96	0.52	0.08	0.34	4.56

purpose of testing whether average penetration ($M = .34$; $SD = .17$) differed statistically from P ($M = .33$; $SD = .20$), a paired-samples t-test was conducted. The results indicated that these two measures did not differ significantly ($t = .18$; $p = .86$).

The other relevant measure that can be estimated from Equation 8.1 is the shopping occasion on which the probability of sequential repeat-buying is equal to zero (Z), that is, when all consumers buying a given group of brands, during a shopping cycle, have stopped buying it at least on one shopping occasion. The values of Z ranged from 0.15 to 86.60 ($M = 13.54$; $SD = 17.23$) across all informational levels and products, and also showed an increase, on average, with increases in informational levels (Level 1 = 8.49, SD = 6.98; Level 2 = 11.81, SD = 8.19; Level 3 = 19.70, SD = 27.42). The parameter Z can be interpreted as a measure of what might be called a *loyalty shopping cycle*, that is, the number of shopping occasions during which the probability of sequential repeat-buying remains above zero. The loyalty shopping cycle would have to be calculated for each brand group (or brand).

The observed decreases in all three measures (P, R, Z) with increases in informational level suggest that they might be positively correlated. Correlation coefficients, relating these measures across all informational levels and products, indicated that P and R were significantly and positively correlated (r_{pr} = .91; p < .000) and were not significantly correlated to Z (r_{pz} = .12; p = .600; r_{rz} = –.14; p = .522). These results suggest that as P, which seems to be associated to penetration level, increases, the rate of decrease of repeat-buying probability (R) also increases, although none of these measures seems related to the number of shopping occasions on which probability is equal to zero (Z).

Another compound measure that might be useful in describing the dynamic properties of repeat-buying is the area of the function, which can be obtained by (P*Z)/2. The area of the function can be interpreted as the sum of penetration level (in proportions rather than percentages) due to successive repeat-buying across all shopping occasions of a loyalty shopping cycle, that is, from the first shopping occasion to the shopping occasion on which probability of sequential repeat-buying is equal to zero (Z). If these values are multiplied by the number of consumers that buy the product category and the average pack size purchased, one can estimate the total amount of sales of a given brand group, during a complete loyalty cycle, that are due to sequential repeat-buying. This value should be half the total number of purchases for a given brand group during a loyalty cycle, that is, (P * Z)* (number of consumers buying the product). The values of area ranged from 0.00 to 13.42 across all informational levels and products, and also showed larger values with increases in informational level of the brands ((Level 1 = 1.05, SD = 1.17; Level 2 = 2.03, SD = 1.51; Level 3 = 4.07, SD = 4.28). The only value of area equal to zero was related to the only positive value of slope, already mentioned above (i.e., margarine, Level 1). Correlation analyses indicated that the values of area were positively correlated to the values of P (r = .91; p < .000) and R (r = .44; p = .038). The high correlation coefficient observed between P and area corroborates Hypothesis 2, which asserts that *higher penetrations should be related to higher amounts of sales*.

Non-sequential buying across shopping occasions

As mentioned previously, as the probability of successive repeat-buying decreases with increases in shopping occasion, the probability of non-sequential buying should increase as shopping occasions increase. In order to examine such possible increases, the probability of non-sequential buyers purchasing a brand at a certain informational level was calculated for each of the first four shopping occasions, for each informational level of each product. On the first shopping occasion the number of non-sequential buyers was equal to zero because all buyers of a brand group, for example, Level 3, were potential sequential repeat buyers for that brand group. From the second shopping occasion onwards, this number could be different than zero, for consumers that bought on their first shopping occasion brands belonging to Levels 2 and 1 could purchase a Level-3 brand. In other words, the type of analysis adopted here requires a starting point, which was defined as the first shopping occasion in the sample. On the third and fourth shopping occasions, consumers that had bought brands belonging to a certain level (e.g., Level 3) but did not do so on all occasions (i.e., on the first and second) could purchase it (Level 3) again. These were included in the number of non-sequential buyers. Then, for example, if a given consumer bought a Level-3 brand on the first shopping occasion, a Level-2 brand on the second occasion, and again a Level-3 brand on the third, these data would be included in sequential buying for Level 3 on the first shopping occasion, in non-sequential buying for Level 2 on the second occasion, and in non-sequential buying for Level 3 on the third occasion.

Figure 8.1 shows the probability of non-sequential buying brands (i.e., dashed lines with white circles) at each informational reinforcement level as a function of consecutive shopping occasions, for each product. In all cases, this probability tended to increase as the number of shopping occasions increases, suggesting a negatively-accelerated function. The similar shapes of the curves across informational levels and products suggest the possibility of describing them with a single equation. The following equation, which is almost a mirrored image of Equation 8.1, was chosen to describe such increases:

$$\text{Non-Sequential Probability} = J + K (\log \text{Shopping Occasion}) \quad (8.2)$$

where J and K are empirically obtained parameters, that can be interpreted as the estimated probability of non-sequential repeat-buying on the first shopping occasion of the period selected for analysis and the estimated rate of increase of non-sequential buying, respectively.

The parameters of Equation 8.2 were calculated for each informational level and each product, which are shown on Table 8.2. Average determination coefficients (r^2) were equal to .82 (SD = .17), .77 (SD = .25), and .78 (SD = .24) for Informational Levels 1, 2 and 3, respectively, indicating that the equation fitted reasonably well with the data. The values of K varied from 0.08 to 0.63 across all informational levels and products, and tended to increase, in average, with increases in informational levels (Level 1 = .20, SD = .09; Level 2 = .36, SD = .18;

Table 8.2 Equation 8.2 parameters for the brand groups classified at each informational level and for all product categories (See text for details).

Product	Info level	r^2	K	Stand. Error	J	Pi
Juice	1	0.78	0.08	0.03	0.01	.12
Cheese	1	0.55	0.25	0.16	0.03	.22
Margarine	1	0.78	0.10	0.04	0.01	−.08
Coffee	1	0.55	0.14	0.09	0.02	.16
Biscuits	1	0.96	0.36	0.05	0.00	–
Tea	1	0.93	0.19	0.04	0.01	.18
Baked beans	1	0.96	0.27	0.04	0.01	.27
Cereals	1	0.87	0.18	0.05	0.01	.11
Juice	2	0.88	0.38	0.10	0.02	.54
Cheese	2	0.96	0.55	0.08	−0.02	.40
Margarine	2	0.96	0.39	0.06	0.02	.48
Coffee	2	0.57	0.28	0.17	0.04	.42
Biscuits	2	0.97	0.63	0.07	0.01	.50
Tea	2	0.64	0.19	0.10	−0.02	.16
Baked beans	2	0.24	0.09	0.12	0.01	.06
Cereals	2	0.97	0.42	0.05	−0.01	.54
Juice	3	0.72	0.10	0.04	0.01	.09
Cheese	3	0.70	0.27	0.12	0.02	.21
Margarine	3	0.98	0.42	0.05	−0.01	.40
Coffee	3	0.96	0.24	0.04	−0.01	.27
Biscuits	3	0.84	0.41	0.13	−0.02	.25
Tea	3	0.76	0.22	0.09	0.01	.44
Baked beans	3	0.99	0.52	0.03	−0.01	.64
Cereals	3	0.83	0.45	0.15	0.03	.34
Kelloggs Corn.		0.92	7.58	1.58	0.14	
Kelloggs brand		0.96	1.22	0.17	−0.05	
Nescafe Original		0.97	0.85	0.1	0.02	
Nescafe brand		0.96	0.59	0.09	0.00	
Heinz Bkd Beans		0.74	0.15	0.06	−0.01	

Level 3 = .33, SD = .14. Sixteen values of K were three times or more the size of their standard errors. The fact that all values of K were positive corroborates Hypothesis 3, which asserts that *the probability of non-sequential buying a group of brands (i.e., penetration level) should increase as the number of shopping occasions increases.*

Values of J (significant regressions) varied from −.02 to 0.04 across all informational levels and products. Although its average value was very close to zero (M = .007; SD = .02), a t-test indicated that it was slightly larger than zero (t = 2.09; p = .048).

Sequential and non-sequential buying probabilities

By definition, the penetration level of a group of brands (or brand) at any given point in time is made up of sequential repeat buyers and non-sequential buyers. Figure 8.1 illustrates the dynamics of these two measures across shopping occasions, indicating that while the probability of sequential repeat-buying decreases, the probability of non-sequential buying increases in similar proportion. Taken together, Equations 8.1 and 8.2 can be used to estimate the proportions of the penetration level associated to sequential and non-sequential buying, at any point in time during a loyalty shopping cycle. If it is assumed that penetration level of a group of brands remains relatively constant across weeks, a reasonable assumption in steady markets (*cf.* Ehrenberg, 1972/1988), one would expect some systematic relations among the parameters of Equations 8.1 and 8.2.

One of these is the prediction that the rate of decrease in sequential buying probability should be similar to the rate of increase in non-sequential buying probability (assuming also that J is equal to zero on the first shopping occasion, which, for practical purposes, seems to be a reasonable assumption). This is to say that R and K should be very similar. A correlation analysis and a paired-samples t-test indicated that R (M = .34; SD = .21) and K (M = .29; SD = .16) were positively and significantly correlated (r = .72, N = 23; p < .000), and that their means were not statistically different (t = −1.36; p = .19).

Another prediction is that when the probability of sequential buying is equal to zero (i.e., shopping occasion equal to Z or $10^{P/R}$, from Equation 8.1), the probability of non-sequential buying should be equal to (J + K (P/R)). If it is assumed that J is equal to zero and K is equal to R (two already tested assumptions), the probability of non-sequential buying (Pi) should be equal to P when the probability of sequential buying is equal to zero. A correlation analysis and a paired-samples t-test relating Pi (M = .29; SD = .18) and P (M = .33; SD = .20)

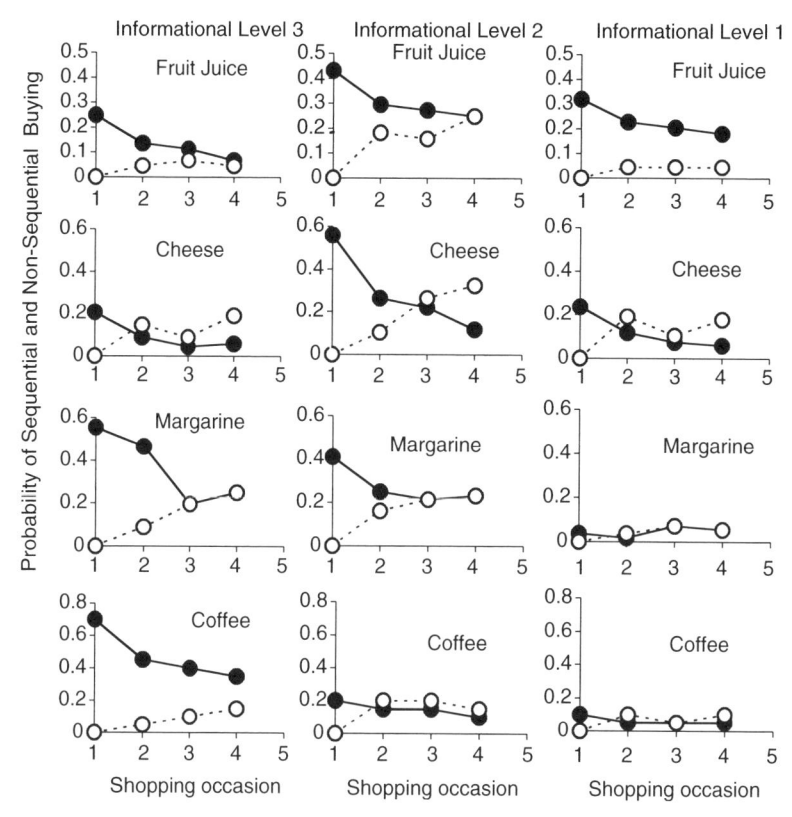

Figure 8.1 Probability of Sequential and Non-Sequential Buying in each Informational Level

indicated that the two measures were positively and significantly correlated ($r = .70$; $p < .000$) and their means were not statistically significant ($t = 1.26$; $p = .22$).

Figure 8.2 illustrates, with data from informational Level 3 for baked beans, all these parameters. As shown in the figure, Equations 8.1 and 8.2 can be used to describe the proportions of sequential and non-sequential buyers of a group of brands across shopping occasions, and to estimate Z, P, Pi, even when these points are not included in the data set. The figure also helps visualize the areas under the functions, which, as mentioned previously, can be used to estimate the total sales due to exclusive and non-exclusive buyers during the loyalty shopping cycle.

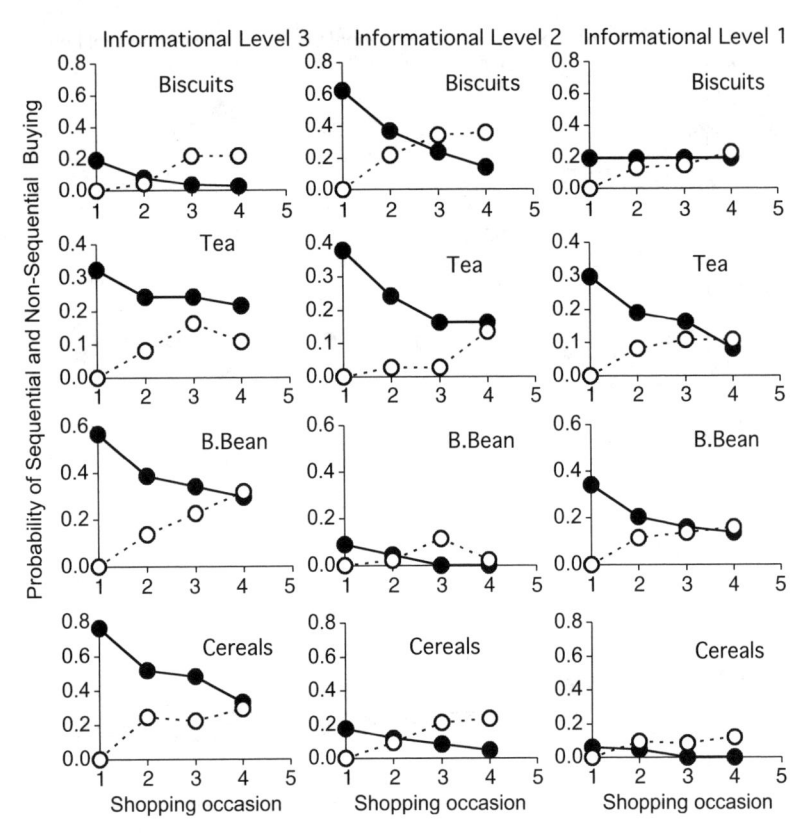

Figure 8.1 Probability of Sequential and Non-Sequential Buying in each Informational Level– *continued*

Dynamics of repeat-buying for brands

With the purpose of testing the applicability of Equations 8.1 and 8.2 to the dynamics of repeat-buying of specific and generic brands (i.e., rather than groups of brands), their parameters were calculated with data from some of the brands that showed the highest numbers of data points in the sample. These were: Kelloggs Cornflakes, Kelloggs (all types of cereals), Nescafe Original, Nescafe (all types of instant coffee), and Heinz Baked Beans. Table 8.1 (bottom part) presents the parameters for the probability of sequential buying (Equation 8.1) for these brands. As the table shows, r^2 ranged from .89 to 1.00, indicating that the equation fitted very well with the data. All values of R were three times or more the size of their standard errors.

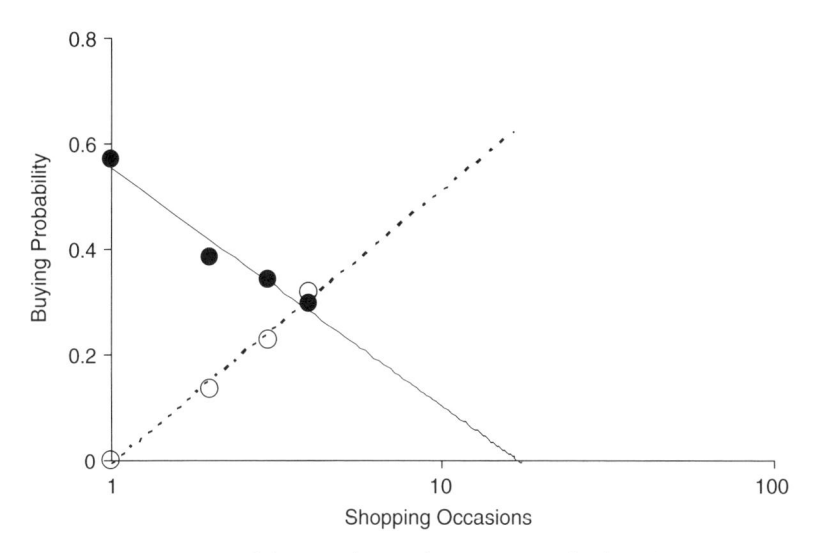

Figure 8.2 Summary of the Data from Information Level 3 for Baked Beans

Table 8.2 (bottom part) shows the parameters for the probability of non-sequential buying (Equation 8.2) for these same brands. As can be seen in the table, r^2 ranged from .74 to .96, indicating that the equation fitted well with the data. Four out of five values of R were three times or more the size of their standard errors (with the exception of Heinz Baked Beans). The goodness of fit of the two equations suggests that they can be used also to describe the dynamics of repeat-buying of specific and generic brands, corroborating Hypothesis 4, which states that *patterns of decrease in successive repeat-buying and of increase in non-sequential buying, with increases in successive shopping occasions, should be similar for groups of brands and for specific brands.*

Discussion

Dynamics of repeat-buying

The relatively constant penetration level of a brand, usually observed from week to week in steady markets, can be viewed as the result of a dynamic cycle of sequential and non-sequential purchases. As the number of shopping occasions for each consumer increases, the probability of sequential repeat-buying decreases while the probability of non-sequential buying increases. The present results demonstrate the possibility of quantifying these probabilities.

The two equations adopted, relating the probabilities of sequential and non-sequential buying to the logarithm of shopping occasions, provided an acceptable description of the data. This was observed for groups of brands, classified on the basis of their differentiation levels, of eight product categories, and for some specific and generic brands. Equations 8.1 and 8.2 have the advantages of being very simple, similar to each other, and containing easily obtainable parameters. Each equation includes two empirically determined parameters, which could be reduced to only one free parameter. This would be the case for Equation 8.1 if P is assumed to be equal to the penetration level of the group of brand (or brand), an assumption that was supported by the present data. One free parameter of Equation 8.2 could also be eliminated if J is assumed to be equal to zero. Although the observed average value of J was very close to zero ($M = .007$; $SD = .02$), this assumption was not completely supported by the present results. A statistical test indicated that J was larger than zero. It should also be noted that if all assumptions were to be accepted (i.e., J is equal to zero, P is equal to Pi and they are both equal to penetration level, and P is equal to R), all relevant parameters could be obtained with the use of only one of the equations.

Equations 8.1 and 8.2 can also be used to determine the duration of the loyalty shopping cycle for each brand or brand group, by allowing for the estimation of the shopping occasion on which sequential repeat-buying is equal to zero (Z). An estimate of the total amount of sales due to sequential and non-sequential purchases during each shopping cycle can also be obtained from the equations by calculating the areas under the graphs.

The high positive correlation observed between the values of intercept (P) and slope (R) of Equation 8.1 ($r = .91$) suggests that brand groups with higher penetration levels also show more rapid decreases in the number of sole buyers across shopping occasions than brands with lower penetration. However, the higher correlation observed between values of intercept (P) and area ($r = .91$) than between values of slope (R) and area ($r = .44$) suggests that the penetration level is more strongly related to the total amount of sales, due to exclusive buyers during a product shopping cycle, than the rate of decrease in the number of exclusive buyers. This finding is perfectly compatible with the phenomenon of double jeopardy, which shows that customers of brands with higher penetration levels tend to show slightly higher purchase frequencies and levels of loyalty than customers of brands with lower penetration levels (Ehrenberg et al., 1990). In the present case, although increases in penetration level (P) were associated to higher rates of decrease in the probability of sequential buying (R), the latter were proportionally smaller than the former. Therefore, brand groups with higher penetration showed proportionally smaller decreases in probability of sequential buying and, thus, have longer loyalty shopping cycles.

There is no theoretical necessity in the equations proposed here. Although their selection was based on some explicit criteria, they were all descriptive, rather than theoretical, criteria. The present results do not necessarily discard the possibility of there being better equations to describe the data. In this vein, the results showed that the fit of Equation 8.1 to the decrease in the probability of sequential buying was slightly better than that observed for Equation 8.2 to the increase in the probability of non-sequential buying. This asymmetry was also corroborated by the statistical rejection of the assumption that J would be equal to zero. The expression *loyalty shopping cycle* has been proposed here to refer to the number of consecutive shopping occasions during which the probability of sequential repeat-buying remains higher than zero (i.e., Z in Equation 8.1). The use of this term may help differentiate this concept from the concept of *product shopping cycle*, which may refer to how often people buy a product during a given period of time. Inter-purchase time and purchase frequency are some of the measures that can be related to product shopping cycles. It should be noted that loyalty shopping cycles are measured in number of shopping occasions rather than in number of weeks or months, as it is usually done for inter-purchase time. The definition of when the cycle starts or which is to be considered the first shopping occasion is arbitrary and will depend on research interests or data available.

Therefore, loyalty cycles are relative to an arbitrary starting point. Loyalty cycles are also relative to each consumer buying pattern, as they are defined with reference to the ordinal position of shopping occasions within each consumer's sequence of purchases. In other words, the first (and second and third, and so forth) shopping occasion for Consumer A may occur during Week 1 whereas that for Consumer B may happen only in Week 5, for Consumer C during Week 4, and so forth. This relativity of loyalty shopping cycles is in accordance to the observation that "studies where consumers are labelled as 'loyal', without specifying the period of observation, are likely to be ambiguous and misleading" (Ehrenberg *et al.*, in press, p. 5). Moreover, if one wants to know the time duration of a loyalty shopping cycle one needs only to multiply the number of shopping occasions of the cycle by the average inter-purchase time for the category.

The observed similarities between the analyses for brand groups and specific brands also represent a relevant outcome of the present research. These results suggest that loyalty shopping cycles of brand groups, classified on the basis of the informational benefit they offer, are similar to those of specific and generic brands. Then, at least with respect to loyalty cycles, brand groups behave similarly to specific brands. This corroborates previous suggestions that brands within a brand group are highly substitutable, which would explain why the majority of consumers make the majority of their purchases within the same informational level of brands (*cf.* Foxall *et al.*, 2004). These results also reinforce the usefulness of the distinctions proposed by the Behavioral Perspective Model, according to which brand differentiation can be interpreted as differences with respect to informational benefits.

Limitations of the present research

The small sample size may limit the generalizability of the present findings. This would be improved by increasing both the number of consumers and the total period of analysis. As different products have different average inter-purchase durations, the number of consumers buying four or more times certain products was quite small (e.g., this value varied from 19 for tea to 59 for biscuits). The total period analyzed was particularly restrictive, for the analyses had to be limited to the first four shopping occasions of each consumer. The small size of our sample may have been responsible for the observation of some non-significant regression analyses, including some unusual results (e.g., a positive slope for Equation 8.1). On the other hand, the results were orderly and replicated across groups of brands, brands, and product categories. This may be a positive consequence of using a small sample, which usually diminishes the probability of finding fortuitous statistically significant results. In addition, it would be valuable in future research to try to relate the patterns of brand choice exhibited in this research to levels of consumers' incomes.

Managerial implications

The possibility that the constructs proposed by the Behavioral Perspective Model could enter meaningfully into managerial decision making (Foxall, 1992) is supported by the present findings which have implications for the behavior of manufacturers and retailers. In the first place, Equations 8.1 and 8.2 can be used to calculate the loyalty-shopping cycle for each brand group or specific brand. This information may serve as a benchmark against which the effects of marketing activities can be compared. This can be done both with respect to loyalty cycles for the same brand in the past or with respect to the loyalty cycles of other similarly positioned brands. By using such measures as reference points, managers can decide whether or not their brands or brand groups are behaving "normally," in the sense of behaving as expected for a brand with such characteristics. This type of analysis has been frequently employed with findings related to consumer buying patterns, such as brand penetration level, purchase frequency and loyalty (e.g., Ehrenberg *et al.*, in press).

Loyalty-shopping cycles can also be used to measure the impact of marketing activities on different groups of consumers. When evaluating the effects of a price promotion or an advertisement campaign, manufacturers could measure separately possible effects on extending sequential repeat-buying (i.e., decreasing R) or attracting "new," non-repeat-buying customers (i.e., increasing K). The sales peak observed during price promotions, for instance, could be separated into possible increases in the duration of the cycle of sequential buying or increases in the number of non-repeat-buying or any combination of both. Although there are some data in the literature indicating that the level of repeat-buying after price promotions does not increase (Ehrenberg *et al.*, 1994), the present results suggest the possibility of a change in repeat-buying patterns during the promotion period. An interesting consequence of using these measures is that the notion of "retaining" one's customers can be conceived as something that applies to each shopping cycle, rather than to some arbitrary unit of time, such as each week or month.

The identification of loyalty cycles could also be useful to plan the duration of promotions. One characteristic of price promotions of fast-moving consumer goods, for example, is that they may not reach many buyers of the promoted brand who, depending on the inter-purchase time, do not buy the product during the promotion period (*cf.* Ehrenberg *et al.*, 1994). Knowing the duration of loyalty cycles allows the manager to predict how many different consumers are likely to buy the product during a given period of time. This can be done by considering that the constant penetration levels of a brand can be divided into sequential repeat buyers and non-sequential buyers during an entire loyalty cycle. In this way, managers can plan the duration of their promotions on the basis of how many different consumers they expect to reach. This can be illustrated with some of the brands investigated here.

First, in the case of Heinz Baked Beans, there were a total of 265 purchases in the category made by 39 different consumers during the 16-week period. The average inter-purchase time for the category was equal to 16.49 days and the duration of the loyalty shopping cycle for Heinz Baked Beans was 4.56 shopping occasions (Z) or 75.19 days (4.56 multiplied by 16.49). Total penetration due to sequential buying the brand during a loyalty cycle is equal to 0.78 (area), which indicates that 30.42 sales during a cycle are due to sequential repeat-buying (0.78 multiplied by 39 consumers). Secondly, in the case of Nescafe (generic), there were a total of 144 purchases in the category made by 19 different consumers during the 16-week period. The average inter-purchase time for the category was equal to 14.78 days and the duration of the loyalty shopping cycle for Nescafe was 28.97 shopping occasions (Z) or 428.18 days (28.97 multiplied by 14.78). Total penetration due to sequential buying the brand during a loyalty cycle is equal to 13.89 (area), which indicates that 263.91 sales during a cycle are due to sequential repeat-buying (13.89 multiplied by 19 consumers).

These examples should, of course, be adapted to the actual penetration numbers of specific product categories, which are very different than the ones observed in our sample. However, they can illustrate the wide differences in shopping loyalty cycles associated to each brand and, in this case, different product categories. The duration of the loyalty cycle for Nescafe is estimated to be more than six times the cycle duration for Heinz in terms of number of shopping occasions (i.e., it is not necessarily related to differences in purchase frequency across products). The success of marketing activities designed to retain loyal customers or to attract new customers could be enhanced by taking into account information concerning loyalty cycles. When using short-term promotions, for example, it may be easier to increase repeat-buying rates for a brand like Heinz, which has a shorter loyalty cycle, than for Nescafe, for which a short-term promotion would not make contact with a proportionally significant number of shopping occasions. On the other hand, with short-term promotions, it may be more appropriate to attempt to attract new customers to Nescafe than try to change present consumers' repeat-buying rates.

Note
1. Previously published in *Journal of Marketing Management*, 2006, 21, 37–61.

References

Alhadeff, D. A. (1982). *Microeconomics and Human Behavior: Toward a New Synthesis of Economics and Psychology*. Berkeley, CA: University of California Press.

Dall'Olmo Riley, F., Ehrenberg, A. S. C., Castleberry, C. B., Barwise, T. P. & Barnard, N. (1997). "The Variability of Attitudinal Repeat-rates". *International Journal of Research in Marketing*, 14, 437–50.

Ehrenberg, A. S. C. (1972/1988). *Repeat-buying: Theory and Applications*. London: North Holland Publishing Company.

Ehrenberg, A. S. C. (1986). "Pricing and Brand Differentiation". *Singapore Marketing Review*, 1, 5–13.

Ehrenberg, A. S. C. (1993). "New Brands and the Existing Market". *Journal of the Market Research Society*, 33, 285–99.

Ehrenberg, A. S. C. & England, L. R. (1990). "Generalising a Pricing Effect". *Journal of Industrial Economics*, 39, 47–68.

Ehrenberg, A. S. C., Goodhardt, G. J. & Barwise, P. (1990). "Double Jeopardy Revisited". *Journal of Marketing*, 54, 82–91.

Ehrenberg, A. S. C., Hammond, K. & Goodhardt, G. J. (1994). "The After-effects of Price related Consumer Promotions". *Journal of Advertising Research*, July/August, 11–21.

Ehrenberg, A. S. C. & Scriven, J. (1999). "Brand Loyalty", in P. E. Earl & S. Kemp (eds) *The Elgar Companion to Consumer Research and Economic Psychology*. Cheltenham, Gloucestershire: Edward Elgar, pp. 53–63.

Ehrenberg, A. S. C., Uncles, M. & Goodhardt, G. J. (in press). "Understanding Brand Performance Measures: Using Dirichlet Benchmarks". *Journal of Business Research*.

Foxall, G. R. (1992). "The Behavioral Perspective Model of Purchase and Consumption: from Consumer Theory to Marketing Practice". *Journal of the Academy of Marketing Science*, 20, 189–98.

Foxall, G. R. (1997). *Marketing Psychology: The Paradigm in the Wings*. London: Macmillan.

Foxall, G. R. (1998). "Radical Behaviorist Interpretation: Generating and Evaluating an Account of Consumer Behavior". *The Behavior Analyst*, 21, 321–54.

Foxall, G. R. (1999). "The Substitutability of Brands". *Managerial and Decision Economics*, 20, 241–58.

Foxall, G. R. (2004/1990). *Consumer Psychology in Behavioural Perspective*, 2nd edn. Frederick, MD: Beard Books. (First published 1990 by Routledge, London and New York.)

Foxall, G. R. (2005). *Understanding Consumer Choice*. London and New York: Palgrave Macmillan.

Foxall, G. R. & James, V. K. (2001). "The Behavioral Analysis of Brand Choice: A Preliminary Analysis". *European Journal of Behavior Analysis*, 2, 209–20.

Foxall, G. R. & James, V. K. (2003). "The Behavioral Ecology of Brand Choice: How and What do Consumers Maximize?". *Psychology and Marketing*, 20, 811–36.

Foxall, G. R., Oliveira-Castro, J. M. & Schrezenmaier, T. C. (2004). "The Behavioral Economics of Consumer Brand Choice: Patterns of Reinforcement and Utility Maximization". *Behavioural Processes*, 66, 235–60.

Foxall, G. R. & Schrezenmaier, T. C. (2003). "The Behavioral Economics of Consumer Brand Choice: Establishing a Methodology". *Journal of Economic Psychology*, 24, 675–95.

Goodhardt, G. J., Ehrenberg, A. S. C. & Chatfield, C. (1984). "The Dirichlet: A Comprehensive Model of Buying Behaviour". *Journal of the Royal Statistical Society*, A147, 621–43.

Herrnstein, R. J. (1961). "Relative and Absolute Strength of Response as a Function of the Frequency of Reinforcement". *Journal of the Experimental Analysis of Behavior*, 4, 267–72.

Herrnstein, R. J. (1970). "On the Law of Effect". *Journal of the Experimental Analysis of Behavior*, 13, 243–66.

Kagel, J. H., Battalio, R. C. & Green, L. (1995). *Economic Choice Theory: An Experimental Analysis of Animal Behavior.* Cambridge: Cambridge University Press.

Keng, K. A. & Ehrenberg, A. S. C. (1984). "Patterns of Store Choice". *Journal of Marketing Research*, 21, 399–409.

Oliveira-Castro, J. M. Foxall, G. R. & Schrezenmaier, T. C. (2005). "Patterns of Consumer Response to Retail Price Differentials". *Service Industries Journal*, 25 (3), 309–35.

Romaniuk, J., Ehrenberg, A. & Sharp, B. (2004). Perceptions of Differentiation. R&D Initiative Report 17.

Scriven, J. & Ehrenberg, A. S. C. (2003). "How Consumers Choose Prices over Time". *Marketing Learning*, 13, 46.

Sharp, B. & Sharp, A. (1997). "Loyalty Programs and their Impact on Repeat-purchase Loyalty Patterns". *International Journal of Research in Marketing*, 14, 473–86.

Uncles, M. & Ehrenberg, A. S. C. (1990). "The Buying of Packaged Goods at US Retail Chains". *Journal of Retailing*, 66, 278–93.

Uncles, M., Ehrenberg, A. S. C. & Hammond, K. (1995). "Patterns of Buyer Behavior: Regularities, Models, and Extensions". *Marketing Science*, 14, G71–G78.

9
Consumer Brand Choice: Individual and Group Analyses of Demand Elasticity[1]

Jorge M. Oliveira-Castro, Gordon R. Foxall and Teresa C. Schrezenmaier

One of the fundamental tenets of behavioral economics is that economic concepts are relevant to and may be profitably used by research in behavior analysis (*cf.* Allison, 1981; Bickel *et al.*, 1995; Hursh, 1984). The analysis of demand has been one of the most useful and frequently adopted frameworks in behavioral economics. This type of analysis usually is based on the parameters of demand curves, which plot the quantity purchased or consumed of a commodity as a function of its price.

In the case of experiments in behavioral economics, demand curves usually relate amount consumed of a reinforcer as a function of some schedule parameter, such as the number of responses required by a fixed-ratio schedule. The two main parameters of a demand curve are the elasticity and intensity (Hursh, 1984) of demand, which, in its simplest form, can be obtained by using the following equation (*cf.* Hursh, 1980, 1984; Kagel *et al.*, 1995):

$$\text{Log Quantity} = a + b \log \text{Price} \qquad (9.1)$$

where *a* and *b* are empirically obtained parameters that represent the intercept and slope of the function, respectively. The advantage of Equation 9.1 is that *a* and *b* can be interpreted as coefficients that measure the intensity and elasticity of demand, respectively. More complex forms for the demand curve have been suggested in the literature (e.g., Hursh *et al.*, 1988; Hursh & Winger, 1995) and will be examined later.

Several experiments conducted with animal subjects have produced results that are compatible with fundamental predictions derived from economic demand theory (cf. Hursh, 1984). According to Kagel et al. (1995), this kind of result extends economic choice theory to non-human animal behavior and, thus, strengthens the arguments against the assumption, commonly held in economic circles, that economic principles are necessarily based on rational evaluations of alternatives. Another, and possibly the most relevant, aspect of these results is the fact that they have been obtained with data for individual subjects. As pointed out by Kagel et al. (1995), most tests of consumer-demand theory have been based on aggregate data, an approach that may lead to serious methodological problems, considering that the theory is a theory about individual consumer behavior. The adoption of aggregate data usually is based on the hypothesis of a "representative consumer", which does not necessarily stand empirical tests (cf. Kagel et al., 1995, p. 71). Therefore, "on a more basic level, the studies reported constitute (arguably) the first real tests of consumer-demand theory" (Kagel et al., 1995, p. 2).

Moreover, when demand curves obtained in the laboratory were compared to those stemming from econometrics and consumer research they showed important similarities, despite the fact that several aspects of the typical market situation are missing in the laboratory (Lea, 1978). These differences between laboratory and marketing conditions, particularly the closeness of the laboratory setting and the use of non-human subjects, may hinder the process of generalization of research findings from one context to the other, which suggests the need to look for additional ways of bridging this gap (cf. Foxall, 2002). One intermediary level of research that fills part of the gap between behavioral economics and marketing analysis is the type of investigation conducted by Battalio et al. (1973), who reported one of the few tests of consumer demand theory using price and quantity data obtained for individual human consumers. They obtained data from institutional patients living in a token economy system. Results indicated that data from individual consumers were consistent with predictions from demand theory.

Considering that a token economy constitutes a less open setting than national economies, one further step to approximate behavioral economics and marketing would be to investigate demand curves for individual consumers making real purchases in existing markets. This type of research has become possible with the availability of consumer panel data, obtained by research firms (cf. Telser, 1962). Panel data are especially valuable for longitudinal studies because changes in purchasing behavior can be monitored very accurately by the continuous measurements, for each individual on each shopping occasion, of the brand name, amount bought, price paid, and so on (Crouch & Housden, 2003). Furthermore, diary panel data are considered to be very precise and less susceptible to errors, especially when based on barcode scanning procedures, than those obtained through consumers reporting their past behavior in surveys (Churchill, 1999).

In the present chapter, demand curves were calculated for separate individual consumers purchasing food products in supermarkets, using data from a consumer panel whose members scanned information concerning their purchases after each shopping trip. As the research investigated consumer behavior occurring in a "natural" economic situation, the basic data do not differ from those used by economists and marketing researchers; the novelty in the present approach lies in the type of analyses that were conducted. The analysis of individual demand curves in natural markets follows the behavior-analytic tradition of focusing on individual behavior, extending this tradition of research to the investigation of one of the fundamental phenomena of economics, namely, demand elasticity.

In addition to reducing the gap between behavioral economics experiments and natural occurring economic phenomena, the investigation of demand curves calculated for individual consumers also may help answer some questions that cannot be addressed by typical group or aggregate analyses of demand found in economics and, specifically, in marketing. This is the case with many econometric models adopted in marketing research to study consumer behavior which use information about each shopping trip of each consumer but estimate model parameters (e.g., elasticity) across consumers. In this type of analysis, several data points from each of many different consumers are simultaneously entered into the equations to calculate empirical parameters (e.g., Guadagni & Little, 1983; Gupta, 1988; Neslin *et al.*, 1985). This methodology may not represent any serious problem for marketing researchers, who are primarily interested in consumer behavior as means to understand the sale volume of brands and products, but it does leave unanswered some relevant questions concerning possible consumer buying patterns.

To illustrate this point, consider the example of demand elasticity coefficients that are calculated for product categories on the basis of panel data where information (e.g., quantity and price) about each consumer purchase is included in the analysis and there are several data points for each consumer, which might be named *overall product elasticity*. In such a case, overall demand elasticity coefficients obtained for the product category, that is, the observed decreases in purchased quantity as a function of increases in prices for the entire category, may result from a combination of intra- and inter-consumer elasticities. *Intra-consumer elasticity* measures the tendency for the same consumers to buy larger quantities when buying products with lower prices, due to price promotions and/or to buying cheaper brands. *Inter-consumer elasticity* measures the tendency for consumers who buy smaller quantities, on average, also to buy more expensive brands, on average. The present chapter attempts to identify and separate these possible choice patterns by analyzing inter- and intra-consumer elasticity coefficients for nine different categories of supermarket products. Inter-consumer elasticity coefficients were calculated across consumers for each product category, using one pair of data points (average amount bought and average amount paid) for each consumer. Intra-consumer elasticity coefficients were calculated across product categories for each consumer, using all pairs of data points obtained in all product categories for each consumer.

The analysis of individual demand curves also can be used to compare results based on data from groups of consumers with those based on data from individual consumers. The present work compares overall elasticity coefficients obtained for product categories based on group data with those based on individual data, considering that the form of a function describing group data is not necessarily the same as the form of the function describing individual data (Myerson & Green, 1995; Sidman, 1952).

Analyses of demand curves calculated for individual consumers also can be used to investigate individual differences in demand elasticity. Recent results suggest that consumers of supermarket products show choice behaviors that are consistent across product categories (*cf.* Ainslie & Rossi, 1998; Andrew & Currim, 2002). Following this line of research, we examine whether individual demand elasticities are consistent across product categories. With the purpose of expanding this type of investigation, we also verify whether individual differences in demand elasticity are consistent across time. In order to do so, demand curves were calculated, for each consumer, using data from the first and the second eight-week periods of the total 16-week sample. Elasticity coefficients obtained for the two periods were then compared.

In the present chapter, all elasticity coefficients were calculated using relative values of quantity and price. In the case of overall product elasticity (all data points of all consumers for each product category), the use of relative values allows for comparisons across product categories which differ with respect to selling units (e.g., package sizes and prices) (cf. Bell et al., 1999; Hursh & Winger, 1995). Relative values of quantity and price were used by dividing each quantity (and price) value by the average quantity (price) in the category. This "normalization" with respect to the category mean also favors the interpretation of the relations between quantity and price because the equation can be interpreted as measuring whether purchases of quantities above (or below) the mean quantity bought in the product category are associated with prices below (or above) the average price paid in the category. For intra-consumer coefficients, quantity bought and price paid were normalized by the average quantity bought and price paid calculated for each consumer for each product category (cf. Neslin et al., 1985). This normalization procedure makes possible the inclusion, in the same equation, of data from the same consumer purchasing in different product categories, which have different scales for quantity and price. In this case, elasticity coefficients would be showing changes in quantity as a function of changes in prices relative to the average quantities and prices that the consumer bought or paid, irrespective of product category. In other words, this type of analysis could indicate, for example, whether consumers tended to pay more or less the average price they paid when buying a quantity above the average quantity they bought, independently of the product category. The same reasoning was applied to inter-consumer coefficients, which were calculated relative to the average quantity (price) bought in the category calculated across all consumers of the category. In this case, the normalization procedure allows for comparisons across consumers in the same category by indicating whether or not consumers that buy above or below the average quantity bought in the category tend to pay prices above or below the average price paid in the category. Such normalization procedures, within a product category and/or consumer, will not affect elasticity coefficients given the use of log-log functions. One disadvantage of this type of procedure is the loss of information concerning the actual levels of consumption and ranges of price, which restricts the interpretation of the results.

Method

Sample and procedure

The market research company, Taylor-Nelson Sofres, provided consumer panel data for 80 British consumers and their total weekly purchases in nine fast-moving consumer goods categories over 16 weeks. Taylor-Nelson Sofres is one of the largest and best-known companies in its field and collects consumer purchasing data from its so-called TNS Superpanel on a range of consumer goods from 15,000 randomly selected British households. Data collection is operationalized as follows: after each shopping trip, members of the panel scan their purchased items into a sophisticated handheld barcode reader by passing the scanner across the barcodes, which nowadays are printed on all packaged supermarket products. The data then are automatically sent to Taylor-Nelson Sofres for central processing without any further voluntary contribution from the panel participants. The retail outlets at which purchases were made also were identified for each shopping occasion and included major U. K. supermarkets such as Asda (a subsidiary of Wal-Mart), Tesco, and Sainsbury.

The nine product categories that served as the basis for this research are: baked beans, biscuits (cookies), breakfast cereals, butter, cheese, fruit juice, instant coffee, margarine, and tea. The following information was recorded on each shopping occasion for each consumer: brand specification (different versions of the same product category were classified as different brands, e.g., Corn Flakes and Rice Krispies by Kelloggs), package size, name of the supermarket/shop, date, number of units, and total amount spent. As the analysis of brand choice requires information concerning actual purchase across several buying opportunities, data from consumers who bought, within each product category, fewer than four times during the 16-week period were disregarded. Table 9.1 shows, for each product category, the number of consumers who made four or more purchases, the total number of purchases, average number of purchases per consumer, average total amount spent (British pounds) per consumer, average amount spent per shopping trip, average price per standard amount (e.g., 100g), average price per package, total number of brands, and average number of brands bought.

Analyses

Overall product price elasticity. Overall price elasticity coefficients were calculated for each product category, using all data points of all consumers in each category, in order to compare the results with those obtained using individual data. Despite the fact that some authors have modeled quantity as a discrete variable (e.g., Gupta, 1988), we followed other investigators, such as Bell et al. (1999), in interpreting quantity and prices as continuous variables. The following version of

Table 9.1 Number of consumers, total purchases, average number of purchases, average total amount spent (British pounds), average amount spent per shopping trip, average price per standard amount (e.g., 100g), average price per package, total number of brands, average number of brands bought, for each product category. Data were collected from February to May 2001, when the exchange rate was, approximately, £1 to $1.43.

Product	Number of consumers	Total purchases	Average purchases	Total spent	Average spent	Average price	Unit price	Total brands	Average brands
Baked Beans	39	265	6.79	4.52	0.62	0.07	.51	32	2.18
Biscuits (Cookies)	59	1125	19.07	14.02	0.74	0.30	.63	230	8.93
Breakfast Cereals	56	691	12.34	20.09	1.56	0.27	1.46	125	5.64
Butter	21	174	8.29	9.84	1.17	0.28	.76	21	2.24
Cheese	45	447	9.93	13.38	1.38	1.91	2.76	95	5.24
Fruit Juice	34	336	9.88	13.99	1.52	0.72	1.05	43	2.91
Coffee	19	144	7.58	18.32	2.51	2.09	2.09	31	2.95
Margarine	50	401	8.02	8.75	1.12	0.19	1.01	55	2.70
Tea	32	199	6.22	11.67	2.02	0.61	1.66	30	1.94

Equation 9.1 was used to calculate the overall elasticity coefficients for each product category:

$$\log Q_{it} = \alpha + \beta (\log P_{it}) + \varepsilon_{it} \tag{9.2}$$

where:
Q_{it} = the quantity bought by consumer i on shopping occasion t divided by the average quantity bought in the product category calculated across all consumers on all shopping occasions,
P_{it} = the price paid by consumer i on shopping occasion t divided by the average price paid in the product category calculated across all consumers on all shopping occasions,

with α and β being estimated regression coefficients, and e_{it} representing the error term. The equation is similar to that used by Kagel et al. (1995), where β can be interpreted as a direct measure of elasticity. We have not attempted to elaborate price elasticity models. We adopted elasticity coefficients as measures of some possible consumer choice patterns. One consequence of this descriptive approach is that we do not expect to obtain high levels of explained variance (r^2) associated with any of the equations.

Inter-consumer and intra-consumer price elasticities. Inter-consumer price elasticity coefficients were obtained for each product category, using one data point for each consumer in each category, based on the following version of Equation 9.1:

$$\log Q_i = \alpha + \beta (\log P_i) + \varepsilon_i \tag{9.3}$$

where:
Q_i = the average quantity bought by consumer i on a given product category divided by the average quantity bought in the product category calculated across all consumers,
P_i = the price paid by consumer i on a given product category divided by the average price paid in the product category calculated across all consumers,

which yielded only one pair of data points per consumer, rather than all data points per consumer, for each product category.

Intra-consumer price elasticity coefficients were obtained using all data points for all product categories for each consumer, based on the following version of Equation 9.1:

$$\log Q_{tc} = \alpha + \beta (\log P_{tc}) + \varepsilon_{tc} \tag{9.4}$$

where:

Q_{tc} = the quantity bought by a given consumer on shopping occasion t in product category c divided by the average quantity bought by that consumer in product category c,

P_{tc} = the price paid by a given consumer on shopping occasion t in the product category c divided by the average price paid by that consumer in product category c,

which yielded one elasticity coefficient for each consumer using data from all product categories.

Individual product price elasticities. Individual product price elasticity coefficients were calculated separately for each consumer buying each of three product categories, based on the same type of data included in Equation 9.4 (but restricted to one product). In this case, all data points obtained for each consumer in each of three product categories were used. The categories were cheese, breakfast cereals, and biscuits (cookies), which showed higher frequency of purchase during the 16-week period of observation, making possible the calculation of individual regression functions. In this case, data points were normalized to individual averages, calculated for each category, as was done for intra-consumer coefficients described above (Equation 9.4). These individual price elasticity coefficients obtained for separate product categories were compared to group elasticity coefficients calculated for each product using Equations 9.2 and 9.3.

Split-sample individual elasticities. Elasticity coefficients were calculated for each consumer using data from each half (i.e., Weeks 1 to 8 and 9 to 16) of the sample. These coefficients were obtained using Equation 9.4, including all purchases across all products for each consumer, during each eight-week period. This was done with the purpose of testing the consistency of individual differences across the two split samples.

Results

Overall product price elasticities

Figure 9.1 presents the demand curve, calculated with all data points from all consumers (Equation 9.2), for each product category. The graphs show log of quantity divided by the average quantity bought in the category as a function of log of price divided by the average price paid in the category. The slopes of the functions depict price elasticity for each category. Table 9.2 presents the parameters of these functions,

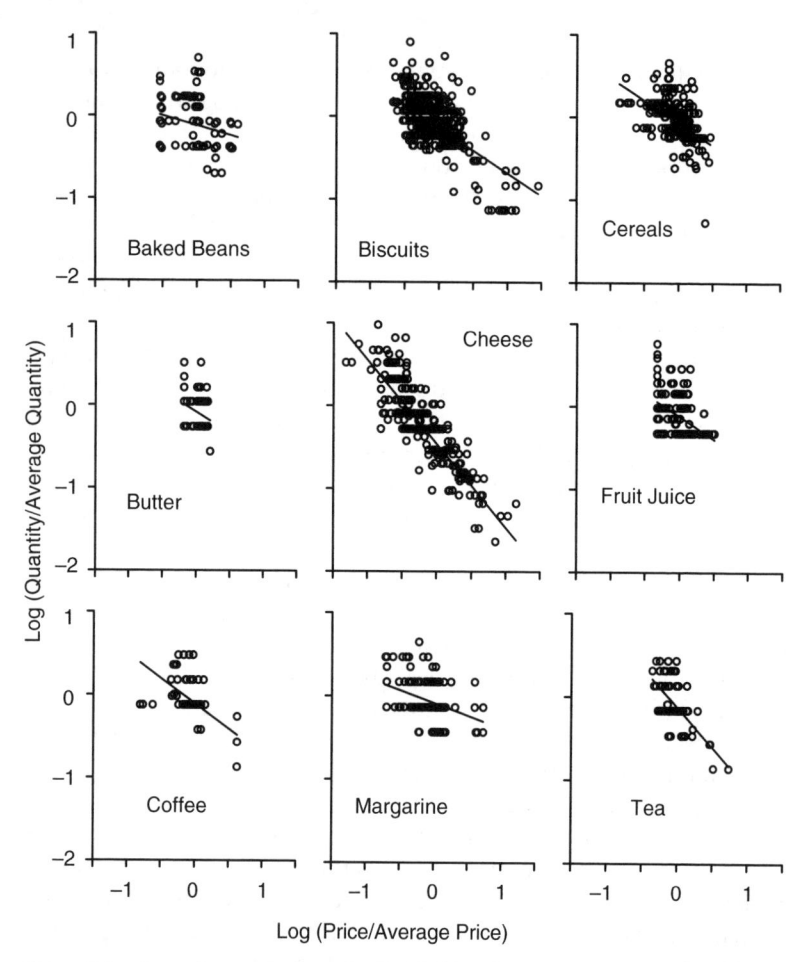

Figure 9.1 Log of quantity bought divided by the average quantity bought in the category as a function of log of price paid divided by the average price paid in the category, calculated with all data points from all consumers (Equation 9.2), for each product category

The slopes of the functions depict overall price elasticity for each category.

obtained with Equation 9.2, for each product category. The *F* statistics show that all regression analyses were significant ($p \leq 0.01$). The values of r^2 varied from .05 to .76, suggesting that there are wide differences across product categories with respect to the influence of variables other than price, which were not investigated here. The values of the intercept (α) were close to zero and ranged from –0.46 to –0.08 across

Table 9.2 Parameters of Equation 9.2, including all data points from all consumers, calculated for each product category
See text for details.

Product	r^2	F*	α	β	Error		t
Baked Beans	.05	14.39	−.12	−.23 [c]	.06		−3.79
Biscuits (Cookies)	.41	764.44	−.14	−.54 [c]	.02		−27.65
Breakfast Cereals	.32	326.66	−.07	−.55 [c]	.03		−18.07
Butter	.06	10.46	−.09	−.52 [c]	.16		−3.23
Cheese	.76	1399.79	−.46	−1.01 [c]	.03		−37.41
Fruit Juice	.18	74.01	−.12	−.55 [c]	.06		−8.60
Instant Coffee	.35	76.33	−.11	−.58 [c]	.07		−8.74
Margarine	.15	69.78	−.08	−.31 [c]	.04		−8.35
Tea	.30	84.76	−.12	−.97 [c]	.11		−9.21

c: $p \leq .01$
b: $p \leq .05$
a: $p \leq .10$
* (1, n) degrees of freedom, where n = (Total purchases − 2); see Table 9.1

product categories. These values indicate that at the average price of the category (i.e., log $P_{it} = 0$) consumers tended to buy a little less than the average quantity for that category. Elasticity coefficient estimates (β) varied from −0.23 to −1.01 across product categories, indicating an inverse relationship between price and quantity demanded. These values also indicate that the demand for all the products was inelastic, that is, increases in prices were accompanied by decreases in quantity demanded, although the decreases in quantity were proportionally smaller than the correspondent increases in price.

Inter-consumer price elasticities

Figure 9.2 presents the demand curve, calculated with one pair of data points from each consumer (Equation 9.3), for each product category. The graphs show log of quantity divided by the average quantity bought in the category as a function of log of price divided by the average price paid in the category. The slopes of the functions depict inter-consumer price elasticity for each category. Table 9.3 presents the parameters obtained with Equation 9.3 for each product category. The F statistics obtained for inter-consumer elasticities showed that seven of the nine regression analyses were significant ($p \leq 0.05$). The values of r^2 varied from 0.09 to 0.68, suggesting again that there are wide differences across product categories with respect to the influence of variables other than price, which were not investigated here. The values of the intercept (α) ranged from 0.20 to 2.55 across product

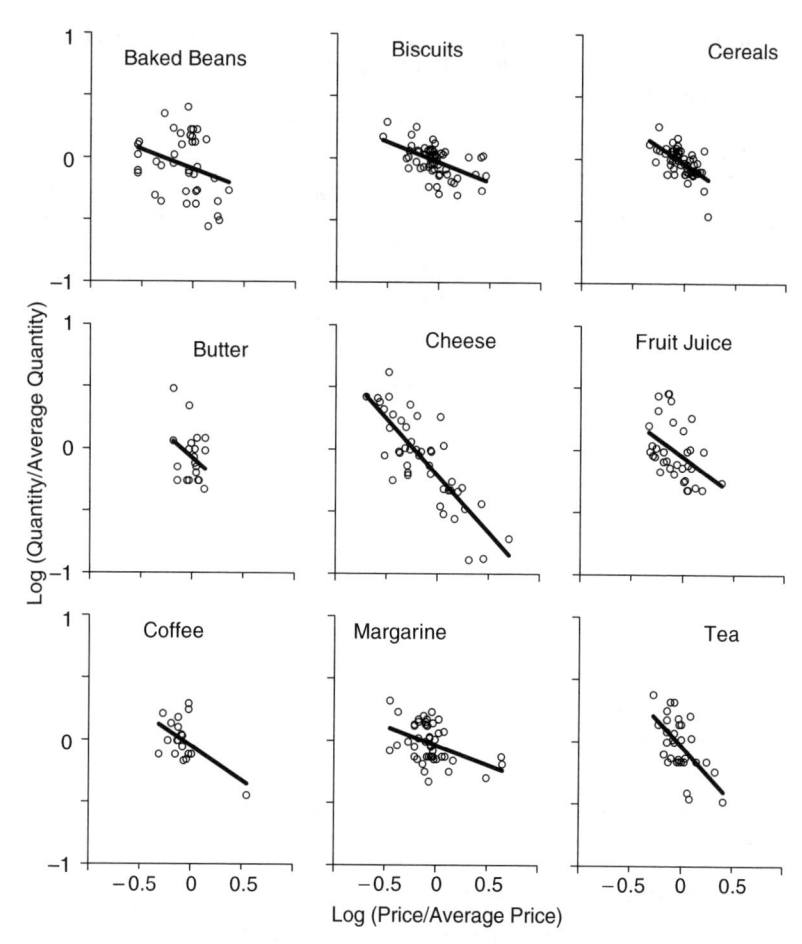

Figure 9.2 Log of quantity bought divided by the average quantity bought in the category as a function of log of price paid divided by the average price paid in the category, calculated with one pair of data points from each consumer (Equation 9.3), for each product category

The slopes of the functions depict inter-consumer price elasticity for each category.

categories. These values indicate that at the average price of the category (i.e., log $P_i = 0$) consumers tended to buy a little more than the average quantity for that category. Elasticity coefficient estimates (β) varied from –0.31 to –0.91 across product categories, indicating an inverse relationship between price and quantity demanded. These

Table 9.3 Parameters of Equation 9.3, including one data point per consumer, calculated for each product category
See text for details.

Product	r^2	F*	α	β	Error		t
Baked Beans	.09		3.68	2.55	−.31 [a]	.16	−1.92
Biscuits (Cookies)	.28		22.53	.33	−.32 [c]	.07	−4.75
Breakfast Cereals	.41		37.16	.47	−.56 [c]	.09	−6.10
Butter	.10		2.20	2.18	−.72	.48	−1.48
Cheese	.68		89.47	.29	−.91 [c]	.10	−9.46
Fruit Juice	.19		7.48	.20	−.60 [c]	.22	−2.74
Instant Coffee	.29		7.01	1.17	−.55 [b]	.21	−2.65
Margarine	.18		10.55	.56	−.31 [c]	.10	−3.25
Tea	.38		18.24	.31	−.91 [c]	.21	−4.27

c: $p \leq .01$
b: $p \leq .05$
a: $p \leq .10$
* (1, n) degrees of freedom, where n = (Number consumers − 2); see Table 9.1

values also indicate that the demand for all the products was inelastic, that is, increases in prices were accompanied by decreases in quantity demanded, although the decreases in quantity were proportionally smaller than the correspondent increases in price. These results demonstrate the occurrence of inter-consumer elasticity in most product categories, showing that, within each product category, consumers who pay higher prices, on average, also tend to buy smaller quantities, on average.

Intra-consumer price elasticity

Table 9.4 shows the parameters of Equation 9.4, calculated for each consumer across all product categories, using measures of quantity and price observed on each shopping occasion relative to the average quantity and average price obtained for each consumer in each product category. Elasticity coefficients were negative for 93.4% of consumers. The estimates of elasticity were significantly different from zero for 57 of the 76 consumers, that is, for 75% of the consumers. For significant regressions, r^2 varied from 0.12 to 0.95, and the values of the elasticity coefficient (β) were all negative ranging from −0.27 to −1.23, with the exception of one consumer (21174) for whom the slope was positive. With the purpose of illustrating the parameters presented in the table, Figure 9.3 presents the demand curves for each of six consumers, calculated with all data points across all products for each consumer (Equation 9.4). The six consumers were chosen from among those who

Table 9.4 Parameters of Equation 9.4, including all data points for each consumer across product categories, calculated for each individual consumer Consumers are listed in ascending order based on the value of p. Degrees of freedom = (1, n), where n = ((N in Split Sample 1 + N in Split Sample 2) − 2); see Table 9.6.

Consumer	r^2	α	β	Error	p
12347	.55	−.10	−.84	.09	< .000
21174	.60	.00	.70	.07	< .000
25927	.37	−.17	−.58	.08	< .000
31639	.54	−.12	−.59	.09	< .000
36968	.33	−.16	−.47	.10	< .000
48996	.13	−.04	−.34	.08	< .000
49461	.78	−.16	−.77	.08	< .000
55814	.36	−.17	−.82	.14	< .000
55815	.30	−.08	−.51	.09	< .000
58275	.19	−.11	−.57	.14	< .000
59984	.36	−.05	−.93	.21	< .000
60695	.48	−.15	−.69	.12	< .000
67380	.50	−.16	−.83	.13	< .000
74108	.37	−.09	−1.02	.21	< .000
78082	.43	−.06	−.48	.07	< .000
86240	.27	−.05	−.57	.10	< .000
86295	.41	−.06	−1.23	.19	< .000
90910	.46	−.09	−.79	.16	< .000
93182	.48	−.07	−.84	.11	< .000
98732	.31	−.05	−.56	.09	< .000
113815	.26	−.06	−.48	.13	< .000
120582	.68	−.17	−1.16	.21	< .000
120587	.25	−.09	−.58	.13	< .000
122718	.51	−.04	−.66	.06	< .000
122753	.20	−.05	−.46	.11	< .000
122990	.43	−.07	−.65	.16	< .000
124244	.41	−.02	−.57	.10	< .000
124559	.30	−.10	−.67	.14	< .000
124933	.47	−.05	−1.06	.20	< .000
126110	.68	−.06	−.61	.06	< .000
126874	.18	−.04	−.30	.07	< .000
127526	.45	−.03	−.80	.18	< .000
128130	.34	−.10	−.51	.08	< .000
130515	.95	−.38	−.98	.07	< .000
130953	.31	−.12	−.52	.09	< .000
131184	.68	−.22	−.72	.08	< .000
131294	.42	−.12	−.74	.11	< .000
131331	.22	−.04	−.47	.08	< .000
131357	.43	−.09	−.69	.11	< .000
132764	.19	−.12	−.27	.07	< .000
133271	.54	−.06	−.63	.06	< .000

Table 9.4 Parameters of Equation 9.4, including all data points for each consumer across product categories, calculated for each individual consumer Consumers are listed in ascending order based on the value of p. Degrees of freedom = (1, n), where n = ((N in Split Sample 1 + N in Split Sample 2) – 2); see Table 9.6. – *continued*

Consumer	r^2	α	β	Error	p
600031	.30	–.12	–.97	.20	< .000
600817	.26	–.07	–.58	.10	< .000
27180	.14	–.08	–.39	.11	.001
75262	.33	–.06	–.89	.24	.001
106715	.44	–.06	–.72	.18	.001
130276	.47	–.15	–.51	.13	.001
130867	.38	–.14	–.66	.18	.001
126831	.21	–.09	–.59	.18	.002
600948	.29	–.05	–.60	.18	.002
29436	.30	–.06	–.69	.22	.004
61529	.13	–.11	–.48	.17	.005
126515	.55	–.06	–.53	.15	.006
26537	.18	–.01	–.52	.18	.007
76872	.12	–.07	–.59	.23	.013
36543	.14	–.03	–.44	.18	.018
10696	.25	–.06	–.43	.19	.036
122025	.12	–.01	–.38	.19	.051
82032	.08	–.06	–.28	.15	.062
122404	.07	–.07	–.19	.11	.073
122016	.05	–.03	–.18	.11	.096
122934	.21	–.05	–.54	.32	.117
600469	.11	–.03	–.33	.21	.134
106627	.03	–.03	–.22	.15	.141
73779	.29	–.05	–.57	.36	.166
118278	.04	–.08	–.18	.14	.215
84030	.17	–.02	–.44	.35	.238
47278	.04	–.05	–.22	.21	.294
129274	.03	–.01	.18	.19	.342
29425	.07	–.04	.42	.44	.361
118411	.05	–.06	–.39	.43	.374
95606	.02	–.04	–.11	.18	.549
23527	.01	–.02	.13	.29	.670
40563	.01	.00	–44.14	149.97	.778
133272	.00	–.05	–.03	.26	.898
132207	.00	–.01	.00	.23	.999

yielded significant regression analyses with the purpose of showing the two highest elasticity coefficients (i.e., more negative; Consumers 86295 and 120582), the average (Consumer 133271) and median (Consumer 31639) coefficients, and the two lowest ones (i.e., less

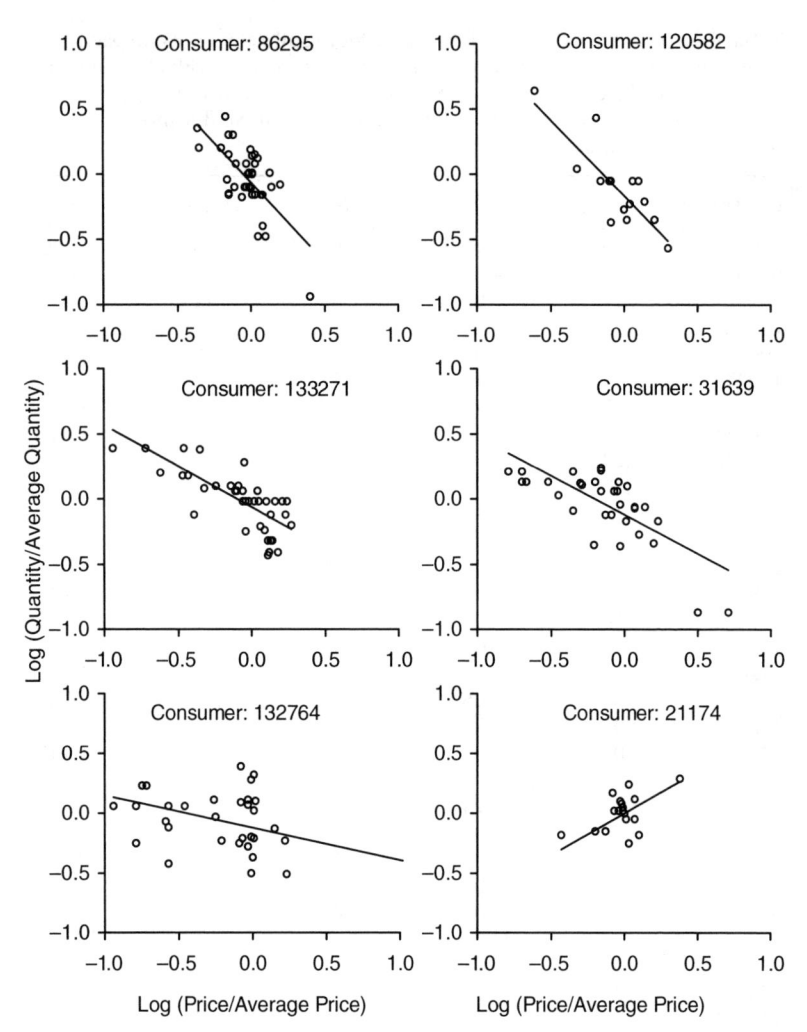

Figure 9.3 Demand curves for each of six consumers, calculated with all data points across all products for each consumer (Equation 9.4)

The six consumers showing the two highest elasticity coefficients (86295 and 120582), the average (133271) and median (31639) coefficients, and the two lowest ones (132764 and 21174) were selected.

negative or positive; Consumers 132764, where two data points equal to log of Price = –0.85 and log of Quantity = 1.02 are not shown, and Consumer 21174). The slopes of the functions depict price elasticity for each consumer across all categories. These results, overall, suggest that the quantity individual consumers buy on each shopping occasion tends to decrease as prices increase, demonstrating the occurrence of intra-consumer elasticity. Such decreases, however, for the vast majority of consumers, are proportionately smaller than the respective increases in price, that is, most of the consumers show inelastic demand.

Individual product price elasticities

With the purpose of comparing product price elasticities obtained from group data with those obtained from individual data, individual elasticity coefficients were calculated for each consumer for the three products that showed the highest frequency of purchase during the 16-week period, that is, biscuits (cookies), breakfast cereals, and cheese. The parameters of Equation 9.4 obtained with relative measures at the individual level were then calculated for each consumer for each of these three product categories. Table 9.5 shows the parameters obtained. As can be seen in the table, for 29 out of 33 consumers who bought both products more than four times during the 16-week period, elasticity coefficients were higher (more negative) for cheese ($M = -1.07$, $SD = 0.48$) than for biscuits ($M = -0.47$, $SD = 0.26$). This difference was statistically significant ($t(32) = 6.31$, $p < 0.000$). These results replicated the tendency observed when group data were used, that is, a higher demand elasticity for cheese than for cookies, observed for overall product elasticities (i.e., Equation 9.2, cheese = -1.01 and cookies = -0.55) and inter-consumer elasticities (i.e., Equation 9.3, cheese = -0.91 and cookies = -0.55).

As also shown in the table, regression analyses indicated higher demand elasticity for cheese than for breakfast cereals for 23 of the 31 consumers who bought both products four or more times. A *t*-test indicated that this difference was statistically significant (cheese: $M = -1.05$, $SD = 0.53$, cereals: $M = -0.54$, $SD = .46$; $t(30) = -3.57$, $p = 0.001$). This analysis replicated the tendency observed for overall product elasticities (cheese = -1.01 and cereals = -0.55) and inter-consumer elasticities (cheese = -0.91 and cereals = -0.56).

As Table 9.5 shows, demand elasticity was higher (more negative) for cereals than for biscuits for 26 of the 42 consumers who bought both products at least four times. A comparison of mean elasticity coefficients, however, did not indicate significant differences in elasticity between these two products (cereals: $M = -0.57$, $SD = 0.50$, biscuits: $M = -0.44$, $SD = 0.34$; $t(41) = 1.21$, $p = .235$). Although a similar difference was observed for inter-consumer elasticities (cereals = -0.56 and biscuits = -0.32), overall elasticities, which were identical and equal to -0.55, also suggested that the two products did not differ.

Table 9.5 Parameters of Equation 9.4, calculated for each individual consumer for each of the following three product categories: biscuits (cookies), cheese, and breakfast cereals

	Biscuits (Cookies)					Cheese					Breakfast Cereals				
Cons.	r^2	α	β	SE	p	r^2	α	β	SE	p	r^2	α	β	SE	p
10696	.20	-.07	-.44	.25	.110						.14	-.01	-.17	.13	.236
12347	.64	-.12	-1.02	.13	<.000	.80	-.23	-.95	.17	.001	.68	-.01	-1.81	.40	.001
21174	.89	.01	.81	.05	<.000						.30	-.02	-.27	.08	.002
25927	.75	-.42	-.89	.08	<.000										
26537	.22	-.01	-.54	.22	.02						.78	-.08	-.78	.17	.004
27180	.14	-.11	-.37	.14	.010	1.00	-.17	-2.11	.00	<.000	.05	-.06	.66	1.25	.619
29425															
29436	.70	-.07	-.71	.14	<.000						.86	-.01	-.65	.13	.008
31639	.87	-.31	-.76	.09	<.000	.20	-.03	-.47	.54	.446	.05	-.03	-.40	.61	.531
36543	.24	-.05	-.50	.24	.054						.16	-.06	-.39	.44	.431
36968	.80	-.32	-.54	.07	<.000	.83	-.45	-2.11	.47	.011					
47278	.12	-.03	-.38	.35	.317	.71	-.18	-1.25	.57	.160	.55	-.05	-.75	.17	<.000
48996	.18	-.04	-.30	.09	.002	.88	-.12	-1.07	.16	.001					
49461	.77	-.10	-.78	.12	<.000	.91	-.27	-.81	.09	<.000	.04	-.09	-.34	.42	.426
55814	.06	-.15	-.45	.55	.431	.75	-.26	-1.04	.12	<.000	.56	-.02	-.43	.14	.017
55815	.44	-.09	-.55	.12	<.000	.87	-.44	-1.24	.20	.001	.23	-.03	-.51	.18	.007
58275						.85	-.80	-.98	.19	.003	.67	-.04	-.71	.13	<.000
59984						.95	.00	.01	.00	<.000	.90	-.03	-1.49	.23	.001
60695	.51	-.12	-.58	.14	.001	.60	-.28	-.85	.24	.008	.11	-.01	-.16	.19	.428
61529	.01	-.10	-.14	.32	.671	.47	-.25	-.86	.26	.005	.57	-.10	-.53	.14	.003
67380						.92	-.54	-1.32	.13	<.000	.35	-.04	-.64	.51	.297
74108	.46	-.03	-.57	.20	.016	.63	-.29	-1.38	.36	.004					
75262	.11	-.01	-.24	.48	.672	1.00	-.30	-1.35	.03	.001					

Table 9.5 Parameters of Equation 9.4, calculated for each individual consumer for each of the following three product categories: biscuits (cookies), cheese, and breakfast cereals – *continued*

Cons.	Biscuits (Cookies)					Cheese					Breakfast Cereals				
	r^2	α	β	SE	p	r^2	α	β	SE	p	r^2	α	β	SE	p
76872	.32	-.09	-.56	.34	.144	1.00	-.39	-1.42	.02	<.000	.19	-.01	.88	.90	.387
78082	.66	-.11	-.53	.09	<.000						.47	-.05	-.53	.14	.001
82032	.53	-.16	-.57	.17	.007										
84030											.74	-.03	-.70	.21	.029
86240	.69	-.07	-.99	.17	<.000						.39	-.05	-.63	.12	<.000
86295	.27	-.02	-.49	.28	.124	.79	-.23	-1.51	.30	.001	.64	.01	.16	.06	.032
90910	.44	-.06	-1.03	.44	.052						.22	-.06	-.45	.25	.093
93182	.29	-.06	-.61	.29	.059	.64	-.24	-1.35	.45	.031	.66	-.06	-.66	.10	<.000
95606	.03	-.02	.09	.21	.694						.03	-.02	-.15	.29	.615
98732	.48	-.06	-.65	.10	<.000	.20	-.06	-.80	.38	.050					
106627	.14	-.04	-.48	.20	.023	.51	-.01	-.94	.65	.286	.02	-.04	-.19	.47	.691
106715	.27	-.07	-.58	.33	.123						.94	-.07	-.97	.10	<.000
113815	.40	-.11	-.57	.15	.001						.08	-.02	.33	.64	.647
118278	.03	-.08	-.12	.39	.776	.01	-.02	-.04	.23	.880	.08	-.12	-.28	.21	.187
118411	.19	-.05	-.38	.45	.461										
120582						.86	-.24	-1.20	.19	<.000					
120587	.29	-.11	-.62	.14	<.000						.47	-.03	-.26	.08	.005
122016	.03	-.02	-.14	.24	.558	.32	-.09	-.60	.50	.318	.02	-.00	-.08	.22	.739
122025	.25	-.06	-.75	.65	.314						.77	-.03	-.88	.28	.049
122404						.50	-.15	-1.25	.38	.007	.57	-.04	-1.30	.27	<.000
122718	.60	-.06	-.63	.07	<.000						.95	-.03	-.72	.11	.024
122753	.03	-.06	-.16	.27	.574	.45	-.10	-.67	.19	.003	.12	-.03	-.44	.46	.367
122934															

Table 9.5 Parameters of Equation 9.4, calculated for each individual consumer for each of the following three product categories: biscuits (cookies), cheese, and breakfast cereals – *continued*

	Biscuits (Cookies)					Cheese					Breakfast Cereals				
Cons.	r^2	α	β	SE	p	r^2	α	β	SE	p	r^2	α	β	SE	p
122990	.60	-.09	-.76	.19	.002										
124244	.27	-.01	-.33	.32	.367										
124559	.81	-.13	-.49	.09	.001						.85	-.12	-.78	.46	.009
124933	.14	-.02	-.38	.36	.326						.09	-.05	-.44	.41	.310
126110	.96	-.08	-.67	.04	<.000	.68	-.22	-1.62	.39	.003	.45	-.01	-1.12	.39	.017
126515						1.00	-.17	-.85	.02	<.000	.08	-.00	-.08	.07	.262
126831	.06	-.06	-.26	.28	.367	.65	-.09	-.62	.18	.015	.63	-.08	-.54	.29	.204
126874	.17	-.06	-.27	.10	.010	.84	-.22	-1.39	.19	<.000	.31	-.03	-.49	.20	.026
127526	.69	-.02	-.54	.26	.171	.92	-.05	-1.06	.14	.001	.77	-.10	-1.47	.57	.124
128130	.49	-.21	-.63	.13	<.000	.78	-.12	-.65	.11	<.000	.02	-.01	.262	.658	.702
129274															
130276	.78	-.33	-.64	.15	.008	.60	-.14	-.79	.29	.041	.78	-.48	-1.31	.26	.002
130515	.95	-.39	-.94	.11	.001	1.00	-.37	-1.04	.09	.001	.94	-.19	-.76	.14	.032
130867						.82	-.46	-.88	.18	.005					
130953	.58	-.19	-.59	.13	<.000	.00	-.04	.02	.32	.950	.49	-.04	-.85	.16	<.000
131184						.91	-.35	-.85	.06	<.000	.61	-.05	-.83	.27	.022
131294	.34	-.06	-.46	.24	.099	.67	-.32	-1.04	.22	.001					
131331	.57	-.05	-.59	.06	<.000	.92	-.33	-1.10	.09	<.000					
131357	.39	.00	.26	.19	.262	1.00	-.03	-2.90	.00	<.000					
132207											.31	-.07	-1.00	.45	.050
132764	.57	-.31	-.46	.08	<.000	.93	-.24	-.81	.07	<.000	.63	-.08	-.93	.36	.061
133271															
133272	.33	.01	.21	.21	.429										

Table 9.5 Parameters of Equation 9.4, calculated for each individual consumer for each of the following three product categories: biscuits (cookies), cheese, and breakfast cereals – *continued*

	Biscuits (Cookies)					Cheese					Breakfast Cereals				
Cons.	r^2	α	β	SE	p	r^2	α	β	SE	p	r^2	α	β	SE	p
600031	.28	-.07	-.52	.26	.076	1.00	-.66	-1.84	.04	<.000	.47	-.03	-.63	.23	.028
600469											.18	-.03	-.30	.19	.144
600817	.01	-.01	-.05	.11	.624	.73	-.29	-1.19	.18	<.000	.40	-.06	-.38	.14	.027
600948	.12	-.02	-.28	.20	.178						.63	-.08	-.85	.25	.011

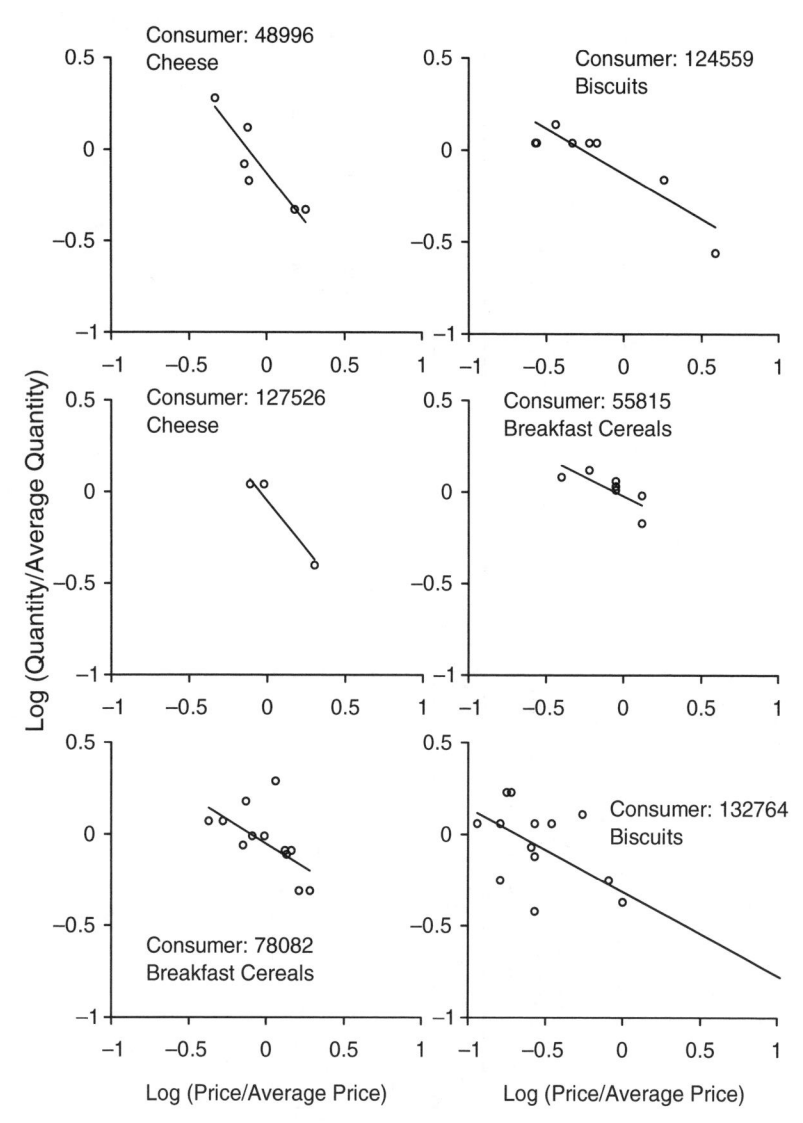

Figure 9.4 Demand curves for six consumers, two for each of the three products, calculated with data points from each of the products for each consumer

Data were chosen on the basis of similarities between individual elasticity coefficients and the average elasticity, calculated across consumers, obtained for each product.

To illustrate the type of function generated with the data presented in Table 9.5, Figure 9.4 shows demand curves for six consumers, two for each of the three products (i.e., cheese, biscuits, and cereals). Data were chosen on the basis of similarities between individual elasticity coefficients and the average elasticity, calculated across consumers, obtained for each product. In the graph that appears at the right-hand corner at the bottom of the figure, two data points (both equal to Log Quantity = –0.85 and Log Price = 1.02) are not shown in order to keep the same scale in all graphs.

With the purpose of testing the consistency of individual demand elasticity across products, correlation coefficients (Pearson), comparing elasticities across pairs of products, were calculated. Correlation coefficients between Cheese and Biscuits, Cheese and Cereals, and Cereals and Biscuits were equal to –0.02 ($N = 33$, $p = 0.927$), –0.25 ($N = 31$, $p = 0.174$), and –0.24 ($N = 42$, $p = 0.132$), respectively. These coefficients indicate that there was no consistency in individual elasticities across products.

Split-sample individual elasticities

Table 9.6 shows the parameters of Equation 9.4 calculated for each consumer across all product categories with data from Split-Sample 1 (1–8 weeks) and Split-Sample 2 (9–16 weeks). Elasticity coefficients were negative, indicating decreases in quantity with increases in prices, for 93.4% and 96% of consumers in Split-Samples 1 (76 consumers) and 2 (75 consumers), respectively. Regression analyses were significant (i.e., $p \leq 0.05$) for 68.4% ($N = 52$) and 60.0% ($N = 45$) of consumers in Split-Samples 1 and 2, respectively. Elasticity coefficients (b) ranged from –44.14 to 1.38 (M = –1.16, SD = 5.04) and from –44.14 to 0.87 (M = –1.07, SD = 5.05) in Split-Samples 1 and 2, respectively. Excluding the largest and extreme value of elasticity (i.e., –44.14 for Consumer 40563 in both samples), coefficients ranged from –5.12 to 1.38 (M = –0.58, SD = 0.70) and from –1.22 to 0.87 (M = –0.49, SD = 0.36) in Split-Samples 1 and 2, respectively. With the purpose of testing for consistencies in demand elasticity across samples, a correlation coefficient (Pearson), relating elasticity coefficients in the two samples, was calculated. The obtained coefficient was equal to 0.99 ($p < 0.000$) when including data from Consumer 40563, and equal to 0.27 ($p = 0.019$) excluding those same data. These coefficients indicate that individual differences in demand elasticity were relatively consistent across samples, that is, those consumers who showed higher elasticity in Split-Sample 1 also tended to show higher elasticity in Split-Sample 2,

Table 9.6 Parameters of Equation 9.4, calculated for each consumer using data from Split-sample 1 (weeks 1–8) and Split-sample 2 (weeks 9–16). Consumers are listed in ascending order of their identification numbers.

Cons.	\multicolumn{5}{c}{Split Sample 1}					\multicolumn{5}{c}{Split Sample 2}			
	N	r^2	α	β	SE	p	N	r^2	α	β	SE	p
10696	10	.51	−.04	−.57	.20	.020	8	.08	−.09	−.26	.35	.496
12347	31	.68	−.05	−1.04	.13	<.000	40	.55	−.14	−.77	.11	<.000
21174	37	.46	−.00	.68	.13	<.000	39	.71	−.01	.72	.08	<.000
23527	10	.01	−.06	−.07	.30	.833	8	.12	.05	.57	.66	.418
25927	48	.38	−.15	−.58	.11	<.000	48	.36	−.19	−.58	.11	<.000
26537	28	.18	−.01	−.55	.23	.024	12	.23	−.00	−.30	.17	.119
27180	23	.00	−.01	−.04	.24	.860	58	.21	−.10	−.48	.13	<.000
29425	9	.46	−.04	1.38	.57	.045	5	.36	.00	−.52	.40	.284
29436	13	.14	−.00	−.49	.36	.200	13	.37	−.11	−.71	.28	.028
31639	19	.59	−.13	−.73	.15	<.000	18	.44	−.08	−.42	.12	.003
36543	18	.30	−.02	−.71	.27	.020	21	.06	−.04	−.26	.23	.268
36968	14	.44	−.14	−.46	.15	.009	30	.29	−.18	−.49	.14	.002
40563	4	.01	.00	−44.14	449.91	.938	5	.02	.00	−44.14	193.61	.834
47278	17	.03	−.05	−.16	.24	.518	12	.06	−.05	−.30	.39	.463
48996	64	.09	−.06	−.25	.10	.016	64	.15	−.02	−.38	.12	.002
49461	14	.77	−.19	−.84	.13	<.000	12	.80	−.12	−.66	.11	<.000
55814	26	.47	−.11	−.82	.18	<.000	35	.30	−.21	−.80	.21	.001
55815	34	.32	−.09	−.48	.12	<.000	46	.30	−.07	−.53	.12	<.000
58275	36	.16	−.03	−.33	.13	.015	37	.30	−.17	−1.09	.28	<.000
59984	16	.52	−.07	−1.10	.28	.002	19	.18	−.04	−.68	.36	.073
60695	20	.27	−.14	−.56	.22	.019	15	.79	−.16	−.82	.12	<.000
61529	27	.18	−.13	−.51	.22	.029	30	.08	−.09	−.42	.28	.14

Table 9.6 Parameters of Equation 9.4, calculated for each consumer using data from Split-sample 1 (weeks 1–8) and Split-sample 2 (weeks 9–16) – *continued*
Consumers are listed in ascending order of their identification numbers.

	Split Sample 1						Split Sample 2					
Cons.	N	r^2	α	β	SE	p	N	r^2	α	β	SE	p
67380	27	.50	-.19	-.82	.17	<.000	20	.54	-.12	-.91	.20	<.000
73779	3	.99	.07	-5.12	.47	.058	5	.35	-.02	-.41	.32	.293
74108	27	.61	-.05	-1.84	.29	<.000	18	.23	-.10	-.60	.28	.044
75262	14	.06	-.03	-.66	.74	.395	15	.50	-.10	-.96	.268	.003
76872	31	.19	-.16	-.71	.28	.015	22	.05	-.05	-.34	.32	.305
78082	31	.22	-.02	-.33	.11	.008	32	.56	-.08	-.56	.09	<.000
82032	18	.00	-.00	-.03	.27	.903	27	.15	-.10	-.38	.18	.043
84030	5	.13	-.04	-.36	.54	.551	5	.30	-.01	-.77	.67	.337
86240	55	.28	-.08	-.58	.13	<.000	41	.28	-.02	-.60	.15	<.000
86295	29	.59	-.08	-1.56	.25	<.000	33	.19	-.04	-.78	.29	.010
90910	19	.55	-.14	-.84	.18	<.000	11	.35	.00	-.78	.35	.056
93182	50	.48	-.06	-.79	.12	<.000	21	.46	-.09	-1.01	.25	.001
95606	16	.00	.02	.01	.26	.964	11	.10	-.12	-.21	.21	.335
98732	43	.31	-.04	-.65	.15	<.000	51	.31	-.05	-.50	.11	<.000
106627	34	.00	-.02	-.00	.20	.999	31	.11	-.02	-.42	.22	.065
106715	8	.75	-.08	-1.16	.27	.005	15	.11	-.08	-.27	.22	.237
113815	27	.38	-.12	-.66	.17	.001	18	.19	-.02	-.29	.15	.071
118278	12	.02	-.03	-.11	.23	.639	31	.05	-.11	-.23	.18	.219
118411	6	.07	-.16	-.37	.71	.626	11	.00	.00	-.03	.60	.966
120582	8	.52	-.15	-1.03	.40	.043	9	.76	-.18	-1.22	.26	.002
120587	30	.18	-.05	-.40	.16	.018	33	.29	-.12	-.66	.18	.001
122016	37	.08	-.03	-.22	.13	.083	24	.01	-.03	-.08	.20	.703

247

Table 9.6 Parameters of Equation 9.4, calculated for each consumer using data from Split-sample 1 (weeks 1–8) and Split-sample 2 (weeks 9–16) – *continued*
Consumers are listed in ascending order of their identification numbers.

Cons.	Split Sample 1						Split Sample 2					
	N	r^2	α	β	SE	p	N	r^2	α	β	SE	p
122025	18	.19	−.03	−.46	.24	.071	15	.02	.03	−.16	.28	.582
122404	21	.03	−.09	−.08	.11	.445	24	.18	−.06	−.44	.20	.042
122718	55	.50	−.03	−.65	.09	<.000	49	.50	−.06	−.64	.09	<.000
122753	31	.62	−.04	−.94	.14	<.000	37	.06	−.05	−.21	.15	.162
122934	6	.06	−.12	−.34	.70	.650	7	.88	−.02	−.88	.14	.002
122990	15	.40	−.08	−.68	.23	.012	10	.48	−.06	−.63	.23	.025
124244	21	.04	−.01	−.28	.30	.363	26	.68	−.02	−.63	.09	<.000
124559	29	.37	−.11	−.78	.20	.001	26	.19	−.08	−.49	.21	.025
124933	18	.46	−.07	−1.18	.32	.002	16	.51	−.03	−.92	.24	.002
126110	17	.69	−.04	−.55	.09	<.000	32	.68	−.07	−.63	.08	<.000
126515	7	.55	−.10	−.54	.22	.055	5	.95	.02	−.29	.04	.005
126831	25	.20	−.11	−.62	.25	.023	21	.22	−.07	−.60	.26	.032
126874	41	.07	−.04	−.17	.10	.094	42	.45	−.04	−.54	.09	<.000
127526	17	.49	−.04	−.86	.22	.002	8	.30	−.03	−.62	.38	.160
128130	37	.23	−.07	−.47	.15	.003	38	.40	−.14	−.52	.11	<.000
129274	18	.02	−.00	.10	.21	.625	20	.14	−.03	.87	.51	.105
130276	14	.54	−.17	−.60	.16	.003	5	.25	−.09	−.22	.22	.390
130515	13	.95	−.38	−.98	.07	<.000						
130867	10	.29	−.12	−.55	.30	.105	14	.44	−.15	−.74	.24	.010
130953	40	.22	−.13	−.49	.15	.002	31	.49	−.11	−.56	.11	<.000
131184	15	.82	−.28	−.73	.09	<.000	30	.62	−.19	−.72	.11	<.000
131294	17	.65	−.10	−.56	.11	<.000	44	.39	−.12	−.93	.18	<.000

Table 9.6 Parameters of Equation 9.4, calculated for each consumer using data from Split-sample 1 (weeks 1–8) and Split-sample 2 (weeks 9–16) – *continued*
Consumers are listed in ascending order of their identification numbers.

			Split Sample 1							Split Sample 2			
Cons.	N	r^2	α	β	SE	p		N	r^2	α	β	SE	p
131331	67	.12	-.05	-.39	.13	.004		76	.32	-.03	-.57	.10	<.000
131357	23	.64	-.10	-.85	.14	<.000		31	.14	-.07	-.39	.18	.037
132207	22	.01	.03	.14	.35	.690		29	.01	-.04	-.15	.28	.594
132764	40	.26	-.14	-.30	.08	.001		30	.08	-.08	-.19	.12	.121
133271	38	.54	-.03	-.66	.10	<.000		51	.56	-.08	-.59	.08	<.000
133272	5	.00	-.02	-.04	.59	.955		10	.00	-.06	-.03	.35	.926
600031	18	.59	-.11	-1.11	.23	<.000		38	.14	-.13	-.77	.33	.023
600469	10	.75	-.04	-.84	.17	.001		12	.11	-.07	-.43	.39	.289
600817	65	.18	-.07	-.40	.11	<.000		37	.47	-.06	-1.01	.18	<.000
600948	14	.42	-.06	-.66	.22	.012		16	.13	-.04	-.51	.35	.169

whereas those with lower elasticity in one sample also tended to show lower elasticity in the other.

Discussion

The present results point to four general empirical conclusions. First, they suggest that demand elasticity coefficients calculated for individual consumers purchasing supermarket food products are compatible with predictions from economic theory and research in behavioral economics. Second, overall analyses of demand elasticity (i.e., based on several purchases of many consumers), typically employed in marketing and econometric research, include effects of inter-consumer and intra-consumer elasticities. Third, when comparing demand elasticities of different product categories, group and individual analyses yield similar trends. And fourth, individual differences in demand elasticity are relatively consistent across time, but do not seem to be consistent across products.

From the laboratory to national economy

In the present investigation of consumers purchasing supermarket food products in a national economy, individual elasticity coefficients (i.e., Equation 9.4) were negative, indicating decreases in purchased quantity with increases in prices (purchasing the same or different brands). Moreover, the large majority of individual coefficients were within the range of 0.00 to −1.00, that is, they indicated inelastic demand. This shows that despite the fact that individuals tend to buy smaller (than the average) quantities when paying higher (than the average) prices, they tend to increase their total spending when paying prices above the usual average price they pay. This inelastic demand for food products observed for individual consumers is in perfect agreement with that obtained using group data in the present chapter (overall product elasticity, see Table 9.2) and those reported in the literature using different estimation methods (cf. U. K. National Food Survey, see Lechene, 2000; Walters & Bommer, 1996). Hence, our findings confirm that quantity demanded is a decreasing function of price and that this functional relationship holds at the level of the individual consumer, which is the fundamental unit of decision making in (economic) consumer theory.

With respect to the form of the function, it is generally accepted that the linear log-log equation adopted here does not describe well experimental demand curves, for elasticity tends to increase when extreme values of prices are used. Hursh has proposed an alternative, two-parameter log-linear equation that has described experimental data quite well (cf. Hursh et al., 1988; Hursh & Winger, 1995). In order to examine the possibility of significant deviations from linearity in the present data, a quadratic term was included in Equation 9.2, and the modified equation was fitted to all data points (i.e., all purchases from all consumers) obtained from each product category. The results indicated significant effects of the quadratic term for only two products, breakfast cereals and cheese, suggesting that it is reasonable to assume linear elasticity for most product categories. This difference in the ability of the linear form of the equation to describe the demand function might be explained by the small price variations observed in the present study, which are typical of real market conditions, when compared to the extreme variations used in experimental settings. However, the fact that the large majority of intercept values obtained in the present study were smaller than zero might be interpreted as supporting a non-linearity assumption. Considering that smaller-than-zero intercepts indicate that at the average price paid (by the group or by individuals) consumers tended to buy quantities a little smaller than the average quantity bought, this suggests that the demand curve is not symmetrically located at the average values of price and quantity. As most intercepts were smaller than zero, this asymmetry favors Hursh's equation indicating that elasticity might increase at extreme prices.

Separating intra-consumer and inter-consumer elasticities

Overall product price elasticity, calculated with data from several purchases of each of a large groups of consumers (e.g., Equation 9.2, Table 9.2), is similar to the most typical econometric analyses found in the marketing literature. This type of analysis of elasticity may be a combination of intra-consumer and inter-consumer elasticities. The finding that, for the large majority of consumers, individual elasticity coefficients were negative and significant demonstrates the occurrence of intra-consumer elasticity (Table 9.4, Equation 9.4). This means that, on different shopping occasions, the same consumer tends to buy smaller (than the average) quantities of a product when paying higher (than average) prices.

Intra-consumer elasticity may be due to their paying different amounts for a given brand (e.g., during and after a price promotion) or buying a differently priced brand. According to typical buying patterns reported in the literature, which show that the vast majority of consumers tend to choose, on each shopping occasion, from a subset of three or four brands (e.g., Ehrenberg, 1988), the changes in prices consumers pay across shopping occasions are most likely the result of a combination of paying different prices for a given brand and buying other, differentially priced brands (*cf.* Foxall *et al.*, 2004). Indeed, these results elucidate more generally the patterns of consumer brand choice identified in studies of aggregate buyer behavior in the marketing literature (*cf.* Ehrenberg, 1988; Ehrenberg *et al.*, 2004; Uncles *et al.*, 1995). Although their research has identified several patterns of consumer choice that have been widely replicated across products and countries, they have not analyzed consumers' responsiveness to price differentials outside promotions and have assumed that the quantity consumers buy on each shopping trip is relatively constant. The finding of intra-consumer elasticity demonstrates that consumers do change the quantity they buy according to the price they pay on each shopping trip, suggesting that some assumptions and conclusions stemming from this type of literature should be re-examined.

The present results also provide evidence for inter-consumer elasticity, which was negative for all nine product categories and statistically significant for seven of them (Table 9.3, Equation 9.3). These negative inter-consumer elasticities indicate that consumers who pay prices above the average price paid in the category tend to buy quantities that are smaller than the average quantity bought in the category. Such an effect may be related to demographic characteristics, such as family size and income, which might determine the quantities consumers need to buy and the prices they can pay. As we did not have information concerning consumers' demographic characteristics, this hypothesis could not be tested. Moreover, inter-consumer elasticity coefficients were all between -0.31 to -0.91, indicating inelastic demand, and were very similar to those obtained for overall product categories and individual consumers.

Taken together, these results demonstrate that overall product elasticity obtained from group data, including several purchases of each consumer, is the result of two different behavioral patterns, namely, intra- and inter-consumer elasticities. Considering that inter- and intra-consumer elasticities could, theoretically, add to each other to inflate overall elasticity coefficients based on disaggregate data, the finding that overall and inter-consumer coefficients were similar should be tested using larger data sets (e.g., more consumers, longer time periods, and more products).

Group *versus* individual analyses of elasticity

One of the main purposes of the present research was to examine possible differences between findings derived from individual data and those obtained from groups of people. This empirical test becomes particularly relevant in the present case in view of the observed patterns of inter-consumer and intra-consumer elasticities. As overall product elasticity coefficients, calculated with data from all purchases from all consumers, were the results of specific combinations of intra- and inter-consumer elasticities, one cannot assume that individual elasticities across products followed the same trends as group elasticities.

Following this line of reasoning, overall product elasticity coefficients, based on all data from all consumers, were compared with those obtained for different individuals across three product categories. Comparisons of elasticity coefficients obtained for the same consumers across different product categories (i.e., Table 9.5) indicated similar trends in elasticity to those observed when elasticity coefficients were calculated with group data, that is, elasticity coefficient for cheese was larger than that for cereals, which in turn was similar to that for biscuits. These similar findings help validate both individual and group analyses of elasticity coefficients, any one of which may be used depending on research or managerial purposes.

Consistency of individual elasticities across products and time

Individual elasticity coefficients obtained for each consumer purchasing each of three products (i.e., cheese, breakfast cereals, and biscuits) were not significantly correlated, indicating that individual differences in elasticity were not consistent across product categories. Results from the literature are not totally clear on this point. Although some authors found significant similarities in consumer choice patterns across product categories, others did not (*cf.* Ainslie & Rossi, 1998; Andrew & Currim, 2002). Such contradictory results have been attributed to methodological differences across studies, for those that have reported significant differences adopted more complex statistical models, including information about consumer preferences, marketing mix effects, and consumer loyalty, than those that reported negative results (*cf.* Andrew & Currim, 2002). Considering that the methodology adopted in the present chapter is more similar to those employed in studies that did not find behavioral consistency across categories, the present results are not totally surprising. The small sample size in the present study did not make possible the use of more complex statistical models.

Individual elasticity coefficients from the two split-sample analyses were significantly and positively correlated indicating that individual differences in elasticity coefficients show some consistency across time. This finding opens new directions for research and applications using information concerning the behavior of individual consumers and helps validate the new procedure adopted here to calculate individual elasticity coefficients, which were based on relative measures from all product categories. The fact that relatively similar individual coefficients were observed in both split-samples suggests that they are reliable measures of individual behavior. The reliability of this measure also is suggested by the fact that several different analyses of elasticity yielded similar results, that is, the large majority of coefficients ranged from –0.20 to –1.00 (although this range tended to increase when fewer data points were used, e.g., individual coefficients for specific products). Values predominantly within this range were observed for overall product elasticity, intra-consumer elasticity across all products with the entire sample, intra-consumer elasticity across all products with half samples, intra-consumer elasticity for individual products (only three products), and inter-consumer elasticity.

Note

1. Previously published in *Journal of the Experimental Analysis of Behavior*, 2006, 85, 147–66.

References

Ainslie, A. & Rossi, P. E. (1998). "Similarities in choice behavior across product categories". *Marketing Science*, 17, 91–106.

Allison, J. (1981). "Economics and operant conditioning", in P. Harzem & M. D. Zeiler (eds) *Advances in analysis of behaviour: Vol. 2: Predictability, correlation, and contiguity*. London: Wiley, pp. 321–53.

Andrew, R. L. & Currim, I. S. (2002). "Identifying segments with identical choice behaviors across product categories: An intercategory logit mixture model". *International Journal of Research in Marketing*, 19, 65–79.

Battalio, R. C., Kagel, J. H., Winkler, R. C., Fisher, E. B. Jr., Basmann, R. L. & Krasner, L. (1973). "A test of consumer demand theory using observations of individual consumer purchases". *Western Economic Journal*, 11, 411–28.

Bell, D. R., Chiang, J. & Padmanabhan, V. (1999). "The decomposition of promotional response: An empirical generalization". *Marketing Science*, 18, 504–26.

Bickel, W. K., Green, L. & Vuchinich, R. E. (1995). "Behavioral economics". *Journal of the Experimental Analysis of Behavior*, 64, 257–62.

Churchill, G .A. Jr. (1999). *Marketing research: Methodological foundations* 7th edn. Fort Worth, TX: The Dryden Press.

Crouch, S. & Housden, M. (2003). *Marketing research for managers* 3rd edn. Oxford: Butterworth-Heinemann.

Ehrenberg, A. S. C. (1988). *Repeat-buying: Theory and applications* 2nd edn. London: Griffin.

Ehrenberg, A. S. C., Uncles, M. D. & Goodhardt, G. J. (2004). "Understanding brand performance measures: using Dirichlet benchmarks". *Journal of Business Research*, 57, 1307–25.

Foxall, G. R. (ed.) (2002). *Consumer behavior analysis: Critical perspectives*. London and New York: Routledge.

Foxall, G. R., Oliveira-Castro, J. M. & Schrezenmaier, T. C. (2004). "The behavioral economics of consumer brand choice: Patterns of reinforcement and utility maximization". *Behavioral Processes*, 66, 235–60.

Guadagni, P. M. & Little, J. D. C. (1983). "A logit model of brand choice calibrated on scanner data". *Marketing Science*, 2, 203–38.

Gupta, S. (1988). "The impact of sales promotions on when, what, and how much to buy". *Journal of Marketing Research*, 25, 342–55.

Hursh, S. R. (1980). "Economic concepts for the analysis of behavior". *Journal of the Experimental Analysis of Behavior*, 34, 219–38.

Hursh, S. R. (1984). "Behavioral economics". *Journal of the Experimental Analysis of Behavior*, 42, 435–52.

Hursh, S. R., Raslear, T. G., Shurtleff, D., Bauman, R. & Simmon, L. (1988). "A cost benefit analysis of demand for food". *Journal of the Experimental Analysis of Behavior*, 50, 419–40.

Hursh, S. R. & Winger, G. (1995). "Normalized demand for drugs and other reinforcers". *Journal of the Experimental Analysis of Behavior*, 64, 373–84.

Kagel, J. H., Battalio, R. C. & Green, L. (1995). *Economic choice theory: An experimental analysis of animal behavior*. Cambridge: Cambridge University Press.

Lea, S. E. G. (1978). "The psychology and economics of demand". *Psychological Bulletin*, 85, 441–66.

Lechene, V. (2000). National Food Survey, Section 6. Institute of Fiscal Studies Working Papers (www.ifs.org.uk), (pp. 89–108). London: Institute of Fiscal Studies.

Myerson, J. & Green, L. (1995). "Discounting of delayed rewards: Models of individual choice". *Journal of the Experimental Analysis of Behavior*, 64, 263–73.

Neslin, S. A., Henderson, C. & Quelch, J. (1985). "Consumer promotions and the acceleration of product purchases". *Marketing Science*, 4, 147–65.

Sidman, M. (1952). "A note on functional relations obtained from group data". *Psychological Bulletin*, 49, 263–9.

Telser, L. G. (1962). "The demand for branded goods as estimated from consumer panel data". *The Review of Economics and Statistics*, 44, 300–24.

Uncles, M., Ehrenberg, A. S. C. & Hammond, K. (1995). "Patterns of buyer behavior: Regularities, models, and extensions". *Marketing Science*, 14, G71–G78.

Walters, R. G. & Bommer, W. (1996). "Measuring the impact of the product and promotion-related factors on product category price elasticities". *Journal of Business Research*, 36, 203–16.

10
Deviations from Matching in Consumer Choice[1]

Sully Romero, Gordon R. Foxall, Teresa C. Schrezenmaier, Jorge M. Oliveira-Castro and Victoria K. James

Introduction

Consumer researchers have established that most buyers of fast-moving consumer goods such as packed foods practice multi-brand purchasing. Analyses of such products show that most consumers tend to purchase a variety of brands within a product category, selecting among a small "repertoire" of brands rather than being exclusively loyal to a single brand (Ehrenberg, 1988). Research generally shows that in stationary conditions (i.e., the absence of any marked short-term trend in sales) (a) only a few consumers acquire a given brand on consecutive shopping occasions; (b) most consumers buy several different brands, selecting them apparently randomly from a subset or "repertoire" of known, tried and tested brands. At the brand level; (c) each brand attracts only a small percentage of 100%-loyal consumers; (d) brands within a product category tend to differ broadly with respect to their penetration levels but tend to be more similar in terms of their average purchasing frequency; and (e) brands with smaller penetration levels (or market shares) also tend to show smaller average buying frequencies and smaller percentages of 100%-loyal consumers (i.e., the effect known as "Double Jeopardy"). These patterns have been demonstrated for a variety of product categories, from food and drinks to aviation fuel, from personal care products to pharmaceutical prescriptions, for patterns of shopping trips and selection of store chains (Ehrenberg, 1988; Uncles *et al.*, 1995; Goodhardt *et al.*, 1984).

Based on these results, a mathematical model was developed which makes it possible to describe the patterns found, the Dirichlet Model (Goodhardt *et al.*, 1984). It focuses on the differences between brands' penetration as explanatory variable, and it has been satisfactorily used to analyze the effects of promotions (Ehrenberg *et al.*, 1994), to evaluate patterns of store loyalty (Uncles & Ehrenberg, 1990), and to predict the insertion of new products into the market (Ehrenberg, 1993). However, as the model's authors conclude, the Dirichlet says little about the variables that account for individuals' patterns of behavior (Goodhardt *et al.*, 1984).

Marketing research has sometimes tended to overlook the effect of price by emphasizing the non-price elements of the marketing mix, concentrating especially on promotional activities (e.g., advertising) that make for brand differentiation. Therefore, price has rarely been used in marketing to systematically explain brand choices other than in the context of promotional campaigns which generally constitute tactical exceptions of marketing strategies (Ehrenberg *et al.*, 1994). However, price is a frequent source of explanation in behavioral economic research, where the economic behavior of animals in experimental conditions has been widely explored, and where price has been seen as the sole index of the varied influences on consumer demand brought about by the marketing system. In this sense, behavioral economists have followed the reasoning and methodology of economics rather than those used by marketing sciences.

Rational choice theory would suggest that consumers would choose the option with the highest utility. In other words, rational choice theory would assume that consumers would purchase just one brand, i.e., they would do the best thing possible under all circumstances. However, as has already been seen, consumers do not tend to act in this way and instead make multi-brand purchase. Operant psychology makes predictions based on observed patterns of behavior controlled by a history of reinforcement, not the foresight expected in economically rational choices (Lea, 1978). In 1990, Herrnstein suggested an alternative theory of choice, the matching law. He stated that although rational choice theory remains unequaled as a normative theory, deviations from it are generally well explained by the matching law, including the issue of non-100% loyalty to a particular choice.

The matching law was developed by behavioral scientists based on the results obtained in choice experiments with non-human subjects. Within the matching law, choice is defined not as an internal deliberative process, but as a rate of temporally distributed intersubjectively observable events (Herrnstein, 1997). In its simplest form, the matching law establishes that, when presented with a choice situation (two opportunities to respond X and Y) organisms allocate their responses according to the rates of rewards available in each alternative

(Herrnstein, 1961, 1970). In other words, the response rate (B) is proportional to the relative rate of reinforcement (R) (de Villiers & Herrnstein, 1976). In this sense, the matching relation takes the form:

$$B_x/(B_x + B_y) = R_x/(R_x + R_y) \qquad (10.1)$$

Where B is the number of responses allocated to options x and y and R is the number of reinforcements contingent upon those responses. Expressed in terms of ratios this relation becomes:

$$B_x/B_y = R_x/R_y \qquad (10.2)$$

A generalized form of the matching law states that the ratio of responses between two alternatives is a power function of the ratio of reinforcements (Baum, 1974; see also Baum, 1979). Expressed in arithmetic terms this relation becomes:

$$(\log)B_x/B_y = s\,(\log)(R_x/R_y) + (\log)b \qquad (10.3)$$

In the generalized matching law, the constants b and s account respectively for the differences among reinforcers in terms of *bias* (e.g., preferences for one reinforcer based on features such as physical placement or color), and *sensitivity* (e.g., responsiveness to the alternative responses) (Baum, 1974). The parameter $\log b$ or *bias* constitutes the intercept of the linear log–log formulation of the law. Deviations of this parameter from unity are interpreted as indicating a consistent preference for one option independently of its reinforcement rate schedule. Such bias is generally a result of experimental artifacts that could make one response less costly than the other.

The exponent s constitutes the slope of the linear log–log formulation, and corresponds to a deviation from strict matching, indicating that the individual favors the richer ($s > 1$, overmatching) or the poorer ($s < 1$, undermatching) schedule of reinforcement more than predicted by the matching law (see Baum, 1974). Furthermore, research using matching analysis with qualitatively different reinforcers (e.g., food and water) has shown to be an exception to the predictions of matching law. When using qualitatively different commodities, as gross complements (i.e., when an increase on the consumption of one product requires the increase of the consumption of a second product, as is the case with food and water), it has been found that choice ratio has an inverse relationship with the reinforcement ratio, showing the exact opposite to what the matching law predicts (Hursh, 1978; see Kagel *et al.*, 1995 for a review). Hence, this particular effect has been named *Anti-matching,* and in operational terms it consists of a result of $s < 0$ in the generalized matching equation (Kagel *et al.*, 1995).

Similar results (see Kagel *et al.*, 1995 for a review) have allowed behavioral economists to conclude that the parameters on the generalized matching equation could be assumed to be an analogous measure of the economic principle of substitutability of reinforcements in the experimental situation (Rachlin *et al.*, 1981; Green & Freed, 1993; Foxall, 1999). The concept of substitutability is referred to as a continuum of possible interactions among reinforcers (Green & Freed, 1993). One end of that continuum is defined by perfectly substitutable commodities, the other by complementary products, and independent products correspond to the middle point between the two. Green & Freed (1993) point out that a definition of substitutability has to consider not only qualitative similarities between the reinforcers, but also their function. In this sense, these authors define substitutable goods as "those that serve similar purposes" (p. 142). Therefore, by definition, commodities that serve different purposes are considered as either complements (in the case that they are used jointly, i.e., tea and biscuits) or independent goods (i.e., tea and baked beans).

Matching and other operant techniques, developed and widely tested and replicated in experimental settings (generally with rats and pigeons) have been used in a wide range of human and more applied situations. Token economies have been used extensively to test operant principles and the similarities between operant and economic predictions (see for example: Ayllon & Azrin, 1968; Kagel, 1972; Kagel *et al.*, 1975). Other relevant studies include those by Conger & Kileen (1974) who used time allocation matching to investigate human social processes and found close approximations to matching, Bernstein & Ebbesen (1978) who examined how people allocate their time between different activities, Buskist & Miller (1981) who used a vending machine to explore VI–VI schedules and Myerson & Hale (1984) who used VI schedules to reduce inappropriate behavior. Within consumer psychology there have been a number of attempts to apply operant techniques, behavioral ecology and matching. These include studies by Hantula and colleagues using simulated malls (e.g., Rajala & Hantula, 2000; Smith & Hantula, 2003).

The molar analysis of behavior provided by the matching law (response frequencies as a function of reinforcement frequencies instead of a molecular stimulus-response analysis) has given a framework for behavior analysts to investigate multi-brand patterns of consumption. The first theoretical attempt to apply matching and melioration to consumer choice was Foxall (1999) who suggests that, in terms of purchasing, the matching law would state that "the proportion of dollars/pounds spent for a commodity will match the proportion of reinforcers earned (i.e., purchases made as a result of that spending)". He also suggests that although matching was developed on and largely tested with VI[2] schedules, ratio schedules[3] may be more suitable to explain consumption/purchase situations. There is general agreement in the literature regarding this (see Myerson & Hale, 1984; Hursh, 1984; Hursh & Bauman, 1987). It is supported by the idea that, to obtain a product, individuals must provide a certain number of responses, for example, 33 to purchase a tin of baked beans (a tin of baked beans would cost 33 pence/cents). Although there has been a debate over whether FR or VR schedules are a more suitable analogue, it is the proposition of this research that FR schedules represent a consumer's choice in a one-week period (the prices are fixed within the shopping trip) while VR schedules represent an aggregation across shopping trips (as prices will vary between weeks) and hence the terms VR3 (across three weeks) and VR5 (across five weeks) have been used to describe particular integrations of the data in ways analogous to the schedules employed in the experimental analysis of behavior (Foxall & James, 2001). The one-week ("FR") and three-week ("VR3") time scales were chosen simply to provide enough data within the 16-week period of available information. They also seem to be different enough to produce noticeable effect across the weeks. The matching law suggests that both concurrent VR–VR and concurrent FR–FR schedules would result in the same behavior patterns: i.e., exclusive preference on the best schedule.

The first quantitative attempt to apply the matching law to the analysis of brand and product choice in real-world conditions was done by Foxall & James (2001, 2003). This preliminary research sought to establish whether (1) Matching (the methodology employed will be discussed further later), (2) Maximization and (3) Downward-sloping demand curves were found in consumers' shopping behavior. The research was undertaken in two phases, a qualitative and a quantitative phase. The qualitative phase allowed the researchers to obtain information about general shopping and purchasing habits of subjects recruited on a convenience basis, and it was particularly important for understanding the degree of substitutability-in-use of different brands of the same product category.

The quantitative phase gave information about the occurrence or non-occurrence of the matching phenomenon at different levels of substitutability through the analysis of prices paid and amount bought. The investigation focused on single subjects' shopping patterns of specific products categories selected from the results of the qualitative research. The purchase choice of substitutes (different brands of cat food), non-substitutes (bottled soft drinks in another) and independent (wine and cola) products were analyzed for one (FR)-, three (VR3)-, and five (VR5)-week periods. The results of this preliminary research showed how consumer choices at product and brand levels could be analyzed using the matching, relative demand analysis and maximization theories and provided evidence of the importance of price on consumer decision making.

Foxall & James (2001, 2003) found near perfect matching, maximization, and very strong downward-sloping demand curves for substitutable products. The qualitative analysis supported these results, since the participants explained how they alternated their choices among the different brands of their repertoire of brands, deciding from week to week based on price dealings or seeking to achieve variety. Similar analyses were performed with brands that were not substantially substitutes. A subject bought two brands of cola on a weekly basis, and he described them as non-substitutes. The results were similar to those found for substitutable products, showing again almost near matching and maximization. The demand curves, however, showed less negative slopes (some were even positive) which is coherent with inelastic demand. Following the conclusions of Kagel *et al.* (1995) anti-matching was expected for grossly complementary products. The results for the maximization and relative demand analyses did not differ substantially from those found for substitutable and non-substitutable brands, but they did differ for the matching analysis. Of particular interest for the present chapter, the results for substitutable brands compared to gross-complements yielded different levels of sensitivity, showing generally the theoretically expected behavior. For commodities that were considered perfect substitutes and independents the results showed an s close to 1 on the logarithmic expression of the matching curve, whereas for grossly complementary products anti-matching was observed, but only for the three-week VR schedule. For the other two analyses, under-matching was found, showing a clear need for further analysis.

Similar analyses were undertaken by Foxall & Schrezenmaier (2003) and Foxall *et al.* (2004) whose research sought to generalize the results found by Foxall & James (2001) on perfect substitutes (different brands of the same product category) by using a sample of 80 consumers, buying nine food product categories over 16 weeks. In this study, the researchers did not approach the participants directly, but used data provided by a consumer panel from a set of randomly selected British households. Following the procedure used by Foxall & James (2001), matching, maximization analysis, and the relative demand curve were carried out on FR (one week) and VR (three weeks) schedules, based on an aggregated analysis across consumers and also weeks, in the case of the VR3 schedule.

Foxall & Schrezenmaier (2003) analyzed patterns of choice for different brands within the same product category. In accordance with Ehrenberg (1988), multi-brand choice patterns were found for the majority of the sample among the different product categories, and only a small number of consumers showed sole buying choices of each brand. Likewise, matching was found and in accordance to the generalized matching law stated by Baum (1974) the parameter s indicated substitutability among the different brands within the consumers' repertoire. For the relative demand analysis, the expected downward-sloping curves were found. Maximization analysis showed a more complicated pattern, since consumers mostly bought the cheapest brand within their repertoire of brands, which was however not necessarily the cheapest among all the brands of the product category. In other words, their repertoire in some cases included only premium, highly differentiated brands, and these consumers bought the cheapest brand within those exclusive repertoires, therefore maximizing in terms on their own consideration set and not in any "absolute" sense.

Foxall et al. (2004) conducted further analyses in order to understand this pattern of maximization in which consumers buy the cheapest brand within their own repertoire of brands instead of the cheapest brand among all the brands available within a product category. In other words, they aimed to investigate why different brands of the same product (that are supposed to be functionally equivalent) are not always perceived by consumers as perfect substitutes for each other. This research constitutes a deeper attempt to integrate behavioral economic theories with the postulates of marketing sciences, since it managed to include ideas of branding (as an extra-functional source of reinforcement) within economic (price-focused) proposals through the differentiation between utilitarian (functional benefits derived from purchase and consumption) and informational (symbolic, usually mediated by actions and reactions of other persons) reinforcements proposed by the Behavioral Perspective Model (Foxall, 1990, 1996).

The results suggested that consumers choose their set of brands within a product category based on both utilitarian and informational levels of reinforcement programmed by the brands. The authors concluded that consumers could be segmented (grouped) through their choices by the combinations provided by this categorization.

However, the analysis performed by Foxall *et al.* (2004) was carried out only at the brand level, where near perfect matching was expected, and the somewhat inconclusive results found by Foxall & James (2001, 2003) on anti-matching warranted further analysis. The current research further investigates matching patterns in consumer choice with different product categories among which different levels of substitutability are expected. It employs the same data employed by Foxall *et al.* (2004). The general expectation guiding the research was that, for more substitutable products, some degree of matching would be apparent, whereas complementary products would exhibit anti-matching.

Method

Sample

Participants were 80 British consumers selected from the Taylor-Nelson Sofres "Superpanel", which comprises some 15,000 households that represent the British population. The Superpanel collects data on all purchases for each of the 15,000 households as and when they shop. Panel members scan the barcode printed on the packaging of their purchases into a sophisticated handheld barcode reader after each shopping occasion. The information recorded for each shopping occasion includes selected brand, actual price paid, quantity bought (package sizes), number of units bought, date, and name of the supermarket/shop. The data are then electronically transmitted to the TNS mainframe computer, and can be used to generate market trends reports. The 80 consumers used in this study were chosen randomly. The data obtained corresponds to nine fast-moving consumer product categories during a period of 16 weeks from the 25th February 2001 to 10th June 2001. The categories used in this research were: tea, instant coffee, butter, margarine, fruit juice, breakfast cereals, baked beans, and biscuits (cookies).

Procedure

Based on the nine product categories available, ten combinations of products were created varying in their level of substitutability. In this sense, a combination of cereals/margarine was expected to exhibit greater mutual independence than the combination biscuits/tea and biscuits/coffee which consumers are more likely to perceive as complementary products. Likewise, combinations such as baked beans/fruit juice and baked beans/cereals were assumed to be more distant from the perfect substitutability end of the continuum than the combination of coffee/tea and margarine/butter. These assumptions were made considering the conceptualization of substitutability proposed by Green & Freed (1993) which emphasizes the products' functionality. Presumptions about the degree of substitutability of each product combination were validated by 11 consumers on a scale of substitutability (see Appendix 3). Results supported the researchers' assumptions (see Appendix 4). The ten combinations in order of substitutability-independence-complementarity were: margarine/butter, coffee/tea, fruit juice/tea, cereals/biscuits, cereals/baked beans, cereals/margarine, fruit juice/baked beans, biscuits/fruit juice, biscuits/coffee, and biscuits/tea. Participants who had bought the two product categories over the 16 weeks were then selected for the analysis of each product combination.

Measures and analysis

The measures and analysis employed in this research consisted of an adaptation of those generally used in behavioral economics and matching research (Herrnstein, 1982; Herrnstein & Vaughan, 1980). Further information about the derivation of the precise measures used – summarized below – can be found in Foxall & James (2001, 2003; Foxall & Schrezenmaier, 2003).

Matching and anti-matching

The matching analysis performed in this research followed the procedure stated by Herrnstein (1997) in matching research with animal and human subjects. As noted briefly earlier, when applied to consumer research, the matching law can be translated as the proposition that the ratio of amount of money (pounds and pence; dollars and cents, etc.) spent for a product/brand to the amount spent on other near perfectly substitutable products (i.e., other brands of the same product category) will match the ratio of reinforcement earned (i.e., purchases made as a result of that spending) of that product/brand to the amount bought of other perfectly substitutable products (i.e., other brands of the same product category) (Foxall, 1999).

However, as stated before in this research some of the reinforcers used are considered to be what Kagel *et al*. (1995) named gross complements (i.e., biscuits/tea; biscuits/coffee); therefore, for those combinations it is expected to find an anti-matching effect rather than matching. On these considerations, the proposition above becomes: the amount of money spent for a product category to the amount spent on another product category (independent or grossly complementary), will show anti-matching with the ratio of reinforcement earned of that product category to the amount bought of another product category (independent or grossly complementary). This was operationalized as follows: the *Response Ratio* was defined as the amount spent for a product category to the amount spent for a second product category: *Amount paid for product category A/Amount paid for product category B*. The *Reinforcement Ratio* was calculated in terms of the physical quantity bought: *Amount bought of product category A/Amount bought of product category B*. Analyses were conducted using logarithmic transformations.

In summary, the s parameter on the generalized equation proposed by Baum (1974) is expected to vary according to the level of substitutability of products. In this sense, it is expected that the slope will decrease from near perfect matching (for substitutable products such as margarine/butter) to anti-matching (for complementary products such as biscuits/tea). Following Baum's (1974) propositions, slopes between 1.10 and 0.90 will be considered near perfect matching. Slopes with values over 1.10 will be considered overmatching whereas any value between 0.90 and 0 will be regarded as undermatching. Values of $s < 0$ will be interpreted as anti-matching.

Schedule analogues

As noted previously schedule analogues in terms of FR and VR3 have been implemented in this research. It is hoped that this distinction will allow exploration of whether consumers consider only the prices of different products available on each discrete shopping trip or whether their choice reflects the expected price-quantity relations over the extended period represented by a series of shopping trips. Generally the prices varied across weeks by pence/cents and not pounds/dollars although some prices did vary more due to promotions.

Results

The matching analysis was conducted for ten different combinations of products that were assumed to vary in their degree of substitutability. Consumers that bought both products within the same week and/or within periods of three weeks on at least three different occasions were identified, and their ratios of response and reinforcement for each period were calculated. Additionally, aggregated analyses (including all data for all the consumers) were performed for the subset of consumers for each combination in the two different schedules of reinforcement. Table 10.1 displays the number and percentage of consumers identified on the original sample of 80 consumers for each combination of products within the two schedules of reinforcement.

Table 10.1 shows that the percentage of consumers buying the two products within each combination generally increased for the VR schedules. Biscuits/fruit juice, (where the percentage remained the same) and biscuits/coffee (the number decreased by one in the VR schedule) were the single exceptions. This pattern is expected since the probability of buying the two commodities over a period of three weeks is larger than buying them within the same week. Therefore, some consumers that were not included for the FR schedules because they had not bought the two products on the same shopping occasion or week, were included on the VR schedule because they bought both products over periods of three weeks. However, a small number of consumers that were considered for the FR schedule analysis were not included for the VR analogues; the reason was that they bought the two products over three consecutive weeks, and therefore, when aggregating their choices over three weeks the results yielded less than two shopping periods (see Appendix 1).

The combination that produced the largest subset of consumers was cereals/biscuits (with almost half of the sample of consumers buying them over the same periods) and the one that yielded the smallest

Table 10.1 Frequencies (fr) and Percentages (%) of consumers for product combination within FR and VR

	FR Schedule		VR Schedule	
Product combination	fr	%	Fr	%
Margarine & Butter	7	9%	10	13%
Coffee & Tea	5	6%	6	8%
Fruit Juice & Tea	8	10%	9	11%
Cereals & Biscuits	37	46%	41	51%
Cereals & Beans	20	25%	27	34%
Cereals & Margarine	30	37%	35	44%
Fruit Juice & Beans	10	12%	16	20%
Biscuits & Fruit Juice	23	28%	23	29%
Biscuits & Coffee	12	15%	11	14%
Biscuits & Tea	17	21%	19	24%

subset was coffee/tea (with less than 10% of shoppers buying both products over the same shopping periods). The reasons for these results could vary from combination to combination (e.g., it may be due to the differences on the products frequencies of purchase). For some product arrangements it could be due to the fact that consumers buy one or the other but not both products categories (which could be the case for margarine/butter and coffee/tea).

Matching analysis

General Results. Figure 10.1 shows the percentage of consumers whose choice patterns indicated overmatching, matching, undermatching and anti-matching, when calculated in terms of a weekly rate (FR schedule) for each product combination which ranged from substitutable to complementary pairs of products. As can be seen in Figure 10.1 (see also Appendix 2), for eight (out of ten) product combinations, undermatching was the most frequent form of choice behavior found. The highest percentage of undermatching was found for a combination of independent products (cereals/margarine = 67%) and the lowest among this group was exhibited by the complements biscuits/coffee (33%). However, for biscuits/tea this percentage did not differ from that found for overmatching (undermatching = overmatching = 35%), and in the case of biscuits/coffee not only was the percentage of under

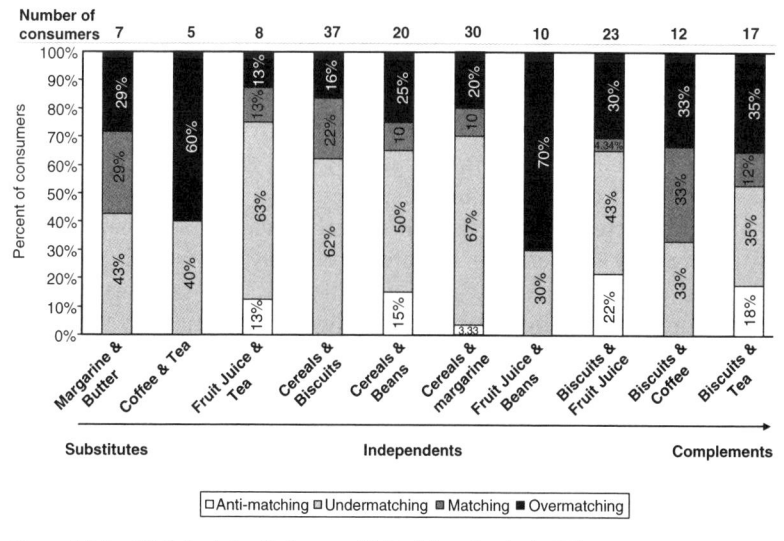

Figure 10.1 FR Schedule: Patterns of Matching Analysis (%)

and overmatching identical, but it was also the same as matching (undermatching = overmatching = matching = 33%). These values indicate that, for different behavioral patterns, approximately the same number of consumers was found. For the other two combinations, undermatching was the second most predominant pattern (fruit juice/baked beans = 30% and coffee/tea = 40%).

The second most frequent pattern of behavior found was overmatching. The highest percentage was shown for the combinations of fruit juice/baked beans (70%) and coffee/tea (60%). As stated before, for two combinations (biscuits/coffee and biscuits/tea) there was a tie in the percentage of overmatching and other forms of behavioral allocation. The arrangement of fruit juice/tea yielded the smallest number of overmatching (13%). For five of the six remaining combinations, overmatching was the second most common performance. Cereals/biscuits constituted the single exception, with only 16% of consumers overmatching, and therefore this pattern was the third and not the second most common form of behavioral allocation. As happened in the case of undermatching, there were two product arrangements where the percentage of overmatching was the same as the one found for other patterns. Thus, for the substitutes margarine/butter, the percentage of consumers showing overmatching was the same as that found for near perfect matching (overmatching = matching = 29%). Likewise, in the case of fruit juice/tea, the number of participants overmatching did not differ from those matching nor from the ones anti-matching (overmatching = matching = anti-matching = 13%).

In general, these two behavioral patterns account for between 67% (biscuits/coffee) and 100% (fruit juice/baked beans and coffee/tea) of consumers' choices. As a consequence, both matching and anti-matching were generally infrequent. However, for three product combinations the frequency of matching was equal to (fruit juice/tea and margarine/butter) or greater than (cereals/biscuits) the frequency of overmatching. Furthermore, as stated previously, for the complements biscuits/coffee the percentage of matching was the same as the one found for over and undermatching. On five of the remaining combinations matching was the least frequent form of behavioral allocation. Specifically in the case of fruit juice/baked beans and coffee/tea there were no consumers who presented either this pattern or that of anti-matching.

Finally, with values between 22% and 0%, anti-matching was generally the least frequent pattern found (see Figure 10.1). The percentage of anti-matching was the lowest on seven combinations, although in some of them this percentage was equal of that found for matching (baked beans/baked beans and coffee/tea) and even overmatching (tea/tea). For the remaining combinations (biscuits/baked beans, cereals/baked beans and biscuits/tea) this form of behavioral allocation was more frequent than matching. This pattern was not particularly linked to the level of substitutability between the product combinations.

Figure 10.2 shows the percentage of consumers whose choice patterns indicated overmatching, matching, undermatching and anti-matching, when calculated over periods of three weeks (VR schedule) for each product combination which ranged from substitutable to complementary pairs of products. The figure indicates that the results for the matching analysis when the data were aggregated over periods of three weeks yielded an increase on the percentage of near perfect matching (values on the slope between 0.9 and 1.1) and the R^2 values (see Appendix 1), when compared to those shown in Figure 10.1. Although the percentage of undermatching for five of the combinations decreased relative to the FR schedules, for nine of the ten product combinations this was the most common form of behavioral allocation. These values varied from 35% (biscuits/baked beans) to 70% for margarine/butter and they were generally slightly smaller for complementary combinations. Only for fruit juice/tea was the number of con-

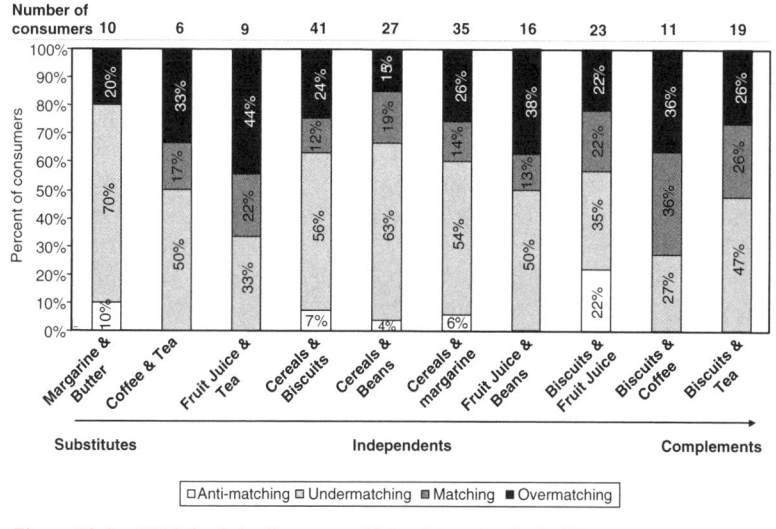

Figure 10.2 VR Schedule: Patterns of Matching Analysis (%)

sumers showing overmatching greater than the one found for undermatching (overmatching = 44% and undermatching = 33%).

Despite the decrease in the percentage of overmatching for five product arrangements in relation to the conc FR FR, this was still the second most common pattern for seven combinations. As can be seen in Figure 10.2, the highest percentage of overmatching was found for fruit juice/tea (44%) where, as has been mentioned, it was the most common pattern. Among those where it was the second most frequent result, the highest value was 36% (biscuits/coffee) and the lowest 22% (biscuits/fruit juice). However, it is important to mention that in some of these cases the percentage of overmatching was the same as that found for matching (biscuits/tea and biscuits/coffee) and in the particular case of biscuits/fruit juice, these two percentages were equal to the number of consumers matching (overmatching = undermatching = matching = 21.73%). Finally, for the cereal/baked beans combination the percentage of overmatching was lower than the one found for matching (overmatching = 14.81% and matching = 18.51%). No consumer showed overmatching in the case of margarine/butter; hence, it was (by trivial definition) the least frequent pattern for that combination.

As has been mentioned, when consumers' choices were aggregated over three-week periods, the results show a greater percentage of near perfect matching than those for the weekly integration of behavior. This was the case for eight of the ten combinations. Thus, for five combinations (cereals/baked beans, biscuits/coffee, biscuits/tea, biscuits/fruit juice and margarine/butter) matching yielded the second greatest percentage of consumers. Once again, in some cases this percentage did not differ from the one of overmatching and in one case it did not even differ from that found for anti-matching. For the remaining combinations, the percentage of matching was greater than that found for anti-matching, which was the most infrequent behavioral allocation.

For eight of the ten combinations, the least frequent pattern was anti-matching (Figure 10.2). The highest percentage of anti-matching was found for biscuits/fruit juice (22%) whereas for five combinations (biscuits/tea, biscuits/coffee, fruit juice/tea, fruit juice/baked beans and coffee/tea) no consumer displayed anti-matching. Hence, no relation with the level of substitutability was found.

Illustrative example: an individual case

Consumer number 93182 was chosen to illustrate the results at an individual level since this shopper uniquely purchased three combinations that differed in their level of substitutability. The following figures illustrate the pattern found for this consumer 93182 where margarine/butter were assumed to be perceived as substitutes (based on the results of the analysis of the substitutability scale – see Appendices 3 and 4 and the procedure section within the method heading), fruit juice/baked beans as independents, and biscuits/fruit juice as complements.

As illustrated in Figures 10.3, 10.4 and 10.5, for this particular consumer the slopes decreased when the data were aggregated over periods

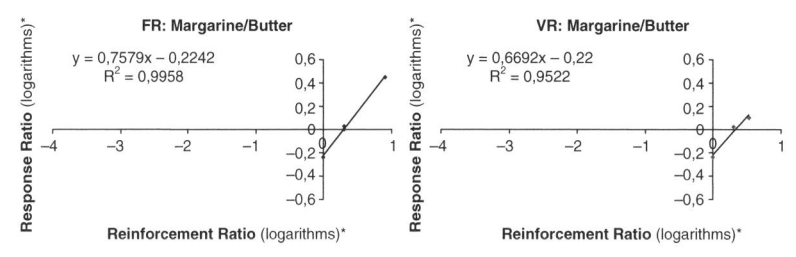

Figure 10.3 Matching Analysis for subject 93182: Substitutable Products (*log10)

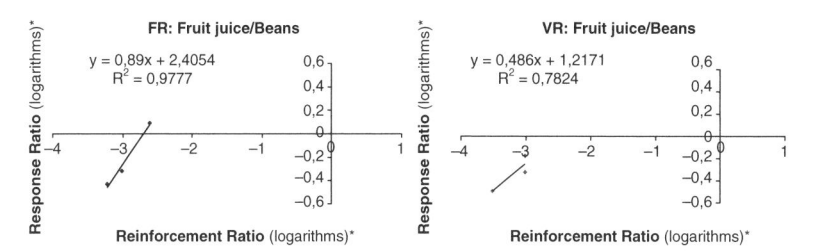

FR: Margarine/Butter: $y = 0{,}7579x - 0{,}2242$, $R^2 = 0{,}9958$
VR: Margarine/Butter: $y = 0{,}6692x - 0{,}22$, $R^2 = 0{,}9522$

Figure 10.4 Matching Analysis for subject 93182: Independent Products (*log10)

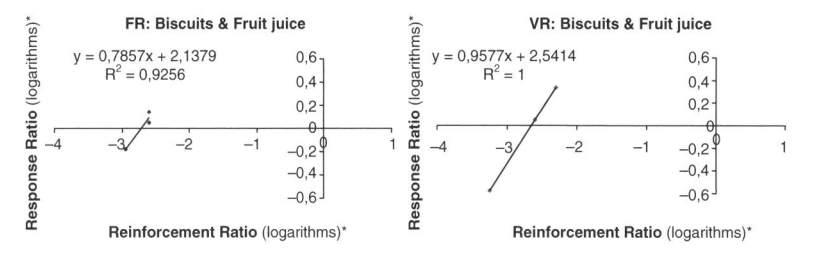

FR: Fruit juice/Beans: $y = 0{,}89x + 2{,}4054$, $R^2 = 0{,}9777$
VR: Fruit juice/Beans: $y = 0{,}486x + 1{,}2171$, $R^2 = 0{,}7824$

Figure 10.5 Matching Analysis for subject 93182: Complementary Products

FR: Biscuits & Fruit juice: $y = 0{,}7857x + 2{,}1379$, $R^2 = 0{,}9256$
VR: Biscuits & Fruit juice: $y = 0{,}9577x + 2{,}5414$, $R^2 = 1$

of three weeks for the substitutable products and for the independent products. By contrast, for the combination of complementary products the slope increased for the conc VR VR. Likewise, and contrary to the predictions, the slopes did not decrease according to the level of substitutability-independency-complementarity. Different patterns emerged for different participants (see Appendix 1).

Aggregated analysis

Table 10.2 summarizes the results of the general equation model found at an aggregated (across all purchases and individuals) level for each product combination. For this analysis the quantity bought and the amount spent for each product category on different shopping occasions were summarized. Then, the ratio of *the total amount bought for one product/total amount paid for both products* and the ratio of *the total amount paid for one product/total amount spent for the two products* during the 16 weeks was calculated. For the concurrent FR FR only the data from those occasions where the consumers bought both products on the same shopping trip were considered. Likewise, for the aggregated analysis of the conc VR VR, the only data used corresponded to those occasions where the consumers had bought both products over periods of three weeks. Each data point in the equation corresponded to the choices of one consumer along the 16 weeks of data collection from the FR and VR schedules.

The slopes varied between –0.668 to 1.030 for the FR schedules. The general tendency of the slope was to decrease with the combinations' level of substitutability (with the single exception of margarine/butter

Table 10.2 Generalized equation: Aggregated level

Product Combination	FR Schedule Slope	Intercept	R^2	VR Schedule Slope	Intercept	R^2
Margarine/Butter	–0.67	0.23	0.20	0.58	–0.21	0.21
Tea/Coffee	1.03	–0.61	0.72	1.08	–0.55	0.88
Fruit juice/Tea	0.65	1.49	0.72	0.81	1.84	0.82
Cereals/Biscuits	0.85	0.07	0.65	0.95	0.03	0.72
Cereals/Beans	0.89	0.58	0.74	1.08	0.51	0.70
Cereals/Margarine	0.84	–0.26	0.45	0.90	0.21	0.58
Biscuits/Fruit juice	0.55	1.45	0.27	0.85	2.20	0.64
Fruit juice/Beans	0.50	1.70	0.31	1	3.00	0.46
Biscuits/Coffee	0.46	–0.52	0.65	0.71	–0.67	0.70
Biscuits/Tea	0.60	–0.29	0.74	0.81	–0.34	0.80

which yielded anti-matching, but the very low R^2 and the small number of consumers that bought both products imply that these results have to be considered carefully). In this sense, highly substitutable products like tea/coffee, exhibit the greatest slope values showing a near perfect matching pattern, whereas for products that were ranked as independents the slope tends to decrease (as it is the case for cereals/margarine $s = 0.842$) indicating undermatching. Finally, for complementary products the slopes were around 0.5 indicating clear undermatching. All the intercept values differed markedly from unity, indicating that some unknown but invariant bias caused some degree of asymmetry between the options. The R^2 values varied from 0.202 to 0.743. For three product combinations (margarine/butter, biscuits/fruit juice and fruit juice/baked beans) this parameter was very low, indicating great dispersion and therefore low adjustment of the data to the model. For the remaining seven combinations, the R^2 was higher than 0.45, denoting a moderate to high adjustment to the model.

A rather different pattern was found for the conc VR VR schedule. In this case the s parameter was generally very high. With the exception of margarine/butter ($s = 0.583$), the values fell in the range of 0.705 to 1.075. For three combinations (tea/coffee, cereals/biscuits and fruit juice/baked beans) the slope indicated near perfect matching. Finally, despite the fact that the s parameter for the remaining six combinations fell on the range of undermatching, they were closer to unity than they were for the FR schedule. As for the weekly-integrated data, the intercept for the VR schedule differed significantly from unity, suggesting consistency in choices due to unknown reasons. With exception of the margarine/butter combination ($R^2 = 0.210$), the degree of adjustment to the model for this schedule of reinforcement was from moderate to high. The values for this parameter yielded between 0.461 (for fruit juice/baked beans) up to 0.878 (for tea/coffee).

Illustrative example: aggregated results

Based on the degree of substitutability assumed by the researcher (and validated by 11 consumers), and the degree of adjustment to the model (R square) the combination tea/coffee was selected as an example of perfectly substitutable goods, cereals/margarine as independents and biscuits/tea as complements. The outcome for the aggregated results are shown in Figures 10.6, 10.7 and 10.8.

The examples illustrate the decrease of the slope of the general matching equation with different degrees of substitutability at an

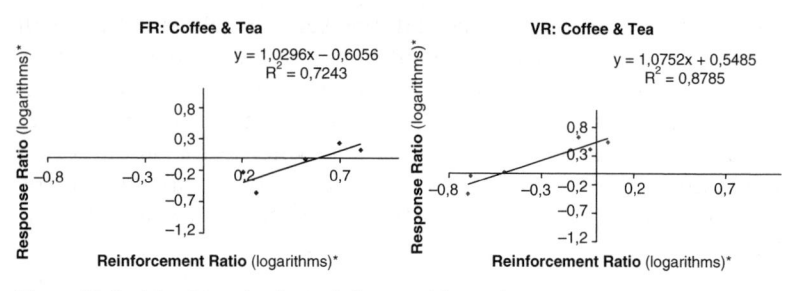

Figure 10.6 Matching Analysis: Substitutable Products

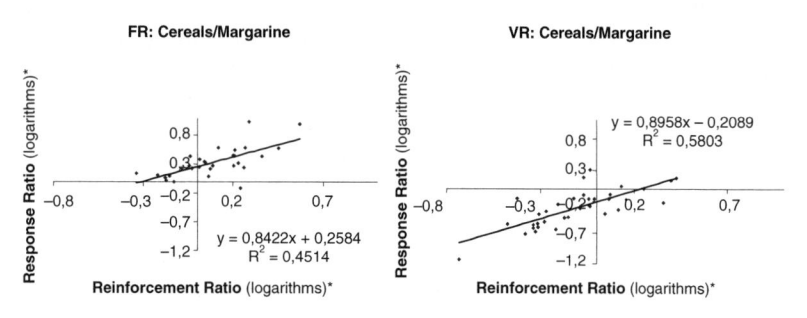

Figure 10.7 Matching Analysis: Independent Products

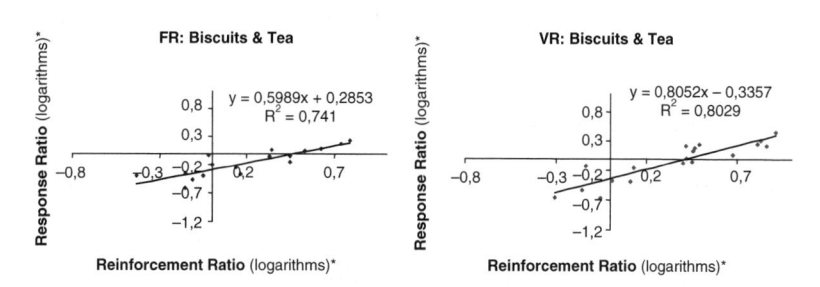

Figure 10.8 Matching Analysis: Complementary Products

aggregated level. As can be seen in the figures above, for the conc FR FR the slope for the combination of coffee/tea (which were assumed to be substitutes) shows near perfect matching, for the independent (cereals/margarine) the slope indicates undermatching although it is close to the matching cut off (0.90) chosen considering Baum's (1974) proposition. For the complementary products (biscuits/tea) undermatching was also found, but in this case the slope was much closer to 0. The illustration also shows how for the conc VR VR these differences among the substitutability continuum were not evidenced, because the slope did *not* vary substantially from one product combination to the other.

Discussion

Individual analysis

The results reported here differ markedly, but as predicted, from those obtained in earlier research that focused on brands rather than product categories (Foxall & James, 2001). The frequencies of over and undermatching (especially when analyses where conducted on a weekly basis) were particularly high. It is noteworthy that product categories that were perceived as substitutes (e.g., margarine/butter and coffee/tea) yielded an unexpected number of cases of overmatching and undermatching compared with the predominant matching patterns found for brands within the same product category. The low percentages of consumers for the most substitutable products (margarine/butter and coffee/tea) suggest that even when consumers practice multi-brand purchasing (as Ehrenberg, 1988, proposed and Foxall & Schrezenmaier, 2003, confirmed) they would not substitute them as easily for a different (although in some respects equivalent) product category. Furthermore, for consumers who bought the two products, relatively few evinced matching in their patterns of choice, suggesting that these consumers do not see them as near substitutes. In other words, it appears that in order to achieve perfect matching the reinforcers have to function as potential substitutes and be seen to belong to the same product category.

At the individual level, different degrees of substitutability did not produce different percentages of matching patterns. Thus, some consumers showed matching with complementary products (e.g., four consumers showed matching on the biscuits/coffee combinations; and others, anti-matching patterns with independent commodities (e.g., three participants performed according to the anti-matching effect with the combination of cereals/beans). Differences in participants' history of reinforcement are suggested by the variety of patterns found for each product combination. A similar source of variation might be found in the fact that different consumers could have different perceptions about the degree of the combinations' substitutability, in terms of products providing different functions for different consumers. This could perhaps be related to their learning history with these products.

In their investigation, Foxall & James (2001) analyzed the data for only one consumer per product combination and they qualitatively explored the participants' degree of substitutability for each product/brand they used. Although for the current research a group of 11 consumers were asked to allocate the combinations along the substitutability continuum in order to validate the theoretical assumptions, the perception of each of the shoppers that took part on the analysis are not available, and therefore it is not possible to contrast their views with their results.

Aggregated analyses over the sample: FR vs. VR schedules

When the data for the conc FR FR analysis were aggregated (the summary of the results from one subject was calculated and therefore each subject constituted a data point), results were more consistent with the expected patterns. For this schedule, the s parameter decreased with changes on the degree of substitutability according to what the theory predicts. In this sense, assuming that the use of multiple consumers minimizes the effect of individual perceptions of substitutability (and perhaps therefore variation in their learning histories), we may conclude that the s parameter is indeed a measure of substitutability at least when data are considered on a weekly basis. Thus, the results for the entire sample seem to demonstrate that, on a single shopping occasion, consumers would match the ratio of amount of money spent on one product to the amount spent on other near substitutable products with the ratio of reinforcement earned of that product to the amount bought of other close substitutable products. Undermatching could then be expected for independent products and slopes nearer 0 for complementary products.

Nonetheless, the anti-matching effect proposed by Kagel *et al.* (1995) for complementary combinations was not found. Although the combinations of biscuits/tea and biscuits/coffee were identified (using the results of the substitutability scale questionnaire) by consumers as complementary products, it seems that those products are still able to achieve their purposes quite independently of the presence of the other. Therefore, even when these product combinations show a very clear deviation from matching, they still do not result in anti-matching. Further research seems to be needed using product combinations with higher levels of complementarity, where the function of one product is truly compromised if the other product is absent. Generally, products whose consumption necessarily increases with the increase of the consumption of another product or which in behavioral terms, need to be presented jointly in the consumption situation to achieve their role as reinforcers. Such combinations of complementary produces (as cereals and milk, shampoo and hair conditioner, coffee and milk) are recommended for future research.

By contrast, when the data was analyzed for periods of three weeks, the slope tended to increase: buyer behavior for independent combinations of which the slopes were generally around 0.80 on the FR schedule, and consequently not high enough to be considered matching, showed near perfect matching on the conc VR VR schedules. Likewise, for complementary products that showed clear undermatching, the slopes increased so that they were closer to unity (although in some cases not high enough to be considered matching, e.g., biscuits/coffee).

Similarly to Foxall & James (2003), results from the current research show that parameter b in both FR and VR schedules differed significantly toward unity, suggesting possible biases of the form of availability of products, and extra-cost associated with each product (e.g., because of their shelf positions in the supermarket).

Conclusions

According to Kagel *et al.* (1995) when subjects are in the presence of complementary reinforcers, results will differ from the matching pattern proposed by Herrnstein (1961) showing what they called "anti-matching". On a consumer setting, at an individual base, Foxall & James (2001) found this effect only when the data were grouped over periods of three weeks. The current research failed to find systematic variations on the s parameter of the generalized matching equation for the different levels of substitutability at an individual level. Moreover, with complementary products the percentage of anti-matching found was relatively low in comparison with other forms of behavioral allocation. There seems to be a need for further research with complementary product combinations that really require each other to achieve their purposes.

However, by aggregating the data (minimizing the effect that individual perceptions, and individual learning histories, could have on behavior), results approached the expected patterns. In this case, the slope of the generalized equation decreased according to the level of substitutability-independence-complementarity, although this effect was found exclusively when occasions were considered on a weekly basis. These results allow the conclusion that, when considered at an aggregated level, consumers seem to consider the prices of different products available within a shopping trip, and behave according to what is predicted by the generalized matching law for different levels of substitutability. Nonetheless, over extended periods, represented by series of three shopping trips, consumers tend to match their choices even with qualitatively different reinforcers.

Further research and implications

This chapter has given an indication of the effects of substitutability and complementarity on matching relationships. Further research with a large dataset is already underway to access the extent and usefulness of these patterns. Without extending this study to this larger dataset, we cannot be certain about the useful extent of these findings in terms of marketing theory, strategy and general marketing practice. This is especially the case as much marketing planning is based on aggregated findings from a large number (often thousands) of consumers. Certainly it would also be extremely useful to look at a wider range of product pairings and, at a deeper level, at the effect of brands and sections of products (for example – sweet and savory biscuits). Making early predictions it seems that the work could affect primarily the pricing structure adopted and the positioning of products, in terms of place (for example if complementary products were not available in the same shop).

Further research could also extend the analysis of the levels of substitutability, independence and complementarity. This could be done initially by using the substitutability scale questionnaire on a wider range of product combinations and using a wider range of participants. It could further employ a split-sample procedure and use economic determinants of substitutability, such as the relationships between quantities consumed of different brands/products.

Alongside further studies using data aggregated across consumers, separate work could also explore more individual patterns, perhaps incorporating a qualitative dimension as in the work of Foxall & James (2001, 2003). This would also allow a better understanding of what the role of verbal behavior might be in research on consumer choice behavior. Certainly the difference between verbal behavior about what might be or has been bought and actual observed purchase patterns might provide valuable information to researchers. Looking at individuals would also allow us to look more closely at individual perceptions of substitutability and determine the best course or action for controlling these, and other aspects of the individuals learning history, in future research.

Notes

1. Previously published in *European Journal of Behavior Analysis*, 2006, 7, 15-40.
2. An interval schedules maintains a constant minimum time interval between rewards (or reinforcements). Fixed interval (FI) schedules maintain a constant period of time between intervals, while a variable interval schedule (VI) the time varies between one reinforcer and the next.
3. A ratio schedule is one in which a specified number of responses have to be performed before reinforcement becomes available. Fixed ratio (FR) schedules keep the number of required responses equal from one reinforcer to the next; variable ratio (VR) schedules allow the required number of responses to change from one reinforcer to the next.

References

Ayllon, T. & Azrin, N. (1968). *The Token Economy*. New York: Appleton-Century-Crofts.

Baum, W. M. (1974). "On two types of deviation from the matching law". *Journal of the Experimental Analysis of Behavior*, 22, 231-42.

Baum, W. M. (1979). "Matching, undermatching and overmatching in studies of choice". *Journal of the Experimental Analysis of Behavior*, 32, 269-81.

Bernstein, D. J. & Ebbesen, E. B. (1978). "Reinforcement and substitution in humans: A multiple-response analysis". *Journal of the Experimental Analysis of Behavior*, 30, 243-53.

Buskist, W. & Miller, H. L. (1981). "Concurrent operant performance in humans: matching when food is the reinforcer". *The Psychological Record*, 31, 95-100.

Buskist, W. & Miller, H. L. (1982). "The study of human operant behavior, 1958-1981: A topical bibliography". *The Psychological Record*, 32, 249-68.

Conger, R. & Kileen, P. (1974). "Use of concurrent operants in small scale research: a demonstration". *Pacific Sociological Review*, 17 (4), 399-416.

de Villiers, P. A. & Herrnstein, R. J. (1976). "Toward a law of response strength". *Psychological Bulletin*, 83, 1131-53.

Ehrenberg, A. S. C. (1988). *Repeat Buying: Facts Theory and Applications*. London: Griffin; New York: Oxford University Press.

Ehrenberg, A. S. C. (1993). "New brands and the existing market". *Journal of Market Research Society*, 33, 285-99.

Ehrenberg, A. S. C., Hammond, K. & Goodhardt, G. J. (1994). "The after-effects of price-related consumer promotions". *Journal of Advertising Research*, July/August, 11-21.

Foxall, G. R. (1990). *Consumer psychology in behavioral perspective*. London and New York: Routledge.

Foxall, G. R. (1996). *Consumer in context: The BPM research program*. London and New York: International Thomson.

Foxall, G. R. (1999). "The substitutability of brands". *Managerial and Decision Economics*, 20, 241-57.

Foxall, G. R. & James, V. K. (2001). "Behavior analysis of consumer brand choice: A preliminary analysis". *European Journal of Behavior Analysis*, 2, 209-20.

Foxall, G. R. & James, V. K. (2003). "The behavioral ecology of brand choice: How and what do consumers maximize?" *Psychology and Marketing*, 20, 811–36.

Foxall, G. R. & Schrezenmaier, T. C. (2003). "The behavioral economics of consumer brand choice: establishing a methodology". *Journal of Economic Psychology*, 24, 675–95.

Foxall, G. R., Oliveira-Castro, J. M. & Schrezenmaier, T. C. (2004). "The behavioral economics of consumer brand choice: patterns of reinforcement and utility maximization". *Behavioral Processes*, 66, 235–60.

Goodhardt, G. J., Ehrenberg, A. S. C. & Chatfield, C. (1984). "The Dirichlet: a comprehensive model of buying behavior". *Journal of the Royal Statistical Society*, A147, 621–43.

Green, L. & Freed, D. E. (1993). "The substitutability of reinforcements". *Journal of the Experimental Analysis of Behavior*, 60, 141–58.

Herrnstein, R. J. (1961). "Relative and absolute strength of response as a function of the frequency of reinforcement". *Journal of the Experimental Analysis of Behavior*, 4, 267–72.

Herrnstein, R. J. (1970). "On the law of effect". *Journal of the Experimental Analysis of Behavior*, 13, 243–66.

Herrnstein, R. J. (1982). "Melioration as behavioral dynamism", in M. L. Commons, R. J. Herrnstein & H. Rachlin (eds) *Quantitative analyses of behavior, Vol. II, Matching and maximizing accounts*. Cambridge, MA: Ballinger, pp. 433–58.

Herrnstein, R. J. (1990). "Rational Choice Theory: Necessary but not sufficient". *American Psychologist*, 45, 356–67.

Herrnstein, R. J. (1997). In H. Rachlin & D. I. Laibson (eds) *The matching law: Papers in psychology and economics*. Cambridge, MA: Harvard University Press.

Herrnstein, R. J. & Vaughan, W. (1980). In J. E. R. Staddon (ed.) *Limits to action: The allocation of individual behavior*. New York: Academic Press, pp. 143–76.

Hursh, S. R. (1978). "The economics of daily consumption controlling food-and-water reinforced responding". *Journal of the Experimental Analysis of Behavior*, 29, 475–91.

Hursh, S. R. (1984). "Behavioral Economics". *Journal of the Experimental Analysis of Behavior*, 42 (3), 435–52.

Hursh, S. R. & Bauman, R. A. (1987). "The behavioral analysis of demand", in L. Green & J. H. Kagel, *Advances in Behavioral Economics: Volume 1*. Norwood, N.J.: Ablex Publishing Corporation, pp. 117–65.

Kagel, J. H. (1972). "Token economics and experimental economics". *Journal of Political Economy*, 80, 779–85.

Kagel, J. H., Battalio, R. C. & Green, L. (1995). *Economic Choice Theory: An Experimental Analysis of Animal Behavior*. Cambridge: Cambridge University Press.

Kagel, J. H., Battalio, R. C., Rachlin, H., Green, L., Basmann, R. L. & Klemm, W. R. (1975). "Experimental studies of consumer demand behavior using laboratory animals". *Economic Inquiry*, 8, 22–38.

Myerson, J. & Hale, S. (1984). "Practical Implications of the Matching Law". *Journal of Applied Behavior Analysis*, 17 (3), 367–80.

Lea, S. E. G. (1978). "The Psychology and Economics of Demand". *Psychological Bulletin*, 85 (3), 441–66.

Rachlin, R., Battalio, R. C., Kagel, J. H. & Green, L. (1981). "Maximization Theory in behavioral psychology". *The Behavioral and Brain Sciences*, 4, 371–417.

Rajala, A. K. & Hantula, D. A. (2000). "Towards a behavioral ecology of consumption: Delay reduction effects on foraging in a simulated online mall". *Managerial and Decision Economics*, 21, 145–58.

Smith, C. L. & Hantula, D. A. (2003). "Pricing effects on foraging in a simulated Internet shopping mall". *Journal of Economic Psychology*, 24 (5), 653–74.

Uncles, M. & Ehrenberg, A. S. C. (1990). "The buying of packaged goods at US retail chains". *Journal of Retail*, 66, 278–93.

Uncles, M., Ehrenberg, A. S. C. & Hammond, K. (1995). "Patterns of buyer behavior: regularities, models, and extensions". *Marketing Sciences*, 14, G71–G78.

Appendix 1 Results for the generalized matching law

Margarine/Butter

FR Schedules				VR Schedules			
Consumer Number	Slope	Intercept	R^2	Consumer Number	Slope	Intercept	R^2
				12347	0.55	–0.23	0.75
55815	1.36	–1.24	0.64	55815	0.89	–1.00	0.57
86295	1.22	–0.36	0.61	86295	1.03	–0.31	0.70
93182	0.76	–0.22	1.00	93182	0.67	–0.22	0.95
98732	0.90	–0.30	0.43	98732	0.71	–0.20	0.93
				124244	0.85	–0.01	0.95
				126874	–0.03	0.07	0.02
129274	0.94	–0.20	1.00	129274	1.02	–0.23	1.00
131294	0.35	–0.30	0.22	131294	0.54	–0.46	0.97
133271	0.62	0.25	0.38	133271	0.65	0.19	0.95
Average	0.88	–0.34	0.61	Average	0.69	–0.45	0.78

Tea/Cofee

FR Schedules				VR Schedules			
Consumer Number	Slope	Intercept	R^2	Consumer Number	Slope	Intercept	R^2
				21174	1.02	–0.48	0.99
59984	1.17	–0.66	0.99	59984	1.24	–0.67	0.98
67380	0.31	–0.27	0.62	67380	0.55	–0.40	0.81
75262	2.23	–1.15	0.98	75262	2.00	–0.80	0.37
131331	1.10	–0.60	0.43	131331	0.43	0.09	0.15
600817	0.45	–0.26	0.93	600817	0.58	–0.33	0.83
Average	1.05	–0.59	0.79	Average	0.96	–0.42	0.63

Fruit Juice/Tea

FR Schedules				VR Schedules			
Consumer Number	Slope	Intercept	R^2	Consumer Number	Slope	Intercept	R^2
27180	0.22	0.50	0.25	27180	3.44	7.24	0.97
76872	1.85	4.10	0.86	76872	0.97	2.18	0.74
82032	0.67	1.49	0.52	82032	0.91	2.02	0.94
				122025	1.17	2.54	0.97
122753	0.68	1.58	0.99	122753	0.45	1.30	0.52
124559	−1.61	−3.42	0.29	124559	2.10	5.04	0.46
				128130	0.39	0.72	0.35
133271	0.51	1.07	1.00	133271	0.43	1.19	0.94
600817	0.98	2.22	0.76	600817	1.41	3.28	0.82
131357	0.87	2.04	0.93				
Average	0.52	1.20	0.70	Average	1.25	2.84	0.75

Cereals/Biscuits

FR Schedules				VR Schedules			
Consumer Number	Slope	Intercept	R^2	Consumer Number	Slope	Intercept	R^2
12347	0.92	0.03	0.82	12347	1.30	0.04	0.94
21174	1.29	0.28	0.80	21174	1.09	0.26	0.77
25927	0.58	0.00	0.47	25927	0.89	−0.02	0.83
27180	0.43	−0.16	0.80	27180	0.50	−0.20	0.99
31639	0.35	−0.11	0.29	31639	0.84	−0.20	0.71
36543	1.06	0.18	0.99	36543	1.05	0.22	0.98
36968	0.77	0.15	0.77	36968	1.18	−0.18	0.70
48996	0.96	−0.05	0.72	48996	0.81	−0.05	0.49
55814	0.83	−0.13	0.41				
55815	0.53	0.09	0.33	55815	0.14	0.12	0.38
60695	0.43	0.19	0.46	60695	1.38	0.19	1.00
61529	0.27	−0.12	0.07	61529	0.61	−0.19	0.46
74108	0.64	0.33	0.03	74108	0.25	0.38	0.20
78082	1.26	0.06	0.93	78082	1.25	0.08	0.90
86240	0.82	0.10	0.78	86240	0.15	0.66	0.22
86295	0.81	−0.01	0.73				
90910	0.66	0.22	0.64	90910	0.93	0.08	0.81
93182	1.45	0.13	0.99	93182	1.34	0.11	0.97
95606	0.28	0.08	0.08	95606	0.61	0.03	0.40
106627	1.19	0.22	0.60	106627	−0.19	0.00	0.04
				106715	−0.96	0.22	0.97
113815	0.23	−0.07	0.01	113815	2.47	0.40	0.84
118278	1.21	−0.05	0.67	118278	1.41	−0.27	0.78

Cereals/Biscuits – *continued*

FR Schedules				VR Schedules			
Consumer Number	Slope	Intercept	R^2	Consumer Number	Slope	Intercept	R^2
122016	0.98	0.04	0.82	122016	0.88	0.14	0.96
				122025	0.28	0.22	0.47
122718	1.04	0.30	0.87	122718	1.20	0.35	0.97
122753	1.09	–0.36	0.87	122753	1.03	–0.34	0.92
				124244	0.07	0.26	0.02
124559	0.46	0.13	0.45	124559	0.48	0.12	0.50
124933	0.35	0.29	0.32	124933	0.88	0.13	0.81
126110	0.47	0.16	0.59	126110	0.50	0.21	0.22
				126831	–0.80	–0.68	0.16
126874	1.19	0.17	0.54	126874	1.23	0.15	0.87
128130	1.08	0.16	0.62	128130	0.81	0.09	0.70
130953	0.54	0.20	0.77	130953	0.58	–0.02	0.67
				131294	0.92	–0.30	0.78
131331	0.75	0.19	0.73	131331	0.48	0.18	0.38
131357	0.87	0.12	0.24	131357	0.27	0.24	0.03
				132207	0.88	–0.10	0.97
132764	0.42	–0.10	0.25	132764	1.49	–0.33	0.44
600031	0.88	0.06	0.89	600031	0.77	0.14	0.81
600817	0.66	0.04	0.28	600817	0.42	–0.05	0.13
600948	1.00	0.35	0.64	600948	0.78	0.36	0.27
Average	0.78	0.08	0.57	Average	0.74	0.06	0.62

Cereals/Beans

FR Schedules				VR Schedules			
Consumer Number	Slope	Intercept	R^2	Consumer Number	Slope	Intercept	R^2
21174	1.50	0.94	0.99	21174	0.49	0.71	0.48
25927	0.54	0.41	0.26	25927	0.55	0.47	0.43
26537	0.10	1.22	0.02	26537	1.55	–0.06	0.95
27180	–0.73	0.22	0.08	27180	0.73	0.19	0.17
48996	0.54	0.35	0.73	48996	0.74	0.25	0.71
55814	–1.79	1.18	0.68	55814	0.89	0.49	0.93
55815	1.54	0.58	0.82	55815	0.71	0.81	0.48
58275	0.36	1.11	0.28	58275	0.96	0.89	0.86
61529	0.21	0.57	0.16	61529	0.61	0.64	0.45
				74108	0.46	1.08	0.11
93182	1.12	0.55	0.70	93182	0.74	0.54	0.67
				95606	0.43	0.83	0.87
106627	0.99	0.80	0.75	106627	1.68	1.07	0.59

Cereals/Beans – *continued*

FR Schedules				VR Schedules			
Consumer Number	Slope	Intercept	R^2	Consumer Number	Slope	Intercept	R^2
113815	0.63	0.66	0.06	113815	0.77	0.47	0.39
118278	1.98	–0.05	0.89	118278	1.99	–0.06	0.89
				122404	0.80	0.06	0.83
122718	0.67	0.46	0.83	122718	0.94	0.60	0.95
				128130	0.14	0.52	0.00
130953	0.75	1.02	0.69	130953	0.25	0.89	0.07
				131294	1.09	–0.25	0.75
131331	0.90	0.55	0.96	131331	0.93	0.57	1.00
131357	–5.21	0.62	0.86	131357	0.50	0.85	0.40
				132207	0.42	0.14	0.85
132764	0.42	0.14	0.83	132764	–0.47	0.22	0.35
600031	0.69	0.31	0.58	600031	0.06	–0.16	0.01
				600469	1.04	0.22	0.87
600817	0.41	0.60	0.20	600817	1.35	0.49	0.63
Average	0.28	0.61	0.57	Average	0.75	0.46	0.58

Beans/Fruit Juice

FR Schedules				VR Schedules			
Consumer Number	Slope	Intercept	R^2	Consumer Number	Slope	Intercept	R^2
				23527	0.68	–2.56	0.13
25927	1.11	–3.22	0.47	25927	1.45	–4.08	0.70
				27180	0.65	–1.62	0.12
29436	1.13	–3.10	0.95	29436	1.11	–3.18	0.62
48996	1.26	–2.97	0.54	48996	0.87	–2.23	0.80
55815	0.49	–1.88	0.35	55815	0.61	–2.20	0.61
58275	1.33	–4.28	0.15	58275	1.13	–3.78	0.37
				74108	1.58	–4.50	1.00
82032	1.29	–4.03	0.85	82032	1.35	–4.25	1.00
93182	0.89	–2.41	0.98	93182	0.49	–1.22	0.78
				113815	1.48	–4.29	1.00
118278	1.72	–4.75	1.00	118278	1.72	–4.76	1.00
				128130	1.07	–3.11	0.41
132207	0.42	–1.52	0.86	132207	0.64	–2.23	0.69
				132764	0.97	–2.75	0.83
				600817	0.80	–2.70	0.64
130867	1.33	–3.16	0.99				
Average	1.10	–3.13	0.71	Average	1.04	–3.09	0.67

Cereals/Margarine

FR Schedules				VR Schedules			
Consumer Number	Slope	Intercept	R^2	Consumer Number	Slope	Intercept	R^2
12347	0.72	0.47	0.55	12347	0.99	0.41	0.31
21174	0.87	0.30	1.00	21174	0.94	0.32	1.00
26537	0.84	0.37	0.98	26537	0.93	0.38	0.99
27180	0.68	0.20	0.72	27180	0.73	0.18	0.99
36543	1.42	−0.07	0.38	36543	0.69	0.19	0.81
48996	1.21	0.31	0.57	48996	1.55	0.17	0.83
55815	2.99	0.36	0.90	55815	0.69	0.43	0.70
61529	1.09	0.00	0.91	61529	1.33	0.00	0.92
67380	0.39	0.08	0.54	67380	0.68	0.11	0.46
74108	0.67	0.36	0.96	74108	−0.04	0.19	0.00
78082	1.10	0.19	0.85	78082	0.53	0.40	0.35
				84030	1.24	0.22	1.00
86240	0.40	1.16	0.11	86240	1.57	0.03	0.78
90910	0.56	0.28	0.98	90910	0.72	0.30	0.99
93182	0.96	0.16	0.99	93182	0.98	0.19	0.96
95606	−0.28	0.36	0.01	95606	−0.02	0.62	0.00
106627	1.30	0.39	0.38	106627	0.83	0.45	0.53
122016	0.52	0.22	0.51	122016	0.63	0.24	0.82
				122025	0.53	0.14	0.68
122718	0.82	0.31	0.95	122718	0.81	0.37	0.98
				124244	0.54	0.00	0.82
124559	0.64	0.80	0.36	124559	0.44	0.36	0.52
124933	0.59	0.16	0.99	124933	0.52	0.25	0.86
126110	0.74	0.30	0.84	126110	1.05	0.23	0.97
126874	0.21	0.30	0.02	126874	1.13	0.17	0.58
128130	0.29	0.15	0.01	128130	0.76	0.19	0.80
				129274	1.12	0.25	1.00
130953	0.55	0.13	0.77	130953	0.32	−0.07	0.38
				131294	2.90	−0.41	0.98
131331	0.63	0.18	0.53	131331	0.54	0.24	0.39
132764	1.20	0.11	0.96	132764	1.26	0.13	0.98
133271	0.27	−0.14	0.13	133271	0.77	−0.33	0.82
600031	0.83	0.10	0.89	600031	0.56	0.03	0.79
600817	0.94	0.18	0.46	600817	0.86	0.12	0.55
				600948	1.14	−0.34	0.80
86295	0.63	0.41	0.83				
Average	0.79	0.27	0.64	Average	0.86	0.18	0.72

Fruit Juice/Biscuits

FR Schedules				VR Schedules			
Consumer Number	Slope	Intercept	R^2	Consumer Number	Slope	Intercept	R^2
25927	0.84	1.97	0.70	25927	0.91	2.11	0.99
27180	0.74	1.75	0.41	27180	0.69	1.48	0.92
29436	2.23	5.80	0.99	29436	1.15	3.32	0.64
48996	0.82	1.82	0.47	48996	0.56	1.15	0.59
55815	0.73	1.72	0.64	55815	0.69	1.62	0.98
				74108	1.06	2.63	0.98
78082	−0.88	−1.99	0.40	78082	1.96	5.43	1.00
82032	−0.33	−0.52	0.02	82032	−0.37	−0.63	0.04
86240	0.73	1.98	0.43	86240	−0.52	−1.14	0.03
86295	−1.36	−2.45	0.93	86295	−0.13	0.11	0.09
93182	0.79	2.14	0.93	93182	0.96	2.54	1.00
106715	−1.17	−3.07	0.72	106715	−1.16	−3.07	0.69
113815	0.99	2.54	0.90	113815	0.83	2.04	0.96
118278	1.32	3.10	0.32	118278	1.46	3.41	0.47
122016	0.65	1.77	0.78	122016	1.23	3.12	0.35
122025	2.25	5.62	0.15	122025	0.89	2.26	0.35
122753	1.15	2.97	0.91	122753	1.09	2.78	0.94
124559	−0.02	0.42	0.12	124559	0.35	1.01	0.22
126874	1.66	4.41	0.76	126874	1.05	2.69	0.83
128130	0.24	0.53	0.05	128130	0.13	0.16	0.04
				132207	0.64	1.80	0.56
132764	0.27	0.67	0.32	132764	−0.01	−0.15	0.00
600817	1.12	2.92	0.85	600817	1.31	3.53	0.87
36968	1.31	3.30	0.53				
47278	0.66	1.37	0.22				
Average	0.64	1.69	0.54	Average	0.64	1.66	0.59

Biscuits/Coffee

FR Schedules				VR Schedules			
Consumer Number	Slope	Intercept	R^2	Consumer Number	Slope	Intercept	R^2
21174	1.74	−1.74	0.76	21174	1.77	−1.69	0.86
25927	0.71	−0.60	0.71	25927	0.72	−0.53	0.97
31639	1.03	−0.80	0.91	31639	1.13	−0.86	0.98
86240	0.95	−0.87	0.71	86240	1.23	−1.08	0.57
86295	1.05	−0.80	0.80	86295	0.95	−0.87	0.71
126874	1.37	−1.48	0.75	126874	0.95	−0.87	0.71
130953	0.81	−0.72	0.35	130953	0.95	−0.87	0.71
131294	0.58	−0.94	0.34	131294	0.68	−1.12	0.72
131331	1.21	−1.23	0.46	131331	0.54	−0.31	0.91
131357	0.64	−0.46	0.95				
132207	1.71	−0.99	0.87	132207	1.57	−0.88	0.96
600817.00	0.95	−0.87	0.71	600817	0.92	−0.78	0.90
Average	1.06	−0.96	0.69	Average	1.04	−0.90	0.82

Biscuits/Tea

FR Schedules				VR Schedules			
Consumer Number	Slope	Intercept	R^2	Consumer Number	Slope	Intercept	R^2
21174	1.72	−1.13	0.98	21174	1.34	−0.86	0.93
27180	0.26	−0.20	0.08	27180	0.38	−0.08	0.26
31639	1.11	0.03	0.96	31639	0.96	0.00	0.97
36543	0.84	−0.38	0.83	36543	0.82	−0.40	7898.00
				74108	0.96	−0.39	0.83
78082	−1.88	−0.64	0.16	78082	1.56	−0.55	0.97
82032	−0.20	−0.52	0.01	82032	0.59	−0.47	0.67
98732	0.84	−0.40	0.79	98732	0.66	−0.29	0.81
113815	−0.04	−0.02	0.00	113815	0.17	0.17	0.87
122025	1.61	−0.22	0.48	122025	0.29	−0.19	0.18
122718	1.35	−0.66	0.44	122718	1.58	−1.00	0.71
				122753	0.95	−0.32	0.97
122990	0.98	−0.49	1.00	122990	0.91	−0.49	0.99
124244	0.65	−0.39	0.82	124244	0.63	−0.49	0.72
				124933	1.53	−0.57	0.94
126110	0.33	−0.43	0.28	126110	0.73	−0.31	0.64
128130	0.38	−0.30	0.14	128130	0.76	−0.39	0.75
131331	1.35	−0.75	0.43	131331	1.01	−0.61	0.40
600817	0.94	−0.29	0.94	600817	1.15	−0.37	0.89
124559	1.61	−0.99	0.90				
Average	0.70	−0.46	0.54	Average	0.89	−0.40	416.39

Appendix 2   Matching patterns percentages

FR Schedule

	Anti-matching Fr	Anti-matching %	Under-matching fr	Under-matching %	Near Perfect Matching fr	Near Perfect Matching %	Over-matching fr	Over-matching %	Fr fr
Margarine&Butter	0	0%	3	43%	2	28.57%	2	28.57%	7
Coffee&Tea	0	0%	2	40%	0	0%	3	60%	5
Fruit Juice&Tea	1	12.50%	5	63%	1	12.50%	1	12.50%	8
Cereals&Biscuits	0	0%	23	62.22%	8	21.62%	6	16.21%	37
Cereals&Beans	3	15%	10	50%	2	10%	5	25%	20
Cereals&Margarine	1	3.33%	20	67%	3	10%	6	20%	30
Fruit Juice&Beans	0	0%	3	30%	0	0%	7	70%	10
Biscuits&Fruit Juice	5	21.73%	10	43.47%	1	4.34%	7	30.43%	23
Biscuits&Coffee	0	0%	4	33.33%	4	33.33%	4	33.33%	12
Biscuits&Tea	3	17.64%	6	35.29%	2	11.78%	6	35.29%	17

VR Schedule

	Fr	%	fr	%	fr	%	fr	%	fr
Margarine&Butter	1	10%	7	70%	2	20%	0	0%	10
Coffee&Tea	0	0%	3	50%	1	16.66%	2	33%	6
Fruit Juice&Tea	0	0%	3	33.33%	2	22.23%	4	44.44%	9
Cereals&Biscuits	3	7.31%	23	56.09%	5	12.21%	10	24.39%	41
Cereals&Beans	1	3.7%	17	62.96%	5	18.51%	4	14.81%	27
Cereals&Margarine	2	5.71%	19	54%	5	14.28%	9	25.71%	35
Fruit Juice&Beans	0	0%	8	50%	2	12.5%	6	37.50%	16
Biscuits&Fruit Juice	5	21.73%	8	34.78%	5	21.73%	5	21.73%	23
Biscuits&Coffee	0	0%	3	27.27%	4	36.36%	4	36.36	11
Biscuits&Tea	0	0%	9	47.36%	5	26.31%	5	26.31%	19

Appendix 3   Substitutability scale

Substitutability Scale

Considering **Substitutability** as the degree to which two products can serve the same purpose, please rate the degree of substitutability of the following commodities. In the following scale *1 corresponds to complete substitutability*, the middle point *4 corresponds to Independency* (where the products serve two completely different purposes), and *7 means that you see the products as complements* (one product needs the other to achieve its purpose).

Product Categories	Substitutes 1	2	3	Independents 4	5	6	Complements 7
Cereals&Beans							
Cereals&Margarine							
Cereals&Biscuits							
Biscuits&Tea							
Biscuits&Coffee							
Biscuits&Fruit Juice							
Fruit Juice&Tea							
Fruit Juice&Beans							
Coffee&Tea							
Margarine&Butter							

Appendix 4 Descriptive statistics – substitutability levels

	N	Minimum	Maximum	Mean	Std. Deviation
Margarine/butter	11	1	4	1.363636	0.924416
Coffee/tea	11	1	5	1.363636	1.206045
Fruit juice/tea	11	1	4	2.363636	1.206045
Cereals/biscuits	11	1	5	2.909091	1.30035
Cereals/beans	11	1	4	3.363636	1.026911
Cereals/margarine	11	4	4	4	0
Fruit juice/beans	11	3	5	4.090909	0.53936
Biscuits/fruit juice	11	4	7	4.727273	0.904534
Biscuits/tea	11	4	7	6.181818	1.07872
Biscuits/coffee	11	4	7	6.181818	1.07872

Author Index

Abarca, N., 73
Ainslie, G., 226, 253
Ajzen, I., 2
Albarracin, D., 3
Alhadeff, D. A., 7, 160, 171
Allison, J., 223
Andrew, R. L., 226, 253
Ayllon, T., 259
Azrin, N., 259

Bartholomew, J., 9
Bass, F. M., 172
Battalio, R. C., 224
Baum, W., 11, 27, 28, 31, 43, 46, 56, 73, 77, 91, 92, 96, 104, 105, 127, 128, 258, 262, 265
Bauman, R. A., 77, 78, 129, 260
Bell, D. R., 127, 151, 167, 168, 178, 227, 228
Bernstein, D. J., 259
Bickel, W. K., 223
Bitner, M. J., 2
Blattberg, R. C., 190
Bolton, R., 167
Bommer, W., 167, 168, 169, 187, 250
Brown, S. W., 73
Buskist, W., 259

Cacioppo, J. T., 2
Chaiken, S., 2
Charnov, E. L., 72
Churchill, G. A., 133, 174, 225
Commons, M. L., 74, 93, 101, 104
Conger, R., 259
Crouch, S., 133, 174, 225
Currim, I. S., 226, 253

Dall, S. R., 73
Dalley, J., 96
Dall'Olmo Riley, F., 125, 200
Davis, J., 7
Davison, M., 25, 26, 28, 29, 30, 77, 78, 91, 105

Dawkins, R., 71, 72
Dawson, S., 2
De Chernatony, L., 126
de Villiers, P. A., 74
Diamantopoulis, A., 187
Dias, M. B., 18
DiFonzo, N., 73
Dow, S. M., 73

Ebbesen, E. B., 259
Ehrenberg, A. S. C., 8, 9, 15, 25, 30–43 passim, 54, 94, 100, 125, 126, 127, 137, 158, 169, 176, 189, 190, 192, 198, 200, 203, 212, 219, 252, 256, 257, 262, 275
Engel, J. F., 2
England, L. R., 126, 200
Epling, W. F., 26, 28, 77, 91

Fader, P. S., 167
Fantino, E., 73
Feyerabend, P., 3
Fishbein, M., 2
Flew, A., 71
Freed, D. E., 28, 31, 33, 76, 105, 106, 259, 264

Gill, T., 73
Glasman, L. R., 3
Goodhardt, G. J., 8, 9, 36, 100, 125, 200, 256, 257
Green, L., 28, 30, 31, 33, 76, 102, 105, 106, 226, 259, 264
Greenley, G., 117
Guadagni, P. M., 167, 225
Gupta, S., 166, 167, 168, 169, 188, 225, 228

Hair, J. F., 154
Hale, S., 77, 259, 260
Hantula, D. A., 19, 72, 73, 93, 95, 259
Hayes, S. C., 44

Herrnstein, R., 4, 10, 25, 26, 29, 30, 33, 41, 56, 59, 68, 73, 74, 89, 93, 101, 102, 103, 104, 106, 109, 110, 129, 135, 148, 257, 258, 264, 277
Heyman, G. M., 30
Hoch, S. J., 168, 169
Housden, M., 133, 174, 225
Houston, A. I., 96, 129
Howard, J. A., 2
Hursh, S., 4, 12, 29–30, 77, 78, 116, 118, 129, 223, 224, 227, 251, 259, 260
Hutcheson, A. M., 73

Ito, M., 73

Jacoby, J., 1, 2
James, V. K., 7, 11, 95, 101, 106, 107, 127, 128, 129, 132, 138, 143, 201, 260, 261, 262, 264, 275, 276, 277, 278
Jary, M., 126
Jeuland, A., 9
Jobber, D., 1

Kagel, J. H., 12, 30, 46, 56, 73, 108, 128, 158, 177, 199, 223, 224, 230, 259, 261, 264, 276, 277
Kacelnik, A., 72
Kamil, A. C., 72
Kau, K., 43
Keng, K., 126
Keith, R. J., 1
Killeen, P., 259
Kotler, P., 1
Kraus, S. J., 2
Krishnamurti, L., 126, 167
Kvanli, A. H., 186

Lacey, H., 6, 117
Laibson, D., 30
Lea, S. E. G., 73, 224, 257
Lechene, V., 187, 250
Little, J. D. C., 167, 225
Lodish, L. M., 167
Logue, A. W., 100, 101
Loveland, D. H., 33, 56, 59, 74, 102, 129, 135, 148

Madden, G. W., 19, 106, 112, 128, 129, 143,
McCarthy, D., 25, 26, 28, 29, 30, 73, 77, 78, 91, 105
McDonald, M., 126
McFarland, D., 129
McNamara, J., 72
Mazur, J. E., 74
Mellgreen, R. L., 73
Michael, J., 44
Miller, D., 1
Miller, H. L., 259
Myerson, J., 77, 226, 259, 260

Narasimhan, 167
Neslin, S. A., 225, 227
Nevin, J. A., 31, 56, 128

O'Shaughnessy, J., 2
O'Shaughnessy, N. J., 2
Oliveira-Castro, J. M., 7, 13, 16, 17, 18, 19, 205

Penrose, E., 30, 119
Petty, R. E., 2
Pierce, W. D., 26, 28, 77, 91
Pohl, R. H. B., 18
Popkowski Leszcyc, P. T. L., 9
Prelec, D., 129
Preston, R. A., 73

Rachlin, H., 11, 29, 30, 31, 60, 74, 77, 78, 106, 110, 115, 126, 129, 259
Raj, S. P., 126, 167
Rajala, A. K., 19, 72, 73, 259
Reichheld, F. F., 8
Reisberg, D., 106
Roberts, W. A., 72, 73, 96
Roche, J. P., 73
Romaniuk, 200
Romero, S., 12
Rossi, P. E., 226, 253

Saad, G., 73
Schrezenmaier, T. C., 7, 11, 127, 128, 129, 201, 261, 262, 264, 275
Schwarz, B., 6, 106, 117
Scriven, J., 8, 125, 200

Sharp, A., 40, 126, 200
Sharp, B., 40, 126, 200
Sheth, J. N., 2
Shettleworth, S., 72, 73
Sidman, M., 226
Simonson, I., 1, 2
Skinner, B. F. S., 3, 4, 29, 71, 92
Smith, C. L., 259
Soriano, M. M., 7, 117
Staddon, J. E. R., 72, 93

Telser, L. G., 186, 187

Uncles, M., 8, 34, 35, 36, 37, 125, 126, 166, 189, 190, 200, 252, 256, 257

Van Parijs, 71, 72
Vaughan, W., 29, 33, 41, 56, 59, 74, 89, 109, 110, 129, 135, 148, 264

Walters, R. G., 167, 168, 169, 187, 250
Watkins, D., 126
Wicker, A. W., 2
Wileman, A., 126
Williams, W., 73
Winger, G., 223, 227, 251
Wisniewski, K. J., 190

Yani-de-Soriano, M. M., 7, 161

Zettle, R. D., 44